BANK
FINAL EXAM

M000315411

STRESS TESTING AND
BANK-CAPITAL REFORM

This is an extremely useful book: thorough and balanced. The reader will learn a lot from Morris Goldstein's insightful and candid review of a large body of theoretical and empirical work and from the lessons he draws about US and EU-wide stress tests. An impressive piece of analysis.

—**Ben Bernanke**, Distinguished Fellow at the Brookings Institution and former Chairman of the Board of Governors of the Federal Reserve System

The best work available on stress tests, capital adequacy, and the leverage ratio. A truly excellent book.

—**Charles Goodhart**, Emeritus Professor at the London School of Economics and former Member of the Bank of England's Monetary Policy Committee

A comprehensive treatment—full of valuable real-world illustrations and with plenty of food for thought on how to improve stress testing, capital adequacy, and regulation. A stimulating read.

—**Stefan Ingves**, Governor of Sweden's Riksbank and Chair of the Basel Committee on Banking Supervision

In this important book, Morris Goldstein challenges the false reassurances of 'reformed' yet inadequate regulations that maintain a dangerous banking system. Delving into the devilish details, he offers a better path.

—**Anat Admati**, George G. C. Parker Professor of Finance and Economics, Stanford Graduate School of Business, and coauthor of *The Bankers' New Clothes*

Takes bank stress tests from the impenetrable to the understandable. Morris Goldstein's reform proposals—presented with clarity and based on a keen appreciation of the facts—will stir up a hornet's nest among apoplectic bankers but will be welcome for those concerned about our next financial crisis.

—**Orley Ashenfelter**, Joseph Douglas Green 1895 Professor of Economics at Princeton University and former President of the American Economic Association

A powerful plea to end the make-believe in dealing with risk in banking.

—**Martin Hellwig**, Director, Max Planck Institute for Research on Collective Goods, and coauthor of *The Bankers' New Clothes*

As we navigate the new regulatory regime of stress-tested bank capital, we are lucky to have Morris Goldstein to guide our way. Bankers, regulators and legislators ignore this timely and impressive volume at their peril.

—**Peter Fisher**, Senior Fellow, Tuck School of Business at Dartmouth, and former Undersecretary for Domestic Finance at the US Treasury

Brilliantly distills the essence from a wide range of empirical studies to show what still needs to be done to make major international banks more resilient. A magisterial book.

—**Philip Turner**, University of Basel and former Deputy Head of the Monetary and Economics Department at the Bank for International Settlements

Marshaling ample data and astute analysis, Morris Goldstein demolishes the repeated claim of Wall Street bankers that much higher minimum capital requirements for our largest banks would do grave harm to the US economy. Anyone serious about how to prevent future financial crises and taxpayer bailouts has to read this indispensable book.

—**Dennis Kelleher**, President, Better Markets

BANKING'S FINAL EXAM

STRESS TESTING AND BANK-CAPITAL REFORM

MORRIS GOLDSTEIN

PETERSON INSTITUTE FOR INTERNATIONAL ECONOMICS
POLICY ANALYSES IN INTERNATIONAL ECONOMICS 106

WASHINGTON, DC
MAY 2017

To my three sons: Daniel, David, and Lewis

Morris Goldstein, nonresident senior fellow at the Peterson Institute for International Economics, has held several senior staff positions at the International Monetary Fund (1970–94), including deputy director of its Research Department (1987–94). From 1994 to 2010, he held the Dennis Weatherstone Senior Fellow position at the Peterson Institute. He has written extensively on international economic policy and on international capital markets. He is the author of *Trade, Currencies, and Finance* (2017, World Scientific Publishing Company), *Managed Floating Plus* (2002), *The Asian Financial Crisis: Causes, Cures, and Systemic Implications* (1998), *The Case for an International Banking Standard* (1997), and *The Exchange Rate System and the IMF: A Modest Agenda* (1995); coeditor of *Debating China's Exchange Rate Policy* (2008) and *Private Capital Flows to Emerging Markets after the Mexican Crisis* (1996); and coauthor of *The Future of China's Exchange Rate Policy* (2009), *Controlling Currency Mismatches in Emerging Markets* (2004), and *Assessing Financial Vulnerability: An Early Warning System for Emerging Markets* (2000).

**PETERSON INSTITUTE FOR
INTERNATIONAL ECONOMICS**
1750 Massachusetts Avenue, NW
Washington, DC 20036-1903
(202) 328-9000   FAX: (202) 328-5432
www.piie.com

Adam S. Posen, *President*
Steven R. Weisman, *Vice President for
  Publications and Communications*

Printing by Versa Press, Inc.

Printed in the United States of America
19 18 17   5 4 3 2 1

**Library of Congress
Cataloging-in-Publication Data**
Author: Goldstein, Morris, 1944– author.
Title: Banking's final exam : stress testing and bank-capital reform / Morris Goldstein, Peterson Institute for International Economics, Washington, DC.
Description: Washington, DC : Peterson Institute for International Economics, 2016. | Includes bibliographical references.
Identifiers: LCCN 2016013416 (print) | LCCN 2016014261 (ebook) | ISBN 9780881327052 | ISBN 9780881327069
Subjects: LCSH: Financial services industry—Risk management. | Asset-liability management. | Banking law.
Classification: LCC HG173 .G65 2016 (print) LCC HG173 (ebook) | DDC 332.1—dc23

This publication has been subjected to a prepublication peer review intended to ensure analytical quality. The views expressed are those of the author. This publication is part of the overall program of the Peterson Institute for International Economics, as endorsed by its Board of Directors, but it does not necessarily reflect the views of individual members of the Board or of the Institute's staff or management.
The Peterson Institute for International Economics is a private nonpartisan, nonprofit institution for rigorous, intellectually open, and indepth study and discussion of international economic policy. Its purpose is to identify and analyze important issues to make globalization beneficial and sustainable for the people of the United States and the world, and then to develop and communicate practical new approaches for dealing with them.
Its work is funded by a highly diverse group of philanthropic foundations, private corporations, and interested individuals, as well as income on its capital fund. About 35 percent of the Institute's resources in its latest fiscal year were provided by contributors from outside the United States. A list of all financial supporters is posted at https://piie.com/sites/default/files/supporters.pdf.

Contents

Tables

Figures

Box

Preface

Following the most serious financial crisis since the Great Depression, bank supervisors and regulators undertook a set of reforms to reduce the likelihood of and harm from a recurrence. Attention has rightly focused on efforts, implemented under the international Basel III agreement and the Dodd-Frank Act in the United States—to improve the quantity and quality of bank capital and to make regular stress-testing of large banks a key element in the supervisory assessment of that capital adequacy.

Despite these improvements, Senior Fellow Morris Goldstein argues in this book that bank-capital requirements and stress tests currently conducted in the United States and the European Union fall short of what is needed to promote financial stability. In Goldstein's view: Minimum and actual capital ratios for the largest banks are still way too low; the metrics used in the stress tests are not good enough at distinguishing fragile from sound banks and at gauging systemic risk; and the contagion and amplification of financial shocks that played such a large role in the global financial crisis of 2007–09 are yet to be integrated satisfactorily into today's stress tests.

In light of these deficiencies, Goldstein puts forward a bold plan for further reform. The plan would be implemented over a ten-year period— first in the United States and, if successful, later globally. Under this plan, minimum tangible leverage ratios (the highest quality of bank capital) would be set at 14 to 18 percent for the eight US banks deemed to be global systemically important (G-SIBs), at 11 to 13 percent for other large banks (those with total assets greater than $50 billion), and at 10 percent for smaller banks. Such an increase in minimum bank-capital ratios is intended to vastly raise the loss absorbency of America's largest banks and to decrease significantly the chance of a future taxpayer bailout. The plan would also supplement these much higher minimum leverage ratios with a risk surcharge based on a set of indicators.

According to Goldstein, this combination of a leverage ratio and an indicator-based risk surcharge would be better than the current system at identifying vulnerable banks and at monitoring systemic risk. It would likewise be easier to understand and less costly to maintain than the more complex current counterpart, while being less susceptible to manipulation by banks. There also would be larger incentives for too big to fail banks to shrink over time their systemic footprint, because the difference in minimum capital ratios between G-SIBs and other banks would be much greater. Finally, Goldstein offers evidence that implementing this plan would not harm good US macroeconomic performance, in contrast to concerns that forcing banks to raise capital would constrain lending and growth.

The Institute has a long history of undertaking relevant policy studies on bank regulation as well as on financial stability more broadly. These studies include Goldstein's 1997 book, *The Case for an International Banking Standard*; his 1998 book, *The Asian Financial Crisis: Causes, Cures, and Systemic Implications*; and his 2000 book (with Graciela Kaminsky and Carmen Reinhart), *Assessing Financial Vulnerability: An Early Warning System for Emerging Markets*. More recently, the Institute has conducted a set of studies on policy recommendations arising out of the global financial crisis. Among them are William Cline's 2010 book, *Financial Globalization, Economic Growth and the Crisis of 2007-09;* the 2013 study edited by Adam Posen and Changyong Rhee, *Responding to Financial Crisis: Lessons from Asia Then, the United States and Europe Now;* the 2015 book edited by Marcus Noland and Donghyun Park, *From Stress to Growth: Strengthening Asia's Financial System in a Post-Crisis World,* Cline's 2017 book, *The Right Balance For Banks: Theory and Evidence on Optimal Capital Requirements*, and a number of shorter studies by Anna Gelpern, Simon Johnson, Adam Posen, Edwin Truman, and Nicolas Véron on financial stability and bank reform in the European Union and the United States.

The Peterson Institute for International Economics is a private nonpartisan, nonprofit institution for rigorous, intellectually open, and in-depth study and discussion of international economic policy. Its purpose is to identify and analyze important issues to making globalization beneficial and sustainable for the people of the United States and the world, and then to develop and communicate practical new approaches for dealing with them.

The Institute's work is funded by a highly diverse group of philanthropic foundations, private corporations, public institutions, and interested individuals, as well as by income on its capital fund. About 35 percent of the Institute's resources in our latest fiscal year were provided by contributors from outside the United States. A list of all our financial supporters for the preceding year is posted at http://piie.com/institute/supporters.pdf.

The Executive Committee of the Institute's Board of Directors bears overall responsibility for the Institute's direction, gives general guidance and approval to its research program, and evaluates its performance in pursuit of its mission. The Institute's President is responsible for the identification of topics that are likely to become important over the medium term (one to three years) that should be addressed by Institute scholars. This rolling agenda is set in close consultation with the Institute's research staff, Board of Directors, and other stakeholders.

The President makes the final decision to publish any individual Institute study, following independent internal and external review of the work. Interested readers may access the data and computations underlying the Institute publications for research and replication by searching titles at www.piie.com.

The Institute hopes that its research and other activities will contribute to building a stronger foundation for international economic policy around the world. We invite readers of these publications to let us know how they think we can best accomplish this objective.

ADAM S. POSEN
President
March 2017

Acknowledgments

This is a long book about a contentious subject in finance. It would not have been completed without the help of colleagues, friends, and family.

Adam Posen and Marc Noland, in their roles as president and director of studies, respectively, at PIIE, lent their wholehearted support to this project from its early days. They also offered valuable suggestions on how to make the book better—without impinging on the book's central message or the author's voice.

Without implicating them in any of the book's policy prescriptions, Stan Fischer, Tim Geithner, Charles Goodhart, Tom Hoenig, and Philip Turner could not have been more helpful: They read and commented upon two earlier versions of the manuscript, they put me in contact with specialists who illuminated topics about which I was less familiar, and they encouraged me to persevere through the challenges that confront all such scholarly endeavors.

I am grateful as well to the following individuals along with two anonymous referees for such useful comments on earlier drafts: Anat Admati, Orley Ashenfelter, Tam Bayoumi, Fred Bergsten, Ben Bernanke, Olivier Blanchard, Bill Cline, Kevin Dowd, Mohamed El-Erian, Peter Fisher, Joseph Gagnon, Martin Hellwig, Patrick Honohan, Gary Hufbauer, Stefan Ingves, Simon Johnson, Dennis Kelleher, Jacob Kirkegaard, Signe Krogstrup, Nick Lardy, Tara Rice, Arvind Subramanian, Ted Truman, Ángel Ubide, and Nicolas Véron. I likewise benefited from a discussion with Jose Vinals and his stress-testing team at the IMF and from conversations with participants at the 2015 London School of Economics conference on stress testing and at the 2016 Yale Financial Crisis Forum.

Anish Tailor provided superb research assistance, including but not limited to his careful work with the book's tables and charts.

Chuck Morris and Kristen Regehr were invaluable in helping me to understand better a host of thorny data issues involving US banks as well as with assessing the links among bank capital, profit rates, asset growth, and capital distributions.

Steve Weisman, Madona Devasahayam, and their colleagues in PIIE's publication department did their usual but highly appreciated magic in transforming the manuscript into its final form. This book benefited greatly from their ideas and their meticulous editing.

Finally, but most important, I want to thank my three sons (Daniel, David, and Lewis), my four granddaughters (Ally, Annie, Catherine, and Lilly), my sister and brother-in-law (Rose and Ed), and my two daughters-in-law (Sarah and Juliette) for their love and unfailing support. They—along with my dear late wife (Peggy) and my deceased parents (Belle and Lew)—have been the joys of my life. And to the most popular question of the last two years— "Is it done yet?"—I can finally answer, "Indeed, it is." I leave it to others to judge the results.

Abbreviations

ABM	agent-based model
ABS	asset-backed security
AFS	available for sale
AIG	American International Group (US insurance company)
AQR	Asset Quality Review (in EU)
BCBS	Basel Committee on Banking Supervision
BHC	bank holding company
BIS	Bank for International Settlements
BOE	Bank of England
BRRD	Banking Recovery and Resolution Directive (in EU)
CA	Comprehensive Assessment (2014 EU-wide stress test plus AQR)
CAFE	corporate average fuel economy standard (in US)
CAPM	capital asset pricing model
CAR	capital adequacy requirement
CCA	contingent claims analysis
CCAR	Comprehensive Capital Analysis and Review (in US)
CCB	capital conservation buffer
CCL	countercyclical capital buffer
CCP	central counter-party
CDS	credit default swap
CEBS	Committee of European Banking Supervisors (in EU)
CET1	common equity tier 1 (bank capital)
CoCo	contingent convertible bond

CRD	Capital Requirements Directive (in EU)
CRR	Capital Requirements Regulation (in EU)
CT1	core tier 1 (bank capital)
DFAST	Dodd-Frank Act Stress Tests (in US)
DSIB	domestic systemically important bank
DTA	deferred-tax asset
EBA	European Banking Authority
EC	European Commission
ECA	European Court of Auditors (in EU)
ECB	European Central Bank
EEA	European Economic Area
EFSF	European Financial Stability Facility (in EU)
EL	expected loss
ESLR	enhanced supplementary leverage ratio (in US)
ESRB	European Supervisory Risk Board (in EU)
ESM	European Stability Mechanism (in EU)
FDIC	Federal Deposit Insurance Corporation (in US)
FDICIA	Federal Deposit Insurance Corporation Improvement Act (US)
FPC	Financial Policy Committee (of the Bank of England)
FSA	Financial Services Authority (in UK)
FSAP	Financial Sector Assessment Program (at the IMF)
FSOC	Financial Stability Oversight Council (in US)
FSB	Financial Stability Board
FVA	fair value accounting
GAAP	Generally Accepted Accounting Principles (in US)
GFSR	*Global Financial Stability Report* (of IMF)
G-SIB	global systemically important bank
G-20	Group of Twenty (systemically important countries)
hold-co	holding company (of bank)
ICBA	Independent Community Bankers of America
IIF	Institute of International Finance
IFRS	International Financial Reporting Standards
IMF	International Monetary Fund
ISDA	International Swaps and Derivatives Association
LCBG	large and complex banking group (in EU)
LCR	liquidity coverage ratio
LGD	loss given default
LLP	loan-loss provisions
LOLR	lender of last resort

LTCM	Long-Term Capital Management (hedge fund)
LTRO	long-term refinancing operation (in EU)
MAA	mixed attribute accounting
M&M	Modigliani-Miller (theorem)
NSFR	net stable funding ratio
NPL	nonperforming loan
op-co	operating company (subsidiary of holding company)
PD	probability of default
PFAS	pawnbroker for all seasons
PM	portfolio manager
PPIP	Public-Private Investment Program (in US)
QE	quantitative easing
ROA	return on assets
ROE	return on equity
RORWA	return on risk-weighted assets
RWA	risk-weighted assets
SCAP	Supervisory Capital Assessment Program
SIB	systemically important bank
SLR	supplementary leverage ratio
SPOE	Single Point of Entry
SREP	Supervisory Review and Evaluation Process
SRISK	measure of systemic risk (from Acharya et al. 2010)
SRM	Single Resolution Mechanism (in EU)
SSM	Single Supervisory Mechanism (in EU)
TA	total assets (of a bank)
TAL	Term Asset-Backed Securities Loan Facility (in US)
TARP	Troubled Asset Relief Program (in US)
TBTF	too big to fail
T1	tier 1 (bank capital)
T2	tier 2 (bank capital)
T1C	tier 1 common (bank capital)
TLAC	total loss-absorbing capacity
TLE	total leverage exposure
VAR	value at risk
WEO	*World Economic Outlook* (of IMF)

Introduction
Scene Setting, Preliminaries, Outline, and Main Findings

Setting the Scene

Bank stress tests—exercises designed to assess whether a bank or group of banks will be adequately capitalized even in an adverse economic scenario—have been conducted by the International Monetary Fund (IMF) since the late 1990s. National central banks and other regulatory authorities ran them even before that, and commercial and investment banks have stress tested their trading books for extreme movements in market prices for even longer.[1]

What put bank stress tests on the front page of major newspapers around the world, however, is of more recent origin. Specifically, a bank stress test (known as the Supervisory Capital Assessment Program, or SCAP) was used as an important tool of crisis management by US authorities in February–May 2009. The SCAP was announced on February 10, 2009, and the test results were released on May 7, 2009, only a few quarters after the fall of Lehman Brothers and at a juncture when anxiety about the viability of some large US financial institutions was still high and there was considerable uncertainty about US macroeconomic prospects.[2] To bolster the credibility of the test, bank-by-bank results were published, a new more stringent definition of high-quality bank capital was introduced (tier 1 common), and a severe loss rate on bank loans (over 9 percent—even higher than during the Great Depression) was employed in the adverse scenario.

Because the US crisis management effort had many important elements beyond bank stress tests, it is difficult to assess the impact of a single reform.[3] Nevertheless, there is by now a consensus that the 2009 US stress test "worked." By "worked," I mean that the test results seemed to persuade market participants—both that 9 of the 19 largest US banks had sufficient capital to weather the storm and that the remaining 10 banks that fell short of the regulatory standard would be promptly recapitalized. Interbank lending spreads, credit default swap (CDS) spreads for pressured banks, and the volatility fear index in the broader US stock market all improved dramatically in the immediate aftermath of the SCAP, and the 10 banks identified as needing additional capital were able to raise, within a month of the test results, almost all ($66 billion of $75 billion) of the aggregate shortfall without additional government funds.

Former Federal Reserve Chair Ben Bernanke (2013, 1) offers the following assessment of the SCAP: "In retrospect, [it] stands out for me as one of the critical turning points in the financial crisis. It provided anxious investors with something they craved: credible information about losses at banks. Supervisors' public disclosure of the stress test results helped restore confidence in the banking system and enabled its successful recapitalization." In his recent memoir, Bernanke (2015, 397) confirms his earlier assessment: "The [SCAP] stress test was a decisive turning point. From then on, the US banking system would strengthen steadily—and eventually, the economy would follow." Alan Blinder (2013, 260) reaches a similar positive verdict on the impact of the SCAP: "Few people realized it at the time, but the successful (May 2009) stress tests were a turning point. The tests marked the end of the acute stage of the financial crisis and the beginning of the return to normalcy—albeit just the beginning. It wouldn't be long before everyone stopped worrying about the survival of the big American banks. Not long after that, these institutions started generating profits again."

Spurred by the enormous cost of the 2007–09 financial crisis and buoyed by the apparent success of the initial stress test, further rounds of US bank stress tests were conducted annually between 2011 and 2016.[4,5] Indeed, such stress tests have now been made a mandatory and permanent part of the US regulatory and supervisory framework.

Senior US regulatory officials—including New York Federal Reserve Bank President William Dudley (2012); Chairman Bernanke (2013); Federal Reserve Vice Chair Stanley Fischer (2014b); and Board of Governors member Daniel Tarullo (2014c, 2016)—have argued that US stress tests made an important contribution to financial stability. They point to the key role stress tests have played in strengthening the capital position of the industry, with the 33 bank holding companies participating in the 2016 Comprehensive Capital Analysis and Review (CCAR) stress test having more than doubled their (risk-based) common equity tier 1 (CET1) capital (ratios) since the first quarter of 2009.[6] Similarly, banks' liquidity position has improved markedly relative to precrisis levels.[7]

US supervisors maintain that the process of looking at the group of large banks together in the stress tests facilitated a more "macropruden-tial" approach to supervision—that is, an approach focusing on the health of the entire banking system and the whole economy as opposed to that of an individual bank. The "horizontal" nature of the tests—that is, exam-ining a number of banks simultaneously—is said to facilitate the identifica-tion of banks that are risk outliers in terms of their valuation practices or portfolios. Forward-looking stress testing is also regarded as better than static Basel-type regulatory approaches at evaluating complex exposures to derivative positions and to funding risks.

Going farther, it is argued that the transparency of the stress tests and the publication of results for individual banks have contributed to market discipline by making it easier for investors, counterparties, analysts, and markets to make more informed judgments about the financial condition of banks. Stress tests are also seen as having upped the ante for sound risk management, as failure to either meet the regulatory capital benchmark or demonstrate that the capital planning process is otherwise up to snuff carries nontrivial reputational cost. And last but not least, stress testing is credited with providing a helpful counterweight to the pressures some-times facing banks to use capital distributions to signal financial strength, even when stressful conditions point to a need to conserve capital.

A second moment in the sun for bank stress tests has been their appli-cation in the European Union, first during the crisis of 2007–09 and later during the debt crisis of 2010–13 and the ongoing effort to create a banking union. The results of the first EU-wide bank stress test were released in October 2009. Additional EU-wide tests were completed in 2010 (July), 2011 (July), 2014 (October), and most recently in 2016 (July).

EU policymakers have regarded the EU-wide stress tests as necessary and helpful for obtaining a more objective assessment of the condition of the banking system. They also argue that concerns about failing the test have prompted banks to raise more capital than would be the case in the tests' absence. They point out that in recent years the (weighted) average risk-based capital ratios for the group of large and complex banks in the euro area were very close to or above those of their global peers (including large and complex US banks), even if this has not (in their view) been adequately reflected in equity prices for European banks.[8]

Release of the first EU-wide stress test results in 2009 was not imme-diately followed by a sharp improvement in confidence in EU or euro area banks. The market response to the 2010, 2011, 2014, and 2016 tests also seemed lackluster. Indeed, if one looks at market indicators of EU banking stress/confidence immediately after the release of the five EU-wide stress tests results it is difficult to discern an independent, positive impact of the tests.[9,10] Appendix I at the end of this introductory chapter summarizes the "event studies" of the market impact of the US and EU-wide stress tests. It shows that the market received the US tests, especially the 2009 SCAP, more favorably than the EU-wide tests.

Preliminaries: Measurement of Bank Capital, the US Comprehensive Capital Analysis and Review, and the Dodd-Frank Act Stress Tests

Some definitions will be useful for readers unfamiliar with the arcane subject of the measurement of bank capital or the distinctions between the two main US stress testing exercises.

Measurement of Bank Capital

This volume makes reference to two types of bank capital ratios. The first—risk-based measures of capital—uses risk-weighted assets in the denominator. The second—leverage ratios—uses either unweighted total assets or total leverage exposure in the denominator. About 85 percent of risk weights reflect credit risk differences across assets; market and operational risk are also taken into account. Risk weights typically fall between 0 and 100 percent but can far exceed 100 percent for some very risky assets.

A simple numerical example illustrates the difference between a risk-based and a non-risk-weighted capital ratio. Suppose that a bank has total assets of $100 and equity capital of $5. Assume that the bank's total assets are composed of cash ($10), federal government bonds ($10), municipal bonds ($10), residential mortgage loans ($35), and commercial and industrial loans ($35). For simplicity, assume that bank regulators set the following risk weights on those assets: cash and federal government bonds (0 percent), municipal bonds (20 percent), residential mortgages (50 percent), and commercial and industrial loans (100 percent).[11] The bank's risk-weighted assets (RWA) are then the weighted average of the bank's assets, that is, RWA = ($10 times 0 percent, plus $10 times 0 percent, plus $10 times 20 percent, plus $35 times 50 percent, plus $35 times 100 percent) = $54.5. The risk-based capital ratio is the ratio of equity capital to RWA; that is $5/$54.5, or 9.2 percent. In contrast, the leverage ratio takes no account of these risk weights; it weights all assets equally. The leverage ratio is then simply the ratio of equity capital (E) to total assets (TA), or $5/$100, or 5 percent. A bank that has a leverage ratio of 5 percent is sometimes said to be "leveraged" twenty times (the reciprocal of the leverage ratio), while one that has a leverage ratio of 10 percent would be "leveraged" ten times.

The ratio of risk-weighted assets to total assets (sometimes called risk-weight density) differs significantly across countries and regions, across different size classes of banks, and over time. A few examples convey the flavor. At end-2015 the average risk-weight density for the eight US "global systemically important banks" (G-SIBs) was 63 percent; the figure for the 12 EU G-SIBs was 34 percent.[12] Among a sample of small EU banks (banks with total assets of less than €30 billion), the average risk-weight density was 62 percent—almost twice the level of the EU G-SIBs (Berger, Hüttl, and Merler 2016). In 1993 the average risk-weight density for a group of 17 major international banks stood at 70 percent; by end-2011 it had fallen to below 40 percent (Haldane 2013). With differences this large, it is easy to understand why regulatory and stress testing issues that deal with the application of risk-weighted capital ratios elicit such strong reaction from banks and their supervisors.

The other main source of differences among capital ratios derives from differences in the quality of bank capital, captured in the numerator of the capital ratio. The highest quality of capital is usually regarded to be common equity because it doesn't need to be repaid, it doesn't require payments of dividends or interest, and it stands last in the seniority line in bankruptcy or insolvency proceedings (Elliott 2010). Tangible common equity—defined as common equity minus intangible assets (goodwill, deferred tax assets, minority interest, etc.)—is of even higher quality than common equity because it has greater loss absorbency. In descending order of quality, this book makes reference to the following risk-based measures of capital:

- common equity tier 1, the equity measure at the center of Basel III,
- tier 1 common, the equity measure used in the earlier US stress tests,
- core tier 1, the equity measure used in the 2011 EU-wide stress test (usually defined as common equity plus government hybrid instruments),
- tier 1 capital, the high-quality capital measure used in the first two EU-wide stress tests,
- tier 2 capital, a lower-quality component of bank capital, and
- total capital adequacy ratio (CAR), the broadest measure of bank capital, consisting of tier 1 plus tier 2 capital.

The Basel Committee on Banking Supervision defines common equity tier 1 as consisting of the following components: (1) common shares issued by the bank that meet the criteria for classification as common shares for regulatory purposes; (2) stock surplus (share premium); (3) retained earnings; (4) accumulated other comprehensive income and other disclosed reserves; (5) minority interest that meets the criteria for inclusion in CET1; and (6) regulatory adjustments.

The noncommon stock elements of tier 1 capital are mainly the kinds of preferred stock that are more like common stock. Tier 2 capital consists mainly of the kinds of preferred stock that are more like debt; it also includes subordinated debt.

This volume examines three leverage ratios (listed in descending order of quality):

- the tangible leverage ratio, defined as the ratio of adjusted tangible equity to adjusted tangible assets (see Hoenig 2016b)
- the Basel III tier 1 leverage ratio, defined as the ratio of tier 1 capital to total leverage exposure
- the tier 1 leverage ratio, defined as the ratio of tier 1 capital to total assets.[13]

Some researchers also employ a more generic set of leverage ratios, defined as the ratio of the book value of equity to the book value of total assets (using various definitions of equity). Total leverage exposure includes both on-balance-sheet assets and off-balance-sheet exposures, such as over-the-counter derivatives, cleared derivatives, repo-style transactions, and other off-balance-sheet exposures.[14] For banks that have large derivative books and that use US Generally Accepted Accounting Principles (GAAP), total leverage exposure is always larger than total assets (see Allahrakha, Glasserman, and Young 2015). For banks in countries that use International Financial Reporting Standards (IFRS), total leverage exposure can be close to or even below total leverage exposure (see Berger, Hüttl, and Merler 2016 and Dowd 2016a).

The supplementary leverage ratio and the enhanced supplementary leverage ratio are the US banking agencies' implementation of the Basel III leverage ratio. The enhanced supplementary leverage applies to the eight largest US bank holding companies that are designated as G-SIBs. The supplementary leverage ratio applies to other large US banks that meet certain size criteria (greater than or equal to $250 billion in total assets, or greater than or equal to $10 billion of on-balance-sheet foreign exposures). Banks that meet these criteria are classified as "advanced-approach" banks. All US banks, regardless of size, have long been required to meet a 4 percent tier 1 leverage ratio. The tier 1 leverage ratio is the leverage ratio used in the US CCAR tests and the Dodd-Frank Act Stress Tests (DFAST).

When comparing capital ratios across banking systems in different countries, it is important to recognize that different treatment of the netting of derivative positions under GAAP and IFRS accounting standards can have sizable effects on all leverage ratios that use either total assets or tangible assets in the denominator (see Goldstein 2016). GAAP allows a much more generous treatment of the netting of derivatives than does IFRS. As a result, total assets of US banks look much smaller under GAAP than under IFRS.[15] As total assets are in the denominator of certain leverage ratios (such as the tier 1 leverage ratio used in the CCAR), tangible leverage ratios and tier 1 leverage ratios for US banks look better under GAAP than under IFRS.

A few numbers convey the flavor. At end-2015, the weighted average tangible leverage ratio for the 8 US G-SIBs under US GAAP was 8.1 percent versus 6.0 percent under IFRS—a difference of over 200 basis points. We can do those conversions because the Federal Deposit Insurance Corporation (FDIC) regularly publishes a Global Capital Index that translates one into the other. Not surprisingly, the netting rule makes a big difference for banks with large derivative positions but not for others. JPMorgan Chase, with its huge derivative book, has a US GAAP tangible leverage ratio of 8.3 percent versus an IFRS one of 6.0 percent—a difference of roughly 230 basis points. In contrast, Wells Fargo, with a much smaller derivative book, has a difference between its GAAP and IFRS tangible leverage ratios of only 30 basis points. And for smaller US banks, the GAAP/IFRS difference does not matter at all.

The Basel III leverage ratio—and other leverage ratios based on it (like the supplementary leverage and the enhanced supplementary leverage) that use total leverage exposure in the denominator—are not subject to this apples versus oranges comparability problem, because Basel III has adopted a uniform netting formula that is a compromise between the GAAP and IFRS treatments. This rule is less generous on netting than US GAAP but more generous than IFRS. The compromise makes Basel III leverage ratios comparable across countries.[16]

Because the stricter minimum capital and liquidity requirements specified under Basel III are to be implemented during a transition period that runs through 2019 (but is different for different elements of the Basel III reform package; see table 4.1 in chapter 4), it has become standard to differentiate between "transitional" Basel III capital ratios and "fully loaded" Basel III ratios. "Transitional" means that the capital ratio in question is measured under Basel III's (more generous) transitional arrangements. "Fully loaded" means that the capital ratio is measured under the assumption that Basel III's final requirements were already in force.

Basel III is frequently described as having three pillars. Pillar 1 sets out minimum regulatory capital requirements, Pillar 2 deals with risk management and supervision, and Pillar 3 addresses market discipline, including disclosure requirements. A Pillar 1 capital requirement is rule based and affords less discretion to supervisors than Pillar 2 measures. After an observation period, Pillar 2 measures can sometimes be upgraded to become Pillar 1 requirements.

The Comprehensive Capital Analysis and Review and the Dodd-Frank Act Stress Tests

Large US banks are now required to participate in two supervisory programs in which stress tests are a key component. The first is the stress testing required by the 2010 Dodd-Frank Wall Street Reform and Consumer Protection Act (known as DFAST). The second is the stress testing included in the wider annual capital plan assessment, the CCAR.

The CCAR covers only large complex US bank holding companies with total consolidated assets of $50 billion or more. It includes not only stress test methodology and results but also a more qualitative assessment of the risk management and capital planning process, including policies covering dividends, common stock issuance, and share repurchases. Such large bank holding companies are subject to both supervisor-led and company-run stress tests. In contrast, DFAST applies to a broader range of financial institutions, encompassing bank holding companies with total consolidated assets greater than $10 billion, state member banks with total consolidated assets greater than $10 billion, and savings and loan holding companies with total consolidated assets greater than $10 billion. All of these institutions are subject to company-run stress tests, but only the subset of bank holding companies with $50 billion or more in total consolidated assets is subject to supervisor-led tests. The focus of DFAST is exclusively on the quantitative outcomes of the stress tests. It does not set any capital hurdle rates or limit any capital actions by the firms; those functions are handled through the CCAR.

The two stress test exercises incorporate the same projections of losses, revenues, balances, and risk-weighted assets, but they use somewhat different capital action assumptions. The DFAST uses a set of capital action assumptions specified in the DFAST rules, whereas the CCAR uses a bank's planned capital actions under the bank's baseline scenario (see Board of Governors press release, October 30, 2015; Lehnert 2015; and Tarullo 2016). The Federal Reserve coordinates the two stress test exercises while seeking to reduce duplication and minimize the burden on banks (see Bernanke 2103, Board of Governors 2014a, and Tarullo 2014c). This study focuses on the CCAR tests because the quantitative results are very similar to those of the DFAST, because the CCAR provides information on capital hurdle rates, and because the qualitative part of the CCAR tests is also of interest.

Outline of the Study

This volume takes a critical look at the bank stress tests conducted by bank supervisors in the United States and the European Union between 2009 and 2016. It seeks to draw the lessons that would be most helpful for the design and conduct of future stress tests, not only in the United States and Europe but elsewhere as well.

A central thesis of the study is that the enormous costs of systemic banking crises, combined with the advantages that stress tests possess over other supervisory tools, make it likely that stress testing will become the central pillar of bank supervision worldwide. At the same time, unless several fundamental weaknesses of bank stress tests are corrected, the tests may fail to distinguish healthy banks from sick ones and produce false reassurance about the safety and soundness of the banking system as a whole.

Some important existing weaknesses in bank stress tests can be remedied within the current stress test and bank regulatory framework. Others cannot. Fixing them will require significant reform of the bank capital regime, first in the United States and ultimately at the global level. This is where the second part of this book, on bank capital reform, comes in. Three elements of the current bank capital regime are most in need of change. First, minimum capital requirements are much too low, despite the advances made under Basel III and the Dodd-Frank Act. Theory and empirical evidence suggest that for the eight US G-SIBs, the minimum capital ratio, expressed as an unweighted leverage ratio, ought to be 14 to 18 percent. The minimums for smaller US banks should be lower, in the 10 to 13 percent range. Current regulatory minimums (for leverage ratios) in the United States are in the 3 to 6 percent range, and the eight US G-SIBs currently have an actual average tangible leverage ratio of about 8 percent (in GAAP terms). For the largest US banks, minimum bank capital requirements are thus only about a third and actual leverage ratios only about half of what they should be.

Second, the existing bank capital regime has made risk-based measures of bank capital the primary regulatory standard and unweighted leverage ratios the supplementary backup standard. But a large body of empirical evidence shows that in terms of ability to distinguish sick from healthy (large) banks, vulnerability to manipulation (by banks), the cost of implementation, and ease of understanding, the leverage ratio is far superior to the risk-based measures. We have it backwards. The leverage ratio should thus be the primary capital standard, and the risk-based measures should serve as a backup. This volume shows how this can be done, at low cost and without giving banks a large incentive to shift into high-risk activities.

Third, although the bank capital regime recognizes that failure of a G-SIB imposes larger losses on society than failure of a smaller bank, the capital surcharges (i.e., the additional capital requirements) G-SIBs face are too low. In terms of risk-based capital measures, the minimum capital ratio requirement for the largest bank in the United States is just 450 basis points more than for a small bank; in terms of a leverage ratio, the maximum surcharge is about 200 to 300 basis points. In addition, on average US G-SIBs maintain lower leverage ratios than non-G-SIBs. To right this imbalance and make expected losses at G-SIBs no higher than for non-too-big-to-fail banks, the difference in minimum leverage requirements between G-SIBs and small banks (banks with less than $50 billion in total assets) should be in the neighborhood of 400 to 800 basis points, not 200 to 300 basis points.

With these shortcomings of the current bank regulatory regime in mind, consider what it means to "pass" a stress test. A bank is deemed to pass the quantitative part of the CCAR test if its capital ratio does not fall below the prespecified hurdle rates not only in the baseline scenario but also in the adverse and severely adverse scenarios. As noted earlier, these capital hurdle rates are typically set at the minimum regulatory standard. In the 2016 CCAR test, for example, two of the key hurdle rates were 4.5 percent for the risk-weighted common equity tier 1 capital ratio and 4 percent for the (unweighted) tier 1 leverage ratio. Both hurdle rates were the same for all 33 of the bank holding companies participating in the test.

But what if this 4 percent hurdle rate for the tier 1 leverage ratio is way below the ratio that would maximize net social benefits for the US economy? What if the risk-weighted common equity tier 1 measure of capital is not the measure that best distinguishes sick from healthy banks? And what if the social consequences stemming from the insolvency of JPMorgan Chase (with its almost $2.5 trillion in total consolidated assets as of end-June 2016) during a severe financial crisis are much more damaging than the insolvency of Zions Bancorporation (with less than $60 billion in total consolidated assets)? If these suppositions are correct, the fact that all 33 bank holding companies passed the quantitative part of the test has less economic significance than it would if more appropriate hurdle rates were set. As in other walks of life, a pass or fail verdict is not necessarily a sufficient statistic for drawing valid inferences about the test takers.

The primary purpose of bank capital reform is broader than improving the quality and credibility of bank stress tests. It is to reduce the probability and severity of banking crises and to reduce the day-to-day distortions that come about if banks—especially the largest too big to fail banks—are permitted to operate with a fragile, debt-heavy, equity-light funding structure that is unlike that in most other nonfinancial corporations

(Admati and Hellwig 2013a, Admati 2016a, 2016b). In this sense bank capital reform, writ large, is more important than the narrower objective of improving stress testing. Bank-capital reform would not only increase the credibility of stress testing, it would also generate large, wider-ranging benefits in terms of bolstering financial stability.

Going in the other direction, effective stress testing can likewise improve the prospects for bank-capital reform. The stigma attached to publicly failing a stress test and having bank supervisors reject a bank's capital plan—including approval for dividend payments and share buy-backs—appears to generate more and faster bank capital raising than would occur in the absence of stress testing. A CEO whose large bank fails the Federal Reserve's annual supervisor-led stress test twice in a row may find his job in jeopardy.

As hinted at earlier, stress tests also have other attributes that help compensate for some of the weaknesses of regulatory capital ratios alone. Whereas Basel capital requirements are backward-looking and rigid in design, stress tests address tail risk in forward-looking scenarios and those scenarios can be custom-tailored to meet the specifics of a given country or region's risk profile. Whereas regulatory capital ratios usually lean heavily on aggregate banking data, stress tests, with their bank-by-bank results and greater granularity, provide the horizontal comparisons that market participants value, especially in a crisis. And whereas the setting of regulatory capital ratios has been heavily dependent on the (low) historical probability of banking crises, stress tests employ the less demanding but often more revealing standard that their adverse risk scenarios have to be "severe but plausible." This standard permits stress tests to consider a wider set of crisis vulnerabilities. Finally, if the hurdle rates are appropriately defined and set at the right level, stress tests also provide a simple and understandable metric with which to evaluate the capital adequacy of banks—namely, a comparison of what the capital ratio would be under adverse conditions with the capital hurdle rate.

In short, more credible stress testing and serious bank-capital reform are complements. Achieving both would represent a quantum jump in crisis resistance at low social cost.

This volume is organized as follows. Chapter 1 explores why many analysts (including me) were not impressed with the outcomes of the five EU-wide stress tests. It highlights several important differences between the designs of the EU-wide tests and those of the US tests.

Chapter 2 reviews the main operational features of the US and EU tests: the coordinating supervisor, coverage, frequency, time horizons, design of the baseline and adverse scenarios, models used, definition and height of hurdle rates for bank capital, outcome metrics, disclosure practices, and remedial actions required or recommended for banks that fail the test.[17] It also summarizes the ways in which bank stress tests have evolved since 2009.

Chapter 3 turns to three fundamental criticisms that have been leveled at stress testing methodology and measurement:

- Whatever their helpful role in crisis management, stress tests were a dismal failure as early warning indicators of systemic banking crises in the global economic and financial crisis of 2007–09.

- Stress tests are too "orderly" and do not capture adequately the chaos, contagion, and adverse feedback and amplification effects from the financial sector to the real sector, all of which make financial crises much more costly than normal recessions.

- Stress tests (following the Basel framework) have relied on risk-based measures of bank capital to measure capital adequacy, at just the time when an increasing share of analysts are concluding that risk-based measures of capital should be deemphasized relative to a simpler but more reliable unweighted measure (a leverage ratio).

Chapter 4 lays out the case for thinking that stress tests should be more ambitious than Basel III in setting out bank capital minimums. Three complementary approaches to assessing socially optimal capital ratios are analyzed: an approach that looks at bank losses during a country's most severe banking crisis, a macroprudential approach that focuses on the banking system's ability to support lending and economic growth and highlights runs by wholesale creditors and fire sales by banks under stress, and a benefit-cost approach that weighs the effects of heightened capital requirements on the availability and cost of bank credit against its contribution to reducing the probability of banking crises. Based on my review of theory and empirical evidence, I conclude that the socially optimal bank capital ratio is likely far above both current levels and the Basel III minimums. An immediate policy implication of this finding is that future stress tests should, over the next decade, gradually increase capital hurdle rates until they closely approximate the socially optimal capital ratio.

Chapter 5 examines three frameworks for estimated appropriate capital surcharges for G-SIBs: an approach that compares systemic importance scores to leverage ratios; the Bank of England's "symmetry and proportionality approach," which derives G-SIB leverage surcharges as a proportion of G-SIB surcharges for risk-based capital measures; and the Federal Reserve's "estimated impact" approach, which compares expected systemic losses for G-SIBs and non-G-SIBs. I conclude that the current capital surcharges for G-SIBs in the United States (and elsewhere) are too low. Future stress tests should therefore increase, over time, the amount of differentiation across different banks, with higher hurdle rates set for banks with the highest expected systemic loss (should they fail).

Chapter 6 draws seven lessons for future bank stress tests, based mainly on the US and EU-wide stress testing experiences of 2009–16.

Chapter 7 sketches the outlines of an improved bank capital regime for the United States. It puts forward a plan for a three-level bank capital structure, with a minimum leverage ratio of 10 percent for small banks (with total assets less than $50 billion), 11 to 13 percent for large banks, and 14 to 18 percent for G-SIBs. Under the plan, banks would have 10 years to meet the final capital targets, and interim targets would be incorporated in stress tests. The plan also includes a recommendation for using a set of risk indicators to construct a risk surcharge. This risk surcharge is meant to compensate for some of the weaknesses of current stress tests and to discourage banks from gaming the unweighted leverage ratio by loading up on unduly on risky assets. I also lay out the advantages of such a plan.

Chapter 8 addresses four potential criticisms of the plan: (1) that such a schedule of much heightened minimum leverage ratio requirements is a step too far for banking reform, with little chance of being implemented; (2) that a much higher capital requirement cum larger G-SIB capital surcharges would generate a marked shrinkage in the sizes of large banks, of the banking system, and of the financial sector as a whole—all with adverse effects on efficiency and economic growth; (3) that such high capital requirements for banks would cause financial activity to migrate to less regulated shadow banks, thereby putting financial stability at risk; and (4) that a much higher equity requirement for bank capital is no longer needed, now that the G-20 economies have reached agreement on a total loss-absorbing capacity (TLAC) initiative, which requires G-SIBs to hold 18 percent of their risk-weighted assets in TLAC instruments (equity plus debt that converts to equity under prespecified conditions) (G-20 2014).

In chapter 8, I also argue that objections 1, 2, and 4 (above) are not persuasive. Objection 3 is more weighty. That risk, however, could be combatted, if necessary, by adopting Mervyn King's (2016) "pawnbroker for all seasons" proposal, aimed at "run-proofing" the financial system. Under this scheme, all financial institutions (banks and shadow banks) that chose to issue liabilities with a maturity of one year or less would have to limit the amount of those short-term liabilities to the sum of reserves at the central bank and the haircut-adjusted value of their assets, as estimated by the central bank (the pawnbroker). The scheme would be phased in over 10 to 15 years. Chapter 8 also includes some brief concluding remarks.

Chapter 9 is a postscript. Shortly after most of the writing for this book was being completed, two developments took place that are particularly relevant for bank-capital reform and stress testing. First and most important, Donald Trump, the newly elected president of the United States, announced that he was in favor of major deregulation of the financial system, including banks. And second, following a review of its stress test program, the Federal Reserve announced a set of reforms to its stress testing procedures (Tarullo 2016). Chapter 9 briefly discusses the likely and/or proposed policy changes and provides my preliminary reactions to them.

Readers whose main interest is in stress testing may want to focus on chapters 1 to 3 and chapters 6 and 9. Readers whose bailiwick is bank-capital reform will find chapters 4 to 5 and 7 to 9 to be of primary interest. Given the importance of both topics for the current debate on whether large US banks are now safe enough, I hope most readers will go for the Full Monty.

Main Findings

This is a long book. I therefore provide a summary of the volume's main findings. Those for stress tests are covered first, followed by those for bank-capital reform.

On Stress Tests

1. Stress tests are here to say. If certain current weaknesses can be remedied, their influence is likely to increase even further relative to other bank supervisory tools.

2. The most successful single stress test over the 2009–16 period was the 2009 SCAP in the United States. So far stress testing has been more successful as a crisis management instrument than as an early warning or crisis prevention mechanism.

3. On the whole, the set of EU-wide stress tests received poorer reception by markets and officials (away from home) than the US tests.

4. There are good reasons for the poor reception of the EU-wide tests. They include lack of authority (in the 2009–11 tests) to compel (rather than just recommend) recapitalization for undercapitalized banks; a weak supporting crisis management cast for stress tests (which produced an anemic recovery from the 2007–09 crisis); outside estimates of capital shortfalls that were consistently higher than those emanating from the stress tests; likely overstatement of capital ratios as a result of low loan-loss provisioning and low credit write-downs; and a failure (in the 2011 EU-wide capital exercise) to specify capital targets in terms of absolute amounts rather than as a ratio. In addition, a leverage ratio test was not introduced until the 2016

test, thereby allowing large German, French, and Dutch banks with high risk-weighted capital ratios but low leverage ratios to fare much better on the tests than they should have. Although the 2014 and 2016 EU-wide tests contained some notable improvements relative to their predecessors, they had major shortcomings of their own. The 2014 test contained neither a leverage ratio test nor an adverse deflation scenario, and it allowed participating banks in some EU countries to inflate their capital ratios by being too lenient on tax-deferred assets and credits. The 2016 test made a major step forward by including data on fully loaded Basel III leverage ratios, but it then took a major step backward by suspending the use of hurdle rates, choosing instead to treat the stress test results as merely an input into the Supervisory Review and Evaluation Process (SREP). This decision is likely to retard future capital raising—just when it is badly needed and when there are justified concerns about a potential Italian banking crisis and the viability of Deutsche Bank.

5. Banks participating in stress tests should account for a substantial part of the banking system's assets. If the country's financial system is not bank dominated, a way needs to be found to assess how fragilities in the nonbank sector and in systemically important nonbanks could affect the banking system. This guideline is particularly relevant in the United States, where the nonbank sector is dominant and played an important role in the 2007–09 crisis.

6. The supervisor coordinating the tests should have not only the resources and authority to obtain the necessary private data inputs from the banks but also the capacity to evaluate independently the quality of those inputs as well as the impact of the shocks assumed in the scenarios on bank capital. Over time supervisors should seek to develop their own suites of models, both to guard against model risk from a particular model or two and to validate the reasonableness of models used by the banks in any bank-run tests.

7. Test coordinators must have the political independence to be able to call the results of the tests as they see them. If instead markets perceive that the tests are "rigged" to produce an overly optimistic and politically convenient pattern of outcomes for bank failures and the aggregate capital shortfall, publication is likely to do little to bolster confidence. This caveat applies with particular force to the EU-wide stress tests, where too many national discretions in the definition of bank capital have weakened its quality and outmoded provisioning and credit write-down practices (in some EU economies) have allowed a large stock of nonperforming loans (now estimated at €950 billion) to languish on banks' books for far too long.

8. Since stress test scenarios are meant to be "what if" exercises, it is not helpful to rule out certain scenarios just because they run counter to current policy objectives. Likewise, it detracts from their credibility if the scenarios cover only a minor part of the relevant risk exposures or the look-back periods used to estimate the impact of the shocks are not long enough to encompass some of the most severe banking crises in the country's history. In short, stress tests are not likely to be reassuring if they do not contain much stress.

9. The quality of the capital contained in the hurdle rate matters, especially in a crisis, when there are more losses to absorb. During the worst of the global financial crisis, the only capital ratios that market participants were interested in were those that had tangible equity in the numerator (see Tarullo 2011). Trying to make stress test results look better by inflating artificially the headline capital ratio—by choosing a low-quality capital measure for the hurdle rate—is a mug's game.

10. Disclosure of bank-by-bank results is essential for obtaining the market discipline effects of stress tests. All US tests except the 2011 CCAR and all EU-wide tests except the initial 2009 test have included bank-by-bank results. There is little indication that stress test disclosure has led to reduced production of information by private firms. The decision by US supervisors not to publish the models they use to translate the impact of shocks on bank capital is the right one. Disclosure of these models would weaken banks' incentives to improve their own models and increase the risk that banks would game their portfolios to fit the properties of the supervisors' models.

11. Linking the results of the stress test with remedial actions to correct undercapitalization is crucial. The innovation of the US CCAR exercises—to embed the stress tests in the capital planning process of banks—is a good one that merits serious consideration in other jurisdictions. Bank supervisors need a mandate to temporarily suspend dividend payments, share buybacks, and parts of executive compensation when capita hurdle rates in stress tests are not achieved as well as the will to enforce that mandate.

12. If severely undercapitalized banks are unable to raise enough capital from private markets and the decision is made not to close them, enough public funds need to be available to make public recapitalization feasible. If there is considerable doubt about their availability, it will be difficult to make stress test results credible, because market participants may well reason that the stress test architects are lowballing the capital shortfalls to match the small amount of recapitalization resources.

13. Bank stress tests do not operate in a vacuum. If the supporting crisis management cast is weak and there is a nontrivial probability that banks will face very large losses, it will be tough to sell reassuring stress test outcomes, no matter how skillful the design of the tests.

14. Official stress test estimates of capital shortfalls will be less credible when outside estimates of these shortfalls are consistently much larger. When the gap between official and private shortfall estimates is large, officials should address the main reasons for this discrepancy.

15. It is troubling that stress tests performed so poorly in the run-up to the worst economic and financial crisis since the Great Depression, failing to provide early warning of the banking system's vulnerability not just in the United States but in almost all the economies that subsequently experienced systemic banking crises in 2007–09. Two corrective actions are called for.

16. First, the authorities need to draw more heavily on early warning models of banking crises and integrate them into the stress testing exercise. These top-down, dual threshold models find that banking system vulnerability is greatest when there is both an abnormally rapid rate of growth in credit to the nonfinancial private sector and an abnormally rapid rise in real property prices. These models performed well in forecasting most of the major systemic banking crises of the past several decades, including the 2007–09 episodes. Fortunately, parsimonious models can be estimated and evaluated in any economy with decent time series data on credit aggregates and property prices.

17. Second, the modeling of the financial sector during a crisis needs to include enough feedback, contagion, and amplification effects that a seemingly moderate shock to the banking system can produce the kind of real economy and bank-capital effects observed in an actual severe crisis. Current stress test models do not incorporate enough elements of the leverage cycle, enough shifts in expectations, enough funding problems, enough fire sales of assets, enough nonlinearities and fat tails, enough interaction between the bank and nonbank financial sectors, and enough adaptation by agents. In addition, there are signs that the outcomes of the past few CCAR tests are becoming too predictable for comfort. These analytical issues are not a technical sideshow. In stress test modeling, they are the main event. Even the most advanced stress testing programs admit that they are in the early stages of dealing with this difficult challenge. Until they get farther, true capital shortfalls are likely to be underestimated.

18. Taking a cue from the macroprudential approach to bank supervision, when stress tests indicate that a bank is undercapitalized, the capital target should be expressed in terms of the absolute amount of capital that should be raised. If instead supervisors allow banks to choose how they will achieve the higher capital ratio, there is a good chance the banks will opt to make much of the adjustment by cutting back on loans, engaging in fire sales of assets, and derisking (i.e., rearranging their portfolio or redoing their internal risk-weight models), all with the aim of reducing their risk-weighted assets. The problem is that these methods of lowering the denominator of the capital ratio will not be the lowest-cost option for the macroeconomy. They will be contractionary.

19. All stress tests should contain a leverage ratio test. Almost all of the largest US banks that ran into trouble during the global financial crisis had risk-weighted capital measures that allowed them to be classified as "well capitalized" on their last reports while low leverage ratios were simultaneously pointing to very thin capital cushions (Hoenig 2012, 2013). The story was similar in Europe. This situation could be avoided in the future by requiring a leverage ratio test. US stress tests have contained a leverage ratio test since 2011. The EU-wide tests added one only in 2016.

20. Since the weight of the evidence points to optimal capital ratios being far above the minimum ratios set under Basel III (as well as under current US regulatory requirements), the message for stress test architects is that they need to be raising capital hurdle rates over time until this gap is eliminated.

On Bank-Capital Reform

1. None of the approaches to estimating optimal capital ratios—be it the bank losses approach, the macroprudential approach, or the benefit-cost approach—is comprehensive enough on its own to provide a good guide. In addition, there is no sense in pretending that estimates of optimal capital carry a high degree of precision. Better therefore to combine the insights from all of these approaches to reach a sensible judgment call on the preferred answer. My call is that the optimal (weighted-average) leverage ratio for US banks should be in the neighborhood of 15 percent—with the eight G-SIBs in the 14 to 18 percent range, other large banks (banks with $50 billion or more in total assets) in the 11 to 13 percent range, and small banks at 10 percent.

2. The consensus in official circles is for a much lower leverage ratio. For US banks, minimum leverage ratios are in the 4 to 6 percent range. The

minimum for the Basel III leverage ratio is 3 percent. Actual leverage ratios (be it tangible equity ratios or tier 1 leverage ratios) for the eight US G-SIBs (in US GAAP terms) currently stand at (a weighted average of) about 8 to 9 percent. The official consensus is wrong: It underestimates the benefits of higher capital ratios and overestimates the costs.

3. When implementing the "losses approach" to bank capital, the consensus relies exclusively on observed losses incurred by banks, with particular attention (rightly) devoted to the 2007–09 global financial crisis. The consensus ignores "counterfactual" losses. By counterfactual losses, I mean the losses that banks would have suffered in the global crisis had there not been such a massive and multifaceted array of government interventions. Without those interventions—including widespread government guarantees, public capital injections into banks and measures to aid the asset-backed securities markets, not just super-easy monetary policy and large fiscal expansion—bank losses would surely have been much higher. Note too that a proper treatment of the counterfactual (for US banks) would include not only the effect of US crisis intervention measures but also those of other G-20 governments since those foreign interventions also helped reduce US bank losses. IMF (2009, 2010b) data indicate that observed (peak) credit write-downs by US banks during the global financial crisis amounted to more than 8 percent of their total assets; counterfactual losses would have been much bigger. The counterfactual is highly relevant because G-20 leaders have pledged publicly not to repeat this extraordinary set of government interventions during any future crisis. Ignoring the counterfactual is a major methodological error and seriously biases downward the consensus' estimate of optimal capital.

4. Another common procedure in implementing the losses approach is to assume that after suffering losses during the upswing of the business cycle, banks can run their capital down very close to zero. This assumption ignores the fact that banks typically maintain capital ratios (for both risk-weighted capital and leverage ratios) considerably above the regulatory minimum at the bottom of the credit/financial cycle (reflecting market pressures to do so). The right question is therefore how much capital would banks need to sustain the losses experienced during the upswing of the credit cycle and still have enough capital left to meet market pressures at the bottom of the cycle (Hanson, Kashyap, and Stein 2011). Correcting this omission of market pressure to hold adequate capital leads to a higher optimal capital ratio than when assuming unrealistically that banks can operate (after credit losses) with near-zero capital ratios.

5. The consensus chooses to measure bank losses during the global financial crisis using an income statement approach rather than a balance sheet approach. Using net income as the preferred measure of losses leads to a lower estimate of the optimal capital ratio because credit losses are offset against bank revenues and those revenues usually do not stay negative for long in a surviving bank, even in a severe crisis. But in severe crisis conditions, when many banks are failing or close to failing, market participants will find it difficult to know which banks will survive long enough to earn those positive revenues over the next year or two. Put in other words, they won't know which banks are "going concerns" and which are "gone concerns." What market participants think about potential bank losses and bank survival matters because that perception is important for bank runs and subsequent fire sales. The better assumption for measuring losses during the worst financial crisis since the Great Depression is to use the balance sheet approach, which yields a higher optimal capital ratio.

6. The consensus also takes little account of either earnings management or survivorship bias in measuring bank losses during the 2007–09 crisis. By earnings management, I mean using discretionary measures—such as taking lower loan-loss provisions and showing lower realization of losses on securities—to smooth net earnings during a crisis and to avoid reporting large(r) losses. By survivorship bias, I mean dropping from the sample some banks that did not survive the crisis. Suffice to say that the studies reviewed in chapter 5 indicate that both of these distortions to observed bank losses were present during the global financial crisis. Even though we don't as yet have a good estimate of their combined effect, there is no question that earnings management and survivorship bias have biased down the consensus estimate of the optimal capital ratio.

7. When looking at peak losses during earlier systemic banking crises, there is a choice between focusing on the average/median in the sample or paying more attention to (relevant) extreme observations. The consensus almost always sticks to the average, even though the worst crises can involve losses many times larger than the mean loss. In a similar vein, the consensus typically measures losses on an annual or semiannual basis, which smooths peak losses relative to quarterly data. While reasonable people could differ on which crisis observations are the most relevant for a future US crisis, the consensus tendency to downplay the extremes leads it to a lower optimal capital ratio.

8. The consensus usually fails to incorporate a key insight from the macro-prudential approach to bank supervision—namely, that the capital ratio that the economy needs both to sustain a healthy rate of bank lending and

to remain solvent against bank losses in a crisis is higher than the capital ratio needed just to absorb losses (BCBS 2010d).

9. Yet another sin of omission committed by the consensus is to see bank capital solely as "solvency" protection and not to take account of the "liquidity" benefits of higher capital. Recent empirical studies (for example, Pierret 2015) show that a bank's capital shortfall under stress influences how much debt it can raise. Similarly, the macroprudential approach highlights that where there is substantial reliance on uninsured wholesale financing, the "run point" for a systemic bank is at a higher capital rate than the solvency point. The message here is that while higher bank capital may not be the main supervisory tool for discouraging runs and fire sales, it helps a good deal—and this benefit needs to be accounted for in estimating the optimal capital ratio.

10. The consensus usually assumes that output losses in systemic banking crises are mostly temporary and do not have a large negative impact on potential output. Recent research has put this assumption in doubt. It finds that during the global financial crisis, the negative effect on potential output in advanced economies was about as large as the effect on actual output (e.g., Ball 2014a, 2014b). This raises the output cost of a systemic bank crisis from the 60 percent of GDP level commonly employed in the consensus to as much as 200 percent of GDP. Ceteris paribus, the higher the output cost of a banking crisis, the higher the optimal capital ratio.

11. The consensus uses historical databases on the unconditional annual probability of a systemic banking crisis (in a large group of advanced and developing countries) to drive its estimate of the benefits of higher capital ratios. This probability is typically assumed to be in the range of 2 to 5 percent. With such a low probability, it does not take much capital before the reduction in the probability of a crisis induced by higher capital ratios hits zero. At that point the marginal benefit from higher capital ratios also hits zero, because that benefit is the product of the change in the crisis probability and the output cost of a crisis.

The rub is that the historical probability of a crisis may not be a good guide to future crisis probabilities. This probability fluctuated sharply across subperiods in the international sample, and it was higher in the United States in 1892–1933 than it was in 1934–2007.[18] The historical probability of large losses at large US banks during the 1986–2005 period provided a very poor forecast (way too optimistic) of the losses experienced by those banks during the 2007–09 crisis (Kuritzkes and Schuermann 2007). Nor does the (average) historical crisis probability fully capture the rise of the US shadow banking system, with its large stock of uninsured, runnable, short-term liabilities and the potential adverse spillover effects on the banking system of another run on these shadow banks. Setbacks to the crisis management arsenal that have taken place in the wake of the 2007–09 crisis also count—for both future crisis severity and probability. Here, former US Treasury Secretary Timothy Geithner (2016) underlines that of 21 financial crisis tools used during the 2007–09 crisis (spanning lending, guarantee, and bank-capital programs), 12 of them could not be activated if needed today. Likewise, monetary and fiscal policy tools are more constrained today than they were in 2007.

A sensible guideline for crisis prevention is to hope for the best but prepare for the worst. A poor substitute is to hope for the best but prepare for the global average.

12. At the heart of the banking industry's opposition to much higher capital requirements is the assertion that higher bank capital requirements will depress bank lending and thereby reduce output and employment in the economy. This assertion is increasingly at odds with the empirical evidence—as well as with the appraisals of senior bank supervisors. I cannot emphasize this enough: Better-capitalized banks lend more, not less, than weakly capitalized ones. One impressive recent study, which looked at 105 large banks from advanced economies over the 1994–2012 period, finds that after holding other factors constant, a 1 percentage point increase in the equity to total assets ratio (i.e., leverage ratio) is associated with a 0.6 percent increase in total lending growth (Gambacorta and Shin 2016; see also Cohen and Scatigna 2014 and Cecchetti 2014 for similar findings). With this empirical finding, a key pillar of the case against much higher capital requirements is taken away.

13. In a parallel fashion, the consensus view of the effect of higher capital requirements on banks' overall funding cost sits on shaky ground. Most estimates either fail to allow for any Modigliani-Miller (M&M) offset or, if they do, focus too much on the cost of new equity and not enough on the cost of raising new debt financing. The M&M theorem (1958) shows that under certain assumptions, shifting a firm's capital structure away from debt toward equity leaves the firm's total funding cost unchanged. Because of favorable tax treatment of debt (relative to dividends), subsidies granted to too big to fail banks, deposit insurance, bankruptcy costs, and principal-agent problems, the M&M theorem does not hold strictly in the real world. Still, its fundamental insight—that higher equity reduces the riskiness of both equity and debt and therefore lowers the required rate of return, blunting any sizable increase in overall financing costs—is a much better approximation than the doomsday claims of the banking industry.

Focusing on the effect of higher capital on debt funding costs makes sense because debt is the dominant form of financing for banks. Gambacorta and Shin (2016) report important new empirical evidence on the effect of higher bank capital on bank funding costs. They use a comprehensive database on 105 large banks in 14 advanced economies over the 1994–2012 period. They find that, all else equal, a 1 percentage point increase in the equity to total assets (leverage) ratio was associated with approximately a 4-basis-point reduction in the average cost of debt funding. They then use this estimate, along with data on the "average" bank in their sample, to calculate the overall change in the cost of bank funding from a 1 percentage point increase in the leverage ratio. Their answer is 3 basis points. They argue that even this modest estimate probably overstates the true effect, because it does not allow the cost of equity funding to fall as the funding mix shifts toward equity.

Using the estimates of Gambacorta and Shin (2016) and Hanson, Kashyap, and Stein (2011) and assuming that 80 percent of the increase in bank funding costs were passed on to bank customers would imply that an 800-basis-point increase in the G-SIB leverage ratio—from its current (weighted-average) level of about 8 to 16 percent—would yield an increase in G-SIB bank lending rates of only 20 basis points.[19] Since G-SIBs represent a little above 60 percent of total consolidated US bank holding company assets, the increase in overall bank lending rates would be lower still—about 12 basis points.[20] And as I show in chapter 7, even when this large increase in minimum leverage requirements for G-SIBs is paired with more modest increases in minimum leverage ratios for large non-G-SIB banks and for smaller banks, the increase in overall bank lending rates is only 14 basis points. The consensus typically assumes an increase in bank lending rates considerably higher than that. All else equal, the lower the increase in bank lending spreads, the higher the optimal capital ratio.

14. It is useful to compare my estimated 20-basis-point increase in G-SIB bank funding costs (linked to much higher capital requirements) to the estimated bank funding effects of too big to fail subsidies for systemically important banks (SIBs). In the IMF (2014a) estimates, the annual too big to fail subsidy was lowest for US SIBs, at roughly 15 basis points in normal periods, but rising to 75 basis points for a distressed SIB. Too big to fail subsidies were higher for Japanese, UK, and euro area banks. As these subsidies are funded by the government, elimination of them should not count as a social cost. The bottom line is that a 20-basis-point-plus increase in G-SIB bank lending rates represents a negligible social cost. And the lower the social costs of higher capital ratios, the higher the optimal capital ratio.

15. To translate any increase in bank funding costs into increases in bank lending rates, the consensus almost always assumes full pass-through. The argument for doing so is that failure to pass on fully the increase in funding costs would induce resources to leave the banking industry, with adverse consequences for economic growth. However, as chapter 8 shows, beyond a certain threshold (which US and EU financial systems have already passed), a larger banking and a large financial system become a drag on economic growth, not a spur to it.

16. The recent empirical evidence is not kind to the full pass-through assumption. Cecchetti (2014) examines the effects of the Basel III capital increases using data for 15 large economies. Comparing indicators of bank performance in 2013 and the average for 2000–07, he finds that profitability, net interest margins, and operating costs were all lower in 2013. His interpretation is that to the extent that capital increases imposed costs, these costs were borne by equity holders in the form of lower dividends and managers in the form of lower compensation (which is included in operating costs). He stresses that contrary to the predictions of pessimists, there was no ballooning of interest margins. In light of Cecchetti's finding of essentially zero pass-through of Basel III increases in funding costs to lending rates, my assumption (below) of 80 percent pass-through—that is, that a 24-basis-point increase in G-SIB bank funding costs would lead to a 20-basis-point increase in G-SIB lending rates—seems conservative.

17. Increases in minimum capital requirements that are phased in gradually and can be funded largely by retained earnings are less costly than increases implemented more quickly and funded largely by new equity issuance. On this I agree with the consensus. But if capital increases are going to be funded mainly from retained earnings, it is crucial to tightly control dividend payments and share buybacks, because those discretionary actions drain bank capital. If US bank supervisors were tougher on controlling dividends and share buybacks in the run-up to the global financial crisis, the needed public bank recapitalization during the crisis would have been much lower.

18. Based on the evidence and considerations outlined above, I see an 800-basis-point increase in leverage ratios for US G-SIBs, phased in gradually over 10 years, as consistent with roughly a 20-basis-point increase in G-SIB bank lending rates. Equivalently, G-SIB lending rates would increase by about 2 basis points a year during the phase-in period.

19. As indicated above, a 20-basis-point increase in G-SIB lending rates translates into only a 12-basis-point increase in overall bank lending rates (because G-SIBs account for 62 percent of total consolidated bank holding

company assets). There is no reason to believe that a 12-basis-point increase in overall bank lending rates would have a large negative impact on the level of US real GDP. It is useful to reference the rule of thumb that says a 100-basis-point increase in the US federal funds rate (which boosts the entire term structure of interest rates) lowers the level of real GDP by about 100 basis points over eight quarters.[21] A similar size increase in the overall bank lending rate should produce just a fraction of that effect given its narrower impact. Banks are responsible for only about a third of the credit extended to the private nonfinancial sector in the United States (Fischer 2015b). On the basis of this rule of thumb, the macroeconomic impact of a 12-basis-point increase in overall bank lending rates spread over 10 years—induced by a cumulative 800-basis-point increase in minimum leverage ratios for G-SIBs—is likely to be so small as to be barely detectable in the macro data.[22] Moreover, such a tiny macro effect could be easily offset by the Fed lowering the path (infinitesimally) for the federal funds rate. The consensus assumes larger output effects. The smaller the (negative) output effects of higher capital ratios, the higher the optimal capital ratio.

20. The primary capital standard for bank regulation should have three properties: It should be better than the alternatives in distinguishing sick from healthy banks; be easy to understand, inexpensive to compute, and difficult to manipulate; and possess superior loss absorbency. By no stretch of the imagination do the existing risk-based measures of capital fit this job description. Indeed, the deficiencies of risk-based capital measures—especially of the internal models approach to setting risk weights—are so serious that the leverage ratio should become the primary measuring rod for capital adequacy, not only in bank stress tests but also more broadly in supervision.

21. Making the leverage ratio king of the hill need not mean that there would be no risk sensitivity in bank supervision or stress tests. To incentivize banks not to load up on risky assets and to compensate for some of the weaknesses of existing stress tests, I propose that large banks be subject to a risk surcharge. This surcharge would be based on a set of indicators, in much the same way that G-SIB capital surcharges are based on a set of systemic risk indicators. One might think of six types of indicators:

- a measure of tail risk dependence,
- the rate of loan growth cum a measure of the overvaluation of property prices,
- market-based measures of bank health (e.g., contingent claims analysis of distance to default, leverage ratios that depend on market value of equity rather than book values),

- risk derived from reverse scenarios, in which one solves for the shocks that will produce a given decline in the capital ratio,

- areas of risk where the supervisors have special concerns (e.g., leveraged loans, commercial real estate, etc.), and

- the ratio of risk-weighted assets to total assets, where risk-weighted assets come from a revised standardized approach to risk weighting.

Banks with high risk scores would be subject to a capital shortage; banks with normal or low scores would not.

22. Each of these risk indicators has strengths and weaknesses. When used in combination, they should do better at identifying dangerous levels of asset risk than a single indicator alone. Tail dependence indicators pick up the crucial difference between a solitary bank failure and simultaneous bank failures. The rate of loan growth has been shown to be a useful early warning indicator of deteriorating credit quality and, when paired with a measure of the overvaluation of property prices, subsequent banking crises. Market-based indicators of bank health often do better at diagnosing bank vulnerability than slower-moving accounting (book value) measures. Reverse scenarios are useful because they are portfolio specific in a way that traditional stress test scenarios are not. Allowing supervisors to assign a relatively high risk weight to asset concentrations that are of particular current concern guards against the risk that the nature of risk changes over time. Finally, the ratio of risk-weighted assets to total assets—if obtained from a revised "standardized" approach to risk weights—combines credit, market, and operational risk, without the "noise" created by manipulation from banks' internal models.

23. The Bank of England's approach to setting G-SIB leverage surcharges as a proportion of G-SIB surcharges for risk-based capital measures—what I call the "symmetry and proportionality" approach—is a highly artificial construct that ought not be replicated. It is based on the faulty assumption that the bank-capital regime must retain both the risk-based capital standard and the leverage ratio as Pillar 1 requirements and that there is only one way of getting both the risk-based standard and the leverage ratio to be binding simultaneously. This approach would prevent authorities from moving the leverage ratio (way) up to its optimal level. It also yields unduly low capital surcharges for UK G-SIBs. On top of that, the Bank of England has concluded that the optimal common equity tier 1 and Basel III leverage ratios (exclusive of G-SIB surcharges) need be only 8.5 and 3.0 percent, respectively, under the dubious argument that the regulatory minimums should not be designed for the riskiest banks in unusually risky situations (Brazier 2015).

24. In contrast, the Federal Reserve's "estimated impact" approach is an appealing way to think about what it means to eliminate too big to fail and how to go about estimating G-SIB capital surcharges (Board of Governors 2015b). Unfortunately, its conclusion that the top surcharge for the largest G-SIB needs to be no higher than 450 basis points is seriously flawed.[23] Once one employs a $50 billion bank as the appropriate non-G-SIB reference bank instead of a $250 billion one; factors in the likelihood that G-SIBs have a higher probability of default than non-G-SIB; and recognizes that the historical data are likely to give too optimistic a picture of future crisis probabilities, the appropriate capital surcharge for the largest G-SIB rises to the neighborhood of 800 basis points. The Fed's current G-SIB surcharge range for risk-based capital measures of 100 to 450 basis points is too low and too flat.

25. The problem is even more pronounced for leverage ratios, where G-SIBs face a minimum leverage ratio (under the enhanced supplementary leverage ratio) of 5 to 6 percent (versus a minimum of 3 to 4 percent for other banks).[24] It is likewise regrettable that US regulatory and supervisory officials have applied essentially the same capital hurdle rate to all bank holding companies participating in the CCAR stress tests, without regard to the large variations in their systemic importance.

26. To remedy the most glaring deficiencies in the existing bank capital regime in the United States, I propose a reform plan. The four existing Pillar 1 bank-capital standards would be replaced with a single (Pillar 1) standard, the tangible leverage ratio. Long-term minimums for the tangible leverage ratio would be established for three different classes of US banks. For G-SIBs the long-term target would be 14 to 18 percent (depending on the bank's systemic importance). For other large banks, the long-term target would be 11 to 13 percent (again depending on systemic importance). For smaller banks, the long-term target would be 10 percent. These long-term targets would be phased in (in roughly equal annual installments) over 10 years. Risk sensitivity would be introduced into the regime via a new (Pillar 2) risk surcharge. This surcharge would sit on top of the basic minimum leverage ratio, and it would have a positive charge for banks whose assets and/or off-balance-sheet commitments were judged to be unusually risky relative to their peers. The new leverage minimums would be translated into the baseline (unstressed) capital hurdle rates in the annual CCAR stress tests. The stressed hurdle rates would be set below the baseline rates, depending on the severity of the scenarios and the model parameters that link the shocks to bank capital. In the middle of the phase-in period, the Federal Reserve would assess the effects of the higher capital standards on the financial system and on the broader US economy. If that assessment

were positive, the second five-year period of hurdle rate increases would proceed as planned; if not, the Federal Reserve would have the authority to propose and enact a slower rate of increase or even to suspend these increases entirely.

27. The plan has a number of important advantages.

28. The plan would deliver a quantum jump in the amount of loss-absorbing, high-quality capital in the funding structure of the largest US banks. It would create enough of a capital cushion to withstand not only the scale of losses suffered in the 2007–09 crisis but the even larger (hypothetical) losses under a no-more-too-big-to-fail scenario with more limited government intervention. This higher capital cushion would also help deter runs on banks by wholesale creditors, who could be more confident that their bank counterparties were unquestionably solvent. The taxpayer would not be on the hook. There would be enough capital left after a severe crisis to provide sufficient loan growth to support a recovery.

29. The plan's proposed range and pace of capital increases are perfectly consistent with maintaining satisfactory macroeconomic performance. Well-capitalized banks lend more, not less, than weakly capitalized ones. As outlined above, the plan's proposed increases in minimum leverage ratios over a 10-year period would likely lead to approximately a 14-basis-point increase in overall bank lending rates. Such a small and gradual increase in bank lending rates would have only a barely detectable effect on the level of long-term US real GDP—and even that effect could be offset by a very small decrease in the federal funds rate.

30. The plan's three-level structure requires the largest increases in bank capital where they are needed most—at the nation's largest and most systemically important banks. These are the same banks that received the lion's share of official assistance during the Great Recession as well as the ones where the existing leverage ratio is actually lower than in smaller banks of less systemic importance. By mandating lower minimum leverage ratios for non-G-SIBs and small banks (including more than 6,000 community banks), the plan is able to reach a 16 percent (weighted average) leverage ratio for G-SIBs while producing an overall (across all banks) weighted-average minimum leverage ratio target of 14½ percent. The overall (weighted average) increase in minimum leverage ratios under the plan is 600 basis points (for the tangible leverage ratio)—significantly below the 800-basis-point increase that would be needed under an across-the-board 16 percent leverage ratio target.

31. The plan offers a new answer to the question of how an unweighted leverage ratio and some risk weighting of assets can best be used in tandem. The conventional dual standard (both Pillar 1) bank-capital model has been a failure. The leverage ratio gets much closer to what one should want from a single Pillar 1 minimum capital requirement. The proposed Pillar 2 risk surcharge framework would compensate for some weaknesses and omissions in the existing supervisor-led stress tests, address the leverage ratio's lack of risk sensitivity, and provide some deterrence against the possibility of banks loading up on risky assets. Crucially, it would be binding without constraining the height of the basic leverage ratio itself.

32. The plan would steepen the leverage surcharge schedule for G-SIBs. If real progress is to be made in ending too big to fail, and direct restrictions on bank size are not the route that the Executive and the Congress want to take to get there, another way has to be found to motivate the largest banks to decrease over time their systemic footprint. The plan would provide the necessary price incentives to induce them to do so.

33. The likely objections to the plan are not persuasive.

34. Proposals for much heightened capital requirements are not necessarily pie in the sky.[25] These proposals have been put forward by both Democrats and Republicans, and by officials as well as academics. Imposing much higher minimum leverage ratios on the largest US banks has also been favored by community banks to level the playing the field. Among such proposals, the plan's proposed minimum leverage ratio schedule falls squarely in the middle of the range. If banks were much better capitalized, they would be on stronger ground in arguing that structural activity restraints (like the Volcker Rule) are not needed. At some point, CEOs of G-SIBs could well come to the conclusion that higher capital ratios are the neatest, least intrusive, and least costly mechanism for satisfying regulators and the public that they are safe enough.

35. The body of empirical evidence strongly suggests that if the plan were to shrink the size of the largest banks, the banking system, and the financial system as a whole, the results would not be adverse for US macroeconomic performance. This is because the United States has already passed the point where, without subsidies, getting bigger generates increasing returns.

36. Of the potential objections, the weightiest one is that heightened capital requirements for banks could induce increased migration to the shadow banking system, where regulation is laxer, with potential unhappy consequences for financial stability. Even though the size of the cash-like

part of the shadow banking system has fallen from its precrisis peak, this risk has to be taken seriously (Stein, Greenwood, and Hanson 2016).

37. In the wake of the crisis, a set of reforms was put in train to reduce the fragility of the shadow banking system. Not enough time has passed to know whether these reforms will be sufficient, particularly as regards runs on shadow banks with short-term liabilities and illiquid longer-term assets. If danger signs emerge (again), I propose a backup contingency initiative to better run-proof the shadow banks. This initiative owes to former Bank of England governor Mervyn King (2016), who calls it the "pawnbroker for all seasons" (PFAS). At the heart of the PFAS is a limit on the amount of short-term (one year or less) liabilities a bank or shadow bank can issue. These liabilities cannot exceed the sum of reserves held at the central bank plus the estimated value of haircut-adjusted collateral positioned with the central bank. This PFAS "liquidity" reform would be a valuable complement to the higher-capital solvency plan outlined in this book. It could replace the liquidity coverage ratio and the net stable funding ratio, which apply only to banks. Like the plan for much heightened capital requirements, the PFAS could be phased in over 10 to 15 years. The reform is streamlined relative to other shadow-bank reforms and would be an effective way to address the migration and "run" vulnerabilities in the present financial system.

38. Although the G-20's Total Loss-Absorbing Capacity (TLAC) initiative also sets higher minimum capital standards for G-SIBs, it is not a good substitute for the plan. Under TLAC, by January 1, 2022 G-SIBs would be required to have TLAC-eligible instruments equal to 18 percent of their risk-weighted assets as well as to 6.75 percent of their Basel III total leverage exposure. Less than half the minimum TLAC requirement is expected to be made up of subordinated debt and long-term bail-in bonds (CoCos) that are to be converted into equity once certain prespecified minimum capital ratio criteria are met. Under the accompanying Single Point of Entry (SPOE) reform, the structure of G-SIBs would also be altered so that "losses" by bank subsidiaries performing critical economic functions can be passed upward to the bank holding company, thereby allowing such subsidiaries to remain solvent and operational.

39. The minimum leverage ratio for G-SIBs under the plan is 14 to 18 percent versus less than 7 percent under TLAC. The plan therefore provides much greater loss absorbency. Equity already in place is superior to a bond that converts to equity under a set of prespecified criteria. Setting the trigger for bail-in bonds at the right level is tricky. Pure equity has no trigger issue; it already is equity. Bail-in bonds have a much higher probability than equity of being bailed out in a severe crisis. Ask yourself: Which

is going to produce the better crisis dynamic: trying to bail in bondholders in a severe crisis when banks are trying to keep their funding sources from drying up, or having a comfortable equity cushion in place and allowing that equity capital to be drawn down to reflect credit losses? Bail-in bonds can become a crisis amplification mechanism during a severe crisis as the price of these bonds collapses and the market for them dries up. Unlike dividends, there can be no suspension of interest payments on CoCos. The worthwhile SPOE initiative can be implemented just as easily under the plan as under TLAC.

40. Last but not least, for all the additional risks the TLAC initiative brings with it relative to the plan, it is not much cheaper in terms of its effects on overall bank lending rates and on the level of real GDP. As suggested above, my best estimate is that increasing the tangible leverage ratio in US G-SIBs from roughly 8 to 16 percent would raise overall bank lending rates by about by 12 basis points over a 10-year period. Adding in the assumed smaller increases in leverage ratios for large non-G-SIB banks and smaller banks would raise the tally for increases in overall bank lending rates to 14 basis points. The Bank for International Settlements (BIS 2015b) recently published the results of its quantitative impact study of TLAC implementation. While it is hazardous to compare bank-capital plans that have many moving parts and that employ quite different assumptions, my back-of-the-envelope calculation is that TLAC would wind up cutting the increase in overall bank lending rates (relative to my plan) by roughly 7 to 12 basis points.[26] If, as argued above and in chapter 4, the macroeconomic effects of a 14-basis-point increase in overall bank lending rates, implemented gradually over a decade, is barely detectable, the macroeconomic savings from a rate rise smaller than that (under TLAC) would be virtually invisible. The conclusion is clear: TLAC is penny wise and pound foolish.

Appendix I

Event and Impact Studies of US and EU-Wide Stress Tests

There is by now a significant and rapidly growing empirical literature that presents "event studies" of the US and EU-wide stress tests. Such studies focus on two questions: (1) Was the announcement of the tests and/or publication of the results followed by positive cumulative abnormal returns on bank equity for the tested banks (and sometimes, for nontested banks as well) and (2) did the announcement and/or publication of the tests and results—be they positive or negative—provide market participants with information that they did not have before? Good reviews of this literature can be found in Candelon and Sy (2015); Fernandez, Igan, and Pinheiro (2015); and Flannery, Hirtle, and Kovner (2015), while MacKinlay (1997) provides a review of the standard methodology for doing such event studies. Unfortunately, the results of these event studies seem to be quite sensitive to the metrics used to judge impact (that is, average cumulative abnormal returns, absolute value of average cumulative abnormal returns, behavior of price-to-book ratios, credit default swap spreads, and trading volumes), to the presence or absence of tests for significant differences between tested and nontested banks, and to the model used to generate expected returns before the event

Flannery, Hirtle, and Kovner (2015) argue that earlier event studies of stress tests are badly flawed because mean returns for tested banks could be zero for two quite different reasons: the abnormal return is very small for all firms or the returns are large in absolute value but positive for some banks and negative for others. They therefore recommend that researchers look at the absolute value of these returns, as well as at trading volumes. When they do so for the DFAST and CCAR tests conducted in 2009–15, they find that disclosure of the results generated new information about stress tested banks. They also find larger effects on tested banks than on nontested ones.

Very few studies compare the results of the US and EU-wide tests on a like-to-like basis. Greenlaw et al. (2012) do an event-study comparison of the market reaction to the 2009 US stress test with that for the 2009 EU-wide test. Drawing on bank equity prices and CDS prices, they found that the markets assessed the US test much more favorably than the EU-wide one. Candelon and Sy (2015) compare the results of the 2009 SCAP and the 2012 and 2013 CCAR tests on the one hand with the results of the 2009, 2010, and 2011 EU-wide tests and the 2012 EU-wide capital exercise on the other. They look only at average cumulative abnormal returns, not the average absolute value of those returns. For those tests (relating to publication of results for the tested banks), the only one with large, positive, and statistically significant average abnormal return is the 2009 SCAP. They find positive, statistically significant, albeit much smaller effects for the 2012 CCAR and the 2010 and 2012 EU-wide tests and a negative, statistically significant effect for the 2012 EU-wide test. They argue that the generalized common view that all EU-wide stress tests were unsuccessful is not accurate, pointing in particular to the estimated positive impact of the 2010 test on returns, with an estimated size roughly half that for the 2009 SCAP.

Ong and Pazarbasioglu (2013) compare crisis stress tests in the United States and the European Union. They regard a crisis stress test as having achieved its objectives if it sets a floor under selected financial market indicators. They find that the 2009 SCAP satisfies this criterion but the early EU-wide stress tests did not.

I do not know of any formal event studies of the 2014 EU-wide stress test. A Bloomberg poll, however, taken shortly after publication of 2014 EU-wide stress test results, found that 51 percent of respondents (investors, traders, and analysts who are Bloomberg subscribers) thought that the results "failed to provide an accurate gauge of their financial stability," 32 percent thought the results were accurate, and 17 percent were not sure.[27] The corresponding figures for the US stress tests were 36, 46, and 17 percent.

Some studies suggest that stress tests conducted under extreme crisis conditions are more apt to be successful than tests conducted under more normal conditions. Of the US stress tests, only the SCAP is considered to be a crisis management test; it was also the first test. On the EU side, because the 2007–09 crisis was followed by the 2010–13 debt crisis, most of the tests had a crisis management element to them.

Glasserman and Tangirala (2015) show that tests convey less new information to market participants once they become more routine and predictable.

All in all, I see little in the event-study evidence to contradict my conclusion that the markets received the EU tests more poorly than they received the US tests.

Endnotes

1. For a review of early stress testing, see Hirtle and Lehnert (2014). Moretti, Stolz, and Swinburne (2008) and Ong (2014) present the IMF's approach to and experience with stress testing. Bernanke (2013) notes that the 2009 SCAP was the first time that US regulatory authorities conducted a stress test simultaneously across the largest banks. Stress tests are also sometimes conducted for nonbank financial institutions of various kinds (including insurance companies). This book is confined to stress tests for banks.

2. Between January 20, 2009 (Inauguration Day) and April 30, 2009, an S&P index of financial stocks averaged a 5 percent daily move; the average during normal periods is less than 1 percent. Just before the SCAP results were released, an unweighted average of five-year credit default spreads for Bank of America, Citigroup, Goldman Sachs, JPMorgan Chase, Morgan Stanley, and Wells Fargo stood at roughly 300 basis points, versus about 25 basis points before the 2007 crisis began and about 450 basis points in October 2008, when the Troubled Asset Relief Program (TARP) was announced. After contracting by more than 8 percent in the fourth quarter of 2008, real GDP growth continued to fall during the first two quarters of 2009, and the unemployment rate rose by about 4 percentage points (from 5 to 9 percent) in the 12 months before February 2009 (see Bernanke 2013, Geithner 2014).

3. The Federal Reserve and the US government provided support to financial institutions during the crisis by guaranteeing liabilities and injecting capital into banks and liquidity into an array of markets. In addition, the Federal Reserve cut interest rates to extremely low levels. See Blinder and Zandi (2010, 2015) and Wolf (2014b) for a recap of these support measures. Chapter 1 examines how the effectiveness of other crisis management policies affects the credibility of bank stress tests.

4. Atkinson, Luttrell, and Rosenblum (2013) estimate that the US financial crisis of 2007–09 cost the United States $6 trillion to $14 trillion in forgone GDP. Better Markets (2015) concludes that the crisis led to $7.9 trillion of actual losses of GDP relative to potential GDP and to $3.6 trillion in reduced GDP potential (primarily as a function of reduced capital stocks and reduced labor hours resulting from the effects of the Great Recession). Ball (2014a, 2014b) finds that the Great Recession had dire effects on advanced economies' productive capacity, as measured by OECD and IMF estimates of potential output. The countries with the deepest recessions experienced the greatest long-term damage. For the 23 countries taken as a group, Ball estimates the loss of potential output relative to the precrisis path at more than 8 percent.

5. All of these tests, except the 2011 one, published bank-by-bank results.

6. The 33 bank holding companies participating in the 2016 CCAR stress test increased their (weighted) average common equity tier 1 capital ratios from 5.5 percent in the first quarter of 2009 to 12.2 percent in the fourth quarter of 2016 (Tarullo 2016).

7. Bernanke (2013) reports that banks' holdings of cash and high-quality liquid securities more than doubled between end-2007 and April 2013.

8. See, for example, ECB (2014b, 2016) and Constâncio (2015). As of end-2015, the weighted-average common equity tier 1 capital ratio for the 51 banks participating in the 2016 EU-wide stress test was 13.2 percent (EBA 2016d). The corresponding figure (as of the first quarter of 2016) for the 33 bank holding companies participating in the 2016 US CCAR test was 12.2 percent (Board of Governors 2016a). The IMF (2016b) reports that the three-month moving average of price-to-book ratios in mid-2016 stood at about 0.6 for euro area banks versus 1.0 for US banks.

9.   See, for example, the charts in Ong and Pazarbasioglu (2013) and ECB (2014a).

10. As a whole the crisis management supporting cast for the EU-wide stress tests was weak, a problem that contributed to the tests' poor market reception (see chapter 1). Nevertheless, several important nonstress initiatives had a positive impact on banks, including the statement by ECB President Mario Draghi in July 2012 that the ECB would do "whatever it takes" to save the euro and the ECB's announcement of three rounds of long-term refinancing operations for EU banks (the long-term refinancing operation in December 2011, the first targeted long-term refinancing operation in September 2014, and the second targeted long-term refinancing operation in March 2016). Acharya et al. (2015) show that one of the main reasons why the Draghi "whatever it takes" statement had such a positive effect on EU banks was that it generated large capital gains for EU banks holding relatively large shares of sovereign EU periphery bonds.

11. In the internal models–based approach to risk weighting, risk weights are estimated using the bank's internal models rather than set by bank supervisors. Nevertheless, the basic concept is the same for understanding the difference between risk-weighted capital measures and unweighted capital measures (leverage ratios).

12. The EU risk-weight density figures are for mid-2015 and come from Berger, Hüttl, and Merler (2016).

13. Although total leverage exposure provides a more comprehensive picture of risk exposures, some analysts do not regard it as a better measure of risk than total assets because of the contentious treatment of future exposure for derivatives; they prefer the simplicity of total assets (see, for example, Ricks 2016).

14. The BCBS (2016, 17–18) defines total leverage exposure as including (1) on-balance-sheet assets, excluding securities financing transactions and derivatives; (2) securities financing transaction exposures with limited recognition of netting of cash receivables and cash payables with the same counterparty under strict criteria; (3) derivative exposures at replacement cost (net of cash variation margin meeting a set of strict eligibility criteria) plus an add-on for potential future exposure based on the current-exposure method; (4) written credit derivatives exposures at their effective notional amount (net of negative changes in fair value that have been incorporated into the calculation of tier 1 capital) reduced by the effective notional amount of purchased credit derivatives that meet offsetting criteria related to reference name level of seniority and maturity; (5) off-balance-sheet exposures, obtained by multiplying notional amounts by the credit conversion factors in the standardized approach to credit risk, subject to a floor of 10 percent; and (6) other exposures as specified in the Basel III leverage ratio framework. See also the footnotes to the FDIC Global Capital Index in Hoenig (2016b).

15. The Liikanen Report (2012, 40) describes the difference between US GAAP and IFRS as follows: "Under US GAAP, companies with derivatives under a single master netting agreement with the same counterparty are allowed the possibility to report assets and liabilities (including cash collateral) on a net basis, even if they do not intend to settle the cash flows on a net basis. The same treatment is allowed for repurchase agreements and reverse repurchase agreements. Unlike the current US standards, there are no such provisions under IFRS that apply to EU banks."

16. The Basel III netting compromise does, however, introduce one additional complexity, namely, that the relationship between total assets and total leverage exposure is different in countries using US GAAP than in countries using IFRS. Total leverage exposure for the eight US G-SIBs (taken as a group) is about 40 percent larger than total assets

(Allahrakha, Glasserman, and Young 2015), because the add-ons to total assets and the less generous treatment of netting of derivatives make total leverage exposure considerably larger than total assets. In contrast, under IFRS, total leverage exposure seems to be roughly the same as total assets. For example, Berger, Hüttl, and Merler (2016) report that for 12 EU G-SIBs, total leverage exposure was 97 percent of total assets; see Dowd (2016a, 2016c) for the figures on major UK banks and Deutsche Bank. This rough equality between total leverage exposure and total assets under IFRS arises because the add-ons to total assets increase total leverage exposure while the more generous treatment of netting under Basel III reduces total assets enough to roughly offset (or sometimes even overwhelm) the positive effect of these add-ons on total leverage exposure.

17. The hurdle rate is the minimum capital ratio that banks must meet in the test's baseline and adverse scenarios in order to have their capital plans approved by the bank supervisor.

18. See Barth and Miller (2017) on historical bank crisis probabilities in the United States from 1837 to 2009. The period between 1934 and 2007 is sometimes referred to as the "quiet period" for financial crises in the United States; see Gorton (2012).

19. There are two alternative approaches to translating increases in bank funding costs into increases in bank lending rates. I call them the "loans only" approach and the "loans plus" approach; see chapter 4 for a discussion and application.

20. By "overall" bank lending rates, I mean lending rates for the banking system as a whole—rather than lending rates for a subgroup of banks.

21. I am grateful to my Peterson Institute colleague David Stockton for sharing that (Federal Reserve) rule of thumb with me.

22. If one takes the 100-basis-point decrease in the level of real GDP linked to a 100-basis-point increase in the federal funds rate as the benchmark and if one assumes that the federal funds rate impacts 100 percent of the private nonfinancial sector, then a 12-basis-point increase in overall bank lending rates should have an effect on the level of real output that is roughly 4 percent as large, that is, the level of real output would decline by about 4 basis points. This 4-basis-point decline is the product of an increase in interest rates (overall bank lending rates) that is 12 percent as large as the assumed (100 basis point) increase in the federal funds rate and an impact of bank lending rates on the private nonfinancial sector that is 33 percent as large as that of the federal funds rate, that is, .12 times .33 equals .0396—or roughly 4 percent as large as in the federal funds rate benchmark.

23. The Fed argues that too big to fail would be eliminated when the expected systemic loss from the failure of a G-SIB is no greater than the failure of a large non-G-SIB. As, by definition, the systemic loss given default is higher for a G-SIB than for a non-G-SIB, the only way to make the expected losses equal for the two is to reduce the probability of default for the G-SIB just enough that it exactly offsets its higher loss given default. If, for example, the failure of a G-SIB would produce twice the systemic loss as the failure of a non-G-SIB, then the probability of default for the G-SIB needs to be half as large as for a non-G-SIB. The role of the G-SIB capital surcharge is to generate that decline in the default probability for G-SIBs. Among G-SIBs the higher the score for its systemic loss given default (relative to the reference non-G-SIB), the higher the surcharge needs to be.

24. The minimum is 4 percent for the tier 1 leverage ratio and 3 percent for the Basel III leverage ratio.

25. See the postscript (chapter 9) for my preliminary assessment of the Trump administration's plans for financial deregulation.

26. See chapter 8 for the assumptions behind this calculation.

27. Yalman Onaran, "ECB's Stress Test Failed to Restore Trust in Banks, Poll Shows," *Bloomberg Business*, November 17, 2014.

Why Were the EU-Wide Stress Tests Not Better Received?

There are many explanations for why the EU stress tests generated a less favorable reaction than their US counterparts. Five factors merit emphasis.[1]

Weak Supervisory Authority

The organizations coordinating the first three EU-wide stress tests—the Committee of European Banking Supervisors (CEBS) for the 2009 and 2010 tests and the European Banking Authority (EBA) for the 2011 tests— were new EU organizations without much clout vis-à-vis national bank supervisors—the same national supervisors that had slipped up on supervision and capital adequacy before the global economic and financial crisis. The CEBS and EBA had relatively small staffs and resources, no long track record of credibility, limited authority to challenge submitted information on bank assets, and no authority to compel (rather than just recommend) recapitalization if banks participating in the test were found to have capital shortfalls (see Posen and Véron 2014).[2] These features lie in sharp contrast to the lead agency running the stress tests in the United States, the Federal Reserve.[3]

No Critical Mass on EU Banking Union, and a More Serious Too Big to Fail Problem

The EU stress tests of 2009-11 were run before a critical mass of opinion had formed on the necessity of establishing an EU banking union.[4] Even putting aside the single (EU-wide) deposit insurance fund (on which there is still no EU-wide consensus), there was no meeting of minds before June 2012 on either bank resolution or EU-wide funding of bank failures. Even today questions remain about whether the multilayered decision process and small starting size of the common resolution fund would be adequate to address the failure of a cross-border EU bank with trillions of dollars of assets.[5] Schoenmaker and Véron (2016, 42) conclude that "banking union is only half-finished as an overarching policy framework" and cite the lack of common deposit insurance and a common backstop for the single resolution fund as key unfinished business. Before the 2009 stress test was completed in the United States, the US Treasury had more than $200 billion left from the initial Troubled Asset Relief Program (TARP) legislation that could be used to recapitalize undercapitalized US banks that could not raise the funds from the private markets.[6]

Note, too, that relative to the United States, big EU banks are much larger relative to both home-country and regional GDP, and banking is more important relative to capital markets. Put in other words, the "too big to fail" problem is much worse in the European Union than in the United States (see appendix 1A for a comparison of some popular indicators of too big to fail banks). When funding for bank recapitalization is in question, it is reasonable for investors to worry that estimated capital shortfalls in stress tests are being lowballed because supervisors do not want to publicize bank problems for which there are no immediate solutions lest they stoke market turbulence.

A Weak Supporting Crisis Management Cast

Over the 2007–16 period euro area economic officials (taken as a group) were less successful relative to their US counterparts in putting together a set of economic policies that make thin the catastrophic tail of the distribution for expected banking sector outcomes.[7]

Table 1.1 shows the Blinder and Zandi (2015) tabulation of the measures the US federal government undertook in response to the 2007–09 financial crisis, Blinder and Zandi (2015, 7) accurately characterize that response as "massive and multifaceted."[8] In the euro area, the supporting cast for stress tests has been less impressive. Critics contend that monetary policy stimulus has not been consistent enough or large enough; that fiscal policy consolidation, especially in the crisis-hit euro area periphery, has been too rapid and too large; that the European Central Bank (ECB) was not as aggressive as the Federal Reserve in intervening directly in financial markets to reduce volatility and to stabilize prices; that debt restructuring for the most debt-laden euro areas economies has been too small; and that

Table 1.1   Cost of US federal government response to the financial crisis
(billions of dollars)

Entity	Originally committed	Ultimate cost
Total	**12,332**	**1,640**
Federal Reserve	**6,699**	**15**
Term auction credit	900	0
Other loans	Unlimited	3
Primary credit	Unlimited	0
Secondary credit	Unlimited	0
Seasonal credit	Unlimited	0
Primary Dealer Credit Facility (expired 2/1/2010)	Unlimited	0
Asset-Backed Commercial Paper Money Market Mutual Fund	Unlimited	0
AIG	26	2
AIG (for special purpose vehicles)	9	0
AIG (for American International Assurance Company, Ltd. [AIA] and American Life Insurance Company [ALICO])	26	1
Rescue of Bear Stearns (Maiden Lane)[a]	27	4
AIG-residential mortgage-backed securities (RMBS) purchase program (Maiden Lane II)[a]	23	1
AIG-collateralized debt obligations purchase program (Maiden Lane III)[a]	30	4
Term Securities Lending Facility (expired 2/1/2010)	200	0
Commercial Paper Funding Facility[a] (expired 2/1/2010)	1,800	0
Term Asset-Backed Securities Loan Facility	1,000	0
Money Market Investor Funding Facility (expired 10/30/2009)	540	0
Currency swap lines (expired 2/1/2010)	Unlimited	0
Purchase of GSE debt and MBS (3/31/2010)	1,425	0
Guarantee of Citigroup assets (terminated 12/23/2009)	286	0
Guarantee of Bank of America assets (terminated)	108	0
Purchase of long-term Treasuries	300	0
Treasury	**1,160**	**40**
Troubled Asset Relief Program	600	40
Fed supplementary financing account	560	0
Fannie Mae and Freddie Mac[b]	Unlimited	0
Federal Deposit Insurance Corporation	**2,913**	**75**
Guarantee of US banks' debt[c]	1,400	4
Guarantee of Citigroup debt	10	0
Guarantee of Bank of America debt	3	0

(table continues)

Table 1.1   Cost of US federal government response to the financial crisis
(billions of dollars) *(continued)*

Entity	Originally committed	Ultimate cost
Federal Deposit Insurance Corporation *(continued)*		
Transaction deposit accounts	500	0
Public-Private Investment Fund Guarantee	1,000	0
Bank resolutions	Unlimited	71
Federal Housing Administration	**100**	**26**
Refinancing of mortgages, Hope for Homeowners	100	0
Expanded mortgage lending	Unlimited	26
Congress	**1,460**	**1,484**
Economic Stimulus Act of 2008	170	170
American Recovery and Reinvestment Act of 2009[d]	808	832
Cash for Clunkers	3	3
Additional emergency unemployment insurance benefits	90	90
Education, Jobs and Medicaid Assistance Act	26	26
Other stimulus	20	20
Tax Relief, Unemployment Insurance Reauthorization, and Job Creation Act of 2010	189	189
Temporary Payroll Tax Cut Continuation Act of 2011	29	29
Middle Class Tax Relief and Job Creation Act of 2012	125	125

GSE = government-sponsored enterprise

a. Net portfolio holdings.
b. Assumes fair value accounting.
c. Includes foreign-denominated debt.
d. Excludes alternative minimum tax patch.

Source: Blinder and Zandi (2015). Reprinted with permission.

creditor economies in the euro area, particularly Germany, led economic policy badly astray.

German leaders and senior officials misdiagnosed the euro area's balance of payments crisis as a generalized debt crisis (Wolf 2014b), failed to recognize the pivotal role of a shortage of aggregate demand in the euro area's dismal growth and employment performance (Wolf 2014b), and (before November 2012) allowed the debt crisis in the euro area periphery to deteriorate into a "bad expectations–led equilibrium" (De Grauwe 2011, 2015). German leadership assumed incorrectly that austerity would by itself generate structural reform, and it underestimated the impact austerity fatigue would have on catalyzing support for populist parties (on both the left and the right) and for populist economic policies. Appendix 1B provides a summary of studies that support the argument that "other" (non-stress-test) crisis management policies were less forceful and less effective in the euro area than in the United States during and after the crisis.

Whatever the explanation, three facts are unassailable. First, the euro area's recovery from the 2007–09 crisis has been anemic. Truman (2016) gauges the strength of recovery from the global financial crisis by the number of years it takes a country or region to return to the peak precrisis level of real GDP measured in local currency. It took the euro area as a whole seven years (until 2015) to return to the precrisis peak level of real GDP (assuming optimistically that Italy and Greece return to their precrisis peaks by 2021) (table 1.2). The corresponding figure for the United States was four years. For the six euro area crisis countries, the average recovery time was 11 years; the fastest recovery there (in Ireland) took seven years.[9] (By comparison, after the 1980s debt crisis, when there was also a synchronous global recession, it took the 11 hardest-hit South American countries plus Mexico just over five years to return to peak precrisis levels of real GDP.) In July 2016 the unemployment rate in the euro area (10.1 percent) was more than twice as high as in the United States (4.9 percent).

Second, the euro area has yet to overcome its deflation problem. Annual headline inflation in the euro area was 0.2 percent as of August 2016.[10] It has been below 1 percent for three years—well beneath the ECB's inflation target of "below, but close to 2 percent." (See chapter 9 for an update on the euro area's inflation performance.)

Third, the 2010–16 period has been marked by high volatility in both euro area sovereign risk and EU bank funding risk. It included several episodes where even more serious crises were prevented only at the last minute by the ECB and euro area crisis management initiatives, including, but not limited to, the Outright Monetary Transactions (OMT) and the Long-Term Refinancing Operation 1 (LTRO1), the creation of the European Financial Stability Fund (EFSF) and European Stability Mechanism (ESM), the ESM banking sector loan to Spain, and the troika support programs for Greece, Portugal, and Cyprus.

Bank stress tests do not operate in a vacuum. Where recovery from a historic crisis is weak, uneven, and uncertain and key policymakers disagree about what measures will stave off continuing underperformance for the regional economy as a whole, it is more difficult to make a sale from stress tests that the banks are out of danger.

Higher Outside Estimates of Capital Shortfalls

Outside estimates of the capital shortfall in the EU banking system have been consistently larger than the shortfalls emerging from the stress tests. Ever since International Monetary Fund (IMF) Managing Director

Table 1.2 Actual and projected recovery to previous real GDP peak in the euro area

Country	Year of precrisis GDP peak	Year in which precrisis peak was or will be reached	Number of years to reach precrisis peak
Crisis countries			
Cyprus	2011	2020(e)	9
Greece	2007	After 2021(e)	14+
Ireland	2007	2014	7
Italy	2007	After 2021(e)	14+
Portugal	2008	2020(e)	12
Spain	2008	2017(e)	9
Other euro area countries			
Austria	2007	2011	4
Belgium	2008	2010	2
Estonia	2007	2016(e)	9
Finland	2008	2020(e)	12
France	2008	2011	3
Germany	2008	2011	3
Latvia[a]	2007	2017(e)	10
Lithuania	2008	2014	6
Luxembourg	2007	2011	4
Malta	2008	2010	2
Netherlands	2008	2015	7
Slovak Republic	2008	2010	2
Slovenia	2008	2018(e)	10
Euro area average	2008	2015	7
Other economies			
European Union	2008	2014	6
United Kingdom	2007	2013	6
Canada	2008	2010	2
Japan	2007	2013	6
United States	2007	2011	4

(e) = estimate

a. Latvia had an IMF program before joining the euro area.

Source: Truman (2016).

Christine Lagarde put a spotlight on the need for "urgent capitalization" of Europe's banks in her August 2011 Jackson Hole speech, there has been a flurry of estimates suggesting that EU banks are significantly undercapitalized.

Acharya and Steffen (2014c, 1), for example, concluded that euro area banks have been severely undercapitalized since the 2007–09 financial crisis. Using book values of equity and assets, they estimated an aggregate EU capital shortfall of €82 billion to €176 billion. If the market values of equity and assets are employed instead, the estimated capital shortfall rises to €230 billion to €620 billion. Acharya and Steffen estimated the capital shortfall during a hypothetical systemic financial crisis (with a 40 percent decline in a market equity index) at €580 billion. Acharya, Schoenmaker, and Steffen (2011) reached similar results.

The IMF (2011b) and OECD (2013) estimated the aggregate capital shortfall for euro area banks at €200 billion to €300 billion and €400 billion, respectively. These estimates are much larger than those in the adverse scenarios of the EU stress tests.[11] They also far exceed the €55 billion Single Resolution Fund agreed to by EU finance ministers in December 2013—even assuming that the European Union follows through with its resolution plan to bail in equity holders and junior bondholders in a bank failure before drawing on public funds.

IMF research by Aiyar et al. (2015) indicated that capital ratios in many EU periphery economies are probably significantly overstated, because loan-loss provisions and credit write-downs are much lower than in US banks. Nonperforming loans (NPLs) in the European Union amounted to roughly €1 trillion at end-2014, more than double the level in 2009. Aiyar et al. (2015, 5) summarize the impaired asset problem in the European Union as follows:

> Write-off rates for European banks remain much lower than those of US banks, despite a much higher stock of NPLs. Results from a new survey of European country authorities and banks indicate that there are serious and interrelated impediments to NPL resolution in the areas of supervision, legal systems, and distressed debt markets, often compounded by informational and other institutional deficiencies. Insufficiently robust supervision can allow banks to avoid dealing with large NPL stockpiles and carry them on balance sheets for much longer than warranted. Weak debt enforcement and ineffective insolvency frameworks tend to lower the recovery value of problem loans. And markets for distressed debt in Europe—with some notable exceptions—are still underdeveloped, preventing the entry of much-needed capital and expertise.

Poor Design of the EU-Wide Stress Tests

The design of the EU stress tests contributed to their poor reception.

Early (2009–11) Tests

The methodology and results of the initial October 2009 test were described in a three-page press release summarizing the presentation made by the Committee of European Banking Supervisors (CEBS) to Economic and Financial Affairs Council (ECOFIN) ministers and governors. No individual bank results were published (making it impossible to distinguish weak from strong banks); the capital benchmark used in the 2009 test was the tier 1 ratio rather than the more demanding tier 1 common or core tier 1 ratio; and since none of the 22 major cross-border banks in the sample saw its tier 1 capital ratio fall below 6 percent even in the more adverse scenario, no capital actions were taken (beyond the government support measures announced during the crisis).

The second stress test, the results of which were released in July 2010, was an improvement. The 55-page report detailed the objectives, methodology, and results; the sample of banks was larger (91 banks, representing 65 percent of European banking assets); and individual bank results were published. In addition, given mounting market concerns over sovereign debt sustainability and banks' holding of government debt, the report provided data on banks' exposures to EU/European Economic Area central and local government debt, and the adverse scenario considered a shock in which the sovereign debt crisis worsened, resulting in losses to banks' trading books. This time seven banks (five in Spain, one in Greece, and one in Austria) saw their tier 1 capital ratios fall below 6 percent in the adverse scenario, leading to an aggregate shortfall of €3.5 billion.

Still, the sovereign debt scenario was widely viewed as inadequate, as 83 percent of sovereign debt exposures were held in the banking book, not the trading book, and no haircuts were assumed for the former. Blundell-Wignall and Slovik (2010) estimated that if the same losses assumed for the trading book were extended to the banking book, losses on sovereign debt exposures would have been €165 billion instead of €26 billion.

Another blow to the credibility of the July 2010 test came in October 2010, when the Irish banking system melted down—at enormous cost to Ireland's public debt position and the Irish taxpayer—just a few months after Ireland's two largest banks (the Bank of Ireland and the Allied Irish Bank) passed the test. The retention of tier 1 capital, as opposed to the tier 1 common measure employed in the US stress tests, also came in for criticism. Federal Reserve Chair Ben Bernanke's reading of the reaction to 2010 EU-wide stress test results (2015, 482) was representative: "European bank regulators conducted a stress test of the continent's banks in July (2010). But, unlike the US stress test of the previous year, investors did not see the results as credible, and Europe's banks remained wary of lending, including to each other."

EU-wide stress test number three was the first one coordinated by the EBA. It included some improvements over the earlier tests. The supporting documents were extensive, and the banks provided additional data. The bank-capital measure used (core tier 1 capital) was tougher than the tier 1 measure used in the two earlier tests, although the effect was offset by the lowering of the stressed bank hurdle rate (from 6 percent in the July 2010 test to 5 percent). According to the EBA's calculations, if the tier 1 definition had been retained, capital ratios would have been 17 percent higher than under the tougher standard. Haircuts on sovereign debt exposures of banks in the trading book were updated to reflect market conditions, and an increase in provisions was implemented for sovereign debt held in the banking book. Market concerns about sovereign debt exposures were allowed to increase the cost of funding in the adverse scenario. The difference between the baseline and the adverse scenarios was larger than in previous tests.

Thirty of the 91 banks in the test fell below the 5 percent capital hurdle rate, with an aggregate shortfall of roughly €27 billion.[12] Sixteen other banks displayed capital ratios of 5 to 6 percent. The EBA issued its first formal recommendation to national supervisory authorities—that banks below the 5 percent threshold promptly remedy their shortfall and that banks with capital ratios above but close to the threshold and with sizable exposure to sovereigns under stress also strengthen their capital positions, including, where necessary, by restricting dividends.

Despite these improvements, the Stoxx Europe 600 banks index fell more than 3 percent (to a two-year low) on the first trading day after the July 2011 EU-wide stress test results were released (see Ahmed et al. 2011). Bloomberg's Europe 500 Bank and Financial Services Index, which had stayed within the 100- to-125-point band for a year leading up to July 2011, fell about 75 points soon after release of the 2011 stress test results, and hovered there for a full year (Vestergaard and Retana 2013).

The 2011 Basel III Monitoring Exercise and the 2012 EU-Wide Capital Exercise

Stung by the poor market reaction to the July 2011 stress test and concerned about the deteriorating sovereign debt situation, the EBA soon undertook two additional banking initiatives (for a full description, see Vestergaard and Retana 2013; I provide a summary of their account).

The first, in October 2011, was the Basel III monitoring exercise. Its aim was to evaluate bank capital in a wide sample of European banks (158 of them) under two alternative standards: the prevailing rules and the Basel III rules that would come into effect in the European Union once the Fourth European Capital Requirements Directive (CRD IV) was implemented.[13] Because Basel III restricts what can be counted as high-quality capital and increases somewhat the risk weights for counterparty and market risk, the monitoring exercise found that bank capital ratios would be much lower under Basel III than under the prevailing EU rules. For example, a 10.3 percent ratio of common equity to risk-weighted assets under prevailing EU rules would turn into a 6.9 percent ratio under Basel III.[14] The other main finding from the monitoring exercise was that more than half the banks did not meet the Basel IIII target ratios for either equity to risk-weighted assets (7 percent) or equity to total assets (3 percent).

The second (post-2011 stress test) initiative was the EU-wide capital exercise, launched in October 2011, with the results revealed in October 2012. It did not include a stress test, but it did assess the capitalization of 70 European banks against an exceptional and temporary capital bench-mark of 9 percent core tier 1 capital. Thirty-seven banks fell below the 9 percent benchmark, with an aggregate capital shortfall of €116 billion. The EBA therefore recommended that national banking supervisors implement recapitalization plans for all undercapitalized banks so that these banks would satisfy the 9 percent benchmark by June 2012. In October 2012 the EBA concluded that the exercise had been a success, as the lion's share of the previously undercapitalized banks had by then attained the 9 percent and backstop measures were being implemented for those that did not.

Both the 2011 stress test and the follow-up EU-wide capital exercise have been widely criticized. Some of the most salient criticism comes from the study by two European economists, Vestergaard and Retana (2013). They argue that the EBA made three major mistakes.[15]

First, the EBA insisted on using only risk-based measures of bank capital despite the accumulating evidence that such measures have very limited ability to discriminate between healthy and sick banks. In this connection the authors point to the empirical work of Blundell-Wignall and Roulet (2013), whose study of a sample of 94 US and European banks over the 2004–11 period found that (risk-based) tier 1 capital ratios had no support as a predictor of default whereas a simple (unweighted) leverage ratio found strong support in the data. Vestergaard and Retana (2013) reported that a leverage ratio of 4.5 percent would have identified all the EU (stress test) banks that failed over the subsequent two years. In contrast, no value of the risk-based core tier 1 measure would have identified the failing banks while still allowing some banks to pass the test.

A second charge by Vestergaard and Retana (2013) is that the EBA selected the core tier 1 capital measure as the pass-fail metric in the July 2011 stress test because it wanted the test to generate two results: relatively few failures and a concentration of these failures among relatively small banks on the periphery of the euro area. If the EBA had instead employed a leverage ratio of 3 percent as the pass-fail metric, 26 banks would have failed (instead of 3 with the core tier 1 ratio), and a number of large German and French banks, including Deutsche Bank, Commerzbank, BNP Paribas, and Société Générale, would have been among them.[16] They showed that German and French banks had much lower ratios of risk-weighted assets to total assets and lower leverage ratios than Spanish and Italian banks[17] and that these differences almost guaranteed that the largest German and French banks would look much better under risk-based capital measures than under unweighted capital measures.[18] They assert that smoke and mirrors were used to hide the fact that the EU banking problem was in large banks at the heart of the eurozone, not in relatively small banks in the periphery.

Major mistake number three, according to Vestergaard and Retana, was to specify the (9 percent) bank-capital target in the 2011 EU-wide capital exercise in terms of a ratio rather than as absolute amounts of bank capital.[19] Doing so opened the door for adjustment strategies favoring asset liquidation and the optimization of risk-weighted assets (that is, decreases in the denominator of the capital ratio), as opposed to asset recapitalization (increases in the numerator)—just what one did not want when economic growth in the European Union was weak. Vestergaard and Retana therefore see it as no surprise that only 38 percent of the reported recapitalization occurred from the raising of new equity capital.

In its own 2013 EU-wide transparency exercise (EBA 2013a), the EBA reports that between December 2011 and June 2013, core tier 1 capital in large EU banks increased by more than €80 billion while risk-weighted assets decreased by more than €800 billion. Of the 170-basis-point increase in the core tier 1 capital ratio, the numerator increased by 80 basis points and the denominator decreased by 90.[20]

Yet a further blow to the credibility of the 2011 EU-wide stress test was the faulty diagnosis of Dexia, the large ($600 billion balance sheet) Belgian-French bank that failed in 2008. In the July 2011 test, Dexia got an easy pass in terms of its capital ratio in the adverse scenario. Just a few months later, the markets regarded Dexia as being in deep trouble because of its exposure to euro area sovereign debt; in October 2011 Belgian and French authorities bailed the bank out, at considerable expense to taxpayers.[21] Dexia's failure raised serious questions about the quality of the stress test and, in particular, the wisdom of relying on risk-weighted assets in the measurement of bank capital. Dexia's core tier 1 capital ratio in the adverse scenario was over 10 percent and its reported ratio at end-2010 was over 12 percent. Yet Dexia's leverage ratio—using unweighted assets in the denominator and either the market or book value of equity in the numerator—was only 0.49 to 1.34 percent, according to Acharya, Schoenmaker, and Steffen (2011).

The 2014 EU-Wide Stress Test and the Asset Quality Review

Some analysts were cautiously optimistic that the 2014 stress test would earn higher marks, because the handicaps and flaws in the earlier tests were expected to be corrected or at least diminished (see, for example, Posen and Véron 2014). The ECB's Asset Quality Review was expected to provide a more objective and harder-nosed evaluation of bank assets, collateral, guarantees, and loans than was possible under national supervisory authorities and would thus provide a better starting point for the stress test. Not only was the ECB regarded as less susceptible to what Posen and Véron (2014) call "banking nationalism," it also had much greater resources, including a flock of consultants and auditors, to assist with the valuation exercise.[22] The fact that some large EU banks participating in the test (including UniCredit, Deutsche Bank, and Intesa SP) had engaged in proactive capital-raising exercises and had increased their loan-loss provisions since the Asset Quality Review was announced lent some credence to this claim.

In addition, the ECB was expected to play a greater role in the 2014 test than in earlier ones, because its new supervisory and licensing powers over large banks give it a large stake in the outcome of the test. Another Dexia-like failure after the 2014 stress test would cause the ECB to suffer a serious reputational loss, and—the argument went—it would need that reputation not only to supervise banks but also to perform its other key function, monetary policy. The ECB would also have stronger authority than its EU-wide predecessors to compel rapid recapitalization (including via dividend and shareholder buyback suspensions) for banks showing a capital shortfall in the test.

In addition, in late 2014 the vicious feedback loop between sovereign risk and banking risk was in less of a crisis than it was in 2011 and early 2012, before the first longer-term refinancing operation and the "do whatever it takes" ECB initiatives, with 10-year sovereign bond spreads for the euro area's periphery having declined to close to pre-2007–09 crisis levels. The methodological note for the 2014 stress test also offered some improvements, including an upgrade in the definition of bank capital from core tier 1 capital to common equity tier 1 capital and a pledge by

EBA Chair Andrea Enria that "the exercise's full transparency will be key to its credibility" (EBA 2014c).

On the skeptical side of the ledger, some observers wondered whether the 2014 EU-wide test would subject banks in the largest EU economies to the same level of scrutiny as banks on the periphery. After all, if the European Commission could not get the largest EU economies to consistently abide by its fiscal policy rules, why should one expect the ECB and EBA to be able to follow an even-handed policy in the Asset Quality Review and the 2014 stress test?

The results of the fourth EU-wide bank stress test were released on October 26, 2014 (EBA 2014e). There were four key findings:

- The aggregate capital shortfall for the 123 banks participating in the test was €24.6 billion.
- Only 24 of the 123 banks were undercapitalized, as indicated by their inability to meet transitional common equity tier 1 capital ratios of 5.5 and 8.0 percent in the adverse and baseline scenarios, respectively.
- All of the undercapitalized banks were in Cyprus, Greece, and Italy.
- The largest banks in France and Germany had ample capital.

The reaction outside the official sector to the 2014 EU-wide test results could be characterized charitably as "mixed," with some analysts and EU bankers regarding the findings as encouraging or definitive and quite a few others seeing the results as a whitewash. Those who were encouraged by the 2014 test results argued that it was a huge improvement over the three previous EU-wide tests. It was a top-down approach, driven and monitored by the ECB; it emphasized the establishment of a level playing field across euro area banks in asset valuation and stress testing; and the combination of the Asset Quality Review with the stress tests increased the reliability and transparency of the results (Beck 2014).

Some of the most glaring discrepancies in asset classification among banks in different euro area economies were regarded as having been identified and corrected through the Asset Quality Review. Even if balance-sheet repair was still seen as a work in progress, the 2014 test was seen as a success in confidence building and transparency. Other supporters praised the decision of the ECB to publish data on "fully loaded" common equity tier 1 capital ratios (to be fully applicable only in 2017), even though the fully loaded ratios were not employed as hurdle rates in the test (see, for example, Véron 2014 and Kirkegaard 2014). Supporters also cited the catalytic effect of the test in inducing EU banks to raise €57 billion of capital after January 1, 2014 and before the October 26 stress deadline (Kirkegaard 2014).

Still others commended the thoroughness of the 2014 exercise (relative to that of "academic" studies without any asset quality review), as well as its contribution to building a real banking union.[23] The European Commissioner for Financial Stability, Jonathan Hill, maintained that the 2014 test delivered "the most stringent scrutiny that European banks had ever faced" and claimed that the adverse scenario in that test was "the most severe anywhere in the world."[24]

Criticism of the 2014 EU-wide test concentrated along three fault lines: There was no leverage test, there was no adverse deflation scenario, and the ECB and EBA allowed participating banks to artificially inflate their capital levels by being too lenient on tax-deferred assets and tax-deferred credits, along with other noncompliance practices relative to fully loaded Basel III standards. Despite the criticism of earlier EU-wide stress tests for not including at least one hurdle rate based on total rather than risk-weighted assets, the ECB and EBA stonewalled on the issue of a leverage ratio test. As with the 2011 test results, this did not prevent outside analysts from estimating what the aggregate shortfall and country-pattern of shortfalls would likely have been had a leverage test been employed in the 2014 test. Acharya and Steffen (2014c) looked at the 39 publicly listed EU banks participating in the 2014 test. They reached three conclusions:

- The aggregate shortfall in the adverse scenario would have been on the order of €450 billion (rather than €20 billion) if a 5.5 percent leverage ratio had been used rather than the risk-weighted 5.5 percent common equity tier 1 ratio.[25]

- The largest capital shortfalls appeared in France (€189 billion) and Germany (€102 billion), not in the euro area periphery (as in the 2011 test).[26]

- The bank-by-bank capital shortfalls identified by their leverage tests were negatively correlated with the shortfalls identified in the official 2014 test results.[27]

In a subsequent paper, Acharya and Steffen (2014b) looked more deeply into why there is such a huge divergence between their shortfall results and those of the 2014 EU-wide test. They conclude that the difference stems mainly from the continued exclusive reliance in the 2014 EU-wide test on risk-weighted capital metrics.[28]

Table 1.3, taken from a study by Vestergaard (2014), provides further confirmation of the high sensitivity of the 2014 EU-wide stress test results to the exclusion of a leverage test. It compares risk-weighted and unweighted capital ratios for some of Europe's largest banks. The main takeaway is that the comfortable capital positions reported for the adverse scenario in the 2014 test evaporate when the risk-weighted capital measure

Table 1.3   Risk-weighted capital ratios and leverage ratios for large EU banks

Bank	CET1 to RWAs (AQR-adjusted, 2013)	CET1 to RWAs (adverse scenario, 2014)	RWAs to TAs (end-2013)	CET1 to TAs (adverse scenario, 2014)
Deutsche Bank	13.3	11.0	16.46	1.81
Commerzbank	10.8	9.1	32.39	2.95
Deutsche Zentral-Genossenschaftsbank AG	9.0	7.3	22.00	1.61
Crédit Agricole	10.8	9.9	18.28	1.81
BNP Paribas	10.5	9.4	30.25	2.84
Société Générale SA	10.7	9.5	25.02	2.38
Banco Santander SA	10.3	10.2	42.78	4.36
Banco Bilbao Vizcaya Argentaria, SA	10.5	9.5	53.53	5.09
Caja de Ahorros y Pensiones de Barcelona	10.2	9.7	44.62	4.33
UniCredit SpA	9.6	8.4	46.18	3.88
Intesa Sanpaolo SpA	11.7	10.0	44.36	4.44
Banca Monte dei Paschi di Siena SpA	7.0	4.7	39.24	1.84

CET1 = common equity tier 1 capital; RWAs = risk-weighted assets; TAs = total assets; AQR = Asset Quality Review

Source: Vestergaard (2014). Reprinted with permission.

is replaced by a leverage test (defined as the ratio of common equity tier 1 to total assets). The leverage ratios for some of the largest German and French banks, including Deutsche Bank, Commerzbank, Deutsche Zentral-Genossenschaftsbank, Crédit Agricole, BNP Paribas, and Société Générale, are very low; with the leverage-ratio metric, these banks' low ratios of risk-weighted assets to total assets are of no assistance in inflating their capital positions. Wolf (2014a) finds that the gap between leverage ratios and the risk-based capital metric used in the 2014 test was wider for Dutch, French, and German banks (banks at the center of the euro area) than it was for Greek, Portuguese, Irish, Italian, and Spanish banks (banks on the periphery).

Criticism of the absence of a deflation scenario was perhaps less wide-spread than criticism of the leverage test, but it was nevertheless strong. Steil and Walker (2014b), for example, maintain that relentlessly falling inflation was clearly bad news for euro area banks, because it increased the real value of borrower debt and the real cost of servicing that debt. It would cause loan defaults and bank losses to rise above the level assumed in the 2014 adverse scenario, which assumed an inflation rate of 1 percent.[29] At the time of the November 2014 stress test, euro area inflation was running at 0.4 percent; it subsequently dipped into negative territory. Steil and Walker (2014b, 2) find it disturbing that at no point (through the end of 2016) was the ECB willing in the 2014 test to contemplate a euro area infla-tion rate lower than it already was (0.3 percent) in September 2014; they therefore conclude that "the ECB is more concerned with the reputational costs of acknowledging the possibility of deflation than with testing accu-rately the ability of banks to withstand it." The fact that only a few months after the release of the 2014 stress test results, the ECB launched a sizable quantitative easing program—aimed in large part at combatting euro area deflation—adds support to this line of criticism.

Criticism number three of the 2014 EU-wide stress test centers on the measurement of bank capital, particularly the numerator of the bank-capital ratio. There are several strands to this line of criticism. All of them share the concern that the ECB and EBA accepted bank-capital figures that overstated the true amount of capital in EU banks.

As part of the global Basel III agreement to upgrade the quality of bank assets (BCBS 2010b), countries agreed to phase out (by 2018) the inclusion of tax-deferred assets in the definition of common equity tier 1 capital.[30] The reasoning behind this decision was clear: Since a bank that was close to going under would not likely have enough taxable profits to offset tax losses, tax-deferred assets could not be regarded as loss absorbing in a crisis and should therefore not be counted as part of the highest-quality bank capital.

The European Union's Capital Requirements Regulation took a similar stance on tax-deferred assets, although it permitted a longer phaseout period than Basel III. Worried about a prospective diminution of bank capital due to the phasing out of tax-deferred assets, four countries (Spain, Italy, Portugal, and Greece) had their legislatures pass laws that allowed their banks to convert their tax-deferred assets into tax-deferred credits Under this scheme to inflate bank capital, if a bank did not earn enough profits to use traditional tax-deferred assets, it would receive a government transfer payment equal to the value of that asset. Moreover, such tax-deferred credits would be counted as part of common equity tier 1. While the ECB was clearly against the use of tax-deferred credits—in large part because of its potentially adverse effect on debt sustainability and the link between sovereign debt and bank debt—it declined, in a 2014 opinion on the Portuguese tax credit plan (ECB 2014c), to make such credits ineligible as high-quality capital for future bank stress tests.[31]

The numbers on tax-deferred assets and credits in euro area banks are not small. The *Wall Street Journal* (Davies 2014) reported that (before the Asset Quality Review), more than 40 percent of the core equity tier 1 capital of Greek banks comprised tax-deferred assets; the corresponding percentages for Portuguese, Irish, Spanish, and German banks were 25, 20, 15, and 10 percent, respectively. Kirkegaard (2014) notes that tax-deferred assets allowed banks participating in the 2014 EU-wide stress test to avoid having to add €126 billion in capital to meet the common equity tier 1 hurdle rate; had they had to add that amount, many more banks would have failed the test.[32]

Despite the considerable resources devoted to the exercise, some analysts were skeptical about the relatively small amount of asset overvaluation found in the Asset Quality Review. Shulock (2014), for example, emphasizes that the €48 billion of asset overvaluation represented only 0.2 percent of the €22 trillion of assets in participating EU banks. He believes this percentage to be implausibly small given both the very weak state of economic activity in most euro area economies and the perceived low quality of loan-loss provisioning.[33]

One scenario for how the ECB and EBA could have arrived at such a low adjustment to asset quality runs as follows. The architects of the 2014 EU-wide stress test were shooting for a "Goldilocks" bottom-line result for the aggregate capital shortfall: not so small that the test would be viewed as nonstressful, but not so large that the shortfall would be beyond the resources of existing national and EU-wide bank rescue funds (and hence threaten market stability).[34] They would have known from their models that the adverse scenario was likely to generate a fall in the bank-capital ratio of, say, 250 to 300 basis points (in the event it turned out to be 260 basis points). If the total decline in the capital ratio was to be kept to, say, no more than 300 to 350 basis points, then the adjustment for asset over-valuation in the Asset Quality Review had to be relatively small (in the event in turned out to be 40 basis points).

Trying to "manage" the outcome of the adverse scenario is hard to do, because the impact of these adverse scenarios is pretty well understood from the earlier US and EU-wide stress test results and the accompanying documentation to these stress tests is now quite comprehensive. In contrast, the Asset Quality Review is a large-scale, one-off exercise whose results cannot easily be dismissed out of hand because no outside analyst has the resources or authority to audit the disaggregate findings of the inspection teams.[35] As such, the margin for "management" of the asset valuation component is much wider.

There continue to be concerns about the comparability of capital ratios both across regions and within the European Union—and not just because of differences in ratios of risk-weighted assets to total assets or tax-deferred assets and credits. When the European Union was drawing up its plans for the Capital Requirements Directive IV and the Capital Requirements Regulation, critics complained that the "silent participation" in German banks and the treatment of the minority stakes of French banks in their insurance subsidiaries were artificially raising bank capital ratios in some large EU economies (Goldstein 2012a).

A 2014 report on the EU banking system by the Basel Committee on Banking Supervision (BCBS 2014a) in its Regulatory Consistency Assessment Program gave fresh impetus to worries about whether EU banks were faithfully implementing Basel III. In this program the BCBS makes a judgment about whether banking supervision in member countries is compliant with the Basel III accord. Previous BCBS assessment reports for Australia, Brazil, Canada, China, Japan, Singapore, and Switzerland found them all to be "compliant." The verdict for the United States (BCBS 2014e) was "largely compliant"—not as good as "compliant" but better than "materially noncompliant" or, even worse, "noncompliant."[36] The BCBS' verdict for the European Union was "materially noncompliant"—the first overall negative rating for any Basel Committee member.[37] All of the areas where the European Union was judged to have important divergences from the Basel framework were related to the calculation of banks' credit risk, where the European Union's Capital Requirements Directive IV and Capital Requirements Regulation permit some risk weights, exemptions, and concessions that are more lenient than those outlined in the Basel minimum requirements.[38]

Even within the European Union and after passage of the Capital Requirements Regulation, nontrivial differences remain in the definition of bank capital. To their credit, EBA Chair Enria and ECB Supervisory Board Chair Danièle Nouy, while emphasizing the progress that has already been made, have been increasingly vocal about the challenges that still remain on this front:

> I...have always argued that we should have aimed for a fully harmonized definition of capital, completely aligned with the Basel standards. However, a number of national discretions and options have been inserted in the legislative texts, which still hamper the comparability of capital ratios across EU banks. Luckily enough, most of these discretions...will gradually fade away. But some will be in place for up to ten years, and some do not have an expiration date. We are talking about deductions from common equity—e.g., goodwill, deferred tax assets, prudential filters on AFS gains and losses—and other technical details.... They can have a sizeable, and often unnoticed, impact on capital levels and their comparability. (Enria 2015, 4)

> It's not so much about how much [capital], it's about the definition of capital. There are too many...national options in the definition of capital in Europe and we have to address that. [...] We may have to go to the legislature, to the European Parliament, to ask for more harmonisation in regulation.[39]

For all of the reasons presented here, I believe that the main conclusions of the 2014 EU-wide bank stress test are not credible. Indeed, I stand on the conclusions that I offered shortly after publication of the 2014 stress test results (Goldstein 2014, 2):

> On the eve of becoming the Single Supervisor for Europe's largest banks, the ECB missed an important opportunity to establish trust in EU banking supervision. By refusing to include a rigorous leverage ratio test, by allowing banks to artificially inflate bank capital, by engaging in wholesale monkey business with tax-deferred assets, and also by ruling out a deflation scenario, the ECB produced estimates of the aggregate capital shortfall and a country pattern of bank failures that are not believable. This was not a case of "doing whatever it takes" to establish credibility, but rather one of avoiding the tough decisions and asking the market to "take whatever."

Also commenting on the credibility of the 2014 EU-wide stress test, Willem Buiter summed it up succinctly: "The AQR [Asset Quality Review] stress test was a fudge."[40]

Not surprisingly, senior ECB banking supervisors do not share the negative assessments of the credibility of the 2014 EU-wide stress test. Speaking just a week after the release of the 2014 results, the ECB

Supervisory Board Chair Nouy concluded that "the comprehensive assessment has been widely received as a credible exercise" (Nouy 2014b, 3). ECB Supervisory Board Vice Chair Sabine Lautenschläger commented as follows: "Think of an athlete at the beginning of his career, who trained extremely hard and achieved an excellent result in his first major tournament.... [H]e clearly cannot afford to rest on his laurels.... This is the situation in which I see the [Single Supervisory Mechanism] after the completion of the comprehensive assessment" (Lautenschläger 2014, 1). ECB Vice President Vítor Constâncio (2015 2) commented: "Due to the inclusion of an [Asset Quality Review] and to an intense 'quality assurance' conducted at the ECB, this exercise was seen as credible by market participants. Evidence of that is, for example, that euro area banks' stock prices reflected the [Comprehensive Assessment] results as soon as these were published." He argued that "market-price-based stress tests," such as the ones used in Acharya et al. (2010), are not credible because they place great emphasis on the "wisdom or whims of the market" and such market-based dependence is subject to substantial volatility.

There seems to be an inconsistency. One cannot simultaneously argue that the 2014 EU-wide stress test results are credible because banks' stock prices reacted in the way one hoped they would and then also claim that the (unfavorable) results of other studies (based on the same banks' stock prices) are not credible because the results are subject to the "whims" of the market. If the wisdom and whims of the market are the credibility test, you don't get to call "credible" only the results that are to your liking. That is not kosher.

The 2016 EU-Wide Stress Test

No EU-wide stress test was conducted in 2015. The results of the 2016 EU-wide stress test results were published on July 29, 2016.

There were three major changes. First, the 2016 test was the first EU-wide test to include results for a leverage ratio (the Basel III leverage ratio) in both the baseline and adverse scenarios. Second, the 2016 test suspended the use of capital hurdle rates and treated the results of the test as merely an input into the broader capital planning process. Third, the 2016 test reduced the number of participating banks from more than 120 in the 2014 Comprehensive Assessment to 51. The three changes represent one important step forward and two important steps backward, leading to a poor overall verdict.

Including the behavior of leverage ratios under alternative macroeconomic scenarios is a long overdue step for the EU-wide tests. Inclusion of baseline and stressed Basel III leverage ratios—in both transitional and fully loaded versions and bank by bank—is therefore very much to be welcomed. At least on this count, it brings the EU-wide test up to best practice.

Suspending the use of hurdle rates and treating the stress test results as merely one among many inputs in the capital planning process seems to be an odd and ill-advised decision, on several counts. The official EBA (2016b, 4) rationale for this decision is as follows:

> The objectives of the EBA's 2011 and 2014 stress tests were to identify possible capital shortfalls and require immediate recapitalization actions. However, after five years of continuous capital raising in the EU banking sector, with average CET1 ratios above 13 percent, the crisis type of stress test seems less relevant.

> Instead of a "capital now" approach, supervisors will use the results of the stress test to assess banks' forward-looking capital planning. Thus, although no hurdle rates or capital thresholds are defined for the purpose of the exercise, CAs will use stress test results as an input to the Supervisory Review and Evaluation Process (SREP). In addition, the publication of capital ratios enables market participants to make their own assessments.

EU banks have €990 billion in nonperforming loans (IMF 2015c). Between the start of the European banking union in November 2014 and July 2016, the Euro Stoxx Bank Index fell by more than 40 percent (Acharya, Pierret, and Steffen 2016). After recovering some ground in the first half of 2015, European bank stocks plummeted again, falling by more than 50 percent, during the first six and a half months of 2016. The June 2016 Brexit referendum exacerbated this rout.[41] UniCredit lost about two-thirds of its market value; RBS was down 56 percent; and the market value of Credit Suisse, Deutsche Bank, and Barclays fell by roughly half. By early July 2016, Deutsche Bank's dollar market value was less than that of SunTrust Banks, and Goldman Sachs' market value was higher than that of Credit Suisse, Deutsche Bank, and UniCredit combined.[42] Equity prices for large US banks were also down sharply over this period, but by significantly less than the large European banks.

Even more pressing, markets and officials were—and still are—wrestling with how to cope with a looming banking crisis in Italy—a threat the *Economist* characterized as one that, if handled badly, could be the euro area's undoing.[43] Italy's nonperforming loans are estimated at roughly €360 billion (approximately 20 percent of its GDP).[44] UniCredit and Banca Monte dei Paschi di Siena—Italy's largest and third-largest banks—have been trading at about 20 percent and 10 percent of their book values, respectively, and the "capital hole" in the system is estimated to be €40 billion.[45] Retail investors own about €230 billion worth of senior and subordinated debt in Italian banks. Real GDP in Italy is forecast to grow just 1 percent in 2016 and 1.25 percent in 2017 and 2018 (IMF 2016a), and Italy is not expected to reach its precrisis (2007) output peak until the mid-2020s.

Seen in this light, the July 2016 EBA argument that the "crisis type of stress test appears to be less relevant" (EBA 2016b) looks unduly optimistic. The fact that the weighted average common equity tier 1 ratio is just over 13 percent for the 51 participating banks should be of limited comfort given the empirical regularity that risk-weighted capital ratios have been much less successful than leverage ratios in identifying weak banks in earlier EU stress tests, as well as in other tests. According to the 2016 EU-wide test, in the adverse scenario, 27 of the 51 participating banks had a stressed fully loaded Basel III leverage ratio below 4 percent, 19 were below 3.5 percent, and 7 were below 3 percent (EBA 2016d).[46] Among the large EU banks that fall below the 3.5 percent stressed leverage ratio are Deutsche Bank, Commerzbank, BNP Paribas, Société Générale, UniCredit, ABN Amro, ING, and Barclays. As expected, Italy's third-largest bank, Monte dei Paschi di Siena, recorded a negative stressed leverage ratio and had to implement a rescue plan only hours before the stress test results were announced.

Although the 2016 EU-wide and US tests used different leverage ratio measures, it is nevertheless notable that the decline in the leverage ratio between the starting and minimum values (in the stressed scenario) was considerably smaller in the EU-wide test (100 basis points for the transitional Basel III leverage ratio) than for the US CCAR test (330 basis points for the tier 1 leverage ratio in the severely adverse scenario). The difference suggests that the adverse scenario in the EU-wide test was probably milder than the severely adverse scenario in the US test.[47]

EU banks raised significant capital since December 2013 (€180 billion of common equity tier 1 capital in the 2016 EU test, according to EBA 2016d). Acharya, Pierret, and Steffen (2016) believe, however, that this capital raising was insufficient. They examine the capital ratios of the 35 banks in the 2016 EU-wide test that are publicly listed, looking at three book leverage ratios: book equity divided by total assets, tangible equity divided by tangible assets, and an International Financial Reporting Standards (IFRS) tier 1 leverage ratio (tier 1 capital divided by tangible assets minus derivative liabilities).

They also track a market capital ratio, defined as market equity to total assets. For the stressed book-capital shortfalls, they assume a less stringent benchmark of 4 percent and a more stringent benchmark of 7 percent. For the market capital ratio, the less stringent and more stringent hurdle rates are again 4 and 7 percent, respectively. They also calculate a "systemic" capital shortfall (SRISK), assuming a global stock market decline of 40 percent, and a 5.5 percent prudential capital ratio, in order to estimate the downside risk of bank stock returns.

Three key findings emerge from research of Acharya, Pierret, and Steffen (2016): (1) The aggregate capital shortfall in a systemic crisis (40 percent market decline over six months) would be €882 billion—up from their estimate of €655 billion following the November 2014 EU-wide stress test; (2) the aggregate capital shortfall using the stressed market capital hurdle rates of 4 and 7 percent would be €314 billion and €845 billion, respectively; and (3) the aggregate shortfall using the stressed IFRS leverage ratios of 4 and 7 percent would be €32 billion and €485 billion, respectively.

Acharya, Pierret, and Steffen (2016) draw several policy implications from their findings: (1) The EU banking system needs a comprehensive recapitalization across almost all its member countries; (2) with an average ratio of market capitalization to book capitalization of about 0.7, market participants are heavily discounting bank asset values; (3) with common equity issuance (via deep discounted rights issues) and haircuts on subordinated creditors, it should be possible to deal with many banks' capital needs; and (4) the banking sectors of Germany, France, and Italy are likely to require public backstops.[48]

European banks are in a precarious position. The key policy questions concern the size of the capital shortfall and what immediate capitalization actions are feasible. The EU official sector can surely not be comfortable with the market's recent assessment of their banks' prospects.[49]

Given this state of affairs, it was extremely unwise to swap the transparent "capital now" policy embedded in earlier EU-wide stress tests for the no capital hurdle rate, protracted capital planning exercise announced in the 2016 EU-wide test. By choosing this strategy, the Single Supervisory Mechanism is giving away the market pressure and leverage advantages linked to publicly disclosing a given capital shortfall and compelling banks to fill it within a specified timetable. Absent the stigma linked to failing the test, weakly capitalized banks will be under less pressure to raise capital before the test. And the lack of announced remedial action immediately after the test—in favor of a behind-the-scenes and perhaps lengthy, heavily negotiated Supervisory Review and Evaluation Process—will increase uncertainty.[50]

EU supervisors are setting up a bad pattern of incentives. Allowing many large banks to continue operating while being seriously undercapitalized risks falling prey to "gambling for resurrection" by bank managers, with unhappy consequences for the size of the capital hole—as US supervisors found out painfully in the US savings and loan crisis.

The real reason that EU bank supervisors suspended use of capital hurdle rates was not that bank-capital needs were close to being met. Rather it was that use of hurdle rates would tie the supervisory authorities to a capital shortfall figure that they currently do not know how to fill (particularly in the Italian case) and that using the stress test results merely as one "input" among several in reaching bank capitalization decisions offers alluring discretion and flexibility.

Admittedly, the European Union is in a tough bind. Going through with a sizable public recapitalization of Italian banks would reveal the 8 percent creditor bail-in provision of its anti-too-big-to-fail Bank Recovery and Resolution Directive (BRRD) to be a paper tiger in its first major test—even as it rationalizes it by a face-saving resort to the "precautionary recapitalization" escape clause in the BRRD agreement. If Italy gets it, others will ask for it, too. Exempting retail investors from the bail-in—even though there may well have been mis-selling of these bank bonds—would also set a precedent for other EU cases and make retail bondholders more like retail depositors. Alternatively, bailing in Italian bondholders risks setting off a funding run elsewhere in the European Union—either now or the next time there is a crisis involving a group of large banks.

The only sensible way to avoid the twin perils of bail-ins of bondholders during a crisis and bail-outs of banks at taxpayer expense is to set a much higher level of equity capital to begin with. In this case the authorities can bail in equity holders with much smaller adverse macroeconomic and moral hazard effects and without setting off a bank funding run.

The 2016 EU-wide stress test reduced the number of participating banks to 51 (from 15 EU and European Economic Area countries), a sharp decrease from the 130 or so banks that took part in the 2014 test. This decision is often viewed as a tradeoff. On the minus side, it reduced coverage from 82 percent of total EU banking assets in 2014 to just over 70 percent in 2016. On the plus side, dealing with a smaller number of more homogeneous large banks may allow the ECB and the Single Supervisory Mechanism to deepen their analysis, especially regarding the development of and greater reliance on supervisor-led models in stress tests.

But there is another aspect of the smaller sample size that tilts the balance decisively toward maintaining the larger group. Since inclusion in the new sample requires meeting a threshold of €30 billion in total consolidated assets, the sample no longer includes any banks from Greece, Portugal, and Cyprus, all of which had banks with capital shortfalls in the 2014 EU-wide test. The banks from smaller EU economies are henceforth to be stress tested by their relevant national supervisory authorities—and the results are not expected to be made public. Banks from some of the EU countries with the weakest banking systems will no longer have the incentive to accelerate their recapitalization efforts because of fear of the public spotlight or the (relatively) tougher Single Supervisory Mechanism oversight attached to the EU-wide tests.[51] Some of the EU countries that have the most to gain from the "discipline" effects of publicly disclosed stress tests will no longer be eligible to participate in those tests. These are not banking systems that will benefit from lighter-touch supervision.

Less than a week after release of the 2016 EU-wide stress test results, the *Financial Times* and Bloomberg published editorials panning the new test. "Without simpler, clearer rules and tests—and clearer consequences for failure—there can be little hope of [change]," wrote the *Financial Times*.[52] "In its latest round of European stress tests, Europe has missed another chance to undertake the honest reckoning that its financial system needs," wrote Bloomberg. "If the continent's leaders want to strengthen their faltering economies, this charade must end."[53]

Appendix 1A

Indicators of Too Big to Fail in EU and US Banks

For 2012, Pagano et al. (2014) report that the 20 largest banks in the European Union had total assets of $23.7 trillion, compared with $12.4 trillion (under GAAP accounting standards) or $17.7 trillion (under IFRS accounting) for the top 20 in the United States. Relative to regional GDP in 2012, the top 20 EU banks accounted for 170 percent versus about 100 percent in the US case. Looking at top-20 bank concentration is informative, because banks just smaller than the top three in EU economies are much bigger in the European Union than in the United States. Using end-2015 data, Schoenmaker and Véron (2016) report that the five largest banks in the European Union had assets equal to 73 percent of euro area GDP; the corresponding figure for the top five banks in the United States was 38 percent.

Cline (2017) presents the ratio of the combined banking assets of the five largest banks relative to individual country GDP in 2015. For the United States, the ratio is 50 percent. For the larger EU economies, the ratios are as follows: France, 310 percent; United Kingdom, 250 percent; Spain, 260 percent; Italy, 130 percent; and Germany, 110 percent. Goldstein and Véron's (2011) figures for top-five concentration figures in 2009 told a similar story. If one looks at total bank assets relative to GDP in 2013, the conclusion is similar: The ratio is 87 percent in the United States and 350 percent in the euro area (see IMF 2014b).

Pagano et al. (2014) show that the ratio of stock market capitalization to bank credit to the private sector is roughly two in the United States, whereas in the largest euro area economies, that ratio clusters well below one. The IMF (2014b) reports that bank loans account for only 12 percent of corporate credit in the United States versus 40 percent in the United Kingdom and 60 percent in the euro area.

Data collected by Goldstein and Véron (2011) and Cline (2015a) show that the European Union's financial structure is much more "bank dominated" than the United States'. The IMF (2014a) estimates that in 2013, subsidies to funding received by too important to fail banks were considerably larger for euro area banks than for too big to fail banks in the United States, Japan, and the United Kingdom (see table 4.2 in chapter 4).

Appendix 1B

The Weak Supporting Crisis Management Cast for the EU-Wide Stress Tests

In this chapter, I argued that the supporting crisis management cast for the EU-wide stress tests was less impressive than the supporting cast for the US tests, and that this difference contributed to the poor market reception to the EU-wide tests. The following studies provide some backing for that assessment.

1. Monetary Policy Stimulus Was Not Consistent Enough or Large Enough.

The Federal Reserve slashed the federal funds rate from 5.25 percent in September 2007 to 0.25 percent in December 2008. For its part, the ECB was, according to Wolf (2014b, 29), "convinced for far too long that the crisis was largely an Anglo-Saxon affair." It therefore lowered its refinancing rate from 4.25 percent in October 2008 to 1.0 percent in May 2009 but then (in what Wolf calls "an action of astonishing myopia") raised rates back to 1.5 percent in 2011 before lowering them in five small steps to 0.25 percent in November 2013 and 0.15 percent in June 2014.

Using departures from a Taylor rule as an indicator of the stance of monetary policy, Federal Reserve monetary policy emerges as considerably more expansionary than ECB monetary policy.[54] The Fed engaged in three large-scale rounds of quantitative easing (to the tune of $3.7 trillion) between November 2008 and October 2014. In contrast, despite weak growth and the growing threat of deflation, the ECB launched a quantitative easing program (of roughly $60 billion a month for a planned one to two years) only in early 2015; it began as a smaller program (of about €13 billion a month), covering covered bonds and asset-backed securities, in October 2014.[55] In December 2015 the ECB announced that it would extend its program of buying bonds and other assets by six months but would not increase the amount of monthly purchases.[56] Federal Reserve Vice Chair Stanley Fischer noted that staff studies indicated that its quantitative easing program lowered 10-year interest rates by as much as 110 basis points and the unemployment rate by perhaps 1.5 percent relative to what they would have been in its absence.[57]

2. Fiscal Policy Consolidation, Especially in the Crisis-Hit Euro Area Periphery, Was Too Rapid and Too Large.

Chari and Henry (2013) present evidence to show that weak eurozone growth performance over the 2010–12 period reflected an overzealous procyclical application of fiscal policy and that growth would have been better protected if Greece, Ireland, Italy, Portugal, and Spain had implemented a decrease in the cyclically adjusted primary deficit that was smaller and more gradual than the sharp cut of almost 4 percent of potential GDP that took place between 2010 and 2012.

Blanchard and Leigh (2013) show that economic growth forecast errors were larger in economies where fiscal policy multipliers were underestimated. According to the IMF's October 2014 *Fiscal Monitor*, the change in the cyclically adjusted fiscal balance between 2009 and 2014 was very similar—a tightening of a little more than 3 percent of potential GDP—for the eurozone as a whole and the United States. The degree of fiscal tightening in the eurozone periphery (with the exception of Italy) was, however, much larger; again, looking at the change in the cyclically adjusted fiscal balance over the 2009-14 period, the amount of fiscal tightening (as a percent of potential GDP) was as follows: Greece (17.5 percent), Ireland (6.2 percent), Italy (2.8 percent), Portugal (6.9 percent), and Spain (6.1 percent); see IMF (2014g). If one instead uses the change in the cyclically adjusted primary balance as the measure of discretionary fiscal policy, the qualitative conclusions are unchanged.

3. The ECB and Other EU Officials Were Not as Aggressive as Their US Counterparts in Intervening Directly in Financial Markets to Reduce Volatility and to Stabilize Prices.

Schildbach and Wenzel (2013) point out that by the fall of 2013, the Fed's balance sheet had grown to more than 400 percent of its summer 2007 level, versus a doubling for the ECB's balance sheet. In addition, they point out that the Fed was much more involved in crucial market segments, whenever it deemed action necessary (e.g., the asset-backed securities market for student, auto, and credit card loans). In comparing the Fed and ECB responses to the crisis, Schildbach and Wenzel (2013, 17) offer the following assessment: "In sum, both the absolute size of the effectual market intervention and the tailwind the central bank provided (and was allowed to provide) more generally to governments and the economy as a whole proved much more overwhelming in the US than in the euro area, thus contributing to banks on the Western shores of the Atlantic emerging faster and stronger from the ashes than their peers on the Eastern coasts."

Alessandri and Haldane (2009) calculate all-in financial support as the sum of central bank money creation, central bank collateral swaps, government guarantees, government insurance, and government capital injections. Over the 2007-09 period, the total was 73 percent of GDP for the United States and 18 percent for the euro area.

Geanakoplos (2010) argues that, despite some significant design problems and tardiness in setting them up, the Term Asset-Backed Securities

Loan Facility (TALF), created by the Federal Reserve, and the Public-Private Investment Program (PPIP), created by the US Treasury, helped limit the downside of the leverage cycle.

4. Debt Restructuring for the Most Debt-Laden Euro Area Economies Was Too Small.

In its 2015 evaluation of public debt sustainability for Greece, the IMF (2015a) concluded that Greece's public debt had become highly unsustainable and could be made sustainable only through debt relief measures that went far beyond what Europe had been willing to consider until then. It projected that Greece's public debt would peak at close to 200 percent of GDP in 2016–17, provided that there was an early agreement on a program, a level that is about 50 percentage points higher than it was in 2010, when Greece entered into its first support program with the IMF, European Commission, and ECB. It estimated Greece's financing need through end-2018 at €85 billion.

The IMF attempted to make its participation in the third support program for Greece contingent on Greece being granted adequate debt relief by its other official creditors. By 2015 Greece had suffered a 25 percent decline in real GDP since 2007. On the positive side, the primary balance in its budget went from a peak deficit of 10.3 percent of GDP in 2009 to balance in 2014 (IMF 2015b); the change in cyclically adjusted primary balance was of a similar magnitude over this period.

Olivier Blanchard (2015a), the IMF's former director of research, has responded to the main critiques of the Greek programs in the following ways: (1) that had Greece been left on its own, the fiscal adjustment and social cost would have been much higher than they were; (2) that delays in debt restructuring reflected contagion risks and lack of firewalls to deal with them; (3) that Greek depositors and households, not just foreign banks, benefited from bank bailouts; (4) that while output declined much more than anticipated, fiscal consolidation explains only part of it; and (5) that opposition to structural reforms was fierce in Greece, and many of the reforms were not implemented.

5. Creditor Economies in the Euro Area—and Particularly Germany—Led Euro Area Policy Badly Astray During the Crisis.

Wolf (2014b) takes the German authorities to task for misdiagnosing the balance of payments crisis as a generalized debt crisis and for not recognizing the pivotal role of a shortage of aggregate demand in the euro area's dismal growth and employment performance. De Grauwe (2011, 2015) also criticizes European leaders for allowing the debt crisis to deteriorate into a bad expectations-led equilibrium, and for blocking a consensus from forming in the ECB Board on engaging in outright monetary transactions. Chopra (2014) maintains that structural policies are likely to be ineffective in a low-growth environment and explains why structural policies and countercyclical macroeconomic policies are better regarded as complements than substitutes.

Wolf (2015) argues that structural reform in Greece over the 2010–14 period was modest and that during the tenure of the Samaris government, Greece failed to deliver on 13 of 14 structural reforms to which it was supposedly committed.

In private correspondence, my Peterson Institute colleague Jacob Kirkegaard has argued that one reason why the euro area has created so much tail risk over the past five years is that creditor countries have consciously allowed market pressure to build up on debtor countries' funding costs as a way to motivate structural reforms that they believe would not be forthcoming under a less confrontational strategy.

Endnotes

1. Although the lion's share of attention accorded to bank stress tests has been directed at the outcomes for the United States and the European Union, stress testing is now widespread. All 27 members of the Basel Committee on Banking Supervision engage in stress testing. The International Monetary Fund (IMF) includes stress tests of banks as an element of its Financial Sector Assessment Programs (FSAPs) and makes an FSAP assessment mandatory at least once every five years for 25 jurisdictions with systemically important financial sectors (see Bernanke 2013).

2. A review conducted by the European Court of Auditors noted that "the European Banking Authority lacked the authority to make or enforce decisions on supervisory convergence and had a limited legal mandate and staff to conduct the 2011 stress tests" (European Court of Auditors 2014, 1).

3. This explanation does not apply to the October 2014 or July 2016 EU-wide tests, as by late 2014 the European Central Bank (ECB) was the de facto lead supervisor for the test. While it was then just assuming the role of single supervisor for Europe's largest banks, the ECB had resources and authorities comparable to those of the Fed, including the authority to compel banks failing the test to recapitalize promptly.

4. In reviewing the euro area experience with bank stress tests, Orphanides (2014, 4–5) notes: "In contrast to the US experience, in the European Union decisions were made at a political level to go ahead with similar stress test exercises but without a coherent plan for the availability of a credible backstop.... In the absence of a credible backstop, the announcement of a stress test should be expected to cause a credit supply retrenchment with all the adverse consequences that would be expected by any policy-induced credit crunch." Angeloni (2014b, 7) offers a similar assessment: "Communicating stress test results is safe only if markets perceive that there is a reliable backstop to the exercise."

5. Writing about the European banking union in the summer of 2014, Hellwig (2014b, 1) concludes that "procedures for the recovery and resolution of institutions in difficulties remain problematic." He argues that "the SRM [Single Resolution Mechanism] provides for a centralized procedure with single-entry resolution for large banks. However, the procedure is complex and provides much scope for participants to veto decisions they do not like. For institutions of the importance and complexity of BNP Paribas or Deutsche Bank, the mechanism will therefore be no more practical and trustworthy than the provisions of the BRRD [Bank Recovery and Resolution Directive]" (p. 18). "The Single Resolution Fund for the SRM is targeted for a level of €55 billion, the German Bank Restructuring Fund for a level of €70 billion, to be reached after many years. These numbers are much too small to ensure interim funding of institutions like Deutsche Bank or BNP Paribas, with liabilities on the order of €2 trillion, a large part of which is wholesale and short term" (p. 19). "The SRM will be able to borrow from the European Stability Mechanism (ESM), but the numbers that have been given there, like those for restructuring or resolution funds, stand in no realistic relation to what is needed to maintain interim funding" (p. 10).

6. Federal Reserve Chair Ben Bernanke (2009) made the following statement shortly after the Supervisory Capital Assessment Program (SCAP) was announced: "We have strongly encouraged institutions requiring additional capital to obtain it through private means.... To ensure that all these firms can build the needed capital cushions, however, the Treasury has a firm commitment to provide contingent common equity, in the form of convertible preferred stock, as a bridge to obtaining private capital in the future."

Sachs and Kabaker (2016) indicate that in addition to public funds left over from TARP, a "placeholder" for $250 billion of additional funding was also included in the president's 2009 budget for "potential additional financial stabilization effort."

7. I say "less successful" relative to their US counterparts because some European officials would emphasize that US officials made the crisis management blunder par excellence when they allowed Lehman Brothers to fail. Henry Paulson (2010, 233), the US Treasury secretary at the time, recalls that he received phone calls from his German and French counterparts (Peer Steinbrück and Christine Lagarde) warning him that the failure of Lehman would be "unthinkable" and "catastrophic." US officials argue that they made heroic efforts to find a buyer for Lehman; that Barclay's planned purchase and assumption of Lehman was nixed at the last moment by its UK regulator; that Lehman did not have adequate collateral to cover the gaping hole in its balance sheet; and that before Dodd-Frank legislation, the Federal Reserve and Treasury had no orderly resolution regime in place for a systemically important nonbank (for accounts of the discussions surrounding Lehman's failure, see Sorkin 2009, Wessel 2009, Paulson 2010, Geithner 2014, and Bernanke 2015).

8. In addition to the size and range of the US crisis response, one can argue that the way in which capital injections were designed under both the (Paulson) capital purchase program and the (Geithner) capital assistance program and the way in which those capital injections were coordinated with the SCAP helped boost confidence in banks and contain the downward spiral in bank equity prices. See Stein (2016) and Sachs and Kabaker (2016) for the thinking behind the design of those capital injections.

9. According to Truman (2016, 4), "It is difficult to avoid the conclusion that the economic decision makers in the euro area failed to recognize and act on what was a euro area crisis."

10. The October 2016 *World Economic Outlook* (IMF 2016b) projected consumer price inflation in the euro area at 0.3 percent in 2016 and 1.1 percent in 2017. The corresponding forecasts for the United States are 1.2 percent in 2016 and 2.3 percent in 2017.

11. The official estimates of the aggregate shortfalls in the four EU-wide stress tests were as follows: 2009 test: no shortfall published; 2010 test: aggregate shortfall of €3.5 billion; 2011 test: aggregate shortfall of €26.8 billion. In the 2011 EU-wide capital exercise, the aggregate shortfall was estimated to be €115 billion. For the 2014 test, the aggregate capital shortfall was €24.6 billion. Since there were no hurdle rates in the 2016, there was no published shortfall. See CEBS (2009, 2010) and EBA (2011, 2012, 2014e, 2016a). Buiter concludes that "the EBA has a long record of stress tests that grotesquely underestimate the capital hole in EU banks" (Willem Buiter, "Four Rescue Measures for Stagnant Eurozone," *Financial Times*, October 24, 2014).

12. The aggregate capital shortfall would have been larger had the EBA not allowed banks to count the €50 billion in fresh capital raised in the first four months of 2011.

13. In the end, the CRD IV was not implemented until June 2013.

14. The contrast between Basel III and prevailing EU rules for other categories of bank capital (that is, tier 1 ratios and total capital ratios) were even more marked than for common equity (see EBA 2012 and Vestergaard and Retana 2013).

15. Other researchers have offered additional criticisms, including that the 2011 stress test did not contain a sovereign default scenario (Ahmed et al. 2011).

16. If the hurdle rate for the leverage ratio had been set at 4.5 percent, 50 of the 70 banks would have failed the 2011 test.

17. German and French banks had an average leverage ratio of roughly 3 and an average ratio of risk-weighted assets to total assets of about 0.3; the corresponding averages for Italian and Spanish banks were roughly twice as high on both counts.

18. These cross-country differences also have implications for the size of the estimated EU-wide capital shortfall. Acharya and Steffen (2014a) show that the largest absolute capital shortfalls show up in the larger countries (France, Germany, Italy, and Spain), not in the smaller periphery countries. In terms of shortfalls relative to GDP, the ranking is, of course, different, with Cyprus leading the pack.

19. IMF (2011b), Goldstein (2012a), and Greenlaw et al. (2012) also made this argument.

20. EBA Chair Andrea Enria (2014b) rejected these criticisms of the 2011 EU-wide stress test and capitalization exercise, as well as the charge that large EU banks are poorly capitalized relative to their US or global peers. He argued that large EU banks stack up reasonably well against their US counterparts on both risk-based capital comparisons and leverage ratios (once one puts them on the same accounting framework), that the 2011 capital exercise generated a large amount of new capital raising, and that EU banks needed to do some asset restructuring.

21. "How Did Europe's Bank Stress Test Give Dexia a Clean Bill of Health?" *Guardian*, October 5, 2011.

22. The *Financial Times* reported that the ECB and national central banks in the European Union were paying €488 million in fees to external advisors for their work on the Comprehensive Assessment; see Claire Jones, Alice Ross, and Sam Fleming, "ECB Bank Audit to Cover Consultants in Cash," *Financial Times*, August 20, 2014.

23. Jacques Gaulard, "The Comprehensive Assessment: Positive Outcome, No Rating Impact," Scope Ratings, October 30, 2014; Phillippe Heim, "Alternative Stress Tests Cannot Compare with Those of the ECB," letter to the *Financial Times*, October 31, 2014.

24. James Obrien, "MEPs Give Cautious Welcome to EU-Wide Stress Test Results," *Parliament Magazine*, November 26, 2014.

25. Kirkegaard (2014) and Véron (2014) also show that there would have been a larger number of undercapitalized banks (including some large German banks) than identified in the 2014 test if even a 3 percent leverage ratio had been used as the hurdle rate.

26. Acharya and Steffen (2014c) conclude that the five largest banking systems in the euro area measured by total assets (France, Germany, Italy, Spain, and Belgium) had an estimated capital shortfall of €432 billion in the adverse scenario versus the €20 billion shortfall implied in the official results.

27. Montesi and Papiro (2015) report a similar finding, comparing the results of the 2014 EU-wide test with those for the 2014 US Comprehensive Capital Analysis and Review (CCAR).

28. Acharya and Steffen (2014a) find that using the projected losses in the adverse scenario employed by the ECB and applying a simple leverage ratio produces results much closer to the Acharya and Steffen (2014a) capital shortfalls than those reported in EBA (2014e).

29. Steil and Walker (2014b) report that the IMF baseline forecast for the euro area was an inflation rate of 0.5 percent.

30. In 2013 no deduction for tax-deferred assets was required; the deduction percentages for the succeeding years was as follows: 2014: 20 percent; 2015: 40 percent; 2016: 60 percent; 2017: 80 percent. Ceilings were also set on what share of common equity tier 1 capital could be accounted for by tax-deferred assets. See De Gunst (2013) for a discussion of the different types of tax-deferred assets and of the intricacies of treating tax-deferred assets and credits in the measurement of bank capital.

31. If the sovereign gets into serious fiscal and debt difficulties, any government guarantees for tax-deferred assets or credits become suspect and so does their loss absorbency for banks.

32. Kirkegaard (2014) indicates that German banks benefitted the most from tax-deferred assets—by €33 billion. The corresponding figures for Spanish and Italian banks were €25 billion and €16 billion, respectively.

33. According to Shulock (2014), the €48 billion estimate of asset overvaluation was not even a generous rounding error. It would be incongruous for EU banks to have valued correctly 99.8 percent of their assets when there is strong evidence that these same banks were making long-standing and strenuous efforts in other areas (e.g., risk weighting, use of tax-deferred assets, etc.) to artificially inflate their capital.

34. As Beck (2014, 2) put it, "The number of banks with (net) capital shortfalls seems exactly what the doctor prescribed—not too low, so that the test would be considered rigorous enough, not too high, in order to not shake the markets."

35. Shulock (2014) notes that the Asset Quality Review reviewed 800 portfolios, 119,000 borrowers, and 170,000 items of collateral.

36. The two areas where the Basel Committee judged US banking regulations to deviate seriously from the Basel III minimums were the securitization framework and the standardized approach to market risk. See Véron (2014) for a broader discussion of these BCBS assessment reports.

37. The BCBS (2014a) assessment covered banks in the nine EU member countries that are also members of the BCBS (Belgium, France, Germany, Italy, Luxembourg, the Netherlands, Spain, Sweden, and the United Kingdom). The BCBS finding of "materially noncompliant" for the European Union led Véron (2014, 1) to remark that "the European Union, which often claims leadership on championing global financial standards, has been found to be the global laggard on a key aspect of banking regulation."

38. See BCBS (2014a) for a summary of the specific problems with the European Union's treatment of credit risk. In addition, although the BCBS does not currently judge them to be material, the report identified other areas where there are differences, including the treatment of investments in the capital instruments of insurance company subsidiaries for the definition of bank capital.

39. Danièle Nouy quoted in Caroline Bingham and Martin Arnold, "Europe's Big Banks Will Need to Raise Capital, Warns ECB," *Financial Times*, February 24, 2015.

40. Willem Buiter, "Four Rescue Measures for Stagnant Eurozone," *Financial Times*, October 24, 2014.

41. "Crisis and Opportunity," *Economist*, July 9–15, 2016.

42. David Reilly, "The Big Bank Bloodbath: Losses Near Half a Trillion Dollars," *Wall Street Journal*, July 7, 2016.

43. "The Italian Job," *Economist*, July 9–15, 2016.

44. "Crisis and Opportunity," *Economist*, July 9–15, 2016.

45. Peter Eavis, "Italy's Plan for Banks Is Dividing Europe," *New York Times*, July 7, 2016; "Avoiding Europe's Next Banking Crisis," Bloomberg, July 7, 2016. Dagher et al. (2016) put forward a methodology for translating estimates of nonperforming loans into banking losses using historical estimates of recovery and provisioning rates.

46. The weighted-average 2015 starting point for the transitional Basel III leverage ratio in the 2016 EU-wide test was 5.2 percent.

47. The decline between the starting and minimum values for the common equity tier 1 measure of capital was 380 basis points in the EU-wide test and 520 basis points in the US test.

48. Amihad and Favero (2016) argue that the Italian government should require banks to issue deep discount rights issues as a coercive way to raise capital and strengthen bank balance sheets. They note that such coercive rights issues were helpful in allowing both Bank Santander (in November 2008) and Barclays (in July 2013) deal with capital shortfalls.

49. See the postscript (chapter 9) for an update of market developments for banks in the European Union and the United States.

50. As Kenneth Lay, then CEO of Enron, put it in 2001: "Investors don't like uncertainty. When there's uncertainty, they always think there is another shoe to drop" (cited in Ong and Pazarbasioglu 2013, 4). In private correspondence, Peter Fisher, a former undersecretary of the US Treasury, offered a similar perspective. He argues that one of the key reasons that the SCAP had such a positive effect on confidence was that it clarified which banks would be saved and which ones would not, something that had been unclear since the fateful Lehman week. In contrast, he maintains that European leaders took much longer to clarify which banks were inside the safe circle and which were not.

51. Schoenmaker and Véron (2016, 5) argue that the Single Supervisory Mechanism provides tougher supervision than do national supervisory authorities: "The ECB appears less vulnerable than national authorities to regulatory capture and political intervention." They also report that Greece and Portugal are among the EU countries with the highest ratios of nonperforming loans. Cyprus had a serious financial crisis in 2012–13.

52. "EU Bank Regulators Need to Do More to Foster Faith," *Financial Times*, August 1, 2016. In addition to criticizing the test for carrying no threshold for passing or failing and providing little clarity about how and when undercapitalized banks will be strong-armed into raising fresh equity, the *Financial Times* editorial bemoaned the lack of attention to the consequences of Brexit and the mounting threat of negative interest rates.

53. "Europe's Stress Tests Fail Again," *Bloomberg View*, August 1, 2016.

54. Simon Kennedy, "Draghi Accelerating on Easy Street Won't Bypass Yellen Soon," Bloomberg Business, February 25, 2015.

55. "ECB Chiefs Target €50 Billion a Month for Landmark Bond Buying Program," *Financial Times*, January 22, 2015.

56. "Investors Are Unimpressed with Further Stimulus Measures in Europe," *New York Times*, December 4, 2015.

57. Reuters, "Fed's Fischer Says Asset Purchase Program Continues to Buoy Economy," February 27, 2015.

2

Operational Features and Evolution of the US and EU-Wide Tests

This chapter examines the key operational features of the US and EU-wide stress tests. It traces the main evolutionary changes in the tests since they first surfaced in 2009, in order to provide insight into the reasoning behind the original design of the tests and the changes made to them to make them more credible and effective.

Operational Features

Tables 2.1 and 2.2 provide snapshots of the main operational features of the US and EU-wide tests, respectively.

Coverage

The tests focus on the largest and most interconnected banks, under the assumption that capital inadequacy there would have the most adverse implications for the wider economy. In the United States, the Comprehensive Capital Analysis and Review (CCAR) uses a simple asset size cutoff. Before 2016 the aim in the European Union was to cover at least half of total banking assets in each member country (with banks selected in descending order of market share). In 2016 the European Union moved to a size cutoff (a minimum of €30 billion in total consolidated assets).

Nonbanks are typically not included, presumably because bank supervisors do not have the same authorization to recommend or mandate corrective action if they fail the test and perhaps also because stress tests for nonbanks would require different scenarios than for banks. In the United States,

(text continues on p. 87)

Table 2.1   US bank stress tests, 2009–16

Stress test	Date	Supervisors	Coverage	Time horizon	Scenarios		Models
	(1)	(2)	(3)	(4)	(5)	(6)	(7)
Supervisory Capital Assessment Program (SCAP)	October 2009	Fed, FDIC, OCC	19 largest domestic bank holding companies (BHCs); 66% of banking system assets	2009–10	Baseline (supervisor-led). More adverse (supervisor-led).	Macroeconomic: real GDP, unemployment rate, housing prices. Market stress scenario: firms with trading assets greater than or equal to $100 billion.	Supervisor models
Comprehensive Capital Analysis and Review (CCAR)	March 2011	Fed, FDIC, OCC	19 BHCs (same as SCAP)	2011–12	Baseline (supervisor-led). More adverse (supervisor-led). Company-run equivalent of above.	Macroeconomic: real GDP, unemployment rate, asset prices. Severe global market shock.[a]	Bank-run models checked by supervisors
CCAR	March 2012	Fed, FDIC, OCC	19 BHCs (same as SCAP)	2012–13	Baseline (supervisor-led). More adverse (supervisor-led). Company-led equivalent of above.	Macroeconomic and financial market: deep recession in US, asset price declines, increase in risk premia, slowdown in global economic activity. Severe global market shock.[a]	Supervisor models and bank-run models

CCAR	March 2013	Fed, FDIC, OCC	18 BHCs; 70% of banking assets	2013–14	Baseline (supervisor-led). Adverse (supervisor-led). Severely adverse (supervisor-led). Company-led equivalent of above.	Macroeconomic and financial market scenarios Interest rate scenarios Severe global market shock[a]	Supervisor models and bank-run models
CCAR	March 2014	Fed, FDIC, OCC	30 BHCs; 80% of assets of all BHCs (including 12 BHCs that did not participate in previous CCARs)	2014–15	Baseline (supervisor-led). Adverse (supervisor-led). Severely adverse (supervisor-led). Company-led equivalent of above.	Macroeconomic and financial market scenarios Interest rate scenarios Severe global market shock[a] Counterparty default[b]	Supervisor models and bank-run models
CCAR	March 2015	Fed, FDIC, OCC	31 BHCs, >80% of assets of all BHCs	2015–16	Baseline (supervisor-led). Adverse (supervisor-led). Severely adverse (supervisor-led). Company-led equivalent of above.	[same as CCAR 2014]	Supervisor models and bank-run models, and models leased from third-party vendors
CCAR	June 2016	Fed, FDIC, OCC	33 BHCs, >80% of assets of all BHCs	2016–17	Baseline (supervisor-led). Adverse (supervisor-led). Severely adverse (supervisor-led). Company-led equivalent of above.	[same as CCAR 2014]	Supervisor models and bank-run models, and models leased from third-party vendors

(table continues)

Table 2.1   US bank stress tests, 2009–16 (*continued*)

	Bank capital				
Stress test	Hurdle rate	Average change in capital ratio (stressed minimum minus starting)	Failures	Disclosure	Remedial actions
	(8)	(9)	(10)	(11)	(12)
Supervisory Capital Assessment Program (SCAP) 2009	Tier 1 (stressed) 6% Tier 1 common (stressed) 4%	Median loss is −7.5% of risk-weighted assets under more adverse scenario	10 of 19 banks needed additional capital	Bank-by-bank results	Firms that didn't meet hurdle rate were required to raise dollar amounts of capital within 6 months; government backup in place if can't raise enough private capital.
Comprehensive Capital Analysis and Review (CCAR) 2011	Tier 1 common (stressed) 5% Tier 1 leverage (stressed) 3% Also must maintain four capital ratios above minimum regulatory requirements.	Not available	Not available	No bank-by-bank results	One month after CCAR report, firms receive detailed assessment of their capital plans, including areas where plans and processes need to be strengthened.

CCAR 2012	Tier 1 common (stressed) 5% Tier 1 leverage (stressed) 3% Also must maintain four capital ratios above minimum regulatory requirements.	Tier 1 common –3.8% (6.3% vs 10.1%) Tier 1 leverage –2.7% (–4.7% vs 7.4%)	4 of 19 firms had one or more stressed capital ratios that fell beneath hurdle rates.	Bank-by-bank results	Federal Reserve notifies BHC if it has any objections to its capital plan; if Fed objects, no capital distributions permitted until Fed gives written approval.
CCAR 2013	Tier 1 common (stressed) 5% Tier 1 leverage 3–4% Also must maintain four capital ratios above minimum regulatory requirements.	Tier 1 common –4.5% (6.6% vs –11.1%) Tier 1 leverage –2.7% (5.3% vs 8.0%)	2 of 18 received objection to capital plan. Two other firms received conditional non-objection to plans.	Bank-by-bank results	Federal Reserve notifies BHC if it has any objections to its capital plan; if Fed objects, no capital distributions permitted until Fed gives written approval.

(table continues)

Table 2.1 US bank stress tests, 2009–16 (continued)

Stress test	Bank capital					
	Hurdle rate	Average change in capital ratio (stressed minimum minus starting)	Failures	Disclosure	Remedial actions	
	(8)	(9)	(10)	(11)	(12)	
CCAR 2014	Tier 1 common (stressed) 5% Tier 1 leverage (stressed) 3–4% Also must maintain four capital ratios above minimum regulatory requirements.	Tier 1 common –5.0% (6.6% vs 11.6%) Tier 1 leverage –3.0% (5.4% vs 8.4%)	5 of 30 received objection to capital plans (of which 4 of 30 had objection on qualitative grounds, and one on quantitative grounds).	Bank-by-bank results	Federal Reserve notifies BHC if it has any objections to its capital plan; if Fed objects, no capital distributions permitted until Fed gives written approval.	
CCAR 2015	Tier 1 common (stressed) 5% Tier 1 leverage (stressed) 4% Also must maintain four capital ratios above minimum regulatory requirements.	Tier 1 common –4.8% (7.1% vs 11.9%) Tier 1 leverage –3.5% (5.2% vs 8.8%)	2 of 31 received objections to capital plans (both on qualitative grounds); one other BHC did not receive objection but has to submit new capital plan.	Bank-by-bank results	Federal Reserve notifies BHC if it has any objections to its capital plan; if Fed objects, no capital distributions permitted until Fed gives written approval.	

CCAR 2016	Tier 1 common (stressed) 5% Tier 1 leverage (stressed) 4% Also must maintain four capital ratios above minimum regulatory requirements.	CET1 –5.1% (7.1% vs 12.2%) Tier 1 leverage –3.3% (5.9% vs 9.2%)	2 of 33 received objections to capital plans (both on qualitative grounds); one other BHC did not receive objection but has to submit new capital plan.	Bank-by-bank results	Federal Reserve notifies BHC if it has any objections to its capital plan; if Fed objects, no capital distributions permitted until Fed gives written approval.

FDIC = Federal Deposit Insurance Corporation; OCC = Office of the Comptroller of the Currency

a. Applies to the six largest firms with significant trading activities.
b. Applies to eight firms with significant trading activity and/or important custodial operations.

Sources: Board of Governors (2009b, 2011, 2012, 2013a, 2014a, 2015b, 2016a).

Table 2.2 EU-wide bank stress tests, 2009–16

Stress test	Date	Supervisors	Coverage	Time horizon	Scenarios		Models
	(1)	(2)	(3)	(4)	(5)	(6)	(7)
First EU-wide stress test	October 2009	CEBS, EC, ECB, national supervisors	22 major cross-border banking groups, covering 60% of total EU banking assets	2009–10	Baseline (supervisor-led) More adverse (supervisor-led)	Macroeconomic: EU real GDP, unemployment rate, property prices (same variables in US).	Supervisor models
Second EU-wide stress test	July 2010	CEBS, EC, ECB, national supervisors	91 European banks, 20 EU member states, covering 65% of EU total banking assets	2010–11	Baseline (supervisor-led) More adverse (supervisor-led)	Macroeconomic: EU real GDP, unemployment rate, property prices, foreign economic activity. Sovereign debt shock to trading book.	Banks' own models, supervisor models
Third EU-wide stress test	July 2011	European Banking Authority (EBA)	90 European banks, 21 EU members	2011–14	Baseline (supervisor-led) More adverse (supervisor-led)	Macroeconomic: Sovereign debt shock to trading book; increased provisions for sovereign debt in banking book.	Banks' own models, supervisor models

Fourth EU-wide stress test and Asset Quality Review (AQR)	October 2014	EBA, ECB, ESRB, EC, national supervisors	123 European banks, covering more than 70% of total EU banking assets	2014–15	Baseline (supervisor-led) More adverse (supervisor-led)	Macroeconomic adverse scenario to include (1) increase in global bond yields; (2) further deterioration in credit quality in EU countries with feeble demand; (3) stalled policy reforms; (4) lack of progress on bank balance sheet repair.	Banks' own models, supervisor models
Fifth EU-wide stress test	July 2016	EBA, ECB, ESRB, SSM, national supervisors	51 European banks, covering around 70% of total EU banking assets	2016–17	Baseline (supervisor-led) More adverse (supervisor-led)	Macroeconomic adverse scenario reflects four system risks: (1) an abrupt reversal of compressed global risk premia; (2) weak profitability for banks and insurers; (3) rising debt loads in the public and non-financial private sectors; (4) prospective stress in a rapidly growing shadow banking system.	Banks' own models, supervisor models

(table continues)

Table 2.2   EU-wide bank stress tests, 2009–16 *(continued)*

Stress test	Bank capital		Failures	Disclosure	Remedial Action
	Hurdle rate	Average change in capital ratio (stressed minus starting)			
	(8)	(9)	(10)	(11)	(12)
First EU-wide stress test	Tier 1 (stressed) 6%	Tier 1 –0.1% (7.8% vs 7.9%)	None announced	No bank-by-bank results published	None
Second EU-wide stress test	Tier 1 (stressed) 6%	Tier 1 –1.1% (9.2% vs 10.3%)	7 banks	Bank-by-bank results; sovereign debt exposures	Remedial actions to be decided by national supervisory authorities.
Third EU-wide stress test	Core tier 1 (stressed) 5%	Core tier 1 –1.5% (7.4% vs 8.9%)	20 banks	Bank-by-bank results; sovereign debt exposures	EBA recommends that national supervisors request all banks failing stress tests to promptly eliminate their capital shortfalls. Also, EBA launches EU-wide capital exercise in October 2011.
Fourth EU-wide stress test	Common equity tier 1: 8% baseline 5.5% (stressed) adverse scenario	Common equity tier 1 –2.6% (8.5% vs. 11.1%); also, decline of 0.4% due to Asset Quality Review	24 banks (14 banks, after 2014 capital raising)	Bank-by-bank results	Banks failing test have two weeks to submit new capital plan. Banks below baseline (adverse) hurdle rate have six (nine) months to achieve hurdle rate.
Fifth EU-wide stress test	No hurdle rate	Common equity tier 1 –3.8% (9.4% vs 13.2%); Fully loaded CET1 –3.4% (9.2% vs 12.6%); Basel III leverage ratio –1.0% (4.2% vs 5.2%)	n.a.	Bank-by-bank results	Results of the tests will be an input into the Supervisory Review and Evaluation Process (SREP).

CEBS = Committee of European Bank Supervisors; EC = European Commission; ECB = European Central Bank; ESRB = European Systemic Risk Board; SSM = Single Supervisory Mechanism

Sources: CEBS (2009, 2010); EBA (2010, 2011, 2014e, 2016d).

the Dodd-Frank Act allows the Federal Reserve to include in its stress tests any nonbank deemed systemically important by the Federal Stability Oversight Council, but the Fed has not yet done so for its supervisory-led tests. Recall that fragility at some nonbanks (Bear Stearns, Lehman Brothers, Morgan Stanley, Goldman Sachs) was an integral part of the global economic and financial crisis, and banks account for only about a third of credit intermediation. An important issue is thus whether future CCAR tests should at least include scenarios that emphasize interactions between the bank and nonbank sectors (see chapter 3). As regards the inclusion of foreign banks in the tests, foreign banks with subsidiaries are increasingly included if they are thought to be important for the functioning of the financial system.[1]

Frequency

Since 2011 US supervisors have been required by legislation to conduct supervisory-led stress tests annually.[2] The European Union has no such requirement (the European Banking Authority [EBA] conducted an EU-wide bank stress test in 2016 but not 2015).

An advantage of requiring annual tests is that it eliminates the option for the authorities to delay a test because they do not wish to disclose the extent of the banking system's fragility. Conducting (supervisor-led) stress tests more frequently than once a year is regarded as impractical, given the large data requirements and the increasingly comprehensive modeling and analytical framework.[3] However, if market conditions worsen significantly after the publication of stress test results, the supervisory authorities can conduct a follow-up exercise with a stricter capital hurdle rate cum recapitalization requirement for banks falling short. The EBA conducted just such a recapitalization exercise a few months after the release of the 2011 EU-wide stress test outcomes.

Scenario Horizons

The usual practice in the US tests has been for the scenarios to cover two whole adjoining calendar years (nine quarters) (see Lehnert 2015); for example, the 2012 (CCAR) stress test results (published in March 2012) covered the 2012–13 period. The EU-wide tests have moved over time to a three-year time horizon (see Henry and Kok 2013 and Constâncio 2015). A two- to three-year horizon fits comfortably with the availability of consensus two-to-three-year-ahead baseline forecasts for the home economy and for its main trading partners (such as in the IMF's *World Economic Outlook*). One way to think of the two- to three-year horizon is as a compromise: not so long as to create unacceptably large forecast errors in the second (third) year, but long enough to allow the shocks to have meaningful effects on the real economy (given the lags in most macro models).[4,5]

Types of Scenarios

Bank stress tests include a baseline scenario and at least one "adverse" scenario that puts banks' capital positions under greater stress. The US supervisory authorities started out (in 2009) with one adverse scenario but were required by the Dodd-Frank Act of 2010 to add a "severely adverse" scenario; they have thus maintained the two-adverse-scenario package ever since. The European Union has stuck to one adverse scenario.

As indicated in tables 2.1 and 2.2, the most popular variables in both the US and EU-wide tests are real GDP growth, inflation, the unemployment rate, housing prices, and equity prices. The maintained assumption is that bank solvency is threatened when there is a recession paired with a collapse of property and equity prices. Over time, the number of variables included in the scenarios has grown to encompass a wider array of interest rates and asset prices and a fuller characterization of foreign economic conditions; for example, the Federal Reserve reports that the macroeconomic scenario for the 2014 CCAR tests (Board of Governors 2014a) contained a block of 48 variables.

"Bespoke" scenarios have also become more common, to reflect either particular market concerns at a point in time or particular structural vulnerabilities of some banks in the test. For example, the EU-wide tests have frequently included a sovereign debt scenario, while the US tests have always included—for the six largest banks with significant trading activity—an adverse global market scenario (meant to capture a severe deterioration in market conditions, like that prevailing between June and December of 2008). The 2016 CCAR included in its adverse and global-market-shock scenarios a period of negative interest rates on short-term US Treasury securities. Starting in 2015, the US tests have also included a counterparty risk scenario. The adverse scenario for the 2016 EU-wide stress test encompassed four kinds of systemic risks: an abrupt reversal of compressed global risk premia, amplified by low secondary market liquidity; weak profitability prospects for bank and insurers in a low-growth environment; rising debt sustainability concerns in the public and nonfinancial private sectors; and prospective stress in a rapidly growing shadow banking sector, amplified by spillover and liquidity risks (ESRB 2016). In addition to the scenarios devised by the supervisors, banks also submit their own scenarios; in the recent CCAR tests, there are two of those bank-designed scenarios, bringing the total to five (three supervisor-designed scenarios plus two-bank designed ones).[6]

The guideline that one often hears about the construction of adverse scenarios is that they should be "severe but plausible." For the US tests, the supervisors have pledged that the severely adverse scenario will reflect, at a minimum, "the economic and financial conditions typical of a severe post–World War II US recession" (Tarullo 2014b)—albeit not necessarily the conditions prevailing during the worst of the global economic and financial crisis of 2007-09.[7] The EU supervisory authorities have not issued a parallel pledge on the minimal conditions for their "adverse scenario," but have emphasized the "substantial" negative impact of the assumed shocks; for example, the adverse scenario in the 2014 stress test resulted in EU GDP being 7 percent below its baseline level in 2016 and in the EU unemployment rate being 2.9 percentage points higher than in the baseline (ESRB 2014). On the more skeptical side of the ledger, the European Union refused to include in either the 2010 or 2011 stress test scenarios either a sovereign default by an EU member country or a euro exit (since these were counter to EU policy objectives)—even though they were arguably a plausible risk at the time. Similarly, as noted earlier, there was no deflation scenario in the 2014 stress test—even though it was a plausible risk that would impact EU banks. Neither the 2016 EU-wide test nor the 2016 US tests included a Brexit scenario.

In the Bank of England's new stress testing regime (Brazier 2015, 4), an effort is being made to make the scenarios more countercyclical:

> The stress test scenario will become more severe as the risks get bigger and less severe as those risks either materialize or shrink. This is ambitious and ground-breaking. And if past cycles are anything to go on, we could be making the test more exacting just as the lenders and their investors are thinking the world is less risky—that this time really is different…. We'll begin with the forecasts made by the Bank of England and the IMF of the UK and global economies…. But it's the second step that's even more interesting…. We'll need to question whether the skew in the distribution of future outcomes is bigger than usual…. If it is, the stress scenario… should be more severe. To gauge this, we will assess indicators of potential imbalances—in credit, in asset prices, and in household and corporate balance sheets.

Only time will tell whether this countercyclical approach to scenario modeling is worthy of imitation in other countries' stress testing frameworks.

Some critics contend that the number of scenarios included in the US and EU-wide stress tests is so small as to make it almost inevitable that they will leave out certain severe but plausible risks (e.g., a liquidity squeeze emanating from fragilities in the nonbank sector, or a fire sale for assets generated by large-scale redemptions from a very large asset manager).[8] In addition, they warn that the repetitive nature of the macroeconomic scenarios in these tests amounts implicitly to "teaching to the test," with the adverse implications that banks are learning how to produce "passable" outcomes, and that the information value of the tests gets smaller and smaller over time (Schuermann 2012, Bookstaber et al. 2013, Glasserman and Tangirala 2015). However, in a recent event study of the US Dodd-Frank Act stress test and CCAR tests, Flannery, Hirtle, and Kovner (2015) find no evidence that the "new information" in US tests is decreasing over time. Finally, some analysts maintain that more meaningful adverse risk scenarios could be identified by conducting "reverse" stress tests; here, one uses an algorithm to search for the scenarios most likely to produce an assumed decline in bank capital ratios, rather than, as in the standard stress test, selecting an adverse scenario and estimating the decline in capital ratios associated with that scenario (Bookstaber et al. 2013, Henry and Kok 2013).[9] While the managers of the US and EU-wide stress tests have not rejected these criticisms/proposals, they apparently feel that these extensions and refinements are not ready for prime time.

Models Used to Estimate the Effects of the Scenarios on Bank Capital

Stress test managers now uniformly speak of relying not on a single model but rather on a set or suite of models. The Federal Reserve uses more than 40 models to project how categories of bank losses and revenues would respond to hypothetical scenarios (Bernanke 2013). In addressing why a multiplicity of models is needed, analysts (Borio, Drehmann, and Tsatsaronis 2012; Bank of England 2013b; Angeloni 2014b) offer the following explanations.

Stress tests involve credit, market, sovereign, liquidity, funding, and operational risks.[10] No single model can handle all these types of risk. Although attention in stress tests often centers on estimates of loan losses, models of bank earnings are no less important, especially as recent studies of bank capital increases over the 2007–12 period show that retained earnings made the largest contribution to such increases (Cohen and Scatigna 2014). Standard macro models are not designed to capture the effect of macro conditions on bank balance sheets. Doing so requires specialized auxiliary or satellite models. As the chance of model error for the conditions examined in adverse scenarios is high, there are advantages in relying on a consensus approach based on the output of a group of models.

"Bottom-up" approaches that rely on banks' own models to estimate the effect of shocks on their performance are good for capturing the granularity and idiosyncratic aspects of individual banks. However, the aggregate capital shortfall from such an exercise needs to be weighted against "top-down" estimates, in which the regulator imposes consistency and uses its own set of models to gauge the impact of the scenarios on bank capital.

Similarly, models that rely on market prices to analyze the relationship between capital ratios and default probabilities—such as the "contingent collateral approach," which the IMF used to good effect in many of its stress tests in Financial Sector Assessment Programs—have some strong advantages over models that rely on book-value data, but they also have shortcomings.[11] Having output from both kinds of models available enhances confidence in the final "judgmental" verdict.

Using a set of models also makes it harder for the banks to game the tests by increasing exposure to risks that a particular model underestimates (see Wall 2013). Supervisory models are also needed to check the reliability of banks' own models, especially as banks may have an incentive to produce test results that mirror their own preferences for capital ratios rather than the minimum capital ratio set by supervisors.

In its EU-wide tests, the European Central Bank (ECB) uses a constrained bottom-up approach: banks implement a common methodology and scenarios defined by the authorities, employing their own internal models (Angeloni 2014b, Enria 2015). The ECB uses a top-down model to conduct quality assurance checks on the bottom-up results the banks submit.

My impression is that the top-down approach dominates in the US stress tests, although banks are also required to generate and publish stress test results based on their own models (cum common scenarios) and separately using bank-specific scenarios. Angeloni (2014b) attributes part of this difference in approach to the much larger number of banks analyzed in earlier EU-wide tests (123 banks in the 2014 EU-wide test versus the 33 banks covered in the 2016 US CCAR). As indicated in chapter 1, for the 2016 EU-wide test, the ECB reduced the number of banks to 51.

Capital Hurdle Ratios

Every test needs a metric by which to judge performance. In bank stress tests, that (quantitative) metric is the capital hurdle rate—the minimum capital ratio banks need to satisfy under the various scenarios. If a bank's capital falls below the hurdle rate, the bank either fails the test and has to raise more capital (as in the pre-2016 EU-wide stress tests), or (as in the CCAR tests) it must revise its capital plan so that it meets the hurdle rate.

If the bank chooses not to submit a revised capital plan or if its revised plan does not gain the approval of the Federal Reserve, the bank fails the test and cannot make dividend payments or engage in share buybacks until it passes the test the following year. As emphasized in chapter 1, the 2016 EU-wide test marked a sharp departure from normal stress test procedure by dropping use of hurdle rates—preferring instead to establish the minimum capital ratio in their Supervisory Review and Evaluation Process (SREP) based on a wider set of considerations.

In the US and EU-wide stress tests, the capital hurdle rate is meant to capture the objective that banks have sufficient capital to absorb losses under "adverse" conditions while still meeting international, regional, and national regulatory minimums for capital adequacy. Minimum international regulatory standards for bank capital are represented by Basel III. Both the United States and the European Union issued final Basel III implementation regulations in mid-2013. In brief, the minimum capital adequacy levels under Basel III are 4.5 percent of risk-weighted assets for common equity tier 1 capital (exclusive of several additional buffers), 6 percent of risk-weighted assets for tier 1 capital, 8 percent of risk-weighted assets for total capital, and 3 percent of total leverage exposure for tier 1 leverage. Since the Basel Committee on Banking Supervision (BCBS) decided to phase in the Basel III requirements over a six-year period ending in 2019 and since the phase-in period is different for different measures of bank capital, meeting the Basel III minimums is a moving and differentiated target (see table 4.1 in chapter 4). Basel III also sets out how the numerator and denominator of each of the capital ratios are to be defined. A strict interpretation of meeting the Basel III minimums in a stress test would mean that banks would have to ensure that none of the four capital ratios fell below the minimums in each year of the test (under the baseline scenario).

The only relevant regional minimum capital standard is the European Union's Fourth Capital Requirements Directive (CRD IV), which went into effect in mid-2013.[12] It mostly mirrors Basel III but has been criticized for not being rigorous enough on the measurement of credit risk, for watering down some of the excluded items in the definition of common equity tier 1 capital, and for making it harder for EU member countries to impose national minimum capital standards that are considerably above the Basel III minimums (see Goldstein 2012a, BCBS 2014d). Members of the European Union are obligated to implement CRD IV. Outside the European Union, there are no limits to how much national minimum capital standards may exceed Basel III.

As noted earlier, the US regulatory authorities have decided to implement a more ambitious minimum for the Basel III leverage ratio (called the supplementary and enhanced supplementary leverage ratios in the United States). In particular, in April 2014, the Federal Reserve finalized a rule requiring large and complex US banks that are classified by the Financial Stability Board as "global systemically important banks," or G-SIBs for short, to have an enhanced supplementary leverage ratio of at least 5 percent for the bank holding company and 6 percent for the insured depository institution (that is, 2 to 3 percentage points above the Basel III minimum) in order to avoid restrictions on capital distributions and discretionary bonus payments. These higher leverage ratio requirements will become effective on January 1, 2018. In the US stress tests, the capital hurdle rate for the leverage ratio has been defined in terms of the tier 1 leverage ratio with total assets in the denominator—instead of total leverage exposure as in the Basel III leverage ratio—and it has been kept at 4 percent. Moreover, neither risk-weighted nor leverage-related capital surcharges for US G-SIBs have yet been incorporated in the US stress tests.[13]

In March 2016 the BCBS released its monitoring report on implementation of Basel III capital standards (BCBS 2016). It indicates that, based on data as of June 30, 2015, all 101 large internationally active banks participating in the study, including 30 G-SIBs, had a common equity tier 1 ratio above the 7 percent Basel III target ratio (i.e., the minimum capital requirement of 4.5 percent plus the capital conservation buffer of 2.5 percent).[14] The average common equity tier 1 ratio for Group 1 banks was 11.5 percent under the fully loaded Basel III standard and 11.9 percent under current transitional arrangements. As for the fully loaded Basel III (unweighted) leverage ratio, all 101 of the Group 1 banks met or exceeded the 3 percent minimum. The weighted-average leverage ratios for the 101 banks (as well as for the 30 G-SIBs) was 5.2 percent for the fully loaded Basel III standard and 5.6 percent under the current transitional arrangements. These results indicate that for large and complex international banks, the fully loaded Basel III capital targets are not acting as binding constraints in stress tests, at least under the unstressed scenario.

As shown in table 2.1, the 2009 Supervisory Capital Assessment Program (SCAP) used a stressed capital hurdle rate of 4 percent for tier 1 common. It was implemented before Basel III was agreed to. The use of tier 1 common (rather than tier 1 as a whole) represented a step toward higher-quality capital.

When the CCAR was introduced, in 2011, the stressed capital hurdle rate was raised to 5 percent and the stressed tier 1 leverage rate of 3 percent was introduced. In the 2012–15 CCARs, the stressed tier 1 common hurdle rate was maintained at 5 percent. As the US tests made the transition (and upgrade) from tier 1 common to common equity tier 1 capital, a 4.5 percent hurdle rate was applied to the latter in both the 2015 and 2016 CCAR tests. In 2014 the stressed hurdle rate for tier 1 leverage was raised to 4 percent, where it remained for the 2015 and 2016 US tests. CCAR participants were not permitted to use advanced approaches for calculating risk-weighted assets in the 2016 CCAR test.

Column 9 of table 2.1 shows the average change in the capital ratio, defined as the difference between its stressed level in the most adverse scenario and the starting level just before the first year of the scenarios. As it is the tier 1 common ratio and the tier 1 leverage ratio (not the tier 1 or total capital ratios) that tend to be binding constraints in the stress exercise, only the former two ratios are presented. The calculations show that the decline in the capital ratio under the most adverse scenario grew (albeit not continuously) over the 2012–16 period, for both the tier 1 common and the tier 1 leverage ratios.[15,16] Table 2.1 also shows that over the longer 2009–16 period, the number and share of banks failing the US stress tests declined. The 2015 CCAR represented the first time that no bank failed the quantitative part of the test, a result that also prevailed in 2016.[17]

Table 2.2 provides similar information on stressed bank capital hurdle rates for the first four EU-wide stress tests. The first two EU tests included a 6 percent stressed hurdle rate but applied it to a lower-quality measure of bank capital (tier 1). Not until 2011 was the hurdle rate defined in terms of core tier 1 capital, and then the stressed hurdle rate was lowered to 5 percent. For the 2014 stress test, the European Union defined the hurdle rate as common equity tier 1 and increased the stressed hurdle rate to 5.5 percent. As the 2014 test did not include a leverage test and the 2016 test contained no hurdle rates at all (for either risk-based capital or leverage ratios), no hurdle rate for the leverage ratio appears in table 2.2. In terms of the change in capital ratios during the adverse scenario, the 2009–16 period shows a movement toward larger declines. Failure rates rose over time (excluding the 2016 test, where, by definition, there were no passes or failures).

Senior US regulatory officials have stated that, unlike a professional golf tournament, US stress tests are not designed with a prespecified failure rate in mind (Tarullo 2014c). As suggested earlier, the failure rate in the quantitative part of a stress test can be "managed" by the test architects via, among other factors, the definition and height of the capital hurdle rate and the specification of the risk scenarios. Taking the 2014, 2015, and 2016 CCARs together, all but one of the failures came in the "qualitative" part of the test, as a result of deficiencies in risk management and capital planning.

Disclosure

Although it is perhaps natural to think of stress test disclosure in terms of the regular publication of bank-by-bank capital ratios, it is useful to remember that progress toward greater disclosure was not linear, that disclosure now covers a much broader spectrum of information about stress tests than just bank capital, and that even today not everything is disclosed.

US and EU-wide stress tests were not conducted every year during the 2009–16 period. The United States had no supervisor-led test in 2010, and the European Union had no EU-wide tests in 2012, 2013, or 2015. When the decision was made to integrate the annual US stress tests with an analysis of the capital planning process in a new CCAR, the initial 2011 CCAR report contained no bank-by-bank results—even though it was published just two years after the widely acclaimed success of such bank-by-bank disclosure in the 2009 SCAP.[18] In the European Union, the Committee of European Bank Supervisors (CEBS) and the European Banking Authority (EBA) appeared to be dragged kicking and screaming into progressively greater disclosure over the 2009–11 period, albeit not enough to satisfy market participants. During 2012–13, when the issue of banking fragility in the European Union was very much alive, market participants looking for an official appraisal of the sensitivity of Europe's banks to tail risk had to be content with the pledge that a "comprehensive" EU-wide stress test cum Asset Quality Review would be forthcoming in the fall of 2014.[19]

Still, when one reads the published materials associated with 2012–16 CCARs, as well as those linked to the 2011, 2014, and 2016 EU-wide stress tests, the disclosure is substantial. The documentation includes, inter alia, the objectives of the test, participating banks, recent trends in bank capital and liquidity, methodology, macroeconomic and market risk scenarios, model approach, treatment of securitizations, data templates, and individual bank losses by type of exposure. Moreover, recent CCARs show not only supervisor estimates of stressed bank capital ratios under the baseline, adverse, and severely adverse scenarios, but the company estimates as well; going in the same direction, stressed capital ratios are given not only under banks' revised capital plans but also under the original capital plans. If a bank fails to pass the qualitative part of the capital plan process, the reasons for its failure are provided. In addition to the multidisciplinary teams that work directly on the stress test, various peer review and advisory panels—in some cases, including outside experts—also are increasingly being brought into the discussion of the design of the tests. All in all, I would hardly call the process a "black box."

Supervisory officials in the United States and the European Union apparently concluded that what they gain from greater transparency and disclosure—in terms of market discipline, improved public confidence during crises, and fuller bank engagement in the exercise—more than compensates for any risk of market turbulence or false complacency associated with publication of the results.[20]

One area where the architects have held out against full disclosure is the publication of the supervisory models used to translate the impact of the shocks on bank capital. The authorities argue that disclosure of these models would both weaken banks' incentives to improve their own stress testing models (the old "teaching a man to fish" argument) and increase the chances that banks would game their portfolios to fit the properties of the supervisory models. Even without publication of the supervisory models, several researchers (Schuermann 2013, Glasserman and Tangirala 2015) have suggested that, as the stress tests have become more routine, banks have become more adept at gaming the exercise (see the discussion in chapter 3).

A second area where disclosure is the exception rather than the norm is in explaining whether and why stress test estimates of capital shortfalls differ from recent estimates made by other analysts, both official (for example, the IMF) and private.[21] Admittedly, there are many reasons (methodology, time periods, sample of banks, etc.) why such a comparison may not be on an apples-to-apples basis. Still, in cases where the stress test results differ markedly from those of outside analysts, there is apt to be a credibility payoff in efforts to explain both the main sources of those differences and the reasons why the official estimates are regarded as accurate.[22]

There is a strong consensus that a stress test that finds individual banks or the banking system as a whole significantly undercapitalized and is not followed by remedial action is not helpful.[23] The unhappy Japanese experience with "zombie" banks in the 1990s is but one case in point. The fact that the CEBS and the EBA had the power only to "recommend" rather than "require" such recapitalization was one of the weaknesses of the first three EU-wide stress tests. The fact that the CCAR program in the United States integrates the stress tests into the capital planning process and gives the Federal Reserve the authority to reject a bank's capital plan and require recapitalization measures is a strong plus. The ECB, in its role as single supervisor for large EU banks, now has similar powers.

Remedial Policy Actions in Response to the Test Results

In planning for its first independent stress test (conducted in 2014), the Bank of England (2013a), set out clearly the measures that banks could be required to take if stress tests identified a need to strengthen their capital. They included the following:

- constraining dividend distributions, share buybacks, or discretionary payments on certain tier 1 capital instruments,
- constraining (variable) remuneration to staff,[24]
- issuing equity or other capital instruments that can definitely absorb losses on a "going concern" basis (outside of resolution or liquidity),
- engaging in liability management exercises, and
- reducing certain risk exposures or business lines.

If the stress tests reveal that the banking system as a whole is significantly undercapitalized, there are likewise remedial policy actions that could be taken. These measures could include activating the countercyclical capital buffer; increasing national minimum capital requirements; constraining dividend payments for all banks; requiring new equity issuance; and, in a deep crisis, using public funds to recapitalize banks that cannot raise enough capital from private sources.

In short, the benefits of disclosure are contingent on there being a policy mechanism in place to deal promptly with any capital problems revealed by the tests. If there is no such mechanism, publication of the results may simply be a recipe for high anxiety.

Evolution of Stress Testing, 2009–16

Given the increasing importance of stress testing in bank supervision and regulation and given that these tests have now been going on for six years plus, it is useful to have an overview from the senior managers about how the stress testing exercise has evolved. In the US case, such overviews have been presented by Bernanke (2013) and Tarullo (2014c); see also the discussion of Tarullo (2016) in chapter 9. Owing perhaps to the multiple institutional changes in the leadership of the EU-wide stress testing exercise over the 2009–16 period, I was not able to find a parallel overview of the evolution of the EU-wide tests by either ECB President Mario Draghi or EBA Chair Andrea Enria. Nevertheless, speeches by senior EU/SSM/EBA bank supervisors (Angeloni 2014a, 2014b; Lautenschläger 2014; Nouy 2014a, 2014b; and Constâncio 2015)—most in the immediate run-up to, or wake of, the October 2014 EU-wide Comprehensive Assessment (i.e., 2014 stress test cum Asset Quality Review)—provide helpful clues about how EU-wide stress testing is changing and where it is headed.

Senior US bank supervisors maintain that the Federal Reserve's basic approach to stress testing has remained pretty constant since the SCAP but underline the following important changes:

- Stress testing has become mandatory in the United States.
- Annual stress tests are now integrated into the CCAR capital planning exercise.
- The adverse and severely adverse scenarios have been expanded and refined, and additional nonmacroeconomic shocks have been added (including the assumed default of each firm's largest counterparty).
- Independent supervisory models have been developed, so that supervisors no longer have to rely on bank models to evaluate the impact of the scenarios on bank capital.
- The static balance sheet assumption has been made an integral part of the tests, so that banks know that they cannot shrink their balance sheets as a way to meet the capital hurdle rate.
- There has been a steady increase in the disclosure of information on bank-specific results, stress test methodology, and stress scenarios.
- Channels for peer review and outside discussion and criticism of the stress test methodology and results have been expanded.[25]

Senior EU bank supervisors also underline improvements in scenario design, econometric modeling, documentation, and transparency. In addition, they signal that several significant changes are under way.

First, the Single Supervisory Mechanism has launched an annual review and evaluation process (to be known as the Supervisory Review and Evaluation Process [SREP]), aimed at ensuring that banks' capital and liquidity positions, internal governance, and risk management are up to snuff. Under this process supervisors will have the power to impose a wide range of measures, from higher capital and liquidity requirements to changes in risk management practices. The SREP appears to broadly resemble the "qualitative" part of the CCAR test, except that decisions will be communicated to banks on an individual basis, not in the context of EU-wide stress tests. It remains to be seen whether EU and Federal Reserve evaluations of risk management at large banks will be on the same page. Deutsche Bank and Santander received clean bills of health in the 2014 EU-wide Comprehensive Assessment while their US subsidiaries had their capital plans rejected (less than five months later) in the 2015 CCAR (Board of Governors 2015c, 3) "due to widespread and substantial weaknesses across their capital planning processes."[26]

Second, using what ECB supervisors have called the gold mine of information on banks that was collected during the 2014 Comprehensive Assessment, the Single Supervisory Mechanism plans to ramp up its peer group analysis of banks. Some of the results might also be used as inputs for future EU-wide stress tests.

Third, relying on joint supervisory teams composed of ECB and national bank supervisors and reflecting the bottom-up approach to stress testing preferred by the EBA and the ECB, supervisory teams will deepen their preparation discussions with large EU banks. As EBA Chair Andrea Enria argued (2015, 9), "in the EU, the bulk of the adjustment actually precedes, rather than follows, the conduct of the stress test exercise."

Fourth, mindful of the warning in the Larosière Report (2009) that convergence of supervision makes little sense if there remain significant cross-country differences in financial regulation in the European Union, the ECB and the EBA will intensify their efforts to achieve a more level playing field, with particular attention to reducing "national discretions" in the definition of bank capital, treatment of sovereign risk weighting, and bank resolution regimes (Angeloni 2014b, Nouy 2014a, Enria 2015). If this effort is successful, it will improve comparability in future EU-wide stress tests.

The Single Supervisory Mechanism also says it will work on improving the measurement of risk-weighted assets. The 2016 EU-wide test was the first to include publication of leverage ratios in the baseline and adverse scenarios (albeit without a hurdle rate). The European Commission will make a legislative proposal to have the leverage ratio become a legally binding standard (Pillar 1 measure) only at the end of 2016, with applicability from January 1, 2018. Whether the suspension of hurdle rates in the 2016 EU-wide test represents a one-time, reversible decision or a permanent change in the EU stress testing regime remains to be seen.

Endnotes

1. Note that in 2014, the Federal Reserve implemented a rule requiring foreign banking organizations with a significant US presence to establish US intermediate holding companies over their US subsidiaries; also, those holding companies are subject to pretty much the same prudential standards applicable to US bank holding companies. Note too that some large banks from countries in the European Economic Area are also included in the EU-wide stress tests.

2. The legislation requires company-run stress tests at least twice a year.

3. See EBA (2014e) for an enumeration and explanation of the substantive data requirements for banks participating in the EU-wide stress tests. The number of data points rose from about 150 per bank in the 2010 EU-wide stress test to 3,500 per bank in the 2011 test, according to Ahmed et al. (2011). The 2014 EU-wide stress test published about 12,000 data points per bank; the 2016 test increased the number to 16,000 per bank. Bernanke (2013) indicates that for the 2013 CCAR, supervisors collected and analyzed loan and account-level data on more than two-thirds of the $4.2 trillion in accrual loans and losses held by the 18 banks participating in the test. In the United States it takes about six months after the submission of the last bank data for stress test results to be published. According to the *Wall Street Journal*, Citigroup (which failed the 2014 CCAR on qualitative grounds) disclosed that it spent $180 million just in the second half of 2014 preparing for the 2015 CCAR. JPMorgan Chase has 500 employees devoted to stress tests (James Sterngold, "Fed Broadens Scope of Stress Tests," *Wall Street Journal*, March 9, 2015).

4. The longer the time horizon, the more likely it is that banks would change their behavior in response to the shocks, including, for example, shrinking the size of their balance sheets. Most stress test exercises place restrictions on how banks can model their response to the scenarios, however, assuming that banks cannot shrink their balance sheet as a way of meeting the bank capital hurdle.

5. Another potential advantage of having a time horizon that is, say, two years or a little longer is that, at least for some baseline scenarios, it provides enough time for bank asset prices to recover from the deep pessimism at the bottom of the cycle.

6. Ben McLannahan and Gillian Tett, "US Lenders Face Higher Stress Test Hurdle," *Financial Times*, June 24, 2016.

7. Of the nine US recessions since 1957, four were "severe," three were "moderate," and two were "mild" (Lehnert 2015). In the average "severe" US recession, the duration is six quarters and real GDP declines by 3.8 percent; in the average "moderate" recession, the duration is four quarters, and the decline in real GDP is 1.0 percent.

8. See Bookstaber et al. (2013), Glasserman and Tangirala (2015), and the discussion in chapter 3. As one answer to this potential problem, Montesi and Papiro (2015) suggest a stochastic simulation framework.

9. Reverse stress tests purportedly focus more sharply on the internal dynamics of bank capital declines than on the declines attributable to external shocks.

10. The 2016 EU-wide test included for the first time a methodology to estimate conduct risk–related losses (EBA 2016b).

11. As Adrian, Covitz, and Liang (2014, 14) note, "Any market-based measure of systemic risk will not be immune to confounding effects of current levels of overall risk pric-

ing. For example, systemic risk measures rely primarily on stock prices or credit default swaps premiums, which reflect the varying market price of risk." In addition, when the market price of risk is low, options-implied risk-neutral probabilities will be low even if the physical probabilities of tail risk have not decreased. Or, as my late good friend and colleague Michael Mussa often remarked, "Markets sometimes go nuts."

12. The CRD IV encompasses both the capital requirements directive and the Capital Requirements Regulation. The former spells out the regulations that must be implemented under national law. The latter specifies the regulations directly applicable to all firms across the European Union.

13. See the discussion of this point in chapters 5 and 9.

14. The 101 large internationally active banks participating in the BCBS (2016) study (called Group 1 banks) each had tier 1 capital of at least €3 billion; the study also included 129 smaller banks (called Group 2 banks). The qualitative conclusions for Group 2 banks were broadly similar to those for Group 1 banks. Group 1 included 30 G-SIBs. The BCBS study also assessed progress in meeting the two quantitative liquidity standards of Basel III, the liquidity coverage ratio (LCR) and the net stable funding ratio (NSFR). The LCR requires global banks to have sufficient high-quality liquid assets to withstand a stressed 30-day funding scenario specified by supervisors. The LCR came into effect January 1, 2015. The minimum requirement is set at 60 percent and then rises in equal annual steps to 100 percent in 2019. The weighted-average LCR for the Group 1 bank sample was 124 percent on June 30, 2015. The NSFR is a longer-term structural ratio, meant to address liquidity mismatches and give banks an incentive to use more stable funding sources. The weighted-average NSFR for the Group 1 banks was 112 percent.

15. It is not clear what is producing this result. Lehnert (2015) shows that both the loan-loss rate and net income (as a percentage of average assets) declined in the CCAR tests over the 2012–15 period.

16. There is enormous variation across banks in the degree to which the capital ratios fall under the most adverse scenario. In 2014, for example, the least affected bank saw its tier 1 common ratio fall by 130 basis points whereas the most affected suffered a decline of 850 basis points.

17. In addition to the two foreign-owned banks (Santander and Deutsche Bank) that failed the qualitative part of the 2015 CCAR, Bank of America received a "conditional non-objection" to its capital plan, which required it to submit a new plan by the end of the third quarter of 2015 to address certain weaknesses in its capital planning process. Goldman Sachs, JPMorgan Chase, and Morgan Stanley met minimum capital requirements on a poststress basis only after submitting adjusted capital plans (Board of Governors 2015a). In the 2016 CCAR, Deutsche Bank and Santander failed the qualitative part of the test, and Morgan Stanley received a conditional nonobjection.

18. In explaining why they did not publish bank-by-bank results in the 2011 CCAR, the Federal Reserve stated that whereas the 2009 SCAP results were generated by a consistent application of independent supervisory models to data submitted by the banks, the 2011 CCAR results relied much more on company-run models that were not consistent across banks. A year later, in the 2012 CCAR exercise, the Fed apparently changed its modeling procedures—and its mind—and published bank-by-bank results.

19. The EBA did publish the results of a Basel III monitoring exercise in April and September 2012 and the EU-wide capital exercise in October 2012, but neither analyzed the conditions of EU banks under an adverse scenario.

20. Itay Goldstein and Haresh Sapra (2014) argue that one cost of stress test disclosure is that it may lead private sector participants to produce less information. Flannery, Hirtle, and Kovner (2015, 11) tested this hypothesis on data for the US CCAR and Dodd-Frank Act Stress Test tests. "We find no evidence to support the theoretical concerns relating to increased disclosure. The information environment for public equity appears, if anything, better for stress tested firms, and we find no evidence for reduced risk-sharing or runs."

21. One exception was the 2009 SCAP (Board of Governors 2009b, 7), which stated: "Another reference for the estimated loss rates in the SCAP is where they stand relative to estimates recently made by other analysts. Unfortunately, many of the loss estimates are not directly comparable.... However, the SCAP estimates appear to be in the middle of the range of those other estimates."

22. Geithner (2014) maintains that the credibility of the SCAP results received a big boost when Bridgewater Associates, a highly regarded hedge fund, announced right after the publication of the SCAP estimates that its own estimates were very close to those of the SCAP.

23. As Orphanides (2014, 3) puts it, "The key for restoring confidence is ensuring that a credible solution is available for any problem that might be identified in the process." Fisher (2012, 6) offers his own favorite remedy for improving regulatory forbearance and eliminating the option bank executives currently have to avoid raising common equity when it is most needed. He suggests that when a bank falls below the specified equity threshold, it should be given 90 days to raise new common equity to restore its ratio. Failure to do so would require the resignations of the bank's CEO and the senior responsible supervisor. "If we could take away management's free option—to plead for forbearance, to double down their leveraged bet on a highly leveraged balance sheet and to avoid dilution—and implement this 90-day rule, I think we would find that banks rarely enter the 90-day period."

24. I cannot resist saying it: If bankers' bonuses were contingent on the bank being judged well capitalized (in terms of a leverage ratio), I suspect that we would suddenly find a turnaround in the industry's view about the social perils of higher bank capital.

25. Bookstaber et al. (2013) maintain that three features distinguish current US stress testing from its precrisis predecessors: the scale and granularity of data collection, the scale and granularity of modeling, and the quantity and quality of disclosure.

26. In an editorial contrasting the evaluations in the 2015 CCAR and the 2014 EU-wide stress test of Deutsche Bank and Santander, the *Financial Times* drew the following conclusion: "For the credibility of Europe, and the European banks themselves, the sooner the EU stress tests become as tough as the US ones the better" ("European Banks Need to Catch Up with US Rules," *Financial Times*, March 16, 2015). As of the third quarter of 2014, the US subsidiary of Santander accounted for about 7 percent of the bank's total assets; the corresponding figure for Deutsche Bank's US subsidiary was roughly 9 percent ("Santander and Deutsche Bank Fall Foul of the Fed," *Financial Times*, March 13, 2015).

3

Criticisms of Stress Testing Methodology and the Measurement of Bank Capital

Just because stress testing is becoming a "cornerstone of a new approach to regulation and supervision of the...largest banks" (Tarullo 2014c) does not mean that there are not serious misgivings about the methodology of stress testing itself. Quite apart from criticisms of individual stress tests in a particular country, some critics have raised objections about the building blocks of the basic approach. Three such concerns merit discussion: (1) the weakness of stress tests as early warning indicators of banking crises, (2) the failure of stress tests to capture adequately the contagion and other dynamics that are characteristic of actual crises, and (3) shortcomings of risk-based measures of bank capital as gauges of capital adequacy.

Stress Tests as Poor Early Warning Indicators of Banking Crises

Whatever their merits as a crisis management tool, bank stress tests have been found seriously wanting as an early warning indicator of banking crises. Borio, Drehmann, and Tsatsaronis (2012, 7) offer the following bold charge:

> To our knowledge, no macro stress test carried out ahead of the (2007–09) crisis identified the build-up of the vulnerabilities. The message was overwhelmingly: "The system is sound." Rather than being part of the solution, stress tests turned out to be part of the problem. They lulled policymakers and market participants into a false sense of security.[1]

Early Warnings before the 2007–09 Global Financial Crisis

As but one example of this failure of bank stress tests to foreshadow the worst financial crisis since the Great Depression, Borio, Drehmann, and Tsatsaronis (2012) point to the clean bill of health given to Iceland's banking sector in the 2008 IMF Financial Sector Assessment Program (FSAP).[2] According to the database on banking crises put together by Laeven and Valencia (2013), 18 countries experienced a "systemic" banking crises during the 2007–11 period (8 more underwent "borderline" banking crises). Since Laeven and Valencia (2013) report that all of these systemic crises (with the exception of Nigeria) started in 2007 or 2008, I looked at the FSAPs (cum bank stress tests) published by the Fund in 2006–07 for the larger economies that were on the Laeven-Valencia list. There were seven: Greece (2006); Denmark (2006, 2007); Ireland (2006); Spain (2006); the United Kingdom (2006); Belgium (2006); and Portugal (2006). The United States did not have an FSAP during this period. According to the IMF's Independent Evaluation Office (IMF 2011c), the IMF repeatedly asked to conduct an FSAP during the 2004–07 period, but the US authorities declined those requests.[3]

What I was looking for in these FSAPs (preferably in the executive summary of the report) was a clear, published warning of a potentially serious banking crisis, along with a recommendation for strong corrective policy response,[4] including (where necessary) prompt application of macroprudential tools. I found little of it.

In the FSAPs for Belgium and Portugal, the banking system gets a pretty clean bill of health; in four other cases (Ireland, Spain, Greece, and the United Kingdom), the assessment is mixed, including some concerns about excessive credit growth and attendant risks, but this is usually softened by reassurance from the generally positive results of the stress tests.[5] Only in the FSAP for Denmark (IMF 2006b) did I see a clear warning that "a very severe scenario could entail significant shortfalls in regulatory capital." From an early warning perspective and taken as a group, there is not a lot here for the IMF to brag about.[6]

What the Bank for International Settlements (BIS) authors are highlighting is the disconnect between the early warning literature on banking crises and the adverse scenarios typically employed in the bank stress tests. The former finds that banking crises typically occur when both credit growth to the private sector and real property prices are well above their norms. Put in other words, these are dual threshold models in which a crisis is indicated when both credit growth and real property prices are at or near the peak (see Borio and Drehmann 2009, Borio 2012, and BIS 2014).[7] The intuition is that credit growth is a proxy for leverage (and lending standards), while property prices are a proxy for collateral (BIS 2014). Borio, Drehmann, and Tsatsaronis (2012) label this close association between banking crises on the one hand and credit and asset price booms on the other the "financial cycle" and show that it has different properties from the normal business cycle, being longer than business cycles (15 to 20 years versus 1 to 8 years); highly synchronized across economies; and sensitive to changes in the macroeconomic and policy environment, including the degree of capital-market liberalization.

A key finding of the early warning literature is that sharp declines in real economic growth or large increases in the unemployment rate (the variables most popular in bank stress tests) do not stand out as good advance indicators of banking crises in advanced economies (over the past three or four decades), because these crises typically begin when output growth is still on the upswing.[8] Once a banking crisis erupts, real output does show a marked fall and this output decline has a negative feedback effect on banks. But it is the banking crisis that causes output to fall, not the other way around. Yes, the adverse scenarios in the stress tests typically include a marked decline in property prices, but abnormal movements in property prices are rarely paired with abnormal movements in credit. A major selling point of these early warning models is that they do seem to have caught the bulk of the systemic banking crises over the past 40 years or so, including the 2007–09 crises in the United States and the United Kingdom and the Asian financial crisis of 1997–98 (BIS 2014).[9,10] The takeaway is that stress tests may well be a good way to differentiate weak banks from stronger ones once a banking crisis is already under way, but they are not apt to see one coming, especially when many other risk indicators (including credit default spreads, interest rate spreads, and equity market volatility) are sending all-clear signals.

Since credit-to-GDP ratios typically fall after banking crises, supervisory officials in the United States and the European Union might well respond that it would not have been useful to include a credit boom scenario in their postcrisis stress tests. Indeed, during the recovery period the concern was to get bank lending up, not down. If credit growth and property prices become elevated in the future, that would be the time—so the argument might go—to include such a scenario in the stress tests.[11] Such a defense would not apply, of course, to stress test exercises conducted before the 2007–09 crisis.

Early Warnings in Asia, 2011–14

Such a defense would also not apply to emerging Asia in 2014. As highlighted in the 2014 BIS Annual Report, red lights were flashing for the credit-to-GDP and property price early warning indicators for an Asian emerging-economy aggregate, composed of Hong Kong, Indonesia, Malaysia, the Philippines, Singapore, and Thailand.[12] The credit-to-GDP indicator was likewise flashing red for China (as well as for Brazil, Switzerland, and Turkey), and it was flashing yellow for Korea. Note also that the BIS early warning indicator for credit booms refers to total credit to the private sector and hence is not affected by sharp shifts between bank and shadow bank financing. In short, a prominent early warning model of banking crises was pointing to high potential vulnerability in much of emerging Asia over the next few years. Press reports indicate that as of the fall of 2016, the BIS was still worried about credit expansion in China—based, inter alia, on its finding that the "credit gap" is currently three times higher than the danger level.[13]

China, Hong Kong, Korea, Malaysia, and Singapore underwent IMF FSAP missions cum bank stress tests during 2011–14. My reading of those reports—sometimes supplemented by looking at the recent Article IV consultation report—is that they are better than the FSAPs conducted in 2004–07 in identifying and highlighting the systemic risk to the banking system caused by very rapid credit growth and highly elevated property prices.[14] But the reports still placed too much confidence in the usually reassuring results of the stress tests, and they were too timid in recommending strong corrective and protective remedial measures.[15] To my mind the 2013 Article IV report for China (IMF 2013a) and the 2013 FSAP for Singapore (IMF 2013b) perhaps best illustrate the Janus-faced nature of these reports. The China Article IV report states early on that "in the near term, the priority is to rein in broader credit growth and prevent a further build-up of risks in the financial sector" (p. 10). In discussing the financial sector, it cautions that "while risks appear manageable for now, history suggests credit expansion of this kind often entails costly cleanup" (p. 11). But when it comes to corrective measures, aside from liberalizing interest rates, the report seems to offer only the broad recommendation to "strengthen regulatory and supervisory oversight, especially in areas experiencing rapid growth such as trusts and wealth management products." I did not see any recommendation for stronger capital buffers and/or other macroprudential tools, even though the 2011 FSAP for China (IMF 2011d, 7) indicated vulnerability of banking system capital to a set of simultaneous shocks.[16]

Turning to the 2013 FSAP for Singapore (IMF 2013b, 1), the first paragraph of the executive summary states that "the most pressing vulnerability appears to stem from the rapid growth of credit and real estate prices in recent years." The report includes staff recommendations for further strengthening banks' capital positions, including through implementation of a countercyclical capital buffer. But that message is seemingly weakened by the stress test findings that current risks are "manageable" (without further capital increases). The recent FSAP reports for Korea and Malaysia show elements of this same tension between risks and policy proposals for strengthening bank and nonbank capital. In the case of Hong Kong, the 2014 FSAP (IMF 2014d) gives the financial sector pretty close to a clean bill of health.[17]

Even when early warning models of banking crises and IMF-run stress tests reach similar verdicts, national bank supervisors may disagree with the findings. The People's Bank of China summarized its own stress test results in a 2014 financial stability report. The tests covered 17 domestic banks that are regarded as systemically important (accounting for over 60 percent of banking assets). The main finding was that "under light, middle, and heavy stress scenarios, the banking system's overall capital adequacy would remain at the relatively high level; even the most serious scenarios would not see capital adequacy fall below 10.5 percent."[18,19]

Failure of Stress Tests to Capture the Dynamics of Actual Financial Crises

A second major criticism of bank stress tests—not unrelated to their poor early warning track record—is that they fail to capture adequately the heightened uncertainty, nonlinearities, contagion (across markets and financial institutions), and feedback effects that make the output loss deeper and the recovery slower for recessions accompanied by financial crises than for normal recessions.[20] The feedback effects from financial sector stress to the real economy tend to be rather weak in the models underlying stress tests, with the result that it takes very large (and sometimes implausible) shocks to generate serious capital inadequacy for banks, as Borio, Drehmann, and Tsatsaronis (2102) emphasize.[21] In contrast, during a real systemic banking crisis, risks can migrate quickly from one institution, asset class, or country to others; insolvency and liquidity risks can reinforce one another, leading to severe funding strains for banks and their customers and to fire sales for assets; and market participants whose claims are not guaranteed may find it logical to "run" to cash or Treasuries until they get better information. On top of this, delays/conflicts in formulating a muscular government response to crisis—be it because of disagreements among members of a monetary union, clashes between the executive branch and the Congress or policy squabbles among different bank supervisory agencies— can undermine confidence in ways that are not evident from earlier time series.[22] For these reasons, Bookstaber et al. (2013, 2) characterize today's approach to stress testing as still essentially microprudential: "It focuses on the resilience of individual banks to specific shocks, rather than on the broader and more complex macroprudential question of how stress might be transmitted among firms, across financial markets, and into the real economy."[23] Three examples illustrate some of the forces at work.

The Run on Repo

The first example comes from the 2007–09 global economic and financial crisis. One of the intriguing questions was how a shock to the relatively small subprime mortgage market wound up generating such a widespread and systemic crisis.[24] While this puzzle has many pieces, part of the answer comes from what Gorton and Metrick (2010a) call the run on repo (the repurchase market). The story they tell is one in which the loss of liquidity at the firms that were the biggest players in the securitized part of the banking system ultimately led to the panic of 2007–08. Weakness in the subprime mortgage market in early 2007 caused repo buyers of securitized bonds to become anxious about the quality of the collateral they were holding. As real estate and mortgage prices continued to slump, that anxiety continued to increase; it was reflected in large-scale selling of collateral and demands for larger haircuts in a widening segment of the huge repo market. Since many of the largest US investment houses and commercial banks were using the repo market to fund themselves, it was not long before the drying up of funds in the repo market led to fears about the liquidity of counterparties in the interbank market. Measures of counterparty risk (such as the spread between the London interbank offered rate [LIBOR] and the overnight indexed swap [OIS] spread) rose to record highs, and repo haircuts continued to climb—tantamount to massive withdrawals from the banking system. The forced rescue of Bear Stearns in March 2008 further stoked fears and induced the contagion to spread to highly rated credit securities unrelated to the subprime markets. Soon the entire securitized banking model came under intense pressure. In the second half of 2008, the panic hit a wider array of asset markets, financial institutions, and the real economy, ultimately contributing to the failure of Lehman Brothers, the AIG bailout, and the government takeovers of Fannie and Freddie.

The 1997–98 Asian Financial Crisis

My second example comes from the Asian financial crisis of 1997–98, where the initial shock was to the economy of Thailand, not one of the world's major trading or investment hubs. Yet after Thailand, the crisis spread quickly to Indonesia, Malaysia, Korea, and the Philippines, leaving in its wake crashes in exchange rates and equity markets, deep recessions, and banking crises.

Analyzing contagion during the Asian crisis, I offered the "wake-up call" hypothesis as an explanation (Goldstein 1998).[25] I posited that Thailand acted as a wake-up call for international investors to reassess the creditworthiness of Asian borrowers. And when they made that reassessment, it was concluded that quite a few emerging Asian economies had vulnerabilities similar to Thailand: large external deficits, appreciating real exchange rates, sizable currency mismatches, weak financial sectors with poor prudential supervision, export slowdowns (in 1996), and declining quality of investment. As currencies and equity markets were written down to reflect this reassessment, the crisis spread. A weighted average of fundamentals that gives greater weight to measures on which Thailand was relatively weak is more consistent with an ordinal ranking of which Asian economies were most affected by the crisis than one predicated on either the extent of bilateral interdependence with Thailand or the strength of fundamentals irrespective of similarities with Thailand (see Goldstein and Hawkins 1998). Ahluwahlia (2000) finds that shared (visible) characteristics with the "ground zero" country—what he calls "discriminating contagion"—were helpful in explaining the pattern of currency crises during the Mexican, Russian, and Asian crises (after controlling for trade and financial interdependence).

The 1998 Failure of Long-Term Capital Management

Example number three derives from the failure of Long-Term Capital Management (LTCM) in 1998. Bookstaber et al. (2013, 11) trace the dynamics of the liquidity crisis cycle:

> The proximate cause of LTCM's collapse was the failure of the Russian bond market. While LTCM did not have much exposure in Russia, it did have high exposure in other markets, such as Danish mortgage bonds. Other investors were heavily invested and leveraged in both markets. When the Russian market failed and these firms received margin calls, their next step was to liquidate what they could, which meant, among other things, selling out of their positions in Danish mortgage bonds. Because this created a contagion into a market where LTCM heavily invested and leveraged, LTCM was caught in an avalanche. If LTCM's risk managers had been asked to do a stress test for the firm's direct Russian exposure, the warning light would likely have remained green. It is only by working through the interactions of heterogeneous agents that the risk would have been manifest.

What is missing from today's stress testing models? Delving deeper into what is missing from today's stress testing models, research conducted over the past half dozen years has emphasized the leverage cycle, the multiple channels of contagion that flow from the systemic interdependence of financial institutions, the risks of predictability and linearity in annual stress testing exercises, the behavior under stress of complex, adaptive networks, and the need for greater use of agent-based models to understand threats to financial stability, among other factors. A sampling of recent research on these issues helps illuminate them.

The Leverage Cycle

Geanakoplos (2010) defines the leverage cycle as huge moves in collateral rates. When leverage is loose, asset prices go up, because buyers can get easy credit and spend more. In contrast, when credit is very difficult to obtain, leverage is constrained and prices plummet. He argues that it is changes in the volatility of news that lead to changes in leverage. Economists ask themselves every day whether the economy is picking the right interest rate; Geanakoplos maintains that they should also be asking whether the economy is picking the right margin (collateral) rates. He sees the 1999–2006 period as the upswing in the leverage cycle and the 2008–10 global financial crisis as the bottom of that cycle. He asserts that what brings an end to all leverage cycles are bad news creating uncertainty and disagreement,[26] sharply increasing collateral rates, and losses and bankruptcies among the leveraged optimists.[27] Geanakoplos (2010) shows that over the 2000–09 period, the Case-Shiller national home price index was highly correlated with an index of down payments for home mortgages. Similarly, he finds a close association over this period between the margin offered by Wall Street banks to hedge funds and AAA-rated security prices.

While leverage cycles are a recurring event in US financial history, Geanakoplos (2010) concludes that the 1999–2009 leverage cycle was the worst one since the Great Depression, for the following reasons: (1) Securities leverage increased and then declined by more than before;[28] (2) housing was subject to a "double leverage cycle," because not only mortgage securities but also their cash flows were subject to the leverage cycle;[29] (3) the standardization/creation of the derivative credit default swap market for mortgages allowed pessimists to leverage more than optimists; (4) the Lehman Brothers bankruptcy highlighted counterparty risk in collateralized borrowing; (5) government laxity, deregulation, and implicit guarantees also increased leverage; and (6) both the ratings agencies and large global imbalances acted to increase leverage.

Bank stress tests take account of the changing value of collateral held by banks throughout the scenario period. But Geanakoplos' (2010) analysis of the wide-ranging adverse effects that the leverage cycle has on the economy suggests that they are addressing only part of the feedback effects of dramatically changing collateral rates.[30]

Channels of Contagion

Hellwig (2014a, 4 and 7) argues that contagion can be induced by a variety of channels associated with the systemic interdependence of financial institutions.

> The most direct channel of contagion involves domino effects through contractual relations. If one institution goes bankrupt, all institutions with claims on the defaulting institution are damaged.... Thus...the insolvency of Lehman Brothers caused the money market mutual fund Reserve Primary to "break the buck" because the roughly $800 million they had lent to Lehman Brothers was impaired.

> We also see contagion effects from the disappearance of an institution as a potential contracting partner. Thus, when Reserve Primary and other money market funds were run upon after the Lehman bankruptcy, they were no longer available as a source of funds for banks, e.g., the Belgian-French bank Dexia or the German bank Hypo Real Estate that had been using the money market to fund the excess coverage for their covered bonds.

> A second contagion channel involves information contagion. Information showing that one institution is in trouble can be relevant for the assessment of other institutions that are believed or known to have similar risk exposures as the institution that is in trouble. Thus, Reserve Primary's breaking the buck caused investors to reassess the risk of all money market mutual funds and to withdraw from these institutions.[31]

> Another channel of contagion...involves markets and prices. An institution that is in difficulties may choose to sell assets in order to get cash or in order to reduce its leverage. Such asset sales put pressure on market prices. If market prices go down, all other institutions that hold these assets in their trading books have to write down their positions. These write-downs reduce these institutions' equity.... This mechanism played an important role in the period from August 2007 to October 2008 and again in the European crisis in the second half of 2010.

> Finally, market breakdowns also play an important role in contagion. Such a breakdown may be due to a breakdown of trading infrastructure. If an institution serves as a market maker, the disappearance of this market maker can have a dramatic negative effect on all institutions that regularly rely on this particular market.... Disappearance of trading facilities can also be the result of a market freeze, as occurred in August 2007 when uncertainty about the proper valuation for mortgage-backed securities and related derivatives caused a breakdown of markets for these securities. For institutions that were funding such securities through short-term debt...

this market freeze created significant liquidity problems that required them to take recourse to the liquidity guarantees of the sponsoring banks.

He concludes that any serious assessment of systemic risk needs to account for each of these channels of propagation and contagion, as well as the interaction among them.

While only a small part of Hellwig's contagion matrix has found its way into formal bank stress tests, analytical work has sought to measure interconnectedness in the financial sector and to appraise its consequences. Adrian, Covitz, and Liang (2014) provide a good survey. Box 3.1 summarizes two recent examples of analytical work on interdependence. In the United States, where the nonbank financial sector dominates the credit intermediation process, there has been an explosion of work on the feedback effects of distress in the shadow banking system on banks and the real economy. In this connection, Federal Reserve Vice Chair Stanley Fischer (2015a, 2) has proposed five lessons from the 2007–09 crisis:

- The crisis first manifested itself in the nonbank sector and was worse for the nonbank sector than for banks.

- Nonbank distress harmed the real economy, as mortgages, auto loans, credit, and securities all became harder to obtain. The resulting credit contraction caused millions of Americans to suffer.

- Many of the problems of nonbanks (insolvency, illiquidity, loss of confidence) were similar to the problems that plagued banks.

- Before the crisis and relative to what was available to deal with banks, the US authorities had few policy levers to provide liquidity or resolve failures of nonbanks.

- Nonbank distress can be transmitted to the bank sector through various channels, including counterparty relationships, disruptions in funding markets, and knock-on effects of asset fire sales.[32]

Pozsar (2014) presents an accounting framework for measuring the sources and uses of short-term funding in the global financial system. He offers a number of salient observations on contagion distinctions between shadow banks and banks:[33]

The fact that international cash pools are constrained to holding mainly public-private and purely private shadow money claims means they always face some counterparty and collateral-related risks in cash portfolios. This is the fundamental reason behind the fickle and finicky nature of the wholesale funding market today.... (pp. 29–30)

From a policy perspective, the fundamental problem at hand is a financial ecosystem that has outgrown the safety net that was put around it

Box 3.1   Financial-sector interdependence and contagion risk

In its *Global Financial Stability Report* of April 2009, the International Monetary Fund (IMF 2009) assessed four complementary approaches to assessing direct and indirect financial sector systemic linkages:

- a network approach, which tracks the reverberation of a credit event or liquidity squeeze throughout the banking system via direct linkages in the interbank market;

- a co-risk model, which draws on market data to assess systemic linkages among financial institutions under extreme events;

- a distress dependence matrix, which looks at pairwise conditional probabilities of distress, taking into account a set of other institutions; and

- a default intensity model, which measures the probability of failures of a large fraction of financial institutions caused by both direct and indirect systemic linkages.

One of the insights from the network analysis is that the origin of the shock makes a lot of difference for contagion. For example, the combination of a severe credit and liquidity shock, originating in either the US or UK banking systems in 2008 could, via contagion, wipe out 100 percent of the capital in the global banking system. In contrast, the same shock occurring in any other advanced economy would wipe out no more than 10 percent.

A Banque de France study by Gabrieli, Salakhova, and Vuillemey (2015) analyzes contagion risk among 73 European banking groups, including all the European banks designated as global systemically important banks. They focus on the consequences of a common shock to the stock market, paired with the default of one of the 73 European banks in the system. They find that in 2008, for some interbank exposure networks, a market shock could have produced losses equal to roughly 30 percent of the European banking system's equity capital and triggered the default of 14 other institutions. They also show that as a result of the bank deleveraging in the postcrisis period and the reduced level of interbank exposures, contagion risk was appreciably smaller in 2012 than in 2008.

---

many years ago. Today we have a different class of savers (cash portfolio managers [PMs] versus retail depositors), a different class of borrowers (risk PMs to enhance investment returns via financial leverage versus ultimate borrowers to enhance their ability to spend via loans), and a different class of intermediaries (dealers who do securities financing versus banks that finance the economy via loans) to whom discount window access and deposit insurance do not apply.... (p. 67)

Adrian (2014, 6) offers a useful perspective on a key contagion mechanism in shadow banks, namely, fire sales.[34]

Per definition, funding sources for shadow banking activities are uninsured and thus runnable.... Shadow banks are subject to runs because assets have longer maturities than liabilities and tend to be less liquid as well. While the fundamental reason for commercial banks is the sequential servicing constraint, for shadow banks the effective constraint is the presence of fire sale externalities. In a run, shadow banking entities have to sell assets at a discount, which depresses market pricing. This provides an incentive to withdraw funding—before other shadow banking depositors arrive. However, the analogy between bank runs and shadow bank runs only goes so far. The reason is that shadow bank entities do not offer deposits, but instead obtain funding in wholesale money markets such as commercial paper and repo.

The IMF sounded yet another warning about the potential risks from contagion emanating from the shadow banking system in its April 2015 *Global Financial Stability Report*. In a chapter analyzing the asset management industry, it argued that while the financial stability risks linked to high-leveraged hedge funds and money market funds are by now well recognized, the risks from less leveraged "plain vanilla" investment products (such as mutual funds and exchange-traded funds) merit greater scrutiny. The Fund's empirical analysis finds that mutual fund investments do appear to affect asset price dynamics, at least in less liquid markets. Going farther, IMF (2015d, 91) underlines that "easy redemption options and the presence of 'first mover' advantage can create risks of a run, and the resulting price dynamics can spread to other parts of the financial system through funding markets and balance sheet and collateral channels."

Predictability and Linearity in Bank Stress Tests

Glasserman and Tangirala (2015) emphasize that in a real crisis, the results of actual shocks to the financial system are not predictable. They therefore find it troubling that as the stress testing process has evolved, its outcomes have become more predictable and therefore arguably less informative.

They focus on projected losses on loans in the US Comprehensive Capital Analysis and Review (CCAR) stress tests. They find that the loss rate distributions in the 2012, 2013, and 2014 tests are similar. Regression analysis confirms that losses by bank and loan category are highly persistent from one year to the next. Glasserman and Tangirala find this similarity surprising given the increasing complexity (over time) of the underlying stress test scenarios

They find that for the 30 bank holding companies participating in the 2014 CCAR, there is a nearly perfect linear relationship between the losses in the adverse scenario and those in the severely adverse scenario. Here, too, they regard the outcome as puzzling, because one might expect to see a nonlinear response of bank portfolios to severe economic shocks.

In other tests they report that the high correlations in projected losses from one period to the next still hold when the trading portfolios of banks (not just their loan losses) are included. They regard this predictability as surprising, because trading losses should be more difficult to forecast than loan losses.

Glasserman and Tangirala acknowledge that if a bank's portfolio and the CCAR stress test scenarios remain reasonably consistent over time, finding high predictability in stress test results from one year to the next should not be startling. They point out that consulting firms and software vendors have helped make the stress testing process more routine by selling their services to banks and that the models the Federal Reserve uses to define scenarios and project losses are being refined and likely change less over time. Still, they worry that the increasing predictability of stress testing results may be an artifact of the process rather than an accurate reflection of potential bank losses during a real crisis. In addition, they argue that the information value of the tests declines as their predictability increases. Using the results from the 2014 Dodd-Frank stress tests, they find no significant correlation between the severity of a bank's reported stress test losses and change in its stock price relative to the market.[35]

Schuermann (2013, 2–3) strikes a similar chord about the risks associated with allowing the US bank stress testing methodology to become too homogeneous, too predictable, and too routine:

> As the Fed's models have become more and more important in deciding the fate of the biggest banks, those banks have focused more and more on trying to mimic the Fed's results rather than tracing out their own risk profiles.... The incentives to get close to the Fed's numbers are powerful enough to stifle genuine creativity, imagination, and innovation by risk managers and their modelers. Deviating from standard industry practice is now increasingly viewed with suspicion and often discouraged by bank supervisors.... If everybody uses the same scenario (which they do) and works hard to get the same numbers (and they are trying), then we have a very narrowly specialized risk machine that is inflexible and unresponsive to unexpected shocks. That is, shocks that weren't previously subject to a stress test. The danger is that the financial system and its regulators are moving to a narrow risk-model gene pool that is highly vulnerable to the next financial virus. By discouraging innovation in risk models, we are sowing the seeds of our next systemic crisis.

Hirtle, Kovner, and McKay (2014) look at the stress test projections made by the 18 largest US bank holding companies and compare them with those made by the Federal Reserve in both the 2013 and 2014 Dodd-Frank stress tests. Although the bank and Federal Reserve projections are made under the same macroeconomic scenario, the results differ, primarily because of differences in the models used to make the projections. The differences between the projections for net income were smaller in 2014 than in 2013, but this convergence masks notable differences across projections in the main drivers of net income, including net loan chargeoffs. The authors also caution that the convergence between bank and Federal Reserve projections over a two-year period (2013–14) provides little assurance that this convergence will continue in future years.

Covas, Rump, and Zakrajsek (2013) perform a pseudo-stress test on a sample of 15 large US bank holding companies using the severely adverse macroeconomic scenario employed in the 2012 CCAR. To capture the nonlinear dynamics of bank losses and revenues during periods of financial stress, they employ a fixed-effects quantile (nonlinear) autoregressive model and compare its performance with that for a linear benchmark model. Quantile regression methods are regarded as particularly useful in situations where extremes are important.[36] They find that the linear specification substantially underestimates loan losses, especially for real estate portfolios. More important, for almost all banks in their sample, the nonlinear model generates bank capital shortfalls that are considerably higher than those implied by its linear counterpart. They argue that the small number of macro factors used in the US stress tests may not be sufficient to capture the full spectrum of risks faced by banks—a feature that calls for paying particular attention to the tails of the distribution for bank capital outcomes.

Behavior of Complex Adaptive Networks under Stress

In thinking about how the financial system behaves under stress, Haldane (2009) suggests that one ought to think of the system as a complex adaptive network—complex because it is composed of a nest of interconnections, adaptive because behavior is driven by interactions between optimizing but confused agents. To Haldane (2009), failure in the electricity grid, degradation of ecosystems, and the spread of epidemics all share important features in common with the disintegration of the financial system under stress that we should learn from.

Haldane maintains that the past 20 years have produced a financial network that has a high and rising degree of interconnection; generates long, fat tails of outcomes; and shares "small world" properties—what he calls "an unholy trinity" (2009, 7).[37] Securitization increased the complexity of the network, by spawning larger nodes, increasing the connections among them, and making it harder to discern the precise source and location of underlying claims. Meanwhile, financial firms' balance sheets and their risk management strategies became more alike, reducing the system's diversity. Increased complexity and lower diversity in turn are said to contribute to a common property of complex, adaptive networks: their "knife-edge," or tipping point, characteristic. Within a certain range, high interconnectedness acts as a shock absorber, because there are more creditors to share a loss, but beyond that range, high interconnectedness acts a propagation or amplification device, because firm failures are then transmitted to many counterparties.[38] Haldane notes that the 1997–2007 period fits this knife-edge property. It was one of seeming robustness (despite many shocks), whereas the 2007–09 period was one of acute financial distress. He observes that in epidemiology, the typical behavioral responses to a spreading infection are "hide" and "flight" and that both had their counterparts in the behavior of financial institutions during the 2007–09 global financial crisis, in the hoarding of liquidity and the flight from troubled assets (fire sales).

Haldane concludes his drawing of parallels between today's global financial network and connected networks in other realms by proposing that some of the policy prescriptions that have worked in the latter would likely also be effective in the former. He makes recommendations in three broad areas:

- *Data and communication*: Put in place a system to help map the global network and communicate to the public about its dynamics.

- *Regulation*: To avert financial contagion, vaccinate the "super-spreaders," by increasing minimum capital requirements, especially leverage ratios, for global systemically important banks.

- *Restructuring*: Implement more widespread use of central counterparties and intrasystem netting arrangements.

Use of Agent-Based Models to Better Understand the Dynamics of Financial Crises

Bookstaber (2012) argues that value at risk (VaR) models and standard stress tests have serious weaknesses for analyzing threats to financial stability and that application of agent-based models (ABMs) might help fill the gaps in standard risk tools:

> A key drawback of both VaR and typical stress testing practices is that they are guided by history...even though it is well known that the nature of crises is to have unanticipated shocks and unexpected interrelationships where the past offers limited guidance...a crisis comes from the unleashing of a dynamic that is not reflected in the day-to-day variations of precrisis times. The effect of a shock on the vulnerability of the financial system... creates a radical shift in markets similar to what is observed in traffic jams

or the panic of crowds. Economic relationships change during these times of stress. Thus, the extreme event reflects the inappropriateness of the risk model, not an extreme draw from it. (p. 3)

In a dynamic stochastic general equilibrium (DSGE) model, risk is introduced through well-specified exogenous shocks that do not change through the actions taken by the agents, whereas in a real crisis, the risk tends to come from the actions of the agents themselves, such as the pulling away of liquidity, the fire sales due to forced liquidations, and the withdrawal of sources of funding. (p. 7)

ABMs use a dynamic system of interacting, autonomous agents to allow macroscopic behavior to emerge from microscopic rules.... The models specify rules that dictate how agents will act based on various inputs. Once the model has specified the initial conditions and the agents' rules, the "world" is set loose and all subsequent events are driven by agent interactions.... The rules are not necessarily based on optimization and assumptions of rationality, but may instead reflect the heuristics that are typically applied based on observations of real-world bounded rationality.[39] (p. 4)

The structure of ABMs overcomes some of the problems that arise in applying DSGE and other traditional models to financial systems in times of crisis.... The building blocks of ABMs are best described through the fundamental characteristics of the agents themselves. Agents are autonomous.... Agents are heterogeneous.... Agents have bounded rationality and operate based on behavioral heuristics.... Agents are interdependent.... Agents adapt.[40] (p. 8)

The key agents for analyzing systemic risk are those that provide funding, those on the other side who are leveraged, and those who are liquidity providers. The first of these can be represented by money market funds and banks, operating in the repo market. The second set can be represented by hedge funds. The third can be longer-term, unleveraged investors, such as asset managers and pension funds.... [T]he rules for agents in the face of a market shock can be determined by looking at their policies and procedures and through interviews with the decision makers in the firms, such as the Chief Risk Officer.... Policy...levers include minimum haircuts and margin requirements for investors, capital and liquidity rules for banks, and loan-to-value ratios for mortgages.... The model should include a range of shocks...a seizing up of liquidity; a fire sale in the face of forced deleveraging with subsequent funding and liquidity effects; a sudden funding impairment.... (pp. 16–17)

ABMs remain outside the mainstream of economic and financial research.... ABMs can be a hard sell. (p. 19)

To sum up, the stresses incorporated in today's bank stress tests are still some distance from the stresses that occur in a real banking/financial crisis. They do not incorporate enough elements of the leverage cycle, contagion, funding problems, fire sales of assets, nonlinearities and fat tails, interaction between the bank and nonbank financial sectors, and adaptation by agents. In addition, there are some tentative signs that the outcomes of the past few CCAR tests are becoming too predictable for comfort.

Architects and managers of bank stress tests acknowledge that getting more feedback effects and more chaos into their models is challenging and that their efforts to do so are still at an early stage. But they also maintain that they are making progress. Adverse liquidity and/or counterparty risk scenarios are now more prevalent than before. Several central banks—including the Bank of England (2013b) and the Bank of Canada (Anand, Bédard-Pagé, and Traclet 2014)—have systemwide models in place that incorporate some kinds of feedback loops and amplification mechanisms.[41] The Federal Reserve (Tarullo 2014c) has disclosed that it is now making greater use in its stress tests of some models heretofore used exclusively to gauge the real economy effects of monetary policy. It routinely includes in its stress test scenarios a severe global market shock, meant to capture the type of nonlinear market dislocations that occurred during the frantic period of June–December 2008. European Central Bank Vice President Vítor Constâncio (2015, 1) has explained that "enhancements in the macro stress testing framework are underway to integrate more realistic dynamic features in the model-framework, allow for banks' reactions, add a proper liquidity stress component, and integrate contagion effects as well as two-way interaction with the real economy." Moreover, many of the real world crisis elements missing from stress tests are now being incorporated in systemic risk monitoring exercises run by the same central banks and official oversight councils that oversee bank stress tests. It is expected that, as those monitoring tools mature, simplified versions of them will find their way into stress testing scenarios and models. Rome was not built in a day.

Shortcomings of Risk-Weighted Measures of Bank Capital

A third major criticism of stress tests is directed at the principal measuring rod for the whole exercise—namely, a risk-weighted measure of bank capital. Putting aside for a moment concerns about the quality of capital that serves in the numerator of the capital ratio, the last five years have witnessed a growing chorus of doubts about the reliability of the risk-weighted assets used in the denominator. This is no narrow technical disagreement; it is rather an assault on what the current chair of the Basel Committee on Banking Supervision (BCBS) has called the "cornerstone" of the Basel framework since it was introduced 25 years ago (Ingves 2014, 2). When Basel I was introduced in 1988, there was only a small set of supervisor-set risk weights.[42] Responding to criticism that Basel I did not include enough risk sensitivity and granularity, Basel II, agreed to in 2004, vastly expanded the number of risk weights by permitting banks to use their own internal models to calculate these weights (subject to supervisory oversight) and by increasing risk-weight gradations in the standard, supervisor-set model to include credit ratings and a host of other refinements.[43]

Major disappointment with the performance of Basel II in the run-up to the global economic and financial crisis of 2007–09 led, in turn, to agreement on Basel III, in 2010. It improved the quantity and quality of bank capital and introduced quantitative liquidity standards. It also included (for the first time in an international agreement) a minimum capital ratio (the leverage ratio) that uses unweighted assets in the denominator. The leverage ratio is meant to serve as a backstop or safety net to guard against flaws in the risk-based capital standards.

Deficiencies of Risk-Based Capital Measures

The main charge of critics (including me) is that the deficiencies of the risk-based capital measures are so serious that the leverage ratio should become the primary measuring rod for capital adequacy, not only in bank stress tests but also more broadly in supervision. Haldane (2012, 2013); Hoenig (2012, 2013); and Mariathasan and Merrouche (2013a, 2013b) forcefully make the case for downplaying—even abandoning—the internal ratings–based approach to risk weighting as a capital requirement. Their main points can be summarized as follows:

1. Risk-based capital ratios did a worse job of predicting bank failures during the 2007–10 crisis (among sizable samples of large, complex global banks) than did a simple leverage ratio (figure 3.1).[44] This finding seems to be robust to the inclusion of macro control variables (see Haldane and Madouros 2012 and Blundell-Wignall and Roulet 2012 for similar findings during 2004–11). The superior diagnostic properties of the leverage ratio seem to be most apparent when the risk of a banking crisis is relatively high (Mariathasan and Merrouche 2013b).

2. Risk-based capital measures misled regulators, investors, and the public about the safety of the 10 largest US banking firms just before and during the global financial crisis.[45] Their average tier 1 capital ratio was more than 7 percent, and regulators classified them as well capi-

Figure 3.1   Risk-based capital ratios and leverage ratios for major global banks, end-2006: Surviving banks versus failed banks

a. Risk-based ratio

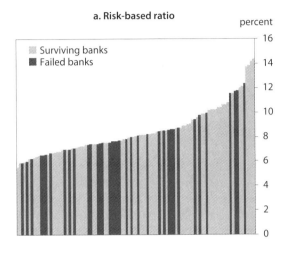

b. Leverage ratio

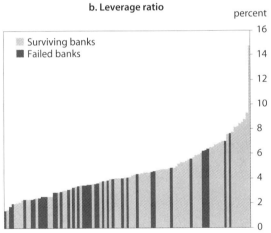

Note: Classification of bank failures/survival is based on Laeven and Valencia (2010), updated by Haldane and Madouros (2012) to reflect failures of government intervention since August 2009.
Source: Haldane and Madouros (2012).

talized (even though many of them needed official support during the crisis). Their average leverage ratio was only 2.8 percent—clearly not enough to absorb a major shock (Hoenig 2013).[46]

3. A tangible leverage ratio (tangible equity to tangible assets) is more closely related to market measures of bank health (such as the price-to-book ratio, the estimated default frequency, credit default swap spreads, and the market value of equity) than is the ratio of tier 1 capital to risk-weighted assets. Using a large, multicountry sample of banks, Demirgüç-Kunt, Detragiache, and Merrouche (2010) report that the relationship between bank stock returns and bank capital is stronger when capital is measured by the leverage ratio than by a risk-adjusted capital ratio. Acharya et al. (2014a) find that ranking banks by their estimated capital shortfall accords well with a market stress test when capital is measured relative to total assets but not when capital is measured relative to risk-weighted assets; Montesi and Papiro (2015) report similar results. They find that the results of the 2011 European Bank Authority stress test would have been positively correlated with results of their market stress tests if capital adequacy had been measured in terms of a simple leverage ratio but that the correlations were negative when a risk-based measure of bank assets was employed. Hagendorff and Vallascas (2013) demonstrate that risk-based capital requirements are only loosely related to market measures of the portfolio risks of banks and that even pronounced increases in portfolio risk generate almost negligible increases in risk-based capital requirements.

4. The ratio of risk-weighted assets to total assets for 17 major international banks fell from more than 70 percent in 1993 to less than 40 percent at end-2011 (at the rate of roughly 2 percent a year), yet neither the record of bank fragility during and before the recent crisis nor the behavior of market-based measures of bank riskiness suggest that bank safety has been on a steady improving trend over the past 20 years (Haldane 2013). In contrast, bank leverage (the inverse of the leverage ratio) rose over this period and is negatively correlated with bank risk weights.

5. Herring (2013) concludes that the experiment with risk-based capital ratios has been a "colossal failure," despite the billions of dollars spent on constructing risk-based assets. As a graphic example of that failure, he notes that the ratio of risk-weighted assets to total assets for three of the four largest banks hardly budged as these banks entered the greatest economic and financial crisis since the Great Depression (when risk was surely highly elevated).[47]

6. The Liikanen Report (2012) finds it "remarkable" that in a sample of Europe's largest banks, the banks with the lowest ratio of risk-weighted assets to total assets are the ones with the highest shares of trading assets in total assets.

7. Drawing on a sample of 115 large banks from 21 OECD countries that were eventually approved for applying the internal risk–based approach to their credit portfolio, Mariathasan and Merrouche (2013a, 2013b) find that the ratio of risk-weighted assets to total assets is lower after regulatory approval is granted. Consistent with theories of risk-weight manipulation, they report that the decline in risk weights is particularly prevalent among weakly capitalized banks, when the legal framework for supervision is weak, and in countries where supervisors are over-seeing many banks using the internal ratings–based approach. They compare the risk-weight manipulation hypothesis to three alternative explanations for declining risk-weight densities: portfolio reallocation, improved risk management, and faulty risk modeling. Their conclu-sion is as follows: "The reduction in average risk weights is driven by more than one of these channels.... However... the only explanation that is consistently supported by the evidence is the one of intentional misreporting" (Mariathasan and Merrouche 2013b, 15).[48]

8. Exploiting the staggered introduction of the model-based approach to risk weighting in Germany and having access to a unique loan-level dataset, Behn, Haselman, and Vig (2016) show that internal risk esti-mates employed for regulatory purposes systematically underpredicted actual default rates; that both default rates and loss rates were higher for loans originated under the model-based approach (relative to the "standardized" approach to risk weights) while corresponding risk weights were significantly lower; and that interest rates were higher for loans originated under the model-based approach, implying that banks were aware of the higher risk associated with these loans and priced them accordingly. Their findings are consistent with serious model-based manipulation of risk weights.

9. Risk weights have produced anything but a level playing field. Banks with the same hypothetical portfolios show very marked differences in risk weights from their internal models, particularly for trading book assets (EBA 2013b, Haldane 2013, Chouinard and Paulin 2014).[49] Banks that use their internal models for calculating risk weights (usually larger banks) typically exhibit much lower ratios of risk-weighted assets to total assets than banks that use standardized risk weights (usually small banks). Large, complex banks can therefore report risk-weighted capital ratios similar to those for smaller banks, even though simple leverage ratios show much lower capital ratios (Hoenig 2013).[50] In some of the largest international banks, risk-weight management has made it possible to drive the ratio of risk-weighted assets to total assets to less than 20 percent. Indeed, in the fourth quarter of 2012, Deutsche Bank reported a ratio of risk-weighted assets to total assets of just 17 percent.

10. The finding that leverage ratios perform as well as or better than risk-based capital measures in predicting bank failure (among large banks) suggests that noise is overwhelming signal in risk weight calculations (Haldane 2013). There are many reasons why this could be so. Risk weights are static and backward looking, and banks may use misleading sample periods for estimating them. As Engle (2009) concludes, (static) risk weights suffer from the risk that risk will change: The Basel Committee on Banking Supervision has acknowledged this de facto by sometimes having to make large changes in the weights—as, for example, in 2009, when the Basel II.5 initiative made major revisions to the risk weights for trading risk and for securitizations. The very low risk weight (7 percent) on AAA collateralized debt obligations before the global crisis surely contributed to the excessive investment in those instruments (Hoenig 2013). In addition, risk weights can be set without taking adequate account of correlations across the portfolio of bank assets. Political factors can be another handicap, as evidenced during the European debt crisis, when risk weights for sovereign bonds were maintained at zero even when sovereign risk was high. Such political influences on risk weights can be counterproductive when efforts are being made on macroprudential grounds to revive bank lending after a crisis, but banks are attracted by the lower risk weight on sovereign bonds.

11. Using a large dataset covering international banks headquartered in 14 advanced countries for the period 1995–2012, Brei and Gambacorta (2014) find that the Basel III leverage ratio is significantly more countercyclical than the risk-weighted regulatory capital ratio (that is, the leverage ratio is a tighter constraint for banks in booms and a looser constraint in recessions).

12. Some observers worry that if an unweighted leverage ratio replaced risk-weighted measures of bank capital, banks would shift unduly into high-risk/high-return assets (see, for example, Lautenschläger 2013). But Hoenig (2013) argues that with more capital at risk and without regulatory risk weights affecting choices, managers would allocate capital in accordance with market risk and returns. And even if gaming and arbitrage were also to affect adversely the signal provided by a leverage ratio, these forces might be less serious than those currently affecting the internal ratings–based approach to risk weights. Sheila Bair (2013, 2), the former chair of the Federal Deposit Insurance Corporation (FDIC) in the United States, offers just such an assessment:

> A simple leverage ratio should be the binding constraint, supplemented with a standardized system of risk weightings to force higher capital levels at banks taking undue risks. It is laughable to think that the leverage ratio is more susceptible to arbitrage than the current

system of risk weightings given the way risk weights were gamed before the crisis, e.g., moving assets to the trading book, securitizing loans to get lower capital charges, wrapping high-risk CDOs [collateral debt obligations] in CDS [credit default swap] protection to get near-zero risk charges, blindly investing in triple A securities, loading up on high-risk sovereign debt, repo financing...need I go on?

Recent Efforts to Reduce the Impact of Artificially Low Risk Weights

For all of these reasons, it seems sensible, at a minimum, to have at least one of the bank capital hurdle rates in stress tests be an unweighted leverage ratio (and to set that leverage ratio at a level where it is binding), just as the Federal Reserve did, starting with the March 2012 CCAR stress test. In discussing the much heralded resilience of Canadian banks during the 2007–09 global crisis, Mark Carney, the former governor of the Bank of Canada and sitting governor of the Bank of England, stated: "If I had to pick one reason why Canadian banks fared as well as they did, it was because we had a leverage ratio."[51] Over time the leverage ratio should become the primary regulatory ratio for bank capital (I offer a proposal for moving in this direction in chapter 7).

The leverage ratio embodied in Basel III is defined as tier 1 capital relative to total leverage exposure. Many analysts (including me) would prefer a definition of the leverage ratio that would include the highest-quality capital in the numerator, in order to benefit from its superior loss absorbency. The favorite in this regard is the ratio of tangible equity to tangible assets. As defined by FDIC Vice Chair Thomas Hoenig (2012, 3), tangible equity is "simply equity without the add-ons such as goodwill, minority interests, deferred taxes or other accounting entries that disappear in a crisis. Tangible assets include all assets less the intangible."

Fortunately, there seems to be movement in the official sector toward reining in the worst abuses of the Basel risk-weighting system—and maybe, at least in the United States—even abandoning altogether the internal ratings-based approach to calculating risk weights. In November 2014 the BCBS (2014c, 1) reported that after completing three earlier studies assessing banks' risk weighting of banking and trading book assets, it concluded that "there are material differences in banks' regulatory capital ratios that arise from factors other than differences in the riskiness of bank portfolios." The BCBS concedes that variances undermine confidence in capital ratios and has initiated a set of policy and supervisory actions to reduce excessive volatility in risk-weighted assets that are based on banks' internal models. One such action is to revise the standardized measurement approach to risk-weighted assets. When that revision is finalized, it will underpin the calculation of a "capital floor," which will ensure that capital requirements based on internal models do not fall below prudent levels. The BCBS is also developing specific proposals to reduce excessive volatility in risk weights deriving from banks' risk modeling practices. Such proposals would narrow the modeling choices available to banks.

Unfortunately, recent press reports suggest that EU banks and EU bank supervisors, among some others, are strongly opposing efforts by the BCBS to get an international agreement on a floor for internal model-generated risk weights, with European Commission Vice President Valdis Dombrovskis reportedly stating that "equalizing risk weights around the world cannot be the answer."[52]

In a May 2014 speech, Federal Reserve Governor Daniel Tarullo (2014b) referred to the Basel II internal ratings–based (IRB) approach to risk-weighted capital requirements as the most prominent example of an outmoded regulatory approach that did not rest on well-specified aims. In the United States the IRB generally applies to all bank holding companies with $250 billion or more in assets. Tarullo noted that the IRB approach was intended to produce a modest decline in weighted capital requirements but that the 2007–09 financial crisis proved this goal to be misguided. Moreover, even with the higher capital ratios mandated by Basel III, he sees the IRB as problematic. The reasoning behind Tarullo's conclusion is worth repeating:

> The combined complexity and opacity of the risk weights generated by each banking organization...create manifold risks of gaming, mistakes, and monitoring difficulty. The IRB approach contributes little to market understanding of large banks' balance sheets and thus fails to strengthen market discipline. And the relatively short, backward-looking basis for generating risk weights makes the resulting capital standards likely to be excessively pro-cyclical and insufficiently sensitive to tail risk.... The IRB approach—for all its complexity and expense—does not do a very good job of advancing the financial stability and macroprudential aims of prudential regulation.

Tarullo argues that the Fed's supervisory bank stress tests provide a much better basis for setting minimum capital requirements. With the Collins Amendment to the Dodd-Frank law providing a standardized statuary floor for risk-weighted capital requirements[53] and the supplementary leverage ratio providing a stronger back-up capital measure, there is "little reason to maintain the requirements of the IRB approach for our largest banks" (Tarullo 2014b, 4).

Tarullo recognizes that having the United States unilaterally abandon the IRB approach to risk weighting in favor of standardized risk weights and reliance on the results of supervisory stress tests is inferior to a plan in which all Basel Committee members make such a move in unison. But he rightly argues that the existing IRB approach to risk weights has created its own serious problems in consistency and transparency.

Endnotes

1. The IMF does not appear to share the reading of Borio, Drehmann, and Tsatsaronis (2012), at least with respect to its Financial Sector Assessment Program (FSAP) assessments. The one-page description of the FSAP on its website notes: "The financial crisis underlined many of the FSAPs' strengths. In countries that had undergone assessments relatively close to the onset of the crisis, FSAP assessments were generally successful in pinpointing the main sources of risk."

2. "The banking system's reported financial indicators are above minimum regulatory requirements and stress tests suggest that the system is resilient" (Borio, Drehmann, and Tsatsaronis 2012, 1).

3. That same IMF Evaluation Office Report (IMF 2011c, 10) also concludes that "the IMF largely endorsed the policies and practices of the largest financial centers at the epicenter of the crisis."

4. I say "published" warning because I am told that IMF FSAP missions typically leave with country authorities confidential memoranda that are not published; since such memoranda are not available to outside analysts, I have to base my commentary on the published reports alone.

5. A few quotations convey the flavor of these reports. The report on Belgium (IMF 2006a, 6) notes: "Stress tests confirm the system's robustness." The Portugal report (IMF 2006e, 5) notes: "Stress testing confirmed that, overall, Portuguese banks would be able to absorb fairly comfortably an array of severe but plausible shocks to the macroeconomic environment." The report on Greece (IMF 2006c, 6, 7) notes: "No immediate threat to systemic stability is perceived, but the financial sector faces challenges. The rapid credit expansion...exposes banks to uncertainties in risk analysis.... In light of rapid credit growth, close monitoring on a timely basis of credit risk is critical...." The report on Ireland (IMF 2006d, 1) notes: "The outlook for the financial system is positive. That said, there are several macro-risks and challenges.... Stress tests confirm, however, that the major financial institutions have adequate capital buffers to cover a range of shocks." The report on Spain (IMF 2006f) notes: "[T]he continued rapid growth of credit is a concern" (p. 1) but that "overall, Spain's financial sector is vibrant, resilient, highly competitive and well-supervised and regulated" (p. 5) and "credit risk was found to be important for some credit institutions but it did not seem to pose a threat to capital adequacy" (p. 74).

6. My assessment is similar to that reached by the IMF's Independent Evaluation Office in 2011 (IMF 2011c) in its report on the performance of Fund surveillance in the 2004–07 run-up to the global economic and financial crisis.

7. The BIS authors also find that debt service ratios can be useful in the near term in anticipating financial strains and crises. The IMF (2011b, 103) seems to concur about the usefulness of these dual-threshold early warning models of banking crisis: "Credit growth and asset-price growth together form a powerful signal of systemic risk build-up as early as two to four years in advance of crises." In chapter 3 of its *Global Financial Stability Report* of September 2011 (IMF 2011b), the IMF provides a useful examination of such early warning models. It is not clear how much weight is given to these models in the IMF's FSAP exercises.

8. Gorton (1988) and Calomiris and Gorton (1991) show that leading indicators of recession did a good job of anticipating banking crises in the United States during the 1857–1914 period but not during the Great Recession.

9. For the euro area just before the 2007–09 crisis, the BIS indicators show some abnormal credit expansion, but not enough to reach the dual threshold (with property prices).

10. Looking at costly asset-price booms and busts in 18 OECD countries over the 1970–2007 period, Alessi and Detkin (2009) also find an important role for credit aggregates. Indeed, they find that a measure of the global credit gap performs better as an early warning indicator of such asset-price booms and busts than any other indicators tested. Bisias et al. (2012) provide a survey of early warning models of systemic risk.

11. A related defense of stress tests is that they are not really designed to predict crises; they merely evaluate how banks would fare given extremely adverse conditions. But by choosing what they regard as the relevant set of risk scenarios, bank supervisors are already engaging, at least partially, in the business of crisis forecasting. In addition, it is doubtful that stress tests could maintain credibility with the public if they repeatedly issued "all is well" verdicts in the face of repeated banking crises, whether they were formally in the crisis prediction business or not.

12. BIS (2014) also suggests that a debt service indicator would also have been flashing red for China and some of these Asian emerging economies. In one such indicator, the BIS assesses debt service at the current level of interest rates. In another it estimates debt service ratios under an adverse scenario when interest rates have increased 250 basis points (reminiscent of the rise in interest rates during the last bout of monetary tightening).

13. "Rapid Growth of China Debt Raises Concern," *Financial Times*, September 20, 2016.

14. Going beyond credit booms and property prices, the recent IMF FSAPs are also better than ones conducted earlier in dealing with liquidity risks and in evaluating various types of contagion.

15. I explain my reasons for suspecting that too much confidence is being placed in the largely optimistic outcomes of stress tests more fully in the rest of this chapter and in chapter 4. In short, the stress tests rely almost exclusively on risk-based measures of capital instead of leverage ratios, and the stress test models themselves do not include either enough adverse feedback effects from the financial sector to the real sector or large amplification effects within the bank and nonbank financial sectors. The stress tests also have no way to validate the asset quality reflected in accounting statements (since they do not perform audits of these accounts).

16. Despite ongoing reform and financial strengthening, China confronts a steady buildup of financial sector vulnerabilities. "Jointly conducted stress tests of the largest 17 commercial banks indicate that most of the banks appear to be resilient to isolated shocks.... However, if several of these shocks were to occur at the same time, the banking system could be severely impacted" (IMF 2011c, 7).

17. The 2014 FSAP for Hong Kong (IMF 2014c) concludes: "Stress tests suggest that banks are well positioned to absorb a significant realization of key risks" (p. 1) and "the sector is well regulated, with the capacity to withstand a diversity of shocks" (p. 6).

18. Reuters, "China Confident After Bank Stress Tests, Even As Growth Slows," April 30, 2014.

19. There are also the views of outside analysts to consider on the risk of banking crises. Speaking in April 2014, Lardy (2014) concluded that the risk of a financial crisis in

China, despite the large run-up in credit, had been somewhat exaggerated. He emphasizes six mitigating factors: (1) bank lending is almost entirely funded by relatively stable (and largely captive) bank deposits, not by wholesale funding sensitive to sudden stops; (2) despite recent growth, the shadow banking sector is still smaller as a percentage of GDP than both the global average and its counterpart in the United States; (3) China still has a plain vanilla financial system, with relatively limited loan securitization; (4) although external debt is on the rise, China's net international investment position is very strong; (5) the rate of credit growth could well moderate in the next few quarters, at it has often done in the past after sharp increases; and (6) the effects of a credit slowdown are likely to be tolerable, because its negative effect on growth is likely to be offset in part by improved credit allocation to the private sector (where rates of return are much higher).

20. See Reinhart and Rogoff (2009) for the differences between banking crises and normal recessions.

21. As Borio, Drehmann, and Tsatsaronis (2012, 7) put it, "The very essence of financial instability is that normal-size shocks cause the system to break down."

22. Anand, Bédard-Pagé, and Traclet (2014) indicate that when the Bank of Canada included liquidity and spillover effects, in addition to solvency risk, in the stress tests for its 2013 FSAP with the IMF, it found that the capital position of Canadian banks was 20 percent lower than when these effects were omitted. For the reasons outlined in the rest of this chapter, I suspect that this is a lower bound on the true effects.

23. Hellwig (2014a, 3) notes that both the IMF's *Global Financial Stability Report* of April 2007 and the BIS Annual Report published in June 2007 "contain fairly accurate accounts of the subprime crisis in the United States but overlook the potential for contagion and therefore very much underestimate the impact of the crisis on the global financial system."

24. I am saying that the initial shock was relatively small, not that the shocks were small after the initial shock had affected other key variables in the system. Geithner (2014) compares the decline in household wealth and the increase in corporate interest rates between 2008 and 1929. He finds that those shocks were much larger in the 2008 crisis than during the Great Depression.

25. I call it a wake-up call because judging from most market indicators of risk, private creditors and rating agencies were asleep about vulnerabilities in the crisis countries before the outbreak of the Thai crisis.

26. Geanakoplos (2010) points to rising delinquencies in the securities market in the last half of 1996 as starting the downward leg of the leverage cycle.

27. Following from those symptoms, Geanakoplos (2010, 117) argues that once the crisis has started, the thematic solution is to contain the bad news, intervene to bring down margins, and carefully inject "optimistic" equity back into the system.

28. As but one of many indicators of changing leverage during the 1999–2009 leverage cycle, Geanakoplos (2010) points out that in 2006, the $2.5 trillion of toxic mortgage securities could be bought by putting $150 billion down and borrowing the remaining $2.35 trillion. In contrast, in early 2009 the buyer might have had to put nearly the whole amount down in cash, even though those same securities collectively might have been worth roughly half as much.

29. Geanakoplos (2010, 112) defines the double leverage cycle as "the feedback from falling security prices to higher margins on housing to lower house prices and then back to

tougher margins on securities and to lower security prices and then back again to housing."

30. Among other effects of the leverage cycle, Geanakoplos (2010) points out that the bankruptcy of one optimist makes it more likely that other optimists will go bankrupt, debt overhang destroys productivity, seizing collateral destroys much value in the process, asset prices can have a profound effect on economic activity, large fluctuations in asset prices over the leverage cycle can lead to massive redistributions of wealth and large changes in inequality, and the inevitable government response to the crisis part of the leverage cycle can create resentment from those that are not bailed out.

31. Bernanke (2015, 399) also emphasizes the role of information contagion in the 2007–09 financial crisis: "Contagion can occur through several channels. When bad news about one institution emerges, for example, depositors naturally wonder whether other institutions with similar asset holdings or business models might be in trouble as well."

32. Although the nonbank financial sector is much smaller relative to banks in Europe than in the United States, Europe's banks are hardly immune from problems in the nonbank sector. See, for example, the difficulties faced by German life insurers and their implications for the banking system (Patrick Jenkins, "Squeeze on German Life Assurers Is a Threat to Financial Stability," *Financial Times*, April 21, 2015).

33. Adrian (2014, 1) defines shadow banking as "maturity transformation, liquidity transformation and credit risk transfer outside of institutions with direct access to government backstops, such as depository institutions, i.e., traditional commercial banks."

34. Shleifer and Vishny (2011) provide a comprehensive treatment of fire sales in finance and macroeconomics. An important building block in fire sale models is investor heterogeneity. If the "natural buyers" for a particular asset face a common shock that reduces their ability to purchase that asset, the remaining (not-so-natural) buyers will be willing to purchase only at a lower price. Investor heterogeneity is also important in the dynamics of the leverage cycle proposed by Geanakoplos (2010, 2014).

35. Flannery, Hirtle, and Kovner (2015) reach a different conclusion: They find no evidence that the information value of US stress tests declined over the 2009–15 period.

36. Ordinary least squares estimates approximate the conditional mean of the response variable (y) given the autonomous values of the predictor variables (x). Quantile regression estimates approximate the conditional median or other quantiles of the response variable given the autonomous values of the predictor variables (see Koenker and Hallock 2011).

37. Haldane estimates that between 1985 and 2005, nodes in the international financial network increased by a factor of about 14 and links increased by a factor of roughly 6. Measures of skew and kurtosis suggest increasing asymmetry and a long tail in the network, and between the largest nation states there were only 1.4 degrees of separation in 2009. Milgram (1967) highlights the small-world property of connected networks, showing that the average number of links between any two individuals was about six (six degrees of separation).

38. See Acemoglu, Ozdaglar, and Tahbaz-Salehi (2015) for a formal model of financial networks in which interconnectedness displays this knife-edge, or "robust yet fragile," property.

39. As an example of such an ABM, Bookstaber (2012) cites Reynolds' (1987) model for the movement of birds in flight based on three simple rules: separation (don't get too close to any object, including other birds); alignment (try to match the speed and direction

of nearby birds); and cohesion (head for the perceived center of the mass of the birds in your immediate neighborhood).

40. As another example of application of an ABM, Bookstaber (2012, 10) refers to an escape panic during, say, a fire in a movie theater. In a simulation with one exit, more people escape when a pillar is posted a few feet in front of an exit, even though intuitively one might think the column would impede the outflow of people. ABM simulations, backed by real-world experiments, indicate that the column provides structure, reducing the number of injured people and increasing the flow. The 2015 decision by the International Swaps and Derivatives Association (ISDA) to amend its standard documentation to allow a 48-hour stay on termination rights in over-the-counter derivative transactions is not unlike the rationale for the column.

41. For example, the Bank of England's RAMSI model allows a weakening of bank fundamentals to lead to higher funding costs or (in the extreme) an exclusion from certain funding markets. Under severe capital losses, capital inadequacy at one bank is allowed to cause losses at other banks (see Bank of England 2013b for discussion of feedback and amplification mechanisms).

42. The initial (1988) Basel I agreement included four risk-weight categories: 0 percent for cash, 20 percent for assets involving banks located in OECD countries, 50 percent for residential mortgage loans, and 100 percent for commercial and industrial loans and personal consumer loans. In addition, national supervisors had the option to assign a risk weight of 10 percent to claims on domestic public sector entities. This small set of risk weights was used to calculate a bank's risk-weighted assets), and the minimum capital requirement was set at 8 percent of a bank's risk-weighted assets (see Tarullo 2008, Mariathasan and Merrouche 2013b).

43. There was also an amendment to Basel I in 1996 to incorporate market risk into the framework. As under Basel II, what mattered for calculating risk weights was no longer just the counterparty but either the asset's external credit weighting under the basic/standardized approach or the banks' internal risk models under the advanced/internal ratings–based approach (Mariathasan and Merrouche 2013b). The internal ratings–based approach had two variants: the foundational internal ratings–based approach and the advanced internal ratings–based approach. Under the former, the bank calculates (for credit risk) the probability of default based on its internal credit risk models, but it takes maturities, the loss given default, and exposure at default from supervisors; under the latter, the bank has the option to also do its own calculations for maturities, the loss given default, and the exposure at default (see Mariathasan and Merrouche 2013b). Haldane (2013) claims that for a large complex bank, the number of risk weights rose from what you count on one hand under Basel I to hundreds of thousands and maybe even millions under Basel II and III.

44. Risk-weighted capital measures tend to perform better when the sample is restricted to, or consists mainly of, small banks (see, for example, Haldane and Madouros 2012). This finding, however, hardly constitutes a reason for keeping risk-based capital ratios as the primary Pillar 1 standard, as total assets of the eight US global systemically important banks account for almost two-thirds of the total consolidated assets of all US bank holding companies; the 33 large bank holding companies participating in the 2016 CCAR test accounted for more than 80 percent of the total consolidated assets of all US bank holding companies; and in the 2007–09 crisis over 90 percent of government support went to banks with total assets of $100 billion or more (Haldane 2010). Rather, this

finding is consistent with the argument that manipulation of risk weights is much more prevalent among large banks than among smaller ones.

45. The Turner Report (FSA 2009) notes similarly that risk-based measures of bank capital for the United Kingdom were not indicating a large rise in leverage between 2003 and 2008 whereas leverage ratios were.

46. Hoenig (2013) also points out that for the US banking industry as a whole, the average tangible leverage ratio decreased from 5.2 percent in 1999 to 3.3 percent in 2007.

47. The exception was Wells Fargo, which saw its ratio of risk-weighted assets to total assets rise sharply during the crisis.

48. Haldane (2013) opines that the downward trend in risk weights is more consistent with the hypothesis that banks have had both the incentives and the ability to game the system in order to artificially boost their capital ratios. Federal Reserve Vice Chair Stanley Fischer (2014b, 2) observes that "any set of risk weights that involves judgments and human nature would rarely result in choices that made for higher risk weights."

49. When Basel II was being designed, its architects held out hope that the internal ratings approach would reduce "herding" and promote stability by permitting greater diversity across banks in their views about credit risk. There is little evidence that such "good" diversification in risk weights has taken place, according to Turner (2012), who cites the widespread acceptance of zero risk weights for sovereign risk in the euro area crisis, among other examples.

50. It has been argued that the fact that banks in emerging economies tend to make greater use of the standardized approach to risk weights than large banks in advanced economies contributes to the former reporting higher ratios of risk-weighted assets to total assets than the latter (see Sheng 2013 on this point for banks in emerging Asia).

51. "Mark Carney Sees Logic in Tougher Cap on Banks' Leverage," *Independent*, September 29, 2014.

52. "Brussels to Push Back on Bank Capital Rules," *Financial Times*, September 29, 2016.

53. Section 171 of the Collins Amendment requires federal banking agencies to establish minimum consolidated capital requirements for all banking organizations that are not less than "generally applicable" risk-based capital requirements (see Tarullo 2014b).

4

What We Have Learned—or Should Have Learned— about the Right Level of Bank-Capital Ratios

The fourth and final criticism of bank stress tests addresses the minimum capital ratios that banks have to meet in stress tests—that is, the height of the hurdle rate. The claim is that the minimum bank-capital requirements in Basel III for both risk-weighted measures and an unweighted leverage ratio are still far too low and that bank stress tests ought to assist the longer-term path toward a more appropriate level of bank capital by using higher hurdle rates. I address this criticism in its own chapter, because the height of minimum capital requirements, both inside and outside bank stress tests, continues to be the most important issue in bank regulation and supervision.

Table 4.1 shows the minimum capital and liquidity ratios agreed to under Basel III, along with the transition path to full implementation. Consider the minimum for risk-weighted capital. If one takes the minimum of a 4.5 percent ratio for common equity tier 1 and adds to it 2.5 percent for the capital conservation buffer, the minimum common equity tier 1 ratio rises to 7.0 percent.

Not shown in the table but also important are the capital surcharges for global systemically important banks (G-SIBs). The Basel Committee on Banking Supervision (BCBS) originally suggested a G-SIB capital surcharge schedule of 1.0 to 2.5 percent but since raised the top end to 3.5 percent. For the most systemic G-SIBs, the surcharge would raise the common equity tier 1 minimum to 10.5 percent. In the United States, the top end of the G-SIB surcharge range is now 4.5 percent, raising the (potential) minimum common equity tier 1 for the most systemic US G-SIBs to 11.5 percent.[1]

Table 4.1 Basel III minimum requirements and phase-in arrangements (percent)

Requirement/arrangement	Basel II	2013	2014	2015	2016	2017	2018	2019
Capital								
Leverage ratio	None	Parallel run (2013–17), disclosures start January 1, 2015					Pillar 1 (3.0%)	
Minimum common equity tier 1 (CET1) ratio	2.0	3.5	4.0	4.5	4.5	4.5	4.5	4.5
Capital conservation buffer (CCB)	None	0	0	0	0.625	1.250	1.875	2.5
Minimum CET1 plus CCB	2.0	3.0	4.0	4.5	5.125	5.75	6.375	7.0
Phase-in of deductions from CET1	None	0	20	40	60	80	100	100
Minimum tier 1 ratio	4.0	4.5	5.5	6.0	6.00	6.00	6.0	6.0
Minimum capital adequacy ratio	8.0	8.0	8.0	8.0	8.00	8.00	8.0	8.0
Capital instruments that no longer qualify as noncore tier 1 or tier 2 capital	n.a.		Phased out over 10-year horizon, starting 2013					
Countercyclical capital buffer (voluntary)	None	0	0	0	0.625	1.250	1.875	2.5
Liquidity								
Liquidity coverage ratio	None			60	70	80	90	100
Net stable funding ratio	None						Introduce minimum standard	

Note: All years as of January 1.

Source: Moody's Investors Service (2014).

Turning to the leverage ratio, the minimum Basel III requirement is 3 percent. For US G-SIBs, the minimum leverage requirement (under the enhanced supplementary leverage ratio) rises to 5 percent for bank holding companies and 6 percent for their insured bank depositories. All banks, regardless of size, are also subject to a 4 percent tier 1 leverage requirement.[2]

By now there is a consensus that the Basel III minimums are better than their Basel II predecessors. The minimum equity requirement in Basel II was only 2 percent; some analysts have concluded that if the Basel II equity requirement had been redefined in terms of its Basel III equivalent (making adjustments for hybrid capital, goodwill, intangibles, deferred-tax assets, and changes in risk weights), the Basel II minimum would have been 1 percent or even lower (see Carney 2014). In addition, Basel II contained no minimum for bank leverage.[3]

Why then do critics—myself included—think that Basel III capital levels are still way too low? In answering that question, I summarize three complementary approaches to estimating the optimal level of bank capital for large US and/or EU banks, all of which point to the desirability of higher minimum capital requirements. The three approaches focus on bank losses during a country's most serious crisis, the implications of a macroprudential approach for capital levels, and a benefit-cost calculus for higher capital levels.

Bank Losses during the 2007–09 Crisis

One popular approach for estimating optimal capital ratios is to look back at the "losses" banks experienced during previous systemic banking crises. Because the 2007–09 global economic and financial crisis was the worst crisis since the Great Depression, it naturally gets the most attention as the preferred benchmark. The basic idea is to see what capital ratio would allow banks to absorb the losses experienced during a severe crisis while remaining solvent and still meeting other criteria, such as maintaining healthy lending growth and meeting market pressures to hold capital in excess of regulatory minimums. All else equal, the larger are past losses, the higher the optimal capital ratio.

Balance Sheet versus Income Statement Approaches

Broadly speaking, two measures of bank losses are used in optimal capital calculations. Under the balance sheet framework, the emphasis is usually on some measure of credit losses, typically either mark-to-market losses, or write-downs.[4] Under the income statement framework, the workhorse metric is net income.[5] Net income losses in a crisis are almost always much smaller than credit losses, because the latter are offset in the income statement by positive revenue from interest-earning activities and noninterest sources of revenue. In this sense the income statement framework is more comprehensive than the balance sheet framework. Net income is closer to the net approach to measuring losses versus the gross approach with credit losses.

To take a concrete example, the IMF (2009, 2010b) estimates that write-downs by UK banks during the 2007–09 crisis represented more than 6 percent of those banks' total assets. The Bank of England (2014b) gauges that over the 2007–13 period its banks suffered an average peak net income loss relative to total assets of less than 2 percent. Using data from the 2014 and 2015 CCAR stress tests, Lehnert (2015) reports that bank revenue offset about 88 percent of loan-loss provisions under the severely adverse scenario.

Another important distinction between the two bank loss metrics is that net income is a flow concept, measured over a period of time (usually at least a quarter and in stress tests usually over a two- to three-year period). In contrast, credit losses are a stock concept, capable of being measured (at least in a mark-to-market sense) at a point in time. This difference is crucial in evaluating which framework better suits the circumstances of banks in a severe crisis, particularly regarding their survival (i.e., whether they should be treated as a "going" concern or, in the absence of strong support from the official sector, a "gone" concern).

Suppose, for example, that during the fourth quarter of 2008, at the worst of the global crisis, bank investors and counterparties, using a comparison of the mark-to-market value of a major bank's assets with its high-quality capital, reached the judgment that the bank was probably insolvent and as such refused to roll over their short-term financing. In the absence of official support, that bank would then not be given the time to replenish its depleted capital by earning new revenue. In this "wartime" scenario, the "in the moment" balance sheet measure of loss would be more relevant than the "peacetime" net income measure, even if the initial mark-to-market estimate of losses subsequently turned out to be too pessimistic.[6] In contrast, if the bank's financial condition had already been stabilized by, say, government capital injections or guarantees or the crisis was a relatively mild one, the net income measure of losses would be more revealing.

These distinctions are directly relevant to the issue at hand. In the June 2009 issue of its *Financial Stability Review*, the Bank of England (2009) reported that between October 2008 and January 2009, the mark-to-market value of UK banks' banking book deteriorated by roughly £350 billion (versus core tier 1 capital of only £200 billion). Senior US bank regulators and crisis managers have indicated that after the fall of Lehman Brothers in 2008, a number of major US financial institutions were on the verge of failing—and would have failed had there not been strong official intervention and financial support.

In the remainder of this section, I discuss estimates of optimal capital ratios using a balance sheet (credit-loss write-down) framework. In chapter 5, when discussing the Bank of England's symmetry and proportionality approach and the Federal Reserve's estimated impact approach to gauging appropriate capital surcharges for G-SIBs, I analyze the application of a net-income calculation of bank losses to optimal capital estimates.

Following Hanson, Kashyap, and Stein (2011), I lean more heavily (for optimal capital calculations) on credit write-downs than on either mark-to-market losses or net income declines, for three reasons. First, there is considerable evidence that during a severe crisis, mark-to-market prices are subject to large uncertainty and liquidity discounts, which cause mark-to-market losses to systematically overshoot the losses incurred over a longer period. According to the Bank of England (2008b), whereas mark-to-market losses on US residential-mortgage-backed securities totaled some $380 billion, the estimated losses from an economic model were less than half as large ($170 billion). The fact that most central banks made a profit on their purchases of distressed assets during the crisis also speaks to this overshooting property of mark-to-market estimates. While credit write-downs are by no means an ideal measure of bank losses, they come closer to an accurate forecast of bank credit losses.[7]

Second, the IMF has published estimates of credit write-downs over the 2008–10 period (on a like-for-like basis) for banks in the United States, the euro area, and the United Kingdom. These estimates facilitate cross-region comparisons. It is highly unlikely that the IMF would have continued to use this bank-loss methodology throughout the 2008–10 crisis period and publish the results in six consecutive issues of one of its flagship publications (the *Global Financial Stability Report*) if the IMF membership regarded this methodology as seriously flawed.

Third, I think the balance sheet framework is more relevant than the net income framework for the circumstances of the 2007–09 crisis. During the nadir of that crisis, there were profound doubts about the survival of the largest financial institutions in the United States (and probably in some other crisis countries as well). As former Federal Reserve Chair Ben Bernanke recalled, "September and October of 2008 was the worst financial crisis in global history. Of the 13 most important financial institutions in the United States, 12 were at risk of failure within a period of a week or two" (Da Costa 2014, 1).[8]

If the (then) chair of the Federal Reserve had, at that moment, serious doubts about the ability of these major financial institutions to continue as going concerns without substantial federal government assistance, it is hard to imagine that private investors in and counterparties of these same institutions would not also have been questioning their viability. As such, using a gross estimate of bank losses that did not assume a positive offset from revenue increases over the medium term would have been entirely rational.[9] In short, in extreme circumstances, credit write-downs are preferred to net income losses as a measure of distress at large banks.[10]

Credit Losses during the Upswing of the Financial Cycle, Market Pressure at the Bottom

Hanson, Kashyap, and Stein (2011) employ just such a balance-sheet/credit-loss approach to US banking losses during the 2007–09 crisis in order to estimate optimal capital ratios. They observe that the four largest US banks had a tier 1 common capital ratio of roughly 8 percent of risk-weighted assets in the first quarter of 2010, near the lower end of the economic cycle—four times the (Basel II) regulatory minimum. They argue that banks were holding that excess because markets (mindful of losses in the crisis) were pressuring them to do so.[11] Hence they regard 8 percent as the market-induced minimum at the lower end of the cycle.

They also note from IMF figures on credit write-downs (IMF 2010b) that US banks lost about 7 percent of total assets during the 2007–09 crisis. They then ask the following question: If banks want to meet the market-induced minimum capital ratio at the bottom of the cycle after suffering a loss equal to 7 percent of total assets, what should the minimum capital ratio be at the top of the cycle?[12] Their answer is 15 percent, because 15 percent minus an asset loss of 7 percent equals a market-induced minimum of 8 percent. Because the ratio of risk-weighted assets to total assets of US banks in 2007–10 was about 70 percent (Le Leslé and Avramova 2012, Schildbach and Wenzel 2013), the minimum capital ratio under the Hanson, Kashyap, and Stein (2011) estimate should actually be more like 18 percent using a risk-based measure of bank capital (18 percent minus a risk-based asset loss of 10 percent equals 8 percent).

Illustrative Calculations of Optimal Capital for Banks in the United States, European Union, and United Kingdom

Suppose we wanted to update and extend the Hanson, Kashyap, and Stein (2011) methodology to account for recent empirical work on the timing of the financial cycle, to obtain estimates of optimal capital not just for US banks but for euro area and UK banks as well, and to gauge optimal capital for leverage ratios as well as risk-based measures of capital. What would we then get?

Following the empirical work in Drehmann, Borio, and Tsatsaronis (2012) and BIS (2014, 2015a, 2016b), among others, the financial cycle can be measured by the deviation of the credit-to-GDP ratio and of housing prices from their long-term real trends. When both the credit ratio and housing prices are above (below) trend, the observation is typically regarded as being in the upswing (downswing) of the cycle; mixed signals denote an intermediate stage. The advantage of using this approach it that peaks in the financial cycle have been shown to be highly correlated with financial crises (and by implication, with large bank losses) (Borio and Drehmann 2009). By picking a low point in the financial cycle as the base period for the optimal capital calculation, one is assuming that banks' credit losses are ahead of them (in the upswing of the cycle) rather than behind them. Based on this empirical work, it appears that the low point in the US financial cycle was in late 2012 to early 2013 (BIS 2014). In the euro area and the United Kingdom, the low point appears to be a little later; 2013 (or even early 2014) seems like a reasonable choice.[13]

For bank losses I use a simple average of the IMF's credit write-down estimates, taken from the October 2009 (IMF 2009) and April 2010 (IMF 2010b) *Global Financial Stability Reports*. The October 2009 estimates were the IMF's highest loss estimates. The April 2010 estimates, while somewhat lower, might still be regarded as close to peak losses. As a share of total bank assets, average peak losses were 7.6 percent for US banks, 3.2 percent for euro area banks, and 6.3 percent for UK banks.[14]

All that remains to implement the Hanson, Kashyap, and Stein (2011) methodology for calculating optimal leverage ratios are the actual capital ratios at the low points in the financial cycle. Let us look first at risk-based measures of capital (despite their serious weaknesses, as outlined in chapter 3). After that, we can proceed to leverage ratios.

When dealing with risk-based capital ratios under the Hanson, Kashyap, and Stein (2011) methodology and when bank losses are measured in terms of total bank assets, one has to convert those losses into losses on risk-weighted assets. This means that countries/regions with low ratios of risk-weighted assets to total assets (i.e., with low risk-weight densities) will show larger risk-weighted losses than those with higher risk-weight densities for a given size of total asset loss. This turns out to be important in any comparison of risk-weighted capital ratios between the United States on the one hand and the euro area and the United Kingdom on the other, because the average risk-weight density for US banks in the 2007–10 period was roughly 70 percent versus 35 percent for euro area banks and 40 percent for UK banks (Le Leslé and Avramova 2012, Schildbach and Wenzel 2013, and Bank of England 2016).

The 2013 Comprehensive Capital Analysis and Review (CCAR) (Board of Governors 2013a) indicates that the 18 bank holding companies participating in that stress test had a weighted-average tier 1 common capital ratio of about 11 percent as of the third quarter of 2012, the assumed low point in the financial cycle.[15] Converting the 7.6 percent total asset bank loss into a risk-weighted asset loss yields a loss of just under 11 percent. Adding the two figures yields an optimal risk-weighted capital ratio of about 22 percent. The optimal risk-weighted capital ratio for the eight US G-SIBs is somewhat higher, at 26 percent, because their tier 1 common capital ratio is a bit higher (11.8 percent) and their risk-weight density (53 percent) lower than that of non-G-SIB CCAR participants.

For euro area banks, the November 2013 *Financial Stability Review* (ECB 2013) shows that as of the third quarter of 2013, 18 large and complex banking groups in the euro area had a median Basel III common equity tier 1 capital ratio of just under 10 percent. For the larger group of 90 significant banking groups in the euro area, the comparable common equity tier 1 ratio was 11.5 percent. Converting the average 3.2 percent total asset bank losses from 2007–10 into losses in risk-weighted terms gives a risk-weighted loss of roughly 9 percent. Adding the 9 percent asset loss to the roughly 11 percent capital ratio generates an estimate of the optimal risk-weighted capital ratio of roughly 20 percent—very close to the US figure.

For major UK banks, the July 2016 Bank of England (2016) *Financial Stability Review* reveals that as of the third quarter of 2013 the average Basel III common equity tier 1 ratio was about 9 percent. The IMF estimated the total asset loss for UK banks in the 2007–10 crisis at about 6.6 percent. Accounting for the risk-weight density of major UK banks of approximately 40 percent during the 2007–10 period and adding the resulting risk-weighted asset loss (about 16 percent) to the capital ratio (9 percent) at the assumed low point in the financial cycle produces an optimal risk-weighted capital ratio of about 25 percent—in the same ballpark as the estimates for US and euro area banks and way above current risk-weighted capital ratios.

The same kind of exercise can be conducted to obtain optimal leverage ratios. Doing so is more complicated than the risk-weighted capital drill for several reasons: There are different leverage ratios with different qualities of capital from which to choose; most leverage measures reflect different treatment of the netting of derivatives under the Generally Accepted Accounting Principles (GAAP) (for US banks) and International

Financial Reporting Standards (IFRS) (for UK and euro area banks), with large effects on the results for banks with large derivative positions (see appendix I in the introductory chapter); the one leverage ratio measure that is cross-country consistent—the fully loaded Basel III leverage ratio—is typically not available before 2014 at the right level of country disaggregation; and published leverage ratios for different regions often apply to different size categories of banks (e.g., G-SIBs versus other groups of large banks).

These challenges notwithstanding, there is enough information out there to produce a rough estimate of optimal leverage ratios. Because most (but not all) leverage ratios use total assets in the denominator, one can use the IMF's total asset loss figures without adjustments.[16]

For the 18 US bank holding companies participating in the 2013 CCAR, the weighted-average tier 1 leverage ratio in the third quarter of 2012 was 8 percent (Board of Governors 2013a).[17] Adding this 8 percent tier 1 leverage ratio (in late 2012) to the loss estimate of 7.6 percent (of total assets) for the 2007–10 crisis yields an optimal leverage ratio of roughly 15 percent.[18]

A higher-quality measure of leverage is the tangible leverage ratio published regularly for US and foreign G-SIBs by the FDIC. For end-2012, the Hoenig (2013) reports that the weighted-average tangible leverage ratio for the eight US G-SIBs was 6.2 percent. Adding this figure to the 7.6 percent loss figure yields an optimal leverage ratio of just under 14 percent.

These estimates of a 14 to 15 percent optimal leverage ratio use US GAAP treatment of derivatives. The FDIC also publishes its tangible leverage ratio figures under IFRS accounting standards. Using IFRS substantially inflates total assets for US G-SIBs with large derivative positions (mainly, JPMorgan Chase, Citigroup, Bank of America, Goldman Sachs, and Morgan Stanley) but not for other US G-SIBs or US non-G-SIBs. Under IFRS accounting the tangible leverage ratio for US G-SIBs drops to 3.9 percent at end-2012. Adding this figure to the 7.6 percent loss rate yields an optimal capital ratio of about 11.5 percent. Using US GAAP accounting thus leads to a 15 percent optimal leverage ratio, whereas using IFRS yields 11 to 12 percent.[19]

Turning to major UK banks, the July 2016 *Financial Stability Review* (Bank of England 2016) reveals that the weighted-average Basel III fully loaded leverage ratio was about 4 percent in 2013. Adding that 4 percent Basel III leverage ratio to the 6.6 percent estimate of bank losses in the 2007–10 crisis yields an optimal leverage ratio for UK banks of roughly 10.5 percent.[20]

We could also draw on the FDIC's tangible leverage ratio for UK G-SIBs in IFRS terms for the second quarter of 2013. It covers Barclays, HSBC,

RBS, and Standard Chartered. This ratio stood at 4 percent, suggesting that the optimal leverage ratio would be about 10.5 percent. Picking a slightly different date for the bottom of the UK financial cycle would not have a large effect on the estimated optimal leverage ratio.[21]

For euro area banks, the November 2013 *Financial Stability Review* (ECB 2013) indicates that the median leverage ratio (total equity to total assets) for 18 large and complex euro area banks was roughly 4.5 percent in the third quarter of 2013. For 72 other smaller but still "significant" euro area banks, the median leverage ratio was a little below 6 percent. The November 2014 *Financial Stability Review* (ECB 2014b) shows that the median tangible leverage ratio at end-2013 was just under 4 percent for the group of large and complex euro area banks and about 4.5 percent for the larger group of other significant banks. The FDIC's (2013) weighted-average tangible leverage ratio for nine euro area G-SIBs in the second quarter of 2013 was 3.4 percent (in IFRS terms). The relevant range of leverage ratios for large euro area banks at the lower point of the financial cycle in 2013 thus appears to be 3.5 to 5.5 percent, with the lower end of the range applicable to the largest and most complex banks (including the nine euro area G-SIBs). Adding this figure to the 3 percent-plus average loss rate for euro area banks during 2007–10 yields an optimal leverage rate of about 6.5 to 9 percent.

Aside from their smaller (reported) loss figures in the 2007–09 crisis, one possible explanation for why optimal leverage ratios turn out to be smaller for EU and UK banks than for US ones in this kind of exercise is that the US has had a regulatory leverage ratio requirement since 1981. In contrast, the EU (and Basel III) leverage requirement does not formally take effect (as a Pillar 1 standard) until January 2018, and the United Kingdom only recently introduced one. The hypothesis is that banks and markets are more inclined to produce higher capital ratios where there is a mandated minimum for that kind of capital. A strong hint that this may be so is that in 2014–16 large US, EU, and UK banks were maintaining very similar capital levels for the ratio of common equity tier 1 to total assets, where Basel III sets a minimum of 7 percent (exclusive of G-SIB surcharges). If this is so, then redoing the optimal leverage ratio calculations once the United Kingdom and the European Union have put in place and adjusted to a formal regulatory leverage requirement is likely to produce optimal leverage ratios across the three jurisdictions that are more similar to one another than estimates using today's figures.

Understatement of Optimal Capital Ratios for EU and Euro Area Banks

Before EU bank supervisors do a jig over their relatively low estimated optimal leverage ratios from this bank-losses-in-crisis exercise, it is useful to place EU progress in achieving appropriate leverage ratios in wider perspective. Among 26 US and foreign G-SIBs included in the FDIC's Global Capital Index, all 6 G-SIBs with the lowest tangible leverage ratios (in IFRS terms) at end-2015 are EU banks, and the median Basel III (fully loaded) leverage ratio for euro area G-SIBs was slightly below 4 percent (ECB 2016) versus about 5.5 percent (in weighted-average terms) for US G-SIBs.

Lax provisioning and write-downs at euro area banks appear to be inflating capital at euro area banks (the 2014 Asset Quality Review exercise notwithstanding), as noted in chapter 1. One indication of this inflation is the "Texas ratio," defined as gross nonperforming loans divided by the sum of tangible equity and loan-loss reserves. According to the May 2016 *Financial Stability Review* (ECB 2016), the average value of the Texas ratio for euro area banks at end-2015 was 60 percent, with some countries showing ratios above 100 percent. In contrast, the Texas ratio for US banks stood below 10 percent; it reached just over 30 percent only at its height, in 2010. Those same lax provisioning and write-down standards at euro area banks would have also caused underestimates of losses during the 2007–09 crisis.

Return on assets—a standard measure of bank profitability—currently stands at about 30 basis points for banks in the core euro area, about a third the figure for US banks (ECB 2016, IMF 2016a). Low profitability is a drag on the ability to build capital via retained earnings.

Both Pagano et al. (2014) and the IMF (2016a) emphasize that the European Union is "overbanked." As one senior IMF official recently put it, "There are simply too many branches with too few deposits, and too many banks with funding costs way above their peers."[22] Very low or negative interest rates and a flattened yield curve are adding to the toll by depressing net interest income (IMF 2016a).

In terms of price-to-book ratios, the market has been valuing euro area banks much below US ones. On top of that, the too big to fail problem is more severe in the European Union than in the United States (see appendix 1A in chapter 1). Given the severity of that problem, Pagano et al. (2014, 9) emphasize that it would be foolhardy for EU bank supervisors to aim for parity on capital ratios with US banks: "One would hope and expect systemically important banks in the EU to have higher leverage ratios than their counterparts in the US, not lower."

The euro area has also gone less far than the United States in integrating leverage ratios into bank supervision: The 2016 EU-wide stress test was the first one to publish baseline and stressed leverage ratios (something the US stress tests have been doing since 2012), and even then no hurdle rate was applied. For all of these reasons, I draw the conclusion from loss-based optimal leverage calculations that large EU banks have quite a ways to go to put their leverage ratios where they should be.

Ignoring Counterfactual Bank Losses and the Liquidity Advantages of Higher Capital

Some observers will consider the optimal leverage ratios estimated in the bank losses approach as too high; others will see them as too low. I think that they are too low, on two grounds.

A Major Methodological Error: Ignoring the Counterfactual

The figures on actual bank losses during the 2007–09 crisis reflect the extraordinary fiscal, monetary, and financial market interventions taken by governments during the crisis. Absent those interventions, bank losses would have been much higher.

Using Moody's models of the US economy, Blinder and Zandi (2015) estimate what US macroeconomic performance would have been without the stunning array of policy responses promulgated by the Fed, the Congress, and two administrations during the 2007–09 crisis. Their conclusions (Blinder and Zandi 2015, 2) are striking:

- The peak-to-trough decline in the real GDP, which was barely more than 4 percent, would have been close to a stunning 14 percent.
- The contraction would have lasted three years, more than twice as long as it did.
- Unemployment would have peaked at just under 16 percent, rather than at 10 percent.
- The federal budget deficit would have ballooned to $2.8 trillion, equal to 18 percent of GDP, compared with the actual peak of 10 percent.
- Today's economy would be far weaker than it is—with real GDP about $800 billion lower, 3.6 million fewer jobs, and unemployment still at 7.6 percent.

A second peek at part of the counterfactual is available from an IMF study by Dagher et al. (2016), who ask what risk-weighted capital ratio would have been necessary to avoid any public recapitalization of banks during the 2007–10 crisis.[23] For US banks their answer is 23 percent of risk-weighted assets. Given their estimate that total assets of US banks were approximately 175 percent of risk-weighted assets (taken from Le Leslé and Avramova 2012), this translates into a required (no public bank recapitalization) leverage rate of roughly 13 percent.[24] As shown in table 1.1, this estimate of an optimal leverage ratio considers only one element of the massive and multifaceted US intervention package implemented during the crisis.

It is inconceivable that bank losses (including multiple bank failures) during the 2007-09 crisis would not been much higher than actually observed under any plausible highly adverse counterfactual policy scenario. It is well to keep in mind too that as large as Blinder and Zandi's estimates of the counterfactual are, they consider only US policy interventions. US banks are counterparties to large banks in other economies and hence also benefited in the crisis by the extraordinary policy measures taken in those economies, especially in the European Union and the United Kingdom. While much more work will need to be done—both to determine how robust the Blinder and Zandi (2015) and Dagher et al. (2016) estimates for the United States are and to make similar calculations for other major economies—I would not be surprised to find that bank loss rates would have been 50 to 100 percent higher than actually observed in the 2007-09 crisis. If they had been, the estimated optimal leverage ratios derived from 2007-09 crisis-related bank losses would be much higher too.

Considering averted—not just actual—bank losses is highly relevant because policy authorities in major economies have emphasized that such extraordinary interventions will not recur in the future. "The G20 leaders have publicly committed not to use public funds anymore to bail banks out" (BIS 2015b, 21). Otherwise—so the argument goes—one would be inviting a high level of moral hazard and would not be addressing forcefully enough the too big to fail problem.

One counterargument to the above conclusion has recently surfaced as part of the unveiling of the quantitative impact study of the Financial Stability Board's total loss-absorbing capacity (TLAC) initiative for G-SIBs. It relies on market discipline (BIS 2015b). The story unfolds as follows. If G-SIBs issued an amount of bail-in bonds roughly equivalent to the amount of regulatory capital they already hold, it would be sufficient to eliminate the possibility of a future public bailout of these institutions; the burden of resolution would fall exclusively on private holders of these bonds.

Drawing on recent empirical work showing that large banks with lower expected government support (as measured by Fitch Rating support floors) take less risk than those with higher government support,[25] the switch from public bailout to private bail-in will (allegedly) lower appreciably the probability of future banking crises. In addition, the switch to private bail-ins would allow governments to use the funds that otherwise might have gone to bank bailouts for targeted fiscal stimuli or to avoid expenditure cuts; avoiding bailouts would also put less upward pressure on sovereign bond yields. With all this going on, there would (allegedly) be no need for minimum bank capital requirements much higher than already exist. The discipline argument could have merit if applied to a large increase in minimum leverage requirements funded by equity, but it strikes me as unpersuasive when applied to TLAC bail-in bonds. (I review the TLAC proposal in chapter 8; see also my proposal in chapter 7.)

As Persaud (2014) forcefully argues, one has to ask who would be holding these bail-in bonds and how the discipline would operate. Banks are ruled out as holders because of potential contagion effects. Retail investors and money market funds are also unlikely, because these bonds are apt to be beyond their risk tolerance and investor mandates. The traditional argument about short-term debtholders providing discipline (by not rolling over their obligations if the issuer takes on too much risk) does not apply, because the TLAC proposal calls for a minimum maturity of at least one year. Even putting aside questions about whether bail-in bonds are good investments for pension funds and insurance companies (see Persaud 2014 on this), how do we know that these holders (presumably selected for the long maturity of their liabilities) would not be bailed out for their losses in a deep systemic crisis like the last one? After all, bondholders, money market funds, and many other creditors were bailed out in the 2007–09 crisis (Ricks 2016). Imagine the outcry if pension funds suffered large losses because of large and widespread G-SIB losses. Alternatively, assume that the main holders are hedge funds, private equity groups, and the like with high risk tolerance. Like Persaud, I do not see them as long-term holders.

Once it becomes clear that the triggers on these bail-in bonds are soon to be pulled, there could be a massive run for the exits. Based on the past, there is little reason to believe that the chaos would be confined to the bail-in bond sector, with no appreciable spillover to other segments of the bond market. With bonds making up more than 90 percent of bank financing, it would be very hard for governments to sit by while bond financing was under enormous strain. More likely, guarantees of one kind or another would be issued to quell the panic. Unlike the scenario depicted in the Bank for International Settlements' (BIS 2015b) contrast between bailout and bail-in, there is no assurance that the bail-in process would be orderly or discipline exercised in a slow, gradual manner rather than abruptly. If in the end the bail-in bond story is susceptible to public bailout, then the whole starting premise of lower risk taking by G-SIBs because of the end of official support, collapses.[26]

Advocates of the bail-in bond discipline story also need to explain why bondholder discipline did not operate effectively in the Great Recession. After all, there were plenty of bonds around at the time, including subordinated debt (the favorite instrument of the bondholder discipline school). In contrast, equity holders—including holders of bank stocks—rarely get bailed out; they did not get bailed out in the last crisis, despite huge declines in the prices of bank stocks. So if we want to reap the advantages of bail-in for the next crisis, why should we be satisfied with costume jewelry when, for only a little more money, we can get the real thing?[27] Let me be clear: I do not prefer bailouts to bail-ins. I just don't see the point of choosing a bail-in strategy that carries many risks and uncertainties when a more reliable bail-in strategy is readily available for only a tiny additional cost.

Liquidity Benefits of Higher Capital Ratios

A second reason to suspect that the loss-related estimates of optimal leverage ratios are too low is that the exercise considers only the link between bank losses and solvency in a severe crisis and not the links among asset price uncertainty, perceived insolvency of banks/nonbanks, funding runs, and fire sales of assets. This is not a technical detail but an issue that cuts to the heart of why the 2007–09 crisis was so severe. It is difficult to explain the depth of the Great Recession without proposing some links among asset price declines, the liability side of bank (and nonbank) balance sheets, the disruption of normal financing patterns, and the decline in output. This issue also explains why the macroprudential approach, reviewed next in this chapter, has such appeal as a framework for thinking about optimal capital regulation.

For now it is helpful to consider why uncertainty and liquidity discounts to asset prices matter in a crisis. Bernanke (2015) and Summers (2000) provide hints. Bernanke (2015, 399–400) discusses the slippery distinction between illiquidity and insolvency in a crisis:

> A firm that does not have the cash to meet its current obligations is said to be illiquid. An illiquid firm need not be insolvent; that is, the value of its assets may still exceed the value of its liabilities. However, in a panic, the distinction between illiquidity and insolvency quickly blurs. On the one hand, depositors and other short-term lenders likely would not run if they did not suspect their bank may be insolvent and thus likely to default. On the other hand, in a panic, even initially sound firms may be forced into insolvency, as fire sales and any economic slump resulting from the panic depresses the value of their assets. Major panics involve both illiquidity and insolvency, and so both short-term lending and injections of capital may be required to end them.

When a serious panic occurs, significant damage to the broader economy is almost inevitable. Amid fear and uncertainty, investors want to hold only the safest and most liquid assets. Lenders become ultraconservative, so credit disappears or remains available only to the best borrowers at high cost and under stringent conditions. The prices of riskier assets, like stocks and corporate bonds, may also fall sharply, reducing household wealth and companies' access to new capital. As credit tightens and asset prices fall, firms and households hit the pause button. Hiring, investing, and spending fall precipitously, pushing the economy into recession.

Summers (2000), writing just after the Asian financial crisis, emphasizes the importance of fundamentals in driving the likelihood of crises, despite the presence of multiple equilibria:

> Imagine that everyone who has invested $10 with me can expect to earn $1, assuming that I stay solvent. Suppose that if I go bankrupt, investors who remain lose their whole $10 investment, but that an investor who withdraws today neither gains nor loses. What would you do? Each individual judgment would presumably depend on one's assessment of my prospects, but this in turn depends on the collective judgment of all the investors.

> Suppose, first, that my foreign reserves, ability to mobilize resources, and economic strength are so limited that if any investor withdraws, I will go bankrupt. It would be a Nash equilibrium...for everyone to remain, but (I expect) not an attainable one. Someone would reason that someone else would decide to be cautious and withdraw, or at least that someone would reason that someone would withdraw, and so forth.

> Now suppose that my fundamental situation were such that everyone would be paid off as long as no more than one-third of the investors chose to withdraw. What would you do then? Again, there are multiple equilibria...but the more favorable equilibria seems much more robust.

> ...this thought experiment captures something real. On the one hand, bank runs or their international analogues do happen. On the other hand, they are not driven by sunspots: their likelihood is driven and determined by the extent of fundamental weaknesses.[28]

Three recent empirical studies back up the conjectures of Bernanke and Summers about an important link between perceived solvency and runs. Examining the short-term balance sheets of 44 US bank holding companies over the 2000–13 period, Pierret (2015) finds that a bank's capital shortfall under stress determines how much short-term debt it can raise. She reports that both the book leverage ratio (capturing pure solvency risk) and the market-to-book ratio (capturing how fast market values fall compared with book ratios) are important factors in explaining US banks' access to short-term funding. Her main conclusion is instructive: "The results suggest that capital not only acts as a loss-absorbing buffer but also ensures the confidence of creditors to continue to provide funding to the banks in a crisis" (p. 1).[29]

Studying a panel of 105 large international banks from 14 advanced economies over the 1994–2012 period, Gambacorta and Shin (2016) find that a higher capital ratio (leverage ratio) reduces the financing constraints faced by banks, not only lowering their cost of debt funding but also allowing them to raise more debt.

In their paper on the 2007 crisis in the asset-backed commercial paper market, Schroth, Suarez, and Taylor (2014) conclude that runs were more sensitive to the capital ratio (leverage) in such conduits than they were to their degree of maturity mismatch.

The relevance of all this for optimal capital calculations is that the final losses at banks observed several years after the crisis is over may not reveal much about how much capital banks need to discourage funding runs, no more than the ultimate cost of government interventions in a crisis reveals how much money was originally needed to make those interventions effective. Blinder and Zandi (2015) estimate the ultimate cost of the US federal government's policy response to the 2007–09 crisis at $1.6 trillion. In contrast, the original cost of that policy response was $12.3 trillion, almost eight times as high.

I am not saying that banks need to have enough capital to cover the most pessimistic tail of asset price declines during a financial panic. After all, as a result of Basel III, we now have two quantitative liquidity standards—the liquidity coverage ratio and the net stable funding ratio—that are meant to give banks a larger liquidity cushion and a less mismatched funding structure (than precrisis) to deal with future liquidity pressures.[30] In addition, we have a lender of last resort—the Federal Reserve for the United States—whose mandate, following Bagehot, should be to lend without limit during a panic to banks that are solvent. As Donald Kohn (2008, 264) the former vice chair of the Federal Reserve, argues, "How far into the tail of the distribution of possible outcomes should intermediaries be required to insure themselves: Shouldn't the Federal Reserve take some of the liquidity tail risk, to facilitate intermediation of illiquid credits, as was intended at its founding?"

Still, just because we have liquidity standards and a lender of last resort does not mean that an additional capital cushion, beyond expected losses, would not be helpful in deterring funding runs (as long as it is not too expensive), much in the same way that a higher stock of international reserves, other things equal, helps deter currency crises.

This is especially so given that there are practical limits to how far liquidity standards and emergency liquidity support can go. Unlike higher capital requirements, a higher liquidity coverage ratio operates (exclusively) on the asset side of the balance sheet. This implies that if one wanted to extend the liquidity coverage ratio beyond its current 30-day own liquidity standard, this extension would presumably come at the cost of less availability of bank lending. In addition, letting liquidity run ahead of solvency is not without its own dangers. As my late colleague Michael Mussa was fond of noting, "There is one thing worse than a solvent bank that is illiquid: It is an insolvent bank that is liquid." The latter is a recipe for gambling for resurrection and, ultimately, much higher bank losses.

As to limits on the lender of last resort, I point to one of the few missteps in the Dodd-Frank Act (Sections 101 and 103), which put unhelpful limits on the Federal Reserve's emergency lending authority. The Federal Reserve can no longer lend in an emergency to an individual institution unless it is part of a program or facility with broad-based eligibility.[31] This restriction is potentially serious, because failure to intervene to address the liquidity problem of a solvent G-SIB could, via contagion, lead to liquidity and solvency problems elsewhere in the economy.

For these reasons, I think the optimal capital calculation should include a capital cushion (perhaps of a few hundred basis points) beyond that dictated by observed/counterfactual losses in a severe crisis. In Summers' terms, this cushion against uncertainty/liquidity discounts during the apex of a crisis would act as a "fundamental" in discouraging funding runs. By making it clearer that a bank was solvent in a severe crisis, a larger capital cushion would also make it easier for the bank to qualify for emergency financial assistance from the lender of last resort if that assistance were needed.[32] As I argue later in this chapter, the social cost of such a cushion seems affordable.

Macroprudential Approach to Banking Supervision

A second route to the higher minimum capital conclusion is via the implications of the macroprudential approach to supervision. Greenlaw et al. (2012) provide a good analysis of the difference between the micro and macro perspectives. They describe the micro approach as focusing on bank capital as a buffer against losses, shielding the deposit insurance agency, and resolving insolvent banks promptly to protect taxpayers. In contrast, the macro approach focuses on maintaining the balance sheet capacity of the banking system to support the economy, averting runs by wholesale creditors on systemic banks, avoiding fire sales and bank deleveraging during periods of stress, and understanding the links between banks and nonbanks.

Greenlaw et al. draw several implications from the macro approach that merit mention. With substantial reliance on uninsured wholesale financing, the "run point" for a systemic bank happens at a higher capital ratio than the solvency point, so such banks need more capital to avoid runs. To support the weaker parts of the financial system during periods of stress, even solvent banks may be required to resist drawing down their capital. When there is a need for recapitalization, the targets should be translated into absolute amounts of capital, thereby eliminating the incentive for banks to meet the target by shrinking their loan base or engaging in fire sales of assets. Stress test scenarios need to consider the liability as well as the asset side of the balance sheet, along with fire sales, common exposures, and runs by wholesale creditors. The relevant bottom line is that to discourage runs that have costly macroeconomic effects, the banking system needs higher capital.

Another important implication of the macro or systemic approach is that one should draw a distinction between the inherent riskiness of an asset and its systemic importance, where the latter arises from the way financial intermediaries' claims are interwoven. Morris and Shin (2008, 252–53) bring out this point clearly:

> A leverage constraint has the potential to prevent the buildup in leverage that leaves the system vulnerable to sudden reversal. The idea is that the maximum leverage constraint is a binding constraint on the upside of the cycle, when funding conditions for banks are ample and banks can increase their leverage easily. The buildup of excessive leverage makes the system vulnerable to an increase in haircuts....
>
> It is important to emphasize here the difference in rationale between the leverage constraint considered here and the traditional risk-based capital requirement.... The credit risk of reverse repos is small, so that under the Basel-style regulation, the required capital is likewise small. However, a leverage constraint would have the effect of mitigating the externalities generated by the fluctuations in funding constraints in a market-based financial system built around secured lending.[33]

Two recent examples illustrate this macroprudential perspective. Boston Fed President Eric Rosengren (2014) lamented the fact that more than seven years after the collapse of Lehman Brothers, US broker-dealers still obtained over half their funding from the short-term repo market. In addition, US money market mutual funds are the largest net suppliers of repurchase agreement financing. Despite some postcrisis reforms to the money market industry, Rosengren does not dismiss the possibility that, as in the 2007–09 crisis, there could again be serious interruptions in repo financing from money market funds, with cascading effects on broker-dealer liquidity. His recommendation is that since highly capitalized institutions are much less subject to runs, there should be an increase in capital for any bank holding company with significant broker-dealer operations.

Rosengren's concern about potential runs from wholesale creditors is not a special case confined to the United States. Greenlaw et al. (2012), drawing on IMF (2010a) research, point out that among 14 advanced economies examined, the United States had one of the lowest ratios of dependence on wholesale funding relative to bank capital; the euro area had a much higher ratio.

A second example—highlighted by Turner (2014) and Shin and Turner (2015)—concerns the (post–2008–09 crisis) shift from bank lending to market-based debt financing by nonfinancial corporations in emerging-market economies. Turner shows that during 2010–13, financing of emerging-market nonbanks by international bonds was about twice as large as cross-border lending by international banks (to these borrowers). Shin and Turner highlight that an important driver of dollar bond issuance by non-US nonbanks has been the lower term premium in global bond markets. In contrast, dollar-denominated international bank lending responds more to short-term interest rates. This shift has resulted in longer maturities and less rollover risk; the concern is that the availability of market funding is very procyclical and that funding strains could develop when interest rates eventually go up significantly in the advanced economies. Indeed, Shin and Turner underscore the now heightened sensitivity of emerging economies to global long-term interest rates. In addition, Turner notes that, on the whole, there is little evidence that the recent surge in capital market borrowing by emerging-market corporates has been accompanied by either increases in their exports or the payoff of earlier external bank loans.

Worries about currency mismatches are particularly high where corporate borrowers (such as property developers in China or utility firms in India) do not have a ready source of foreign exchange earnings and/or currency-hedging facilities are limited. These key trends in emerging-market external financing will not leave emerging-market banks unaffected. Turner (2014) draws attention to the fact that nonfinancial corporate deposits in some emerging economies stand at over 20 percent of the banking system's total assets. If these firms lose access to nonbank financing, they may have to run down their bank deposits, causing funding problems for banks.[34] In addition, if the economy slows in the face of external interest rate contagion, recovery of domestic loans by emerging-market banks may also suffer. These risks point to the desirability of increased bank capital.

Benefits and Costs of Much Higher Bank-Capital Requirements

Yet a third road to the conclusion that regulatory bank-capital requirements are not high enough is via benefit-cost evaluations of the Basel III minimums and/or of (hypothetical) much higher minimums. The benefits are typically taken to be a lower probability and cost of (systemic) banking crises, with the attendant lower output and employment losses and lower fiscal costs (with most of the fiscal cost coming not from net resolution costs for distressed financial institutions but rather from the reduced tax revenue associated with weaker output growth).[35] The costs of higher capital requirements are assumed to be higher bank funding costs, higher interest rates on bank loans, and reduced availability of bank loans, with negative effects on economic growth.[36,37] Some analysts go farther, translating both the costs and benefits of higher capital ratios into levels of real GDP, thereby allowing them to solve for the capital ratio that maximizes net benefits in terms of GDP (BCBS 2010a, Cline 2017).

Perhaps not surprisingly, the banking industry's evaluation of this benefit-cost calculus is much less favorable than that of both the official sector and, by now, most finance academics.[38] Indeed, while not denying that bank capital was (with hindsight) too low in the run-up to the Great Recession, the industry has often taken the view that it is too difficult to get a good estimate of the benefits of higher bank capital on banking crises (IIF 2010) while simultaneously producing many estimates of the costs of higher bank capital (and accompanying financial regulation) for banks and the wider economy. In contrast, many supporters of higher capital standards have argued that the costs of inadequate bank capital after the 2007–09 global crisis should by now be self-evident and that finding theoretical and/or empirical evidence for large social costs of higher bank capital is a stretch (Admati and Hellwig 2013a).

Illustrative of how wide the gulf between industry and official estimates of the impact of higher capital requirements is, in 2010 the Institute of International Finance (IIF 2010) estimated that full implementation of banking reform (of which higher capital standards in Basel III were the most important element) would (via higher lending spreads and lower loan volumes) drive down G-3 GDP growth by 60 basis points a year over the 2011–15 period. In contrast, based on the analysis of the Macroeconomic Assessment Group composed of nearly 100 macroeconomic modeling experts from the world's largest central banks, supervisory institutions, and international financial organizations, the FSB and BCBS (2010b) concluded that the negative growth impact of the higher Basel III bank capital requirements would be on the order of 5 basis points per year for five years—about 1/12th the IIF's estimate (Cecchetti 2014).

Why the Social Costs of Higher Bank Capital Are Low

In making the case that the social costs of higher bank capital are low, Admati and Hellwig (2013a, 2013b) and other proponents stress the following arguments based on first principles. Unlike reserve requirements, bank capital is not something that banks must hold in a strong box, at the expense of higher lending; capital requirements are about how banks are permitted to fund themselves. True, because of favorable tax treatment of debt (relative to dividends), subsidies granted to too big to fail banks, deposit insurance, bankruptcy costs, and principal-agent problems, the Modigliani-Miller (1958) theorem about the total cost of financing being invariant to the mix of debt and equity does not hold strictly in the real world. Still, its fundamental insight—that higher equity reduces the riskiness of both equity and debt and therefore lowers the required rate of return, blunting any sizable increase in overall financing costs—is a much better approximation than the doomsday claims of the banking industry. In any well-functioning financial market, required rates of return are a function of risk, and the risk on any security depends on the firm's overall funding mix. Empirical studies that adopt the assumption that the required return of equity is fixed and independent of the funding mix to arrive at high estimates of the cost of stricter equity requirements are seriously flawed. Contrary to what one often hears, the argument for much higher equity requirements does not depend on the proposition that the funding mix of banks is irrelevant. Instead, it is based on the argument that the overall benefit-cost ratio for society would be more favorable if the funding mix for banks were tilted more toward higher equity, because overborrowing by banks leads to a fragile and inefficient financial system (Admati and Hellwig 2013a).

There is no reason why higher capital requirements must reduce bank lending. If banks are required to meet higher capital requirements by specifying these requirements in terms of absolute amounts of capital (rather than by deleveraging to meet a ratio) and higher capital is obtained by a combination of new equity issuance, retained earnings, and a temporary suspension of dividend payments, the effects on the economy are likely to be benign. With more equity, banks have more funds, which they can use to make more loans. Any adverse selection and signaling effects of new equity issuance can be minimized by increasing capital requirements across the board. The dilution argument against higher equity is overstated. With increased equity issuance, the shareholder gets a smaller piece of a bigger pie rather than a larger piece of a smaller pie. Whether the former combination is inferior to the latter depends on what return the bank earns on the new financing relative to its borrowing cost (Admati and Hellwig 2013b). If banks have higher equity and still decide not to make more loans, it is likely that they have incentives to focus on other investments, perhaps because risk-weighted capital metrics penalize business loans relative to, say, investment in government bonds. Bank credit crunches typically occur when banks have very low levels of equity, not high ones. More equity increases the ability of banks to continue lending in downturns because they are under less financial stress.

Considerable empirical evidence is available on the cost of higher equity requirements. Several groups of studies merit mention.

Bank Capital and Macroeconomic Performance

The first group of studies looks at observed capital ratios on the one hand and various measures of macroeconomic performance on the other. It contains both time series and cross-section evidence, at various levels of aggregation. Almost uniformly these studies find no evidence that lower capital ratios hurt economic performance. In fact, the evidence is far more supportive of the reverse conclusion.

A few examples underline the point. Examination of more than 100 years of data from the United States (including data from before the establishment of the Federal Reserve) and the United Kingdom, including subperiods in which ratios of bank equity to bank assets were more than five times higher than today's minimum (leverage) requirement, finds no statistically significant link between higher bank equity on the one hand and interest rate spreads on bank loans or economic growth on the other (Hanson, Kashyap, and Stein 2011; Miles 2011). Drawing on an even longer set of historical data for Switzerland, Junge and Kugler (2013) reach the same conclusion.

Bank Capital and Loan Growth

In a similar rebuff to the banking industry's claims, researchers find that loan growth was actually higher for better-capitalized banks. EBA Chair Andrea Enria (2015) finds evidence for this relationship for EU banks during the 2011–12 banking crisis; Cohen and Scatigna (2014) find the same relationship for an international sample of large banks over the

2009–12 period.[39] Drawing on a sizable sample of large international banks, Cohen (2013) reports that asset growth over the 2009–12 period was higher for banks that had higher starting capital ratios in 2009. He finds no independent effect of the change in the capital ratio on asset growth.

A particularly strong set of evidence indicating that better-capitalized banks lend more than weakly capitalized ones comes from the BIS study by Gambacorta and Shin (2016). They look at 105 consolidated banking institutions from 14 advanced economies (11 G-10 countries plus Austria, Australia, and Spain) over the 1994–2012 period. These banks represent over 70 percent of worldwide banking assets. The authors find that, after holding other factors constant, a 1 percentage point increase in the equity to total assets ratio is associated with a 0.6 percent increase in total lending growth. They conclude that "these results indicate that a larger capital base reduces the financing constraint faced by banks, allowing them to supply more loans to the economy" (p. 19).

Bank Capital, Funding Costs, and Loan Rates

Another group of studies uses one or more finance or accounting models to estimate the impact of hypothetical or planned increases in minimum capital requirements on banks' overall funding costs and/or lending rates. Those increases in costs are then fed into either a large econometric model of the economy or a production function to gauge the impact on economic growth. In the former case, the increase in lending rates reduces investment and consumption and, in turn, the level of GDP (see, for example, BCBS 2010a, 2010b; Fender and Lewrick 2015). In the latter case, the higher relative price of capital induces substitution away from it, and the smaller volume of capital produces a lower level of output (see, for example, Miles, Yang, and Marcheggiano 2012 and Cline 2017).

When it comes to estimating the impact of higher capital on banks' weighted-average funding costs, practices range from back-of-the-envelope calculations to dependence on loan pricing formulas to more formal econometric studies using the Fama-French (2004) expanded version of the (Lintner-Sharp) capital asset pricing model.

Two examples are illustrative of this literature. After conducting time series regressions for US banks that finds no statistically significant link between loan spreads and capital ratios, Kashyap, Stein, and Hanson (2011) conclude that they cannot reject the Modigliani-Miller full offset.[40] They then focus on a prominent deviation from Modigliani and Miller—namely, that interest payments on corporate debt are tax deductible while dividend payments on equity are not. Using illustrative figures for the interest rate on debt, they simulate the effects of a 10 percentage point increase in capital ratios on the weighted (debt plus equity) average cost of capital. In the first case, equity replaces long-term debt; in the second case it replaces short-term debt. Their bottom line is that the increases to the weighted cost of capital are modest: 25 to 35 basis points for a 10 percentage point increase in capital (leverage) ratios (or a 2.5- to 3.5-basis-point increase for a 100-basis-point increase in the capital ratio).[41]

Elliott, Salloy, and Santos (2012) introduce a loan pricing formula that expresses the notion that the interest rate on a bank loan needs to cover the cost of capital and other funding sources, expected credit losses, and administrative expenses.[42] They then use this loan pricing formula to estimate the increase in bank lending spreads that would result from the Basel III reforms. In so doing, they assume a 50 percent Modigliani-Miller offset, a 12 percent required rate of return on equity, and a 10 percent cut in expenses. They conclude that Basel III would raise US bank lending rates by 28 basis points.[43]

In studies that use the loan pricing formula approach, two important factors are the assumptions made about the required rate of return on equity and operating expenses. Many studies assume (incorrectly) that the required rate of return on equity remains unchanged (usually at its historical average for the 1993–2007 period of 15 percent), even as the capital ratio increases substantially.[44] According to estimates by the Basel Committee on Banking Supervision (BCBS 2010a), reducing the required rate of return on equity from 15 to 10 percent narrows the loan spread needed to recover the cost of a 100-basis-point increase in the capital ratio from 15 to 7 basis points. The *Financial Times* reports that the world's 12 largest investment banks recorded an average return on equity of 6.7 percent in 2015.[45]

Supporters of retaining the historical return on equity maintain that if banks were not to do so in the face of a rise in the cost of their liabilities, the resulting profit decline would induce resources to leave the banking industry and that such a shrinkage would be bad for economic growth. However, as I show in chapter 8, recent empirical research has overturned the finding of a positive link between finance and growth (at all levels of financial depth). It shows that beyond a certain threshold (which US and EU financial systems have already passed), larger banks, a larger banking system, and a larger financial system as a whole become a drag on economic growth, not a spur to it.

Most earlier studies also assumed that banks do not respond to a rise in financing costs by cutting expenses, an assumption that is suspect. The BCBS (2010a) estimates that a 4 percent reduction in operating expenses would be sufficient to offset the effects of a 1 percentage point increase in the capital ratio. Eliott, Salloy, and Santos (2012) note that banks can respond to cost increases in at least eight ways: lowering returns to shareholders; reducing funding costs (e.g., paying less for deposits and borrowed funds); reducing expenses; decreasing expected credit losses; limiting regulatory impacts through technical means; rationing credit; raising prices for credit; and restructuring their business. Their work suggests that there is more than one path to arriving at the conclusion that an (across the board) 800-basis-point increase in leverage ratios would generate a 20-basis-point increase in overall bank lending spreads.

In discussing how European banks should respond to recent challenges, including negative interest rates, Nouy (2016, 3) notes:

> Banks could expand their noninterest business operations. And we indeed observe that banks compensate for lower interest income by increasing their fees. There is at least some evidence that banks tend to offer fee-based products to clients as substitutes for interest-based products.... The role of interest income seems to be slowly decreasing. Another option for banks would be to cut their costs and increase their efficiency.[46]

In interpreting the results on the cost of higher bank-capital ratios, Fender and Lewrick (2015) make two points that bear repeating. First, many lending rate estimates—including the much-referenced study by the BCBS (2010a)—are too high, because they fail to incorporate any Modigliani-Miller offset.[47]

Second, the impact of higher capital on bank lending and GDP need not be negative. Fender and Lewrick (2015) cite empirical studies by Gambacorta and Shin (2015) and Buch and Prieto (2014) that find a positive long-term relationship between bank capital and loan volume. Their results suggest that "higher capitalization levels tend to have no negative effects on spreads and output in the long run" (Fender and Lewrick 2015, 54–55).

Effect of Higher Capital Ratios on Debt Funding Costs of Banks

The most powerful piece of recent empirical evidence on the impact of higher bank capital on bank funding costs appears in the BIS study by Gambacorta and Shin (2016), who draw on a comprehensive database of 105 large banks in 14 advanced economies over the 1994–2012 period. They examine the impact of a higher leverage ratio on the average cost of debt funding, holding other factors (macroeconomic controls, the lagged dependent variable, bank-specific characteristics, and bank or time fixed effects) constant.[48] They find that a 1 percentage point increase in the equity to total assets ratio is associated with approximately a 4-basis-point reduction in the average cost of debt funding. They then use this estimate—along with data on the average bank in their sample—to calculate the overall change in the cost of bank funding caused by a 1 percentage point increase in the leverage ratio. Their answer is 3 basis points—and they argue that even this modest estimate probably overstates the true effect:

> As small as this estimate of 3 basis points is, there are reasons to believe that even this modest number is an overestimate, as we have assumed for simplicity that the cost of equity funding remains fixed at 10 percent, even as the funding mix shifts toward equity. Overall, the conclusion based on our sample is that a shift in the funding mix toward equity results in an overall change in the funding cost of the bank that is small, and possibly even negligibly small. (p. 16)

An 800-Basis-Point Increase in G-SIB Leverage Ratios: Effect on G-SIB Funding Costs and G-SIB Lending Rates

Suppose, following the estimates of Gambacorta and Shin (2016) and of Hanson, Kashyap, and Stein (2011), that each 100-basis-point increase in capital ratios generates no more than, say, a 2.5- or 3.5-basis-point increase in banks' overall funding cost. Suppose further that the leverage ratio rises by 800 basis points for US G-SIBs—the increase that would be necessary to raise the average tangible leverage ratio (in US GAAP terms) and the average tier 1 leverage ratio (for US G-SIBs) from their current levels of roughly 8 and 9 percent, respectively (see table 7.1 in chapter 7) to a target of, say, 16 percent. Assume further that the annual increases in the required leverage ratios occur evenly, at a pace of a little less than 1 percent (0.8 percent) a year. We would then be talking about a cumulative increase of G-SIB funding costs over a period of, say, 10 years of approximately 24 basis points. If we assume that G-SIBs pass on 80 percent of their increase in funding costs to customers, the cumulative increase in G-SIB lending rates would be roughly 20 basis points. And since G-SIBs represent just over 60 percent of US total (bank holding company) assets, the increase in overall bank lending rates would be smaller yet—about 12 basis points.[49]

Comparing Increases in G-SIB Funding Costs to the Too Big to Fail Interest Rate Subsidy

One way to put (estimated) increases in G-SIB funding costs in perspective is to compare them to estimated annual bank funding effects of too big to fail (TBTF) subsidies for systemically important banks (SIBs). The IMF (2014a) and Acharya, Anginer, and Warburton (2014) made these estimates, using a variety of analytical approaches, including comparison of yields on similar bonds for similarly capitalized SIBs and non-SIBS, comparison of credit ratings for SIBs and non-SIBs, and collateral claims analysis of SIBs and non-SIBs.[50] They produce separate estimates for different regions (the United States, the euro area, Japan, and the United Kingdom), for commercial banks and investment banks, and for normal and distressed/crisis periods. They find that the average annual interest subsidy for US SIBs over the 1990–2010 period was 28 basis points; at the peak of the 2007–09 crisis, it rose to 120 basis points.[51]

In the IMF (2014a) estimates, the annual too big to fail subsidy was lowest for US SIBs—at roughly 15 basis points in normal periods, rising to 75 basis points for a distressed SIB. The IMF (2014a) estimates of the too big to fail subsidies were higher for Japanese and UK SIBs (60 basis points in the collateral claims analysis) and highest for euro area SIBs (90 basis points); see table 4.2. Estimated subsidies were also higher for US SIBs that were (previously) investment banks than for other US SIBs. Taking SIBs as a group across the United Sates, euro area, United Kingdom, and Japan, the estimated too big to fail subsidies are suggestive of annual bank funding discounts that are as large as or larger than the estimated cumulative funding effects of much heightened capital requirements.[52]

Admati (2014) argues that such estimates of too big to fail subsidies likely underestimate their size, because large banks have more opaque structures than small banks or nonbank corporations and this greater opacity makes it harder to measure the significant risks that they undertake.[53] She concludes that since the subsidy comes from public funds, reducing or eliminating it does not represent a social cost.

One can go farther. If risk taking by too big to fail banks generates large negative externalities, then merely offsetting the existing funding subsidy to those firms is not sufficient. One should instead be considering a tax on those banks to disincentivize such excessive risk taking.

Lessons for the Effects of Higher Capital Requirements from the Basel III Reform

Yet another group of studies—motivated in part by the uncertainties and limitations of the other approaches—concentrates on particular historical episodes when minimum bank-capital requirements were increased significantly to ascertain the likely implications for bank funding cost and loan availability. One such episode that has attracted considerable attention is the 2009–13 period, which is attractive for study on at least five grounds.

First, the increase in minimum (risk-weighted) capital requirements was considerable (even if it did start from an extremely low point). Basel III raised the minimum for common equity tier 1 capital from 2 to 7 percent of risk-weighted assets (exclusive of G-SIB surcharges). In terms of Basel III

Table 4.2   Summary of the estimates of implicit too big to fail subsidies

Estimation method	Advantages	Shortcomings	Average subsidy value for SIBs (in 2013)
	Contingent claims analysis approach		
Difference between the fair-value CDS spread computed from equity prices and the observed CDS spread	Controls for bank characteristics Controls for economies of scale and scope	CDS data available only for a limited number of banks CDS data may not be reliable during market turmoil Assumes equity holders are not bailed out	Euro area: Around 90 basis points Japan: Around 60 basis points United Kingdom: Around 60 basis points United States: Around 15 basis points
	Ratings-based approach		
Estimation of rating uplift from government support, which is translated into a credit spread based on the historical relationship between credit ratings and bond spreads	Controls for bank characteristics Controls for economies of scale and scope Effect of moral hazard is limited	Relies on credit ratings Ratings are slow to adjust	Euro area: Around 60 basis points (60 basis points for a distressed SIB) Japan: Around 25 basis points (75 basis points for a distressed SIB) United Kingdom: Around 20 basis points (75 basis points for a distressed SIB) United States: Around 15 basis points (75 basis points for a distressed SIB)

CDS = credit default swap; SIBs = systemically important banks, defined as global SIBs plus the three largest banks by asset size in each country. Basis point estimates are for a one-year period.

Source: IMF (2014a).

fully loaded equivalents, the percentage increase was larger still (Cecchetti 2014).

Second, the actual (fully loaded Basel III) common equity tier 1 capital ratios held by the world's largest banks increased markedly over this period, with the average for 103 large global banks increasing by 4.5 percentage points between end-2009 and end-2013, from 5.7 percent (of risk-weighted assets) to 10.3 percent (Cecchetti 2014). The increase in the numerator of that capital ratio was also over 4 percent; the increase in the capital ratio was thus not driven by a decrease in the denominator.

Third, this period was a challenging one for bank recapitalization, with the memory of bank failures and near failures still fresh in investors' minds, the recovery from the global crisis of 2007–09 still relatively weak, and a sovereign debt and bank funding crisis in the euro area.

Fourth, and going somewhat in the other direction, Basel III allowed a gradual phase-in of the heightened common equity requirement, with the process mandated to start in 2013 but not required to be completed until 2019. This gave banks some leeway to build much of the required capital via (perceived less costly) retained earnings rather than to have to rely principally on other mechanisms.[54]

Fifth, the 2009–13 period offers a comprehensive dataset on how the world's largest banks adjusted to higher capital requirements and the accompanying bank performance and macroeconomic outcomes. Because the sample of 94 banks assembled by Cohen and Scatigna (2014) includes significant institutions from the main global financial centers, as well as banks from smaller centers and emerging economies, the findings are broad and permit some important regional differences to be identified.[55]

The most thorough analysis of the 2009–13 bank capital adjustment is by Cecchetti (2014), who updates the bank data reported in Cohen and Scatigna (2014) and analyzes it in concert with recent BIS information on bank performance and macroeconomic outcomes.[56] His main conclusions merit emphasis:

- Although banks had until 2019 to meet the Basel III equity requirement, end-2013 capital requirements already exceeded the 2019 requirement—an outcome that Cecchetti attributes to the working of market discipline in tough times, as banks sought to demonstrate their strength to investors by meeting future requirements early.

- With the exception of European banks, there was an increase in banks' total assets, not the asset shrinkage typically forecast by the banking industry to be the handmaiden of higher capital requirements.[57]

- There was considerable regional variation in changes to the composition of assets. US and euro area banks reduced their riskiness (as measured by the changes to the ratio of risk-weighted assets to total assets), and in so doing raised their risk-weighted capital ratios; the reverse was true in the rest of the world.

- The main driver of the rise in capital ratios for the sample as a whole was an increase in capital itself, with the remainder made up by a decline in risk-weighted assets.

- For the sample as a whole, retained earnings accounted for approximately two-thirds of the increase in capital. Of the remaining one third, net capital issuance accounted for the largest component.

Table 4.3 Profitability of major global banks (percent of total assets)

Country	Pre-tax profits		Net interest margin		Operating costs	
	2000–07	2013	2000–07	2013	2000–07	2013
Australia	1.58	1.28	1.96	1.79	1.99	1.11
Brazil	2.23	1.62	6.56	3.55	6.21	3.28
Canada	1.03	1.06	1.74	1.65	2.73	1.78
China	1.62	1.86	2.74	2.38	1.12	1.01
France	0.66	0.32	0.81	0.92	1.60	1.16
Germany	0.26	0.10	0.68	0.99	1.36	1.55
India	1.26	1.41	2.67	2.82	2.48	2.36
Italy	0.83	−1.22	1.69	1.58	2.27	1.84
Japan	0.21	0.68	1.03	0.77	0.99	0.60
Russia	3.03	2.04	4.86	4.15	4.95	2.68
Spain	1.29	0.50	2.04	2.32	2.29	1.75
Sweden	0.92	0.77	1.25	0.98	1.34	0.84
Switzerland	0.52	0.36	0.64	0.61	2.39	1.90
United Kingdom	1.09	0.23	1.75	1.12	2.02	1.55
United States	1.74	1.24	2.74	2.32	3.58	3.03

Source: Cecchetti (2014). Reprinted with permission.

- Profitability, net interest margins, and operating costs were all lower (on average for the 15-country sample) in 2013 than in 2000–07 (table 4.3).[58] Cecchetti's interpretation is that to the extent that capital increases imposed costs, they were borne by equity holders in the form of lower dividends and managers in the form of lower compensation (the latter is included in operating costs).[59] He stresses that contrary to the predictions of the pessimists, there was no ballooning of interest margins.

- For macroeconomic indicators, Cecchetti looked, inter alia, at bank lending spreads and credit growth (figures 4.1 and 4.2). The main takeaway is that with the noteworthy exception of the euro area, lending spreads are down, while the ratio of bank credit to GDP is up more frequently than it is down.

- Cecchetti offers two explanations as to why euro area banks consistently appear as outliers. The first is the one I stressed in chapter 1: EU bank supervisors (particularly in the 2011 capital exercise) left open the door for undercapitalized banks to engage in serious deleveraging and risk weight manipulation by specifying capital targets in terms of a ratio rather than (as in the 2009 US SCAP) as an absolute amount of capital. It should be no surprise that much of the capital increase for EU banks took the form of lower total assets and lower risk-weighted

Figure 4.1   Lending spreads in selected economies, 2007–14

basis points

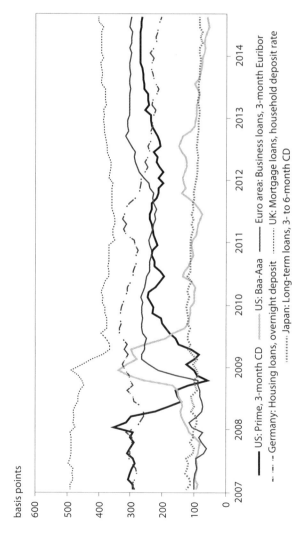

US: Prime, 3-month CD ——— US: Baa-Aaa ·········· Euro area: Business loans, 3-month Euribor
—··—·· Germany: Housing loans, overnight deposit ········· UK: Mortgage loans, household deposit rate
············ Japan: Long-term loans, 3- to 6-month CD

Source: Cecchetti (2014). Reprinted with permission.

Figure 4.2   Ratio of bank credit to GDP, 2006 and 2013

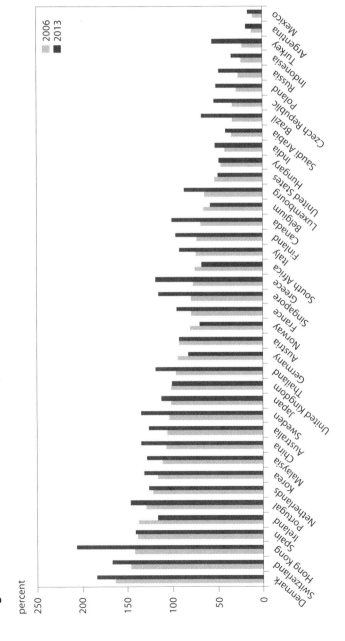

Source: Cecchetti (2014). Reprinted with permission.

assets rather than new equity issuance. The second explanation is that EU banks were suffering from a debt overhang, which made equity holders and managers reluctant to expand and/or to raise new equity because of fears that the fruits of that expansion would accrue to creditors rather than themselves (Squam Lake Working Group 2009, Admati and Hellwig 2013a, 2013b).[60]

Putting all of this together, Cecchetti (2014, 6) argues that the "jury is in" on the effect of higher capital standards:

> With the benefit of hindsight, even the optimists were too cautious. Capital has increased rapidly (in 2009–13) with very little impact on anything but bank profitability (and possibly managers' compensation). Lending spreads and interest margins are nearly unchanged, while (outside Europe) loan volumes and credit growth have remained robust. So, in the end, the macroeconomic impact has been small.[61]

The optimistic reading of the 2009–13 episode of bank capital increases in the United States has been echoed for banks in emerging Asia. Drawing on the Cohen and Scatigna (2014) database, McCauley (2014) reports that emerging-market banks raised their capital ratios over the 2009–2012 period by 1.1 percentage points. Their return on assets widened not because net interest margins grew but because operating costs fell, among other factors. Emerging-market banks did not shrink their loan books.[62] Indeed, loan growth rose by almost half over this period. McCauley's (2014, 3) conclusion is worth highlighting: "The evidence to date from Asia and the Pacific is that banks have managed to raise their capital ratios without raising the cost of credit in aggregate or by seriously restricting its availability."

Effects of Higher Bank Funding Costs on the Level of GDP

I turn next to the impact of higher bank funding costs on the long-run level of GDP. Not surprisingly, different assumptions about the Modigliani-Miller offset and the extent to which financing cost increases are passed through to bank customers (rather than absorbed by the banks) make a huge difference to estimates of the effect of increase in capital ratios on long-run GDP.

The BCBS (2010a) standard assumption—used in many optimal capital calculations—is that a 1-percentage-point increase in the (risk-weighted) capital ratio leads to a fall in long-run GDP of 12 basis points. By contrast, Miles, Yang, and Marcheggiano (2012)—who assume a 45 percent Modigliani-Miller offset—estimate a 5-basis-point decline, even assuming full pass-through of cost increases.

In my opinion the most helpful benchmark for gauging the effect of increased bank funding costs on the long-run level of GDP in the United States is the estimated effect of increases in the federal funds rate. A rule of thumb is that a 100-basis-point increase in the federal funds rate (which boosts the entire term structure of interest rates) reduces the level of real GDP by about 100 basis points over eight quarters.[63] A similar increase in the overall bank lending rate should deliver just a fraction of that effect, given its narrower impact.

Suppose we use this rule of thumb to estimate the effect on the level of US real GDP arising from a 20-basis-point increase in G-SIB lending rates—spread over a 10-year period—induced by a cumulative 800-basis-point increase in G-SIB leverage ratios. To begin with, we need to recognize that a 20-basis-point increase in G-SIB lending rates represents only about a 12-basis-point increase in overall bank lending rates because G-SIBs account for 62 percent of total consolidated bank-holding company assets in the United States.[64] Assume that the federal funds rate impacts 100 percent of financial activity in the nonfinancial private sector; as Stein (2013) puts it, monetary policy gets in all the cracks of the financial system. Fed Vice Chair Stanley Fischer (2015a) has indicated that banks hold only one-third of the nonfinancial credit market debt in the United States; if we assume that a 1 percent increase in overall bank lending rates has roughly one-third the impact on the level of US GDP as a 1 percent increase in the federal funds rate, then a 12-basis-point increase in overall bank lending rates would generate only about a 4-basis-point decline in the long-run level of US GDP (.12 times .33 equals .0396)—a small amount.[65] In short, increases in overall bank lending rates on the order of 12 to 15 basis points—induced by an 800-basis-point increase in leverage ratios for G-SIBs, combined with smaller increases (in leverage ratios) for large non-G-SIB banks and for smaller banks—is likely to be so small as to be barely detectable in the macro data. Moreover, any macro effect could be easily offset by the Fed lowering the path (infinitesimally) for the funds rate. The main point is that since the impact of the fed funds rate is broader than that for bank lending rates, the 100-basis-point rule of thumb, appropriately scaled, sets an upper bound on what the long-run GDP impact in the United States could conceivably be. Estimates that suggest a much larger impact than that for the United States seem highly suspect.[66]

Benefits of Higher Bank-Capital Requirements

I look next at the expected benefits of higher capital requirements.[67] The basic idea is to calculate the expected yearly output gain associated with reducing the expected cost of a crisis, where that cost is the product of the probability of a crisis times the output loss (expressed as a share of the precrisis level of GDP).

Reduced Probability of a Banking Crisis

Suppose that the historical record indicates that the median output loss in a systemic banking crisis is 60 percent of GDP. Then the annual expected benefit of reducing the probability of a systemic banking crisis by 1 percent is 0.6 percent of GDP.[68]

A banking crisis can be defined in various ways. The most popular approach is to use an existing database on systemic and borderline banking crises, as Reinhart and Rogoff (2009) and Laeven and Valencia (2013) do. Laeven and Valencia (2013) define a banking crisis as systemic if (1) there are significant signs of financial distress in the banking system (as indicated by significant bank runs, losses in the banking system, and/or bank liquidations) and (2) significant banking policy intervention measures are taken in response to significant losses in the banking system. Once a crisis is defined and its average or median cost is known, the trick is to map the relationship between the probability of a crisis and the level of bank capital (BCBS 2010a). One way to do so is to rely on reduced-form econometric studies that estimate the historical link between banking crises and the level of bank capital, after holding other factors constant. A second way is to treat the banking system as a portfolio of securities and then use estimates of the volatility of asset prices and correlations of default across banks to derive a relationship between the probability of a crisis and bank capital. A third (albeit less popular) approach is to examine the link between declines in per capita income and declines in bank assets and to define a crisis as a case in which the decline in bank assets is equal to or greater than the existing level of bank capital (Miles, Yang, and Marcheggiano 2012).

A crucial feature of the modeling of the relationship between the probability of a crisis and the level of bank capital is that beyond a certain point it shows diminishing returns to higher levels of capital (i.e., the relationship between the two is concave).[69] In contrast, in modeling the effect of higher bank capital on lending rates and output, it is assumed that the relationship is linear. Once the decline in the probability of a crisis induced by higher capital hits zero, it does not matter how high the cost of a crisis is, because the expected cost is the product of the probability and the cost.

BCBS (2010a) examines a sample of banking crises from 1980 to 2009 in which the unconditional (annual) probability of incurring a banking crisis is about 4 percent or so.[70] With such a low probability, it does not take a huge amount of capital to reduce the crisis probability to such a low point that further increases in the capital ratio do not further reduce the probability of a crisis. This is typically decisive for the optimal level of capital, which is normally defined (in this branch of optimal capital theory) as the level of the capital ratio that maximizes the (positive) difference between the marginal benefits and the marginal costs. It should be no surprise then that estimates of the optimal capital ratio (translated into a leverage ratio) tend to be low (in the range of 3 to 8 percent).[71]

Effects of a Systemic Banking Crisis on Actual versus Potential Output

Evidence is accumulating that the output losses in banking crises are much larger than previously thought. Most of the earlier estimates of these losses assumed that they were mostly temporary (i.e., that the crisis did not have a large negative impact on potential output).

Haldane (2010) looks at the present value of output losses for the world from the 2007–09 crisis, assuming different shares of these losses (100, 50, and 25 percent) were permanent. When 50 percent of the losses are assumed to be permanent, losses amount to 170 percent of the world's 2009 GDP. This figure is much higher than the 60 percent output loss typically assumed in much of the earlier optimal capital literature.

Ball (2014a, 2014b) examines the effects of the Great Recession on potential and actual output in OECD countries. His two main findings are that (1) in most countries the loss of potential output from the Great Recession was almost as large as the loss of actual output and (2) in countries hardest hit by the recession, the growth rate of potential output is much lower today than it was before 2008.

Fender and Lewrick (2015) note that if one averages the estimates of Haldane (2010) and Ball (2014b), the loss of output for banking crises occurring during the Great Recession rises to about 200 percent of GDP. They then recalibrate the average output loss over the entire 1980–2014 period and find that the average output loss for a systemic banking crisis is 100 percent of GDP, not 60 percent.

This figure is also likely to be an underestimate. Using data on US recessions, Blanchard, Cerutti, and Summers (2015) find that potential output was seriously damaged not only during the Great Recession but in other recessions as well, with losses particularly marked during recessions generated by supply shocks (which in their classification include banking crises). This finding suggests that the output loss figures should be revised upward not just for the Great Recession banking crises but also for earlier banking crises (albeit not by the same percentage).

Figure 4.3   Occurrence of banking crises

number of systemic banking crises starting in a given year

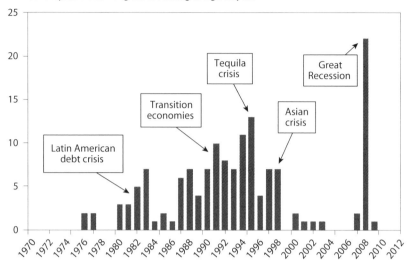

Source: Laeven and Valencia (2013).

Reasons for Skepticism about GDP-Based Estimates of Optimal Capital Ratios

Despite these large adjustments to estimates of output losses during banking crises, the implications for the (GDP-based) optimal capital ratio are likely to be relatively modest as long as the average crisis probability for the entire sample remains low. Some analysts take comfort from the "low" (3 to 8 percent in terms of leverage ratios) estimates of optimal capital ratios derived from this latter GDP-based branch of the literature. I do not, for five reasons.

First, the low average probability of systemic banking crises hides substantial variation in this probability across time—and these variations affect the optimal capital ratio. As Laeven and Valencia (2013) put it, banking crises occur in waves. The frequency of banking crises was particularly high not only in 2008 but also in 1987–98 (figure 4.3).[72] Striking a similar chord, Barth and Miller (2017), examining US banking crises over the entire 1892–2014 period, conclude that the optimal leverage ratio is much closer to 20 percent than to 5 percent.

Second, as Ricks (2016) notes and I discuss in chapter 8, the contemporary monetary landscape, especially in the United States, is very different than it was in say, the 1970s and 1980s. The rapid growth of shadow banking and, in particular, that sector's rapidly rising share of runnable, short-term private money claims in the (decade long) run-up to the 2007–09 crisis demonstrated a new source of financial fragility, with important potential spillover effects on the probability of future banking crises.[73] This shadow banking problem is not reflected adequately in the pre-1995 banking crisis data, and the post–2007–09 crisis reforms have not fully dealt with this vulnerability. Absent bolder reforms to this sector, there is no assurance that future banking crisis probabilities will be as low as suggested by the historical data.

Third, relying on the historical average of crises to guide capital adequacy decisions would have led—and probably did lead—US bank supervisors badly astray in the run-up to the 2007–09 crisis. The catastrophic tail of the loss distribution for US banks over the 1986–2005 period was simply not fat enough to generate the kind of capital ratios needed to protect against the huge banking losses that subsequently occurred (Kuritzkes and Schuermann 2007).

Fourth, the bottom-line conclusion of the optimal capital theory proponents—that current leverage ratios have made the banking system "safe enough"—flies in the face of recent market measures of bank risk. Sarin and Summers (2016a, 1; 2016b) examine stock price volatility, options-based estimates of future volatility, beta (from the capital asset pricing model), credit default swaps, earnings-price ratios, and preferred stock yields for major banks in the United States and worldwide. They conclude: "To our surprise, we find that financial market information provides little support for the view that major institutions (read banks) are significantly safer than they were before the (2007–09) crisis and some support for the notion that risks have actually increased."[74]

Fifth, the optimal capital approach embodies a different risk tolerance than some other approaches to assessing capital adequacy. When it comes to crisis prevention, it is often said "hope for the best, but prepare for the worst." Most of the optimal capital literature instead invokes "hope for the best, but prepare for the historical global average."[75] In contrast, the prevailing guidelines for adverse stress test scenarios are that they should be "severe but plausible." Plausible is a lower bar than likely—and one that has been adopted in view of the demonstrated perils of relying too heavily in the past on the historical average of crises. Similarly, the loan-loss approach can be thought of as akin to a minimax strategy, in which one prepares against the possibility of the worst crisis reoccurring. As Haldane (2010, 9) notes, when it comes to selecting which crises to focus on to guide crisis prevention, "paranoia can sometimes be an optimal strategy."[76]

Conclusions

No one should assign a high degree of precision to estimates of optimal capital ratios. None of the three approaches to estimating them (the bank losses approach, the macroprudential approach, and the cost-benefit approach) is comprehensive enough to cover all the relevant criteria that should weigh on such a choice. I therefore base my evaluation on the combined results of all three.

In addition, there are contentious theoretical and empirical issues over which reasonable people could differ, including: how best to measure bank losses in a severe crisis, the role of higher bank capital versus liquidity standards and emergency lender of last resort lending by the central bank in meeting funding runs during a crisis, the appropriate sizes of the Modigliani-Miller offset and the pass-through of funding cost increases to bank lending spreads, the preferred model for translating increases in bank lending spreads into decreases in the long-run level of output, the role of too big to fail subsidies in evaluating the social costs of higher capital requirements, and the inferences that can be drawn from average past banking crisis probabilities for future ones. Still, when all is said and done, the weight of the evidence points strongly to the desirability of much higher minimum capital ratios for large banks.

I think both the literature and the current consensus on optimal capital requirements underestimate the benefits of higher capital ratios by, inter alia, (1) not taking adequate account of what bank losses would have been in the absence of massive and far-reaching government crisis intervention measures during the 2007–09 global financial crisis, (2) not recognizing the liquidity and run-discouraging benefits of higher capital, and (3) not paying enough attention to the permanent output losses in past banking crises. Likewise, the costs of much heightened capital requirements have been much overstated by (1) ignoring the accumulating evidence that higher capital ratios lead to more bank lending, not less; (2) underestimating the beneficial effects of higher capital ratios on the availability and cost of debt financing (and not just new equity financing); (3) overestimating the pass-through of higher funding costs on to bank lending spread and (4) overestimating the effect of higher bank lending spreads on output. In addition, the literature often confuses private costs (to the banking industry) with social costs. If my central estimate—that an 800-basis-point increase in leverage ratios for US G-SIBs, implemented over a 10-year period, would be consistent with a cumulative increase in overall bank lending rates of only about 12 basis points—is right, then the macroeconomic costs of a quantum jump in loss absorbency are very small.

Endnotes

1. If the "voluntary" countercyclical capital surcharge were employed to its full extent (2.5 percent), the all-in top-end common equity tier 1 minimum for the most systemic US G-SIBs could (theoretically) be 14 percent.

2. In the 2016 CCAR test, the 33 participating BHCs were all subject to a 4 percent minimum tier 1 leverage ratio. In the CCAR tests undertaken in 2012–15, participating BHCs were subject to either a 3 or 4 percent minimum tier 1 leverage ratio (with the 3 percent minimum reserved for BHCs that had a high composite supervisor rating and had implemented the Federal Reserve Board's market-risk rule).

3. Some BCBS members, including the United States, include leverage requirements as part of their national banking regulation.

4. Some studies (e.g., Dagher et al. 2016) prefer instead to derive losses from nonperforming loans, adjusted for estimated recovery rates and loan-loss provisions.

5. According to Investopedia, a write-down is defined as reducing the book value of an asset because it is overvalued compared to its market value. This should be done when the carrying value of the asset can no longer be justified as fair value and the likelihood of receiving the cost (book value) is questionable at best. To remind, loan-loss provisions/reserves are meant to cover expected losses, whereas bank capital is meant to cover unexpected losses. When nonperforming loans increase, loan-loss provisions should also increase, and, ceteris paribus, net income falls. Falls in net income reduce retained earnings and deplete bank capital. Under the balance sheet framework, loan losses show up in the allowance for loan losses (loan-loss reserves), thereby reducing assets; the balancing item on the liability side is then a reduction in shareholders' equity, that is, a fall in bank capital. See Farag, Harland, and Nixon (2014) for a fuller description.

6. This distinction between wartime and peacetime situations of banks owes to Schuermann (2015), although he uses the terms to contrast a case in which bank supervisors (and stress test managers) do not have market credibility with a case in which they do. I use the terms in a more generic way.

7. One shortcoming of write-downs is that the propensity to recognize losses in bank financial statements for a given stock of nonperforming loans seems to differ significantly across countries (Aiyar et al. 2015). In other words, some losses will be hidden before they are reflected in write-downs. The same weakness also applies to estimates of bank losses derived from nonperforming loans since countries are sometimes tardy in classifying loans as nonperforming; similarly, banks can extend new loans to borrowers in difficulty just so they don't default on existing ones—a practice known as "evergreening"—without regard to the borrowers' prospective creditworthiness.

8. Vickers (2012, 12) expresses a view similar to that of Bernanke: "The term 'market failure' hardly lives up to what we have seen since 2007. The whole financial and hence economic system was on the verge of collapse."

9. Recall, too, that many smaller US financial institutions failed during the global financial crisis. Bulow, Goldfield, and Klemperer (2013) report that of the 413 US banks insured by the Federal Deposit Insurance Corporation (FDIC) that failed over the 2008–11 period, the loss to the FDIC, as a share of those banks total assets, was 14 percent or more in 90 percent of cases.

10. The 2009 Supervisory Capital Assessment Program (SCAP) used net income of banks in its stress test scenarios, but the results were announced after banks' capital positions had been bolstered by Troubled Asset Relief Program (TARP) capital injections, a three-year FDIC guarantee on new unsecured debt issues had been put in place, and the London G-20 Summit (of February 2009) had made it clear that G-20 leaders were not willing to countenance the failure of any more Lehmans. Put in other words, the SCAP results were released only after strong official flanking measures were taken to assure the market that the authorities viewed these banks as going concerns.

11. Because banks typically hold capital in excess of the regulatory minimum, there is a possibility that an increase in the regulatory minimum might not lead to an increase in actual capital ratios. Bridges et al. (2014) show, however, that increases in the regulatory minimums usually lead to increases in actual capital ratios, because banks tend to restore their buffers after an increase in the regulatory minimum. Gorton (2012) shows that banks' capital ratios during the 1881–1915 period were actually higher in countries without capital requirements than in those with them.

12. Looking only at bank losses as a guide to optimal capital is equivalent to assuming that banks can continue to operate at very low capital ratios after the crisis depletes their capital almost to zero. I find this assumption untenable.

13. The estimate for the euro area is an average that conceals a good deal of cross-country variation among its members.

14. The 7.6 percent loss figure for US banks is the simple average of the 8.2 percent (estimated) losses reported in the October 2009 *Global Financial Stability Report* and the 7.0 percent (estimated) losses from the April 2010 report.

15. The Federal Reserve did not switch to a common equity tier 1 measure until 2014 (see Board of Governors 2016a). The discrepancy between tier 1 common and common equity tier 1 is not large enough to significantly affect the estimates.

16. The exception is the Basel III leverage ratio, which uses total leverage exposure in the denominator. Total leverage exposure is typically larger than total assets for countries that use the US GAAP but approximately equal to it for countries that use IFRS accounting. I am grateful to Kevin Dowd for helpful conversations on this point.

17. The tier 1 leverage ratio is defined as tier 1 capital divided by total assets.

18. The tier 1 leverage ratio is the leverage ratio used in the US CCAR and DFAST stress tests. I was unable to find an officially blessed figure for the fully loaded Basel III leverage ratio for large US banks.

19. The estimate of the optimal leverage ratio for US banks would not be much affected by changing the date of the low point in the financial cycle from, say, late 2012 to either 2011 or 2014, because the tier 1 average ratio moves up slowly over this period.

20. The United Kingdom uses IFRS accounting standards. Dowd (2016c) notes that total leverage exposure for an average of major UK banks is very close to their total assets. No adjustments to bank losses are therefore needed to account for the difference between total assets and total leverage exposure exposure.

21. Dowd (2016a) compares different measures of leverage for UK banks over the 2007–15 period.

22. The quotation is from Peter Dettels, deputy director of the IMF's Monetary and Capital Markets Department ("IMF Urges 'Deep Reform' at European Banks," *Financial Times*, October 6, 2016).

23. Implicit in the Dagher et al. (2016) analysis is the assumption that, historically, post-crisis bank recapitalizations brought banks to the minimum level of capital needed to restore viability.

24. The analogous leverage ratio necessary to avoid public recapitalizations for 75 percent of the US banks affected would have been 10 percent. Vickers (2012) notes that €4.5 trillion of taxpayers' money was deployed to rescue banks in the European Union during the 2007–10 crisis.

25. See Afonso, Santos, and Traina (2014) and references cited in BIS (2015b).

26. In addition to the issue of ultimate bailout of bail-in bonds, I argue in chapter 8 that the size of the TLAC buffer is too small. Although all-in TLAC equal to 23.5 percent of risk-weighted assets sounds like a lot, it is much smaller once one accounts for the relatively low average ratio (40 percent) of risk-weighted assets to total assets for the 30 G-SIBs, which means that TLAC will represent less than 10 percent of G-SIBs' total assets. If the TLAC buffer proves too small, the chances of a public bailout increase. In chapter 7, I call for a considerably higher minimum average leverage ratio for US G-SIBs.

27. Later in this chapter I explain why a large increase in minimum leverage ratios is unlikely to be costly for the macroeconomy.

28. Morris and Shin (2009), extending Summers' (2000) example, show that successful coordination is achieved where the threshold and cost of coordination are both low.

29. Holmstrom and Tirole (1997) anticipated this conclusion by introducing a model where poorly capitalized firms are hit earliest and hardest when there is a credit crunch or a liquidity squeeze.

30. Morris and Shin (2009, 230) conclude that liquidity requirements on banks reduce the potential for runs through two channels: "They make debtor banks more robust to withdrawals, and they make creditor banks less trigger-happy."

31. See also Geithner (2016) and the discussion in chapter 5.

32. After studying Lehman's balance sheet just before its collapse, Cline and Gagnon (2013, 13), concluded that the firm was deeply insolvent. Wessel (2009) argues that after the government rescues of Bear Stearns, Fannie Mae, and Freddie Mac, Bernanke and Paulson were concerned about political backlash to any further bailouts. Paulson allegedly told Bernanke and Geithner, "I'm being called Mr. Bailout. I can't do it again."

33. Morris and Shin's (2008) point on a leverage ratio limiting the buildup of leverage during the upswing of the financial cycle also dovetails nicely with Geanakoplos's (2010) concern about the marked fluctuation in haircuts during the leverage cycle.

34. This example illustrates why looking at banks' loan to deposit ratios as a measure of stability can be misleading if one does not specify the kind of deposits (retail versus wholesale).

35. See, for example, BCBS (2010a, 2010b); Miles, Yang, and Marcheggiano (2012); Fender and Lewrick (2015); and Cline (2017) on the effect of higher capital ratios in reducing the probability of banking crises, and Reinhart and Rogoff (2009) on the fiscal costs of banking crises. Berger and Bouwman (2013) provide strong empirical evidence for US banks that higher capital ratios (measured as simple leverage ratios) increase the survival probabilities of medium-size and large banks during banking crises and the survival probabilities of small banks at all times (during crises and normal times). Using contingent claims analysis, Haldane (2012) estimates that a capital surcharge of about 7 percent for systematically important banks would reduce 90 percent of their expected

losses. Admati and Hellwig (2013b) and Admati (2016a, 2016b) emphasize that the benefits of higher bank capital extend well beyond just reducing the probability of crises.

36. On the effect of higher capital requirements on bank funding costs and/or lending spreads, see BCBS (2010a, 2010b); Kashyap, Stein, and Hanson (2010); Elliott, Salloy, and Santos (2012); Fender and Lewrick (2015); Gambacorta and Shin (2016); and Cline (2017).

37. Opponents of much higher capital requirements for banks also often argue that banking should rely more heavily on debt financing than nonfinancial sectors. Cline (2017), for example, emphasizes that as deposits amount to about half of assets for large (US) banks and much more for smaller banks, the deposit-taking nature of the banking sector inherently means that the ratio of debt (including debt to depositors) to assets will tend to be much higher than in most other sectors. Admati and Hellwig (2013b) concede that the Modigliani-Miller theorem is less important for deposits but maintain that its analytical approach is essential to the other borrowing that banks do, including short-term borrowing from money market funds and hedge funds, and to their equity. They note that banks do business with the same investors that buy shares and bonds of other corporations and that banks' funding mix affects funding costs and risks borne by investors in much the same way as it affects nonbank firms. While deposit taking may help explain why leverage is higher at banks than at nonfinancial firms, it does not explain why it is socially optimal for banks to have equity holdings that are so low relative to their total assets.

38. See, for example, the comparison of estimates of the impact of capital increases on bank lending spreads in Fender and Lewrick (2015).

39. Enria (2015, 2) observes that "there is plenty of evidence that banks that have been faster in complying with the new (Basel III capital) requirements are those that have experienced a greater growth in lending volumes, gaining market shares and attracting cheaper financing. Also at the micro-level, a positive correlation between the level of bank capital and loan growth is well established at the EU level, as well as in each Member State. Indeed, it is the group of banks with proper and credible capital buffers that have been able to maintain lending levels during the most difficult period of the crisis." Cohen and Scatigna (2014, 2) report that "banks that came out of the financial crisis with higher capital ratios and stronger profitability were able to expand lending more." Mervyn King (2013, 4), the former governor of the Bank of England, reached a similar conclusion: "Those who argue that requiring higher levels of bank capital will necessarily restrict lending are wrong. The reverse is true. It is insufficient capital that restricts lending. That is why some of our weaker banks are shrinking their balance sheets. Capital supports lending and provides resilience. And without a resilient banking system, it will be difficult to sustain a recovery."

40. Using data for US banks, Cline (2017) estimates a Modigliani-Miller offset of 45 percent.

41. Kashyap, Stein, and Hanson (2010) and Hanson, Kashyap, and Stein (2011) first assume that new equity displaces long-term debt and that the only effect on the bank's weighted-average cost of capital derives from the lost tax shield on debt. If the coupon on debt is 7 percent and the corporate tax rate is 35 percent, each percentage point of increased equity raises the weighted-average cost of capital by .07 times .35 = .0245 percent, or 2.45 basis points. Hence an 800 percentage point (across the board) increase in the capital requirement (leverage ratio) boosts the weighted-average cost of capital—and overall loan rates—by roughly 20 basis points. In their second case, they assume that equity replaces short-term debt, which they see as reflecting both capital and liquidity attributes. They

therefore assign the short-term debt a "money premium" of 100 basis points. Redoing the same calculation for this type of debt yields an increase in the weighted-average cost of capital of 28 basis points. Admati and Hellwig (2013b) argue that these kind of calculations overestimate the cost of higher bank capital because these are private, not social, costs.

42. The loan pricing formula of Elliott, Salloy, and Santos (2012, 25) is

$$L^* (1-t) \geq (E * re) + ((D * rd) + C + A - O) * (1-t),$$

where L is the effective interest rate on the loan, including the annualized effect of fees; t is the marginal tax rate for the bank; E is the proportion of equity backing the loan; re is the required rate of return on marginal equity; D is the proportion of debt and deposits funding the loan; rd is the marginal interest rate on debt; C is the credit spread, equal to the probability-weighted expected loss; A is the administrative expense and other expense related to the loan; and O is other income and expense items related to the loan.

43. The Elliott, Salloy, and Santos (2012) results for Basel III are not directly comparable to other cost of finance estimates, because they include not only capital increases but also the introduction of two new liquidity standards.

44. McKinsey and Company (2014) report that the average return on equity for a sample of the 500 largest global banks was 10 percent over the 1980–2014 period.

45. "Investment Banks Getting Hit from Two Sides," *Financial Times*, February 22, 2016.

46. Later in this chapter, I discuss the role of noninterest income in differentiating a "loans only" from a "loans plus" approach to the link between increased financing costs of banks and increases in their lending rates.

47. According to Fender and Lewrick (2015, 55) the BCBS (2010a) estimates are "(intentionally) biased upwards because they do not take into account that higher capital ratios will—over time—tend to reduce banks' funding costs.... Indeed, more recent studies confirm the conservative nature of the LEI [long-term economic impact] estimate, which—if anything—looks more conservative now than it did back in 2010." For "conservative," read a relatively low assessment of the benefits and relatively high assessment of the costs.

48. Gambacorta and Shin (2016) define the cost of funds as the total interest rate paid over the total level of debt (excluding equity and reserves). An advantage of the approach used by Gambacorta and Shin (2016) is that it sidesteps the problems (including "low risk anomaly") that have been encountered when researches have attempted to ascertain the size of the Modigliani-Miller offset by relying exclusively on equity returns of banks; see Baker and Wurgler (2015). See Fama and French (2004) on difficulties in applying the capital asset pricing model.

49. I consider most other estimates of the effect of increases in bank capital ratios on banks' overall funding costs less reliable than the Gambacorta and Shin (2016) and the Hanson, Kashyap, and Stein (2011) estimates. Cecchetti and Schoenholtz (2014) conclude that the relevant range is 3 to 9 basis points per 100-basis-point increase in the (risk-weighted) capital ratio. Translating an 800-basis-point increase in the US G-SIB leverage ratio into its risk-weighted capital equivalent (about 1,400 basis points) and selecting the lower end of their range would produce a cumulative increase in G-SIB funding costs of about 42 basis points (before making any assumptions about pass-through). As an example of an estimate that I regard as being at the very high end of the scale, the BCBS (2010a) multipliers imply that if the required rate of return on equity after a large capital

increase were 10 percent, then the same G-SIB leverage ratio increase that I assume above would imply an increase in G-SIB lending rates of roughly 100 basis points.

50. Collateral claims analysis uses balance sheet data and market prices of traded securities to assess the implied value and volatility of assets, credit risk, and contingent liabilities for a firm or bank (see IMF 2014a).

51. The banking industry (e.g., Goldman Sachs 2013) claims that a comparison of bond yields for US SIBs and non-SIBs shows that the average too big to fail subsidy is negligible or even negative since 2009. More careful study of those yields shows that once the comparison is properly adjusted for differences in bond characteristics (e.g., duration) and differences in leverage between SIBs and non-SIBs, a nontrivial positive too big to fail subsidy is apparent for the 2009–13 period (see IMF 2014a and Acharya, Anginer, and Warburton 2013).

52. Using the IMF (2014a) estimates, the unweighted average of the too big to fail funding discount across the four regional groups of SIBs (US, euro area, Japan, and UK) during normal times is 55 basis points. For US G-SIBs, the estimated subsidy in normal times (15 basis points) would offset about 60 percent of my estimated increase in G-SIB funding costs under a hypothetical 800-basis-point increase in G-SIB leverage ratios.

53. Freixas and Rochet (2008) provide a good example of such hard to measure subsidies to too big to fail banks. They note that the practical effect of a policy of ambiguity on lender of last resort assistance to banks really amounts to a transfer of wealth from small banks to too big to fail ones, because in a crisis the liabilities of too big to fail banks are almost always covered by the government or central bank whereas small banks are rescued only if they are solvent.

54. Myers and Majluf (1984) argued long ago that issuing new equity is the most costly method of increasing capital, because outsiders may view it as a signal that insiders see the shares as overvalued. The "pecking order" model of capital (also due to Myers) maintains that firms will finance investments out of cash whenever they can, sell debt only if cash flows are inadequate, and raise new equity only as a last resort. Hanson, Kashyap, and Stein (2011) argue that frictions in financial markets make a strong case for gradually phasing in much heightened capital requirements.

55. The Cohen and Scatigna (2014) sample includes all of the 29 institutions identified by the Financial Stability Board as G-SIBs. It covers almost two-thirds of the assets of the top 1,000 global banks listed by *The Banker* magazine.

56. Cecchetti previously served as chair of the Macroeconomic Assessment Group that produced the well-known BCBS (2010b) report with the FSB on the impact of the Basel III capital requirements.

57. Like Cohen (2013) and Cohen and Scatigna (2014) before him, Cecchetti (2014) reports that credit growth is higher for better-capitalized banks. He reports that a simple cross-sectional regression of bank credit growth (in 2006–13) on the level of the capital ratio (in 2006) yields a slope coefficient of 16.3. A one standard deviation increase in the initial capital ratio implies credit growing by an additional 44 percent over the 2006–13 period.

58. Operating costs are down for 14 of the 15 countries shown in table 4.3. The net interest margin fell in 11 countries and pretax profits fell in 11.

59. Cohen and Scatigna (2014) report that dividend payout ratios in their bank sample declined from 40 percent of net income in 2005–07 to 30 percent in 2010–12. For US banks, the decline was much larger (from 58 to 21 percent).

60. An example that is often used to illustrate debt overhang is that a homeowner with a mortgage that is well under water will not likely spend money for home repairs—even if those repairs boost the selling price of the home by several times the cost of the repair—because he fears that the benefits of the repairs will go exclusively to his creditors if he has to sell the house. Admati et al. (2015, 1) emphasize shareholder-creditor conflicts as a key reason why banks resist increases in capital ratios even when the costs are low: "In the absence of prior commitment or regulation, shareholder-creditor conflicts give rise to a leverage ratchet effect, which induces shareholders to resist reductions and favor increases in leverage, even when total value maximization calls for the opposite." Johnson and Kwak (2009) highlight the web of subsidies and underpriced government guarantees that allow too big to fail banks to operate with socially inadequate capital ratios, as well as the oversized political influence that such banks have had in persuading the US Congress to implement banking deregulation that protects these subsidies and guarantees. This is a matter of privatizing gains from excessive risk taking and socializing the losses. Stein (2016) notes that bank management has private information and that equity issuance may therefore send a negative signal to the market. As such, in restoring a capital ratio, banks may exhibit a preference for asset shrinkage over equity issuance, even when the former is not in the social interest. Thus there is an adverse selection reason why banks avoid raising new equity on top of the debt overhang argument. Stein concludes from the 2009 SCAP experience, however, that when banks have little choice but to issue equity, they can do so with little market impact.

61. Cecchetti (2014) does offer a qualification to this conclusion, noting that one of the reasons the macroeconomic impact of capital and liquidity increases has been so small is that monetary policy was unusually easy over this period. He cautions that the ability of central bank policymakers to offset any further capital-induced increases in costs could be limited by the zero nominal interest rate lower bound. Over the 10-year transition period to much higher capital requirements, I assume that the Fed will have regained its more normal interest rate stance, allowing it to move interest rates in both directions, as it sees fit.

62. Chouinard and Paulin (2014) report that in Canada total credit continued to expand in the postcrisis period, even as banks built up their capital levels.

63. I am indebted to my Peterson colleague David Stockton for supplying this rule of thumb.

64. See Board of Governors of the Federal Reserve, National Information Center, for total consolidated assets of US bank holding companies. I use figures for end-2015.

65. This framework, relying on the relationship between the federal funds rate and the long-run level of GDP, can also accommodate the two different approaches to translating increases in bank funding costs into increases in bank lending rates. The "loans only" approach assumes that banks recover all of the increase in funding costs exclusively by raising lending rates. Thus, for example, if funding costs increase by 10 basis points and the bank has a loan-to-asset ratio of 40 percent, loan rates rise by 25 basis points. In the case of Goldman Sachs, which has a loan-to-total assets ratio of only 10 percent, the loans-only approach would (implausibly) imply an increase in loan rates of 100 basis points. In this approach, there is a large increase in loan rates built on a narrow base (loans only). Using data for the United States for 2012–14, Cline (2015a) finds that bank loans accounted for only 13 percent of financing to the nonfinancial private sector (where financing is defined as the sum of loans by banks and nonbanks, bonds and debt securities, and stock market capitalization). Employing the fed funds framework

and Cline's (2015a) 13 percent share for bank loans, a 25-basis-point increase in loan rates would translate into about a 3-basis-point decline in the level of GDP (.25 times .13 equals .0325). The second approach, which I call "loans plus," assumes that increases in bank funding cost are recovered across a broader spectrum of the bank's activities, including noninterest income. Here, a 10-basis-point increase in funding costs leads to a 10-basis-point increase in loan rates, but also to the equivalent of a 10-basis-point increase in nonloan revenues (so that the weighted average is 10 percent). With the loans-plus approach, the increase in lending rates is smaller because funding cost recovery is being shared across a wider base. But since the output decline depends on the *product* of the interest rate increase and the spillover share to the nonfinancial private sector, the output effects will be similar—at least for the case of the United States. Using Fischer's (2015a) estimate that banks provide about one-third of the financing to the nonfinancial private sector, and assuming a 10-basis-point increase in loans-plus rates, the estimated output decline is again about 3 basis points (.10 times .33 equals .033). Given that US G-SIBs have a loan-to-asset ratio of about 35 percent, that they have substantial non-interest sources of revenue (including investment banking fees and commissions, trading revenue, and custodial/fiduciary fees), that certain segments of the loan market (e.g., loans to corporates) are likely to be highly price elastic (since corporate can also issue bonds), and that increases in US loan spreads over the 2009–13 period are not consistent with the predictions of the loans-only approach, I strongly prefer the loans-plus approach and use it for my estimates of induced increases in loan rates. I am grateful to Pat Parkinson and Lev Ratnowski for helpful discussions on this issue. When applying the "loans-only" approach to translating increases in G-SIB funding costs into increases in overall loan rates, one should use loan shares—not total asset shares—as weights. The share of G-SIBs in total banking system loans—at 47 percent—is considerably lower than G-SIB share of total consolidated bank-holding company assets (at 62 percent).

66. Using a supply-side production function approach, my Peterson Institute colleague Bill Cline (2017) estimates that a 62-basis-point increase in lending spreads at US banks (resulting from a hypothetical across-the-board 1,500-basis-point increase in the leverage ratio) would lower the long-run level of US GDP by 223 basis points. This estimate seems to suggest that a 62-basis-point increase in overall bank lending rates would have a considerably larger negative effect—indeed, almost four times larger (223 basis points versus 62 basis points)—on the level of output in the US economy than would an increase in the federal funds rate of the same size (62 basis points). I find this conclusion implausible. Cline (2017) criticizes application of the Federal Reserve's rule of thumb to the bank-capital problem as inappropriate. He argues that the federal funds framework is not dealing with a long enough time period to capture the full effects on investment. In responding on its website to the frequently asked question of how monetary policy affects inflation and employment, the Fed emphasizes that adjustments to the federal funds rate are the primary way it influences conditions in financial markets, that changes in the funds rate are passed on to other short-term interest rates, that short-term interest rates influence long-term rates, that long-term rates reflect current and expected future values of short-term rates, and that changes in financial conditions affect economic activity; see www.federalreserve.gov/faqs/money_12856.htm. It is also worth pointing out that the average maturity of US commercial and industrial loans in 2016 was about nine quarters—not the much longer maturity that Cline (2017) seems to imply. Cline (2017) offers no evidence that his production function methodology tracks better the output effects of interest rate changes than does the fed funds rule of thumb. Most of the lit-

erature on optimal bank capital does not employ a production function supply-side approach to estimating the output effects of much heightened capital requirements.

Because Cline (2017) employs a steady-state analysis without any time dimension, he is not able to draw any distinctions between a large capital increase undertaken over, say, one year, and the same capital increase spread over a decade. In contrast, the literature shows that spreading the capital increase over a longer period is likely to be less costly, because more of the capital increase can be generated from retained earnings. In the plan discussed in chapter 7, I call for the equivalent of a 600-basis-point increase in the tangible leverage ratio, to be implemented over a 10-year period. The assumed increase in overall bank lending rates would then be only 1.4 basis points a year (one-tenth of the cumulative14-basis-point increase).

Another significant weakness of the production-function approach to estimating optimal capital ratios is that it does not lend itself easily to estimating optimal capital requirements for different size banks. Cline (2017) implies that this might not be so important because, according to his estimates, medium-sized banks had losses in the crisis not significantly different from large banks. The evidence I present on that issue in chapter 7 reaches a different conclusion on the role played by the largest banks in the 2007–09 crisis. But even if the probability of default were roughly the same between, say, US G-SIBs and smaller banks, the loss given default would surely be much higher for G-SIBs, and it is the product of the two that matters for getting the expected loss in a G-SIB to be equal to that of a non-G-SIB bank. As shown in chapter 5, the Federal Reserve uses just such an "estimated impact approach" to measure progress on ending too big to fail. I regard the implication in Cline (2017) that the optimal capital ratio for a large and complex BHC like JPMorgan Chase is the same as that for a much smaller regional bank or an even smaller community bank as simply untenable. For work on systemic importance scores, see chapter 5.

67. For good explanations of the standard methodology for quantifying those expected benefits (in terms of output), see BCBS (2010a); Miles, Yang, and Marcheggiano (2012); Fender and Lewrick (2015); and Cline (2017), among others.

68. Admati (2016a) takes strong exception to the popular view that the only benefit of higher bank capital is to reduce the probability of a banking crisis. She argues that the pattern of too big to fail subsidies and guarantees leads to an inefficient and highly distorted banking system every day. She also argues that higher capital reduces the severity of banking crises (see chapter 6).

69. In BCBS (2010a), the annual probability of a banking crisis is calculated to be 3.2 to 8.0 percent (depending on the model) at a risk-based capital ratio of about 6 percent; by the time the risk-based capital ratio rises to 15 percent (roughly the equivalent of a 9 percent leverage ratio at a risk-weight density of 60 percent), that probability of a crisis falls to between zero and 1 percent. In a recent study, the Federal Reserve Bank of Minneapolis (2016), using data on peak nonperforming loans during the most severe banking crises among advanced economies during the past 40 years or so, finds that the marginal benefits of a higher capital ratio don't decline to zero until the leverage ratio is much higher (above 20 percent). Similarly, examining US banking crises over the entire 1892–2014 period, Barth and Miller (2017) find that marginal benefits usually exceed marginal costs even at leverage ratios above 20 percent.

70. Cline (2017) reviews the empirical literature on the annual probability of banking crises. Drawing on the Laeven and Valencia (2013) and Reinhart and Rogoff (2009) databases,

he cites average annual probabilities over the 1985–2009 period of 3.6 to 5.2 percent for all BCBS countries and 4.1 to 5.2 percent for G-10 countries. The corresponding average annual probability for industrial countries during the 1977–2015 period is significantly lower—about 2.6 percent.

71. See BCBS (2010a); Miles, Yang, and Marcheggiano (2012); Fender and Lewrick (2015); and Cline (2017). Looking at a sample of 15 studies, Cline (2017) reports that the median estimate for the optimal ratio of capital to risk-weighted assets was 13 percent. Assuming an average ratio of risk-weighted assets to total assets of, say, 50 percent for advanced economies, this estimate would translate into an optimal leverage ratio of just over 6 percent. In his own estimates for the United States, Cline (2017) concludes (using a risk-weight density of 0.6) that the optimal tangible leverage ratio is between 7 and 8 percent. As emphasized throughout this volume, I regard the consensus estimate of the optimal capital ratio as much too low.

72. Writing in December 2006, Larry Summers noted that over the 1986–2006 period, the United States experienced some kind of financial crisis approximately once every three years (Wessel 2009). Summers' definition of a crisis differs from that of Laeven and Valencia (2013). The point is that the probability of a crisis is highly dependent on the sample period and the level of country aggregation.

73. Even though shadow banking's share of runnable, private money-like claims has fallen sharply since the 2007–09 crisis, it could well rise again significantly, especially in an environment of rising interest rates; see Hanson (2016).

74. Sarin and Summers (2016a, 2016b) highlight that the ratio of market value of common equity to assets (on both a risk-adjusted and risk-unadjusted basis) has declined significantly for most banks. They regard their findings as most consistent with the explanation that the franchise value of major banks has also declined significantly. They do not regard their results as calling into question the desirability of the increase in capital ratios that was mandated by postcrisis regulations, but they do speculate that regulatory policy could be partly responsible for the decline in franchise value.

75. Dagher et al. (2016) and the Federal Reserve Bank of Minneapolis (2016) stand as notable exceptions to this (prepare for the global average) practice. They study the worst banking crises among advanced economies over the 1970–2011 period and ask what leverage ratio would have been necessary to fully absorb peak losses (that is, to prevent a public bailout). The higher the share of crises one wants to avoid, the higher the leverage ratio needs to be. Because it sets the target for the share of crises to be avoided at a very high level, the Federal Reserve Bank of Minneapolis (2016) finds a high optimal leverage ratio—about 15 percent. Dagher et al. (2016) implicitly set the target somewhat lower (than the Minneapolis Fed) and find that capital in the range of 15 to 23 percent of risk-weighted assets would have been sufficient to absorb losses in the majority of past banking crises in advanced economies; if a US risk-weight density of 60 percent is used to transform RWA into total assets, the Dagher et al. (2016) findings imply that a leverage ratio of 9 to 15 percent would be appropriate; if one uses a lower risk-weight density of say 40 percent, then the appropriate leverage ratio falls to 6 to 9 percent. The trick in this branch of the optimal capital literature is to decide which of the "worst" historical crises are relevant benchmarks for a future US banking crisis. If one rules out the two or three worst historical crises as not so relevant, then, of course, the optimal capital ratio falls. Nevertheless, these two studies indicate that a "prepare for the worst" methodology typically yields higher estimates of the optimal capital ratio than a "prepare for the global average" one.

76. I am not saying that the GDP-based optimal capital literature generates no value added; I think it does. I also commend the BIS for the recent work it has been doing (Fender and Lewrick 2015) to incorporate the higher estimated cost of crises (permanent output effects) into its optimal capital estimates and for having the courage to say publicly that the effect of capital increases on lending rates need not be negative. But one also has to be aware of the limitations of this branch of optimal capital approach, particularly of the high dependence of the estimates on the average crisis probability. If we were confident that the historical record contained all the relevant information we needed to evaluate capital adequacy, we would not need to conduct stress tests. Moreover, a key maintained assumption in stress tests is that risks change over time, so the historical record of crisis probabilities may not be a good guide to future probabilities.

5

Estimating Capital Surcharges for Global Systemically Important Banks

Even when one has a handle on what the right capital ratio ought to be for relatively large banks, a question remains about the right capital ratio for the very largest and most systemically important banks. In this chapter I therefore review three leading approaches to addressing that question. My main conclusion is that the existing schedule of capital surcharges for global systemically important banks (G-SIBs) is too low and too flat.

Capital Ratios Relative to Systemic Importance Indicators for G-SIBs versus Non-G-SIBs

Rationale and Size of the G-SIB Capital Surcharges

At the core of the current international approach to determining capital surcharges for G-SIBs is the construction of an index of systemic importance. Banks with higher scores on this index are presumed to merit a higher capital charge. If banks with the highest systemic scores are observed to be holding less capital than those with lower scores, the conclusion would be that a misalignment in relative capital ratios exists and needs to be promptly remedied.

Because such a high proportion of the losses in the 2007–09 global crisis occurred in very large financial institutions (Haldane 2010) and because the rescue/resolution of troubled large financial institutions had to rely on (unpopular) taxpayer funding (like the Troubled Asset Relief Program [TARP]), the global crisis put the spotlight on the too big to fail problem. In response, bank regulators and supervisors adopted a more differentiated approach to their task. Perhaps the best example of that approach is in the United States. As Federal Reserve Governor Daniel Tarullo (2014c, 2) explains:

> Section 165 (of the Dodd-Frank Act) requires that "in order to prevent or mitigate risks to the financial stability of the United States," the Federal Reserve Board is to establish for all bank holding companies with at least $50 billion in assets prudential standards that "are more stringent" than generally applicable standards and that "increase in stringency" is based on a variety of factors related to the systemic importance of these institutions. These standards must cover capital, liquidity, risk management, resolution planning, and concentration limits.[1]

Higher minimum capital requirements for SIBs and G-SIBs promote financial stability in two ways. First, a higher minimum amount of self-insurance internalizes the negative externalities associated with greater size and connectivity and reduces the risk of failure cum subsequent taxpayer liability. Second, if the bank decides to shrink in size and complexity in order to avoid qualifying for the higher systemic capital surcharge, its failure would then generate smaller social costs, because the bank would have a smaller systemic footprint.

In 2011 the Basel Committee on Banking Supervision (BCBS) came up with a set of 12 financial indicators to identify G-SIBs, the Financial Stability Board (FSB) published its first annual list of G-SIBS, and the BCBS agreed to a G-SIB capital buffer of up to 3.5 percent of risk-weighted assets. No G-SIB capital buffer was applied to the supplementary tier 1 leverage ratio agreed to under Basel III. In 2013 the BCBS updated its G-SIB identification methodology. The 2015 G-SIB list, published in November 2015, contained 30 banks worldwide, 8 of which were US bank holding companies (table 5.1).

US bank supervisors and regulators have gone beyond the international G-SIB capital surcharges. In 2014 the Federal Reserve agreed on a minimum supplementary leverage ratio for G-SIBs of 5 percent for bank holding companies and 6 percent for bank subsidiaries in a holding company. These ratios are to be implemented beginning in July 2018. In July 2015 the Fed increased the top end of the G-SIB surcharge to 4.5 percent of risk-based assets. Table 5.2 shows the (risk-based) surcharges for the eight US G-SIBs. Only JPMorgan Chase qualifies for the 4.5 percent top-end surcharge. The phase-in of these risk-based G-SIB capital surcharges began on January 1, 2016 and becomes fully effective on January 1, 2019.

Table 5.1   Global systemically important banks (G-SIBs), as of November 2015, allocated to buckets corresponding to required level of additional loss absorbency

Bucket	G-SIBs in alphabetical order within each bucket
5 (3.5 percent)	(Empty)
4 (2.5 percent)	HSBC JPMorgan Chase
3 (2.0 percent)	Barclays BNP Paribas Citigroup Deutsche Bank
2 (1.5 percent)	Bank of America Credit Suisse Goldman Sachs Mitsubishi UFJ FG Morgan Stanley
1 (1.0 percent)	Agricultural Bank of China Bank of China Bank of New York Mellon China Construction Bank Groupe BPCE Groupe Crédit Agricole Industrial and Commercial Bank of China Limited ING Bank Mizuho FG Nordea Royal Bank of Scotland Santander Société Générale Standard Chartered State Street Sumitomo Mitsui FG UBS UniCredit Group Wells Fargo

Source: Financial Stability Board.

Table 5.2 Risk-based capital surcharges for US global systemically important banks

Bank	Risk-based capital surcharge (percent)
JPMorgan Chase	4.5
Citigroup	3.5
Bank of America	3.0
Goldman Sachs	3.0
Morgan Stanley	3.0
Wells Fargo	2.0
State Street	1.5
Bank of New York Mellon	1.0

Note: Surcharges began in 2016 and are to be fully phased in by 2019.

Source: Federal Reserve.

Systemic Importance Indicators and Leverage Ratios

Table 5.3 shows the 12 systemic importance indicators and the total systemic importance scores for 12 US bank holding companies, each with assets over $250 billion; 8 of the 12 are designated as G-SIBs. There are five categories of systemic risk indicators, each carrying a weight of 20 percent. The higher the score in the last column, the higher the level of systemic importance for the bank. The highest total systemic importance scores are recorded by the eight G-SIBs. JPMorgan Chase, Citigroup, and Bank of America (in descending order) have the highest scores. Allahrakha, Glasserman, and Young (2015) report that the eight US G-SIBs already have enough capital to meet the fully loaded Basel III risk-based capital minimums, inclusive of the Basel G-SIB surcharges.

A striking finding emerges when one turns to unweighted capital ratios (tier 1 leverage ratios), however, and compares them to banks' systemic importance scores (figure 5.1). The US banks with the highest total systemic importance scores tend to have lower (tier 1) leverage ratios than the median large non-G-SIBs.[2] So on the capital metric that best distinguishes sick from healthy (large) banks, the systemically most important US banks have, on average, lower capital than large banks with lower systemic importance—just the opposite of what one should want in a well-designed bank capital regime. This fact ought to be troubling to US regulators and supervisors.

Table 5.3 Systemic importance indicators reported by large US bank holding companies (billions of dollars)

Bank holding company (stock ID)	Size Total exposures	Interconnectedness Intrafinancial system assets	Intrafinancial system liabilities	Securities outstanding	Payments activity	Substitutability Assets under custody	Underwriting activity
Weight (percent, across)	20	6.7	6.7	6.7	6.7	6.7	6.7
JPMorgan Chase (JPM)	3,570	422	544	599	321,458	21,320	508
Citigroup Inc. (C)	2,895	421	513	596	300,783	11,096	331
Bank of America (BAC)	2,696	294	220	489	83,705	136	390
Wells Fargo (WFC)	1,961	110	129	508	28,761	2,400	86
Goldman Sachs (GS)	1,518	337	107	310	9,585	866	371
Morgan Stanley (MS)	1,283	535	182	231	9,812	1,369	262
US Bancorp (USB)	525	11	22	139	6,918	959	17
PNC Financial Services (PNC)	425	18	13	68	2,004	161	10
Bank of New York Mellon (BK)	410	79	230	61	166,279	23,590	6
HSBC N.A. Holdings (HSBC)	406	36	55	50	1,061	43	49
State Street (STT)	345	30	209	43	59,122	20,411	—
Capital One Financial Corp. (COF)	336	14	2	94	914	3	2

(table continues)

Table 5.3 Systemic importance indicators reported by large US bank holding companies (billions of dollars) *(continued)*

Bank holding company (stock ID)	Complexity			Cross-jurisdictional activity		2013 systemic importance score
	Amount of over-the-counter derivatives	Adjusted trading and available-for-sale securities	Level 3 assets	Foreign claims	Total cross-jurisdictional liabilities	(percent)
Weight (percent, across)	6.7	6.7	6.7	10	10	10
JPMorgan Chase (JPM)	68,004	446	69	693	674	5.05
Citigroup Inc. (C)	59,472	130	46	839	742	4.27
Bank of America (BAC)	54,887	203	32	387	246	3.06
Wells Fargo (WFC)	4,880	128	37	70	130	1.72
Goldman Sachs (GS)	50,355	138	43	347	319	2.48
Morgan Stanley (MS)	43,611	316	23	353	470	2.60
US Bancorp (USB)	106	13	4	3	34	0.35
PNC Financial Services (PNC)	252	26	11	5	2	0.30
Bank of New York Mellon (BK)	1,158	39	0	87	164	1.50
HSBC N.A. Holdings (HSBC)	5,194	40	4	43	1	0.38
State Street (STT)	1,141	54	8	7	125	1.48
Capital One Financial Corp. (COF)	63	16	4	9	2	0.19

Note: Systemic risk scores are based on size, interconnectedness, substitutability, complexity, and cross-jurisdictional activities. This table shows bank holding companies with assets over $250 billion. The eight gray-shaded bank holding companies were G-SIBs as of 2013. HSBC North America is a holding company for the US operations of HSBC Holdings, plc, incorporated in the United Kingdom.

Source: Allahrakha, Glasserman, and Young (2015).

Figure 5.1 Tier 1 leverage ratios (percent)

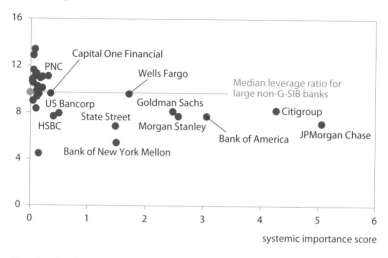

Note: Peer banks that are not G-SIBs have a higher median tier 1 leverage ratio of close to 10 percent.
Source: Allahrakha, Glasserman, and Young (2015).

In his comparison of tangible leverage ratios for different size categories of US banks (expressed under both US Generally Accepted Accounting Principles [GAAP] and International Financial Reporting Standards [IFRS]), Hoenig (2016b) finds a (seeming) negative relationship between bank size and capital adequacy. Using data for end-2015, Hoenig (2016b) reports the following tangible leverage ratios (in IFRS terms) for different size/systemic importance categories of US banks (table 5.4):[3]

- US G-SIBs: 5.97 percent
- 10 largest non-G-SIBs: 8.76 percent
- 10 largest banks with assets less than $50 billion: 8.31 percent
- 10 largest banks with assets less than $1 billion: 9.76 percent

By way of contrast, these four groups of US banks have risk-based (tier 1) capital ratios that are more similar to one another (all falling in the 12.8 to 14.2 range) and G-SIBs no longer show up as a low-capital outlier compared with most of their smaller brethren. Once again, leverage ratios are sending a very different signal about capital adequacy and its link to systemic risk than are risk-based measures.[4]

Like their US counterparts, EU G-SIBs have systemic importance scores that are higher than non-G-SIBs, although the differences in leverage ratios

(text continues on p. 205)

Table 5.4 FDIC Global Capital Index, December 31, 2015

Institution[a]	Basel risk-based capital			Self-reported Basel III leverage ratio[d] (percent)	Tangible capital				
					GAAP		IFRS estimates[e]		
	Tier 1 capital[b] (billions of dollars)	Risk-weighted assets (billions of dollars)	Tier 1 capital ratio[c] (percent)		Total assets (billions of dollars)	Leverage ratio[e] (percent)	Total assets (billions of dollars)	Leverage ratio[f] (percent)	
	(1)	(2)	(3)	(4)	(5)	(6)	(7)	(8)	
			US G-SIBs						
Bank of America	181	1,602	11.28	6.40	2,147	7.58	2,787	5.78	
Bank of New York Mellon	21	170	12.29	4.90	3,394	4.44	405	4.31	
Citigroup	177	1,191	14.82	7.08	1,731	8.80	2,294	6.57	
Goldman Sachs	82	578	14.11	5.90	861	9.22	1,582	5.00	
JPMorgan Chase	200	1,485	13.50	6.50	2,352	8.27	3,254	5.93	
Morgan Stanley	67	384	17.37	5.80	787	7.72	1,427	4.22	
State Street	15	100	15.33	5.80	245	5.67	252	5.52	
Wells Fargo	165	1,303	12.63	7.70	1,788	8.52	1,855	8.20	
US G-SIBs (total in billions of dollars, percent weighted average)	907	6,814	13.31	...	10,306	8.09	13,855	5.97	

Institution[a]	Components of tangible capital			Price-to-book	
	Total equity[g] (billions of dollars)	Goodwill and other intangibles (billions of dollars)	Deferred tax assets (billions of dollars)	Price-to-book ratio[h] (percent)	Price-to-adjusted tangible book ratio[h] (percent)
	(9)	(10)	(11)	(12)	(13)
	US G-SIBs *(continued)*				
Bank of America	256	77	24	0.75	1.32
Bank of New York Mellon	38	21	0	1.26	3.21
Citigroup	222	28	48	0.75	1.19
Goldman Sachs	87	4	4	1.00	1.12
JPMorgan Chase	248	55	3	1.09	1.48
Morgan Stanley	75	10	6	0.90	1.18
State Street	21	7	0	1.44	2.46
Wells Fargo	193	44	0	1.61	2.17
US G-SIBs (total in billions of dollars, percent weighted average)	1,140	247	86	1.05	1.4

(table continues)

Table 5.4 FDIC Global Capital Index, December 31, 2015 (continued)

Institution[a]	Basel risk-based capital				Tangible capital			
					GAAP		IFRS estimates[e]	
	Tier 1 capital[b] (billions of dollars)	Risk-weighted assets (billions of dollars)	Tier 1 capital ratio[c] (percent)	Self-reported Basel III leverage ratio[d] (percent)	Total assets (billions of dollars)	Leverage ratio[e] (percent)	Total assets (billions of dollars)	Leverage ratio[f] (percent)
	(1)	(2)	(3)	(4)	(5)	(6)	(7)	(8)
Foreign G-SIBs								
Agricultural Bank of China Limited (China)	186	1,692	10.96	6.33			2,740	6.24
Banco Santander (Spain)	80	636	12.55	4.73			1,456	3.24
Bank of China Limited (China)	198	1,641	12.07	7.03			2,590	7.86
Barclays (UK)	78	528	14.69	4.50			1,651	4.76
BNP Paribas (France)	83	684	12.21	4.00			2,166	3.99
BPCE Group (France)	57	425	13.34	5.00			1,267	4.64
China Construction Bank (China)	220	1,651	13.32	7.28			2,826	7.65
Crédit Agricole Group (France)	85	553	15.29	5.60			1,845	4.49
Deutsche Bank (Germany)	63	432	14.65	3.50			1,769	3.01
HSBC (UK)	153	1,103	13.90	5.00			2,410	6.97
Industrial & Commercial Bank of China (China)[i]	274	2,036	12.48	7.48			3,421	7.88
ING Bank (Netherlands)	50	349	14.45	4.40			914	5.45
Nordea Bank (Sweden)	29	156	18.50	4.60			703	4.30

Royal Bank of Scotland (UK)	68	358	19.10	5.60	1,202	5.58
Société Générale (France)	54	387	14.00	4.00	1,449	3.37
Standard Chartered (UK)	43	303	14.12	5.50	640	6.69
UBS (Switzerland)	45	212	20.99	4.00	942	4.10
UniCredit (Italy)	49	424	11.50	4.63	935	3.81
Foreign IFRS (total in billions of dollars, percent weighted average)	1,814	13,569	13.37	…	30,925	5.68

(table continues)

Table 5.4   FDIC Global Capital Index, December 31, 2015 *(continued)*

Institution[a]	Components of tangible capital			Price-to-book	
	Total equity[g] (billions of dollars)	Goodwill and other intangibles (billions of dollars)	Deferred tax assets (billions of dollars)	Price-to-book ratio[h] (percent)	Price-to-adjusted tangible book ratio[h] (percent)
	(9)	(10)	(11)	(12)	(13)
Foreign G-SIBs (continued)					
Agricultural Bank of China Limited (China)	187	4	13	0.76	0.84
Banco Santander (Spain)	107	32	30	0.75	2.15
Bank of China Limited (China)	209	3	3	0.71	0.73
Barclays (UK)	97	12	7	0.67	0.89
BNP Paribas (France)	109	15	9	0.74	0.97
BPCE Group (France)	71	6	7	...	...
China Construction Bank (China)	223	3	4	0.79	0.81
Crédit Agricole Group (France)	106	17	7	...	...
Deutsche Bank (Germany)	73	11	10	0.50	0.72
HSBC (UK)	198	25	7	0.90	1.11
Industrial & Commercial Bank of China (China)[i]	277	5	3	0.82	0.84
ING Bank (Netherlands)	53	2	1	1.01	1.07
Nordea Bank (Sweden)	34	3	0	1.33	1.49

Royal Bank of Scotland (UK)	80	10	4	0.74	0.91
Société Générale (France)	68	6	8	0.67	0.92
Standard Chartered (UK)	49	5	1	0.61	0.70
UBS (Switzerland)	57	7	13	1.34	2.06
UniCredit (Italy)	58	6	17	0.64	1.15
Foreign IFRS (total in billions of dollars, percent weighted average)	2,054	171	144	0.74	0.92

(table continues)

Table 5.4 FDIC Global Capital Index, December 31, 2015 (continued)

| | Basel risk-based capital | | | | Tangible capital | | | |
| | | | | | GAAP | | IFRS estimates[e] | |
Institution[a]	Tier 1 capital[b] (billions of dollars)	Risk-weighted assets (billions of dollars)	Tier 1 capital ratio[c] (percent)	Self-reported Basel III leverage ratio[d] (percent)	Total assets (billions of dollars)	Leverage ratio[e] (percent)	Total assets (billions of dollars)	Leverage ratio[f] (percent)
	(1)	(2)	(3)	(4)	(5)	(6)	(7)	(8)
Other foreign G-SIBs								
Credit Suisse (Switzerland; CHF, US GAAP)	53	295	17.99	4.50	820	4.18		
Mitsubishi UFJ FG (Japan; JPY, local GAAP)	120	943	12.76	4.64	2,459	5.40		
Mizuho FG (Japan; JPY, local GAAP)	66	526	12.51	3.90	1,625	4.43		
Sumitomo Mitsui FG (Japan; JPY, local GAAP)	77	566	13.68	4.72	1,558	5.38		
All foreign G-SIBs (total in billions of dollars, percent weighted average)	2,131	15,900	13.40	...	37,387	5.55		

Institution[a]	Components of tangible capital			Price-to-book	
	Total equity[g] (billions of dollars)	Goodwill and other intangibles (billions of dollars)	Deferred tax assets (billions of dollars)	Price-to-book ratio[h] (percent)	Price-to-adjusted tangible book ratio[h] (percent)
	(9)	(10)	(11)	(12)	(13)
Other foreign G-SIBs (continued)					
Credit Suisse (Switzerland; CHF, US GAAP)	45	5	6	0.96	1.29
Mitsubishi UFJ FG (Japan; JPY, local GAAP)	143	10	1	0.68	0.75
Mizuho FG (Japan; JPY, local GAAP)	78	6	0	0.76	0.84
Sumitomo Mitsui FG (Japan; JPY, local GAAP)	92	7	1	0.68	0.76
All foreign G-SIBs (total in billions of dollars, percent weighted average)	2,412	200	152	0.74	0.90

(table continues)

Table 5.4 FDIC Global Capital Index, December 31, 2015 (continued)

	Basel risk-based capital			Self-reported Basel III leverage ratio[d] (percent)	Tangible capital			
					GAAP		IFRS estimates	
Institution[a]	Tier 1 capital[b] (billions of dollars)	Risk-weighted assets (billions of dollars)	Tier 1 capital ratio[c] (percent)		Total assets (billions of dollars)	Leverage ratio[e] (percent)	Total assets (billions of dollars)	Leverage ratio[f] (percent)
	(1)	(2)	(3)	(4)	(5)	(6)	(7)	(8)
US BHC by group size[j]								
US G-SIBs	907	6,814	13.31		10,306	8.09	13,855	5.97
Ten largest non-G-SIBs	209	1,765	11.81		2,184	8.80	2,194	8.76
Ten largest less than $50 billion[k]	30	233	12.78		328	8.31	328	8.31
Ten largest less than $1 billion[k]	1	7	14.17		10	9.76	10	9.76

	Components of tangible capital			Price-to-book	
	Total equity[g] (billions of dollars)	Goodwill and other intangibles (billions of dollars)	Deferred tax assets (billions of dollars)	Price-to-book ratio[h] (percent)	Price-to-adjusted tangible book ratio[h] (percent)
Institution[a]	(9)	(10)	(11)	(12)	(13)
US BHC by group size[i] *(continued)*					
US G-SIBs	1,140	247	86	1.05	1.40
Ten largest non-G-SIBs	267	75	7	1.18	1.82
Ten largest less than $50 billion[k]	35	6	3	1.29	1.79
Ten largest less than $1 billion[k]	1	0	0	...	...

FDIC = Federal Deposit Insurance Corporation

a. Global systemically important banks (G-SIBs) are defined by the Financial Stability Board and include eight US bank holding companies (BHCs). Foreign G-SIBs report in local currencies, which are converted into US dollars by SNL Financial.

b. Tier 1 capital is equity capital less unrealized gains on available-for-sale debt securities, unrealized losses on available-for-sale equity securities, disallowed preferred stock, disallowed goodwill, disallowed servicing assets, disallowed deferred tax assets, and other tier 1 capital components.

c. Tier 1 capital ratios and underlying data are calculated and reported under Basel III capital standards for all G-SIBs.

d. Basel III leverage ratios are self-reported by institutions in published financial statements and presentations. They have not been reviewed for accuracy.

(table continues)

Table 5.4 FDIC Global Capital Index, December 31, 2015 (*continued*)

e. Differences in accounting requirements for netting and offsetting of assets and liabilities result in significant differences in banks' total assets. The ability to offset under International Financial Reporting Standards (IFRS) is limited in comparison with Generally Accepted Accounting Principles (GAAP), especially for derivatives traded with the same counterparty under an International Swaps and Derivatives Association (ISDA) master netting agreement. US GAAP permits the netting of derivative receivables and payables, and the related cash collateral received and paid when a legally enforceable master netting agreement exists between a firm and a derivative counterparty. US GAAP discloses gross derivative assets and liabilities and the offset amount applied to derivatives in the notes to the consolidated financial statements rather than in the consolidated balance sheet. To narrow the difference in total assets between IFRS and US GAAP reporting institutions, the US G-SIBs IFRS estimates follow the methodology used by ISDA in its Netting and Offsetting Report (May 2012, http://www2.isda.org/functional-areas/research/studies/) and adds the disclosed offsetting amount applied to derivatives back to total assets in order to calculate total assets. Total assets are as reported in the consolidated balance sheet while the offset applied to derivatives is as reported in the notes to the consolidated financial statements on derivatives in each firm's 10-Q report.

f. The leverage ratio is the ratio of adjusted tangible equity to adjusted tangible assets. Adjusted tangible equity, adjusted tangible assets, and adjusted tangible book subtract goodwill, other intangibles, and deferred tax assets.

g. Equity capital is the basic GAAP measure of net worth, defined as total assets minus total liabilities.

h. Median price-to-book ratios and price-to-adjusted tangible book ratios are used instead of averages for subgroups and for US BHC size groups. Current quarter data are not available for Mizuho FG; third quarter 2015 ratios referenced as proxy. Data are not available for six bank holding companies with assets less than $1 billion, as well as for BPCE Group and Crédit Agricole Group.

i. Current quarter goodwill and other intangible assets data are not available; second quarter 2015 figures referenced as a proxy.

j. Bank holding companies that are owned by a foreign parent or reported a net loss in fourth quarter 2015, and thrift holding companies that did not file a full FRY-9C report as of fourth quarter 2015 were excluded.

k. The ten largest US bank holding companies with assets less than $50 billion and the ten largest US bank holding companies with assets less than $1 billion reported de minimis derivative exposures. We assume that total assets and the adjusted tangible equity to adjusted tangible assets ratio are essentially the same under US GAAP and the IFRS estimate.

Source: FDIC Global Capital Index, Capitalization Ratios for Global Systemically Important Banks (G-SIBs), December 31, 2015, www.fdic.gov/about/learn/board/hoenig/capitalizationratios4q15.pdf.

across size categories appear to be smaller than in the United States. A European Banking Authority report (EBA 2014e) that looked at end-June 2013 data for 173 EU banks reported that the weighted-average, fully loaded Basel III leverage ratio for 41 large banks (each with tier 1 capital in excess of €3 billion) was 3.3 percent, versus 3.9 percent for the remaining 132 smaller banks in the sample. Here, too, then, the very banks that, on systemic risk grounds, one would want to have the highest capital ratios have lower ratios than banks with less systemic risk.

The Bank of England's "Symmetry and Proportionality Approach"[5]

The Financial Policy Committee's Conclusions, the Critical Risk Weight, and the Underlying Rationale

In October 2014 the Financial Policy Committee (FPC) published a report (Bank of England 2014a) explaining why a leverage ratio framework should be introduced in the United Kingdom before the date required by the Basel III timetable. The report also provides the FPC's conclusions on what the height of the (basic) leverage ratio should be; the size of appropriate supplementary leverage ratio surcharges for G-SIBs, other major domestic UK banks, and building societies; and the size and operation of a countercyclical leverage ratio surcharge.[6] The report's recommendations include the following:

- The minimum leverage ratio requirement should be set at 3 percent.
- Supplementary leverage ratio surcharges should be set at 35 percent of the corresponding risk-weighted systemic risk surcharges for these firms, thereby preserving the relationship between the 3 percent minimum leverage requirement and the 8.5 percent minimum tier 1 risk-weighted capital requirement (inclusive of the capital conservation buffer).[7]
- The countercyclical leverage ratio surcharge should be set at 35 percent of the risk-weighted surcharge.

Explaining the basis for its conclusions, the FPC argues that all capital ratios have flaws and that the best prospects for success will occur when the leverage ratio is used in tandem with risk-based capital measures. After going through the litany of shortcomings of risk-based capital measures in the run-up to the 2007–09 global crisis (much along the same lines as the shortcomings described in chapter 3), the FPC maintains that adding a leverage ratio requirement would give banks better protection against risks that are hard to model. At the same time, it emphasizes that the leverage

Figure 5.2 The critical risk weight

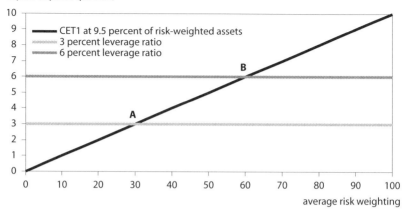

capital required (percent)

Note: This figure depicts the problem of getting *both* a minimum risk-weighted capital standard (common equity tier 1 [CET1]) and a leverage ratio to "bind" in a bank capital regime (like Basel III) with two Pillar 1 capital standards. In the figure, the binding capital standard is the one that is highest on the y-axis. The "critical risk weight" is the point at which both the risk-weighted capital measure (CET1) and the leverage ratio are binding. At a 3 percent minimum leverage ratio, the critical risk weight occurs at an average risk weight of 31.6 percent (point A). For any bank with a risk weight of 31.6 percent or less, the leverage ratio is the binding constraint. At a minimum leverage ratio of 6 percent (point B), the critical risk weight occurs at a risk weight of 63.2 percent. The IIF (2015) reports that among a sample of 41 major banks (all G-SIBs plus domestic SIBs from China, Canada, and Australia), the average risk weight was 44 percent. This implies that a minimum leverage ratio of 6 percent would be the binding capital constraint on a majority of global banks—contrary to what the IIF (2015) argues was the intent of Basel III. In the text, I show why this argument is not persuasive.
Source: IIF (2015). Reprinted with permission.

ratio suffers from the defect that it has no risk sensitivity. It also questions whether the leverage ratio will continue to be able to identify weak banks much better than the risk-based measures once the leverage ratio itself becomes a regulatory requirement (that is, they posit that Goodhart's law could soon be at work).[8]

Next, the FPC highlights a practical problem that any dual capital regime (i.e., one that employs both a risk-based capital standard and a leverage ratio) must face: how to ensure that both minimum capital targets are binding. The problem is depicted in figure 5.2, adapted and modified from the Bank of England (2014a) report and from an IIF (2015) study. The capital requirement is on the vertical axis and the ratio of risk-weighted asset to total assets (called the average risk weighting) is on the horizontal one. The binding capital requirement is the one that is higher on the vertical axis. Suppose that the minimum leverage ratio is set at 3 percent. At very low risk weights, only the leverage ratio bites. However, as the average risk weight rises, one eventually reaches a point at which the risk-weighted capital measure becomes the binding constraint. At point A, where the two lines intersect, both capital requirements are binding and both requirements imply the same amount of capital; the Bank of England (2014a) calls this the "critical risk weight." In figure 5.2 the critical risk weights occurs at an average risk weighting of just over 30 percent—below the risk weighting (just over 40 percent) that the IIF (2015) cites as the average for its sample of 41 systemically important banks.

What happens when the leverage ratio is raised to, say, 6 percent? At 6 percent (point B), the critical risk weight rises to 63 percent. This means that the risk-weighted capital requirement is binding on a minority share of banks. At a 9 percent leverage ratio, the critical risk weight rises to over 90 percent and the risk-weighted measure ceases in practice to have any force. The bottom line here is that if both capital requirements in a dual regime are to bite, the minimum requirements between the two must be maintained in strict proportion. In addition, if the risk-based requirement is a single-digit one, the minimum leverage requirement will have to be set (well) below the level that some supervisory authorities and analysts (including me) would otherwise regard as optimal.

The FPC reviews the evidence on what the appropriate minimum requirements ought to be for both a tier 1 risk-based capital measure and a leverage ratio (defined as tier 1 capital divided by total exposure). Its answers are 8.5 and 3.0 percent, respectively. The relationship between these two minimums (3.0 percent divided by 8.5 percent, or roughly 35 percent) provides the magic constant that is used thereafter to derive the relevant G-SIB surcharges for the leverage ratio;[9] all the G-SIB surcharges related to the leverage ratio are set at 35 percent of the surcharges that already apply to the risk-based capital measures. Thus, for example, if the risk-based G-SIB surcharge is 1.0 percent for a smaller G-SIB, then the symmetry and proportion approach implies that its leverage ratio counterpart should be roughly 0.35 percent (35 percent of 1.0 percent). Likewise, if the countercyclical capital buffer, when activated, for the risk-weighted capital measure is 2.5 percent, then the appropriate surcharge for the leverage ratio is 0.8 percent. When the countercyclical capital buffer is activated during a credit boom period, the symmetry and proportionality approach yields a minimum G-SIB leverage ratio of just under 5 percent for the largest G-SIB—seemingly the same level as the minimum under the enhanced supplementary leverage ratio in the United States.[10]

Given that the UK regulatory authorities have only recently adopted a minimum leverage ratio, given that the framework includes a surcharge for G-SIBs, and given that these new capital requirements have been incorporated into the Bank of England's 2015 and 2016 stress testing exercises, this would ordinarily be an occasion for applause. Unfortunately, although the policy change is unquestionably in the right direction, the design seems badly flawed. Symmetry and proportionality have been permitted to run amok, with the result that both the minimum leverage ratio and the G-SIB surcharge that relates to it are way too low.

My critique centers on five issues: dual versus single capital regimes, the thinking behind the critical risk weight, the treatment of losses in deriving the optimal capital ratio, identification of the thresholds that distinguish surviving from failing banks, and the inclusion of the countercyclical capital buffer in the minimum leverage ratio and its G-SIB surcharge.

Dual versus Single (Pillar 1) Bank Capital Regimes

For my money, the FPC presents a too idealized picture of a dual bank capital regime. The US experience serves as a relevant counterpoint. The United States has had a leverage ratio requirement for US banks since the early 1980s and has been running a dual regime since 1991 (see Bailey 2014). In the run-up to the Great Recession, risk-based capital ratios were sending out a much more benign message about the vulnerability of large US banks than were leverage ratios (Hoenig 2012).

Unfortunately, US regulators bet on the wrong horse; when the crisis came, the amount of loss-absorbing capital was far short of what would have been necessary to avoid a taxpayer-funded recapitalization of those banks.[11] Had the United States been operating under a single capital regime and had the sole capital metric been the leverage ratio, preventive and corrective action could arguably have been undertaken before the crash.

Looking at the correlation between leverage ratios and risk-based capital measures for the European Union's 20 largest banks, Pagano et al. (2014) tell a similar story. The correlation between the two measures of bank capital was positive and high in the 1990s; it broke down in the early 2000s and became negative during the run-up to the 2007-09 crisis. Regulators were apparently focused on the wrong bank capital metric. The FPC does not address this problem of conflicting signals when selling the virtues of a dual regime.

In a dual capital regime, one would expect to give greater weight to the capital measure that has the better forecasting record in identifying problem banks—in much the same way that one weights individual indicators in constructing a composite early warning indicator (see, for example, Goldstein, Kaminsky, and Reinhart 2000) or picking the cues for a fast and frugal decision tree (see Aikman et al. 2014). Not so in the FPC's preference for the risk-based measure, despite overwhelming evidence to the contrary. In Bank of England (2014b), the FPC cites no fewer than 10 empirical studies that show the leverage ratio outperforming risk-based capital measures in distinguishing between sick and healthy (large) banks and in maintaining bank lending during a crisis. Not a single empirical study is put forward that favors risk-based capital measures.

Similarly, a study by the BCBS (2010d) that looks at the differences between severely stressed large banks and other banks before the crisis in a group of advanced economies finds that for each of four different measures of leverage (total capital/assets, tier 1 capital to assets, common equity to assets, and tangible common equity to tangible assets), mean leverage ratios for stressed banks were always lower than for nonstressed banks and in many cases these differences were statistically significant. In contrast, it finds "little evidence that risk-based capital ratios were consistently higher for the group of nonstressed banks before the crisis."

Aikman et al. (2014) examine failure and survival patterns among 116 large global banks during 2007–09. They identify four indicators that could be used as cues in a fast and frugal decision tree for bank vulnerability. At the top of the list is the leverage ratio; the other three are a market-based capital ratio, a wholesale funding indicator, and the loan to deposit ratio. The regulatory risk-based capital ratio does not make the cut.

In trying to make its case that the risk-based capital ratios should remain the senior partner in a dual regime, the FPC notes that while the leverage ratio outperforms risk-based measures for US banks, it is superior by a lower margin for large US banks than in other jurisdictions where the leverage ratio has no regulatory status, suggesting that Goodhart's law is taking a toll and that a dual regime delivers superior performance. Yet in what is probably the most careful empirical study of the performance of a leverage ratio versus a risk-based capital measure among a large sample of US banks (both large and small) over the 2001–11 period, Hogan, Meredith, and Pan (2013) challenge that judgment:

> We find that the RBC (risk-based capital) ratio is significantly less accurate than the capital (leverage) ratio as a predictor of bank performance. Regressing bank performance on the capital and RBC ratios together, we find that capital is a statistically significant indicator of performance even after accounting for the RBC. The RBC ratio, on the other hand, is almost never statistically significant regardless of whether capital is included in the regression. (p. 25)

> We find that using capital and RBC ratios together does not improve the accuracy of our estimations of bank performance.... We therefore conclude

that RBC regulation has the potential to create significant harm with little or no added benefit. The Fed should abandon its use of the RBC ratio and return to the simple and effective capital ratio as a measure of risk. (p. 26)

Faced with this formidable body of empirical evidence, it is perplexing that the FPC opted for a leverage ratio (3 percent) that is low enough that risk-weighted capital requirements would be the binding constraint for a majority of UK firms most of the time.

The Critical Risk Weight

I see two problems with the critical risk weight. First, the FPC does not offer any empirical evidence that, in cases where the leverage ratio is the binding constraint, banks will load up significantly on risky assets. Second, even if there were such a tendency, the FPC does not demonstrate that the symmetry and proportionality approach is the only or best way to deal with this potential problem.

Using a panel of more than 500 EU banks from 27 countries over the period 2005–14, Grill, Lang, and Smith (2015) examine the change in portfolios for banks that are constrained by the Basel III leverage ratio (under a dual capital regime). The Basel III leverage ratio is not formally binding in most of these countries until 2019; the authors assume that banks acted early to implement the new regime as soon as it was announced in 2010. They find that "empirical results suggest increased risk taking is modest— between 1.5 to 2 percentage points compared to what banks would have done under a solely risk-based framework. Further results show that banks can increase risk by much more than this and distress probabilities will still significantly decline" (p. 39).

The European Central Bank (ECB) found these results important enough to include them as a special feature of its November 2015 *Financial Stability Review*. Its summary of the main findings (ECB 2015b, 1) is as follows:

> Using a simple theoretical model, it is shown that the increased incentive to take on more risk is more than outweighed by the increase in loss-absorbing capacity from higher capital, thus leading to more stable banks. These results are confirmed within an empirical analysis on a large sample of EU banks. The empirical estimates suggest that banks bound by the LR (leverage ratio) increase their risk-weighted assets to total assets ratio by around 1.5–2 percentage points more they otherwise would, i.e., without an LR requirement. Importantly, this small increase in risk-taking is more than compensated for by the substantial increase in capital positions of highly leveraged banks, which results in significantly lower estimated distress probabilities for banks bound by the LR.

Although the ECB study does not examine what the change in risk taking would be under a leverage-ratio-only capital regime or what it would be for much higher minimum leverage ratios, it serves as a cautionary tale against the assumption that any sizable increase in the leverage ratio would automatically generate a large switch in bank portfolios.

The FPC also conveys the impression that anyone favoring a minimum leverage ratio much above 3 percent—say, 9 percent—and at all worried about the leverage ratio's absence of risk sensitivity faces only two unpalatable choices. One would be to supersize the axes of figure 5.2 so that a 9 percent minimum leverage ratio is paired with a 25 percent minimum risk-based capital ratio, thereby preserving the 35 percent proportionality constant and the 35 percent critical risk weight. Since the main reason why the leverage ratio was added to both Basel III and the UK regulatory arsenal is the growing recognition of the inadequacies of the risk-based measures, doubling down on the risk-based minimum hardly seems appealing. The second choice would be to impose the higher minimum leverage ratio as the sole regulatory bank capital metric and let risk sensitivity be damned. Although I think the prospect of banks going out the day after the leverage ratio is enthroned as the one and only king and loading up on every risky asset they can find is overdone, ignoring this risk seems imprudent.

Upon closer examination the dilemma posed by the critical risk weight seems to be wholly a creation of the constraints that the FPC has artificially imposed by assuming that the risk-based minimum and the leverage ratio must both be Pillar 1 capital standards. As I show in chapter 7, it need not—and indeed should not—be this way. In brief, one can make the leverage ratio the only Pillar 1 minimum capital requirement and set its level wherever the theory and evidence on optimal capital standards says it should be. At the same time, one can simultaneously construct as a Pillar 2 measure a set of risk indicators that would form the basis for a risk surcharge. Those indicators might include the ratio of risk-weighted assets to total assets from a revised standardized approach to risk weighting, but it would be only one indicator among many and would not dominate the total risk score. Most important, this risk surcharge—just like the G-SIB surcharge—could sit on top of the basic leverage ratio. Hence both the leverage ratio and the risk surcharge would be binding, without forcing the level of the leverage ratio itself to be lower than would otherwise be desirable. This risk surcharge would have two purposes. One would be to compensate for some of the inadequacies of the current stress testing framework. The other would be to discourage banks from gaming the leverage ratio by shifting unduly into higher risk assets and activities. In sum, the alleged critical risk-weight constraint is no constraint at all if one is willing to think a little outside the prevailing Basel III box. And why not? This is meant to be banking supervision, not synchronized swimming.

Bank Losses and the Financial Policy Committee's Optimal Capital Ratios

Using losses sustained during a previous banking crisis is one of the standard methodologies for estimating optimal capital ratios. Still, the way in which the FPC employs that methodology leads me to question its conclusions. In looking at the historical evidence on bank losses during past crises, the FPC relies on both its own survey of losses and a BCBS (2010d) study that reviewed bank losses during the 2007–09 crisis as well as in some earlier banking crises. Both the FPC and the BCBS rely exclusively on a net income measure of losses. The BCBS defines losses as the ratio of net income to risk-weighted assets, while the FPC opted for pretax net income plus unrealized net gains and losses for the numerator and either total leverage exposure or total assets in the denominator. The BCBS looks mostly at annual data, the FPC at half-yearly data. The FPC focuses on losses between the first half of 2007 and the second half of 2013 for alternative samples of UK and international banks; the BCBS focused on the period between the third quarter of 2007 and the fourth quarter of 2009. I see a number of potentially serious problems.

No Counterfactual

Neither study makes any effort to estimate what bank losses would have been had there not been the massive and comprehensive set of government interventions during the crisis. The BCBS study notes that it was not able to estimate a no-policy-intervention counterfactual and that the results are hence more optimistic (that is, losses are smaller) than they would be if they had been adjusted for such interventions. The FPC study hardly mentions the policy intervention problem—even though UK policy interventions in the 2007–09 crisis were sizable, with the Bank of England's June 2009 Financial Stability Report placing (actual and potential) financial system support measures (from the central bank and the government) at more than $2 trillion (or 88 percent of annual GDP at the time). If one adds in the financial system support measures adopted by the United States and the euro area, the total rises to more than $14 trillion.[12] In view of this omission, the FPC's conclusion that the mean peak losses during the crisis for UK and international banks were roughly 2 percent (of 2006 total assets or total exposure) seems highly suspect.

Earnings Management and Survivorship Bias

Both studies suffer from measurement problems with net income that could bias down the results. Let me mention two of them.

There is a long-standing body of literature on earnings management by firms, including banks. Because managers apparently believe that lower reported volatility in earnings improves their stock price performance (and perhaps also their remuneration),[13] they have an incentive to smooth net earnings. According to this literature, the two main vehicles for implementing earnings management are loan-loss provisions and realization of security gains and losses (see Cohen et al. 2014). Since loan-loss provisions show up as an expense on the income statement, banks can inflate net income during a financial crisis by taking low loan-loss provisions. Reporting lower losses on securities during a crisis will also inflate net income. Although supervisors oversee such practices, the literature suggests that banks, especially large banks, retain considerable discretion over how they treat these items in their income statements. In empirical studies economists estimate normal loan-loss provisions and then treat the difference between normal and actual loss provisions as earnings management. Most empirical studies find that earnings management is prevalent at large banks and that it has a positive effect on net income during downturns, including during financial crises. Flannery, Kwan, and Nimalendran (2010) find that opacity at banks increased markedly during the 2007–09 financial crisis.

Herring (2013) studied accounting practices at large banks during the 2007–09 crisis. He points out that if a bank wanted to increase the discretion it had in valuing assets and liabilities during the crisis and avoid the large asset losses indicated by fair value accounting, there were two popular routes open to it. One way (under fair value accounting) is to try to classify more of its assets as Level 2 (marked-to-matrix) and Level 3 (marked-to-model), and less of them as Level 1 (marked-to-market).[14] A second (under mixed attribute accounting) is to move assets/liabilities from trading securities or available-for-sale securities to held-to-maturity securities.[15] Herring (2013) reports that both accounting tactics were used during the last crisis:

> During the recent crisis, in which liquidity in many secondary markets deteriorated markedly, a substantial volume of assets was shifted from Level 1 to Level 2 and especially to Level 3. (p. 7)

> During the crisis the standard setters on both sides of the Atlantic permitted financial institutions to exercise some flexibility in reclassifying assets to shield them from the necessity of applying FVA [fair value

accounting]. Ordinarily, managerial intent is determined when an asset is booked and the asset will be valued in that way until it matures or is sold. But in the face of enormous political pressure from both Europe and the United States, the standard setters permitted institutions to real-locate assets from trading or available to sale to held to maturity. Some institutions took aggressive advantage to shield their balance sheets and income statements from FVA. For example, during the third quarter of 2008 Deutsche Bank avoided more than $800 million in losses from write-downs in its bond and marketable loan portfolios by shifting assets to a more favorable category and was thus able to report third quarter profit of $93 million rather than a loss of $700 million. Similarly, Citigroup reclas-sified debt with a carrying value of $60 billion into held-to-maturity in the fourth quarter of 2008 to limit the negative effect of further declines in net income and shareholders' equity from FVA. (p. 9).

The second measurement problem is "survivorship bias"—the practice of dropping from the sample banks that did not survive the crisis. The BCBS (2010d, 9) study acknowledges this problem: "The analysis conducted in this report is subject to survivorship bias, as losses from banks that failed are not always captured in the analysis. This biases down the estimates." It is not known whether the bank samples the FPC looked at in calculating losses were also subject to survivorship bias.

Survivorship bias has been shown to have a significant effect in artifi-cially boosting returns. David Swensen (2011), the successful manager of Yale University's endowment fund, concludes that when survivorship bias and backfilling bias are accounted for, mean annual returns of hedge funds can drop from an average of roughly 14 to 3–4 percent.[16]

The FPC study does not address earnings management and survivor-ship bias at banks. I was unable to find outside estimates of how large they were likely to be for UK and international banks. I therefore classify those potential downward biases to net income as question marks. To its credit, the FPC definition of net income did appear to cover unrealized net gains and losses. The BCBS (2010d) study acknowledges that some of its bank loss figures exclude mark-to-market variation of available-for-sale assets.

If earnings management and survivorship biases cause net income during a crisis to be overstated—or if loan-loss provisioning is delayed long enough to push losses into periods beyond those classified as the crisis period—the tail of peak losses will look thinner than it really is and compar-isons of crisis-on and crisis-off periods will be distorted. The effect will be to distort the inference that can be drawn from these losses for optimal leverage ratios.

Means/Medians versus Extremes

Done right, stress testing is all about (relevant) extremes, not means and medians. It is about looking carefully at the tail of loss distributions, looking for the weakest link among large banks when economic conditions are at their worst in living memory. Seen in this light, the FPC's focus on the mean and median of peak losses during the past crisis seems ill advised.[17]

The 2009 Supervisory Capital Assessment Program (SCAP) included loss-rate assumptions and scenarios that were severe. It assumed a two-year loss rate for commercial bank loans of 9.1 percent (figure 5.3)—larger than that experienced during the Great Depression. Such a loss-rate assumption was not in the extreme tail of the loss distribution. It was more pessimistic than any loss actually experienced over the previous 87 years. In the same spirit, the assumed rise in the unemployment rate was more severe than any recession since the 1930s. The global market shock scenario in the 2011 Comprehensive Capital Analysis and Review (CCAR), which applies to the six bank holding companies with the largest trading and private equity exposure, assumes that the change in market risk factors that occurred between June and December 2008 took place in one day.

In contrast, when researchers have been confident that a rather meager loss experience provides the basis for equally meager capital requirements, that confidence has sometimes proved to be unwarranted. Perhaps the best example is the study by Kuritzkes and Schuermann (2008), who look at more than 300 US large bank holding companies over the 1986–2005 period. Their measure of bank losses was the ratio of net income to risk-weighted assets—the same measure used in both the BCBS (2010d) study and the Fed's estimated impact study (discussed later in this chapter). They conclude that "for the largest banks, i.e., those with at least $10 billion in assets, the (8 percent Basel I total capital) regulatory capital cushion is consistent with an annual default probability of 0.12 percent (99.8 percent confidence level)" (p. 4) and that "based on the empirical record, if banks held at least 8 percent capital, they would be unable to withstand an adverse risk-weighted asset event in about two quarters out of every 10,000" (p. 31). The main problem in this study is that the loss experience in the Texas (1980–89) and Northeastern (1990–92) banking crises was not a good basis for judging the loss distribution in the 2007–09 systemic banking crisis.[18]

The FPC published the range of losses incurred during the recent crisis for the UK and international bank samples, but it emphasizes the mean and median of peak losses as the most relevant statistics. The mean of peak losses (relative to total assets) for UK banks was about 2 percent, but the range went from just above zero to 9 percent. In its sample of international

Figure 5.3   Commercial bank two-year loan loss rates, 1921–2008

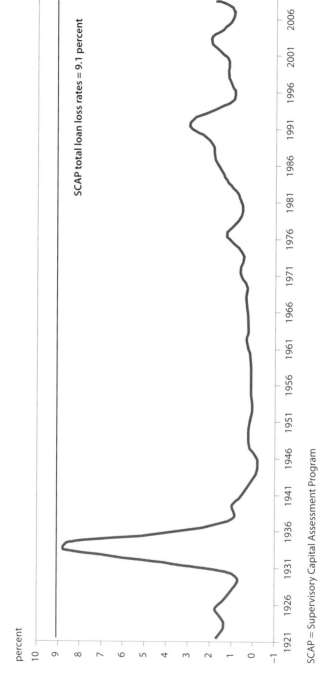

SCAP = Supervisory Capital Assessment Program

Note: The 9.1 percent loss rate assumed in the 2009 US SCAP stress test is higher than the loss rates observed in the United States during any time over the preceding 87 years, including during the Great Depression.

Source: Board of Governors (2009a, 2009b).

banks, the range was from just above zero to over 6 percent (relative to total leverage exposure). In the BCBS (2010d) study, the range is even larger relative to mean losses.[19] Considering losses (relative to risk-weighted assets) during the recent crisis, the mean is 5 percent, but the range goes from less than 1 to 26 percent.[20] Looking at historical peak losses in other crises (before the 2007–09 crisis), the BCBS reports a mean peak loss of 7 percent but a range of less than 1 to 29 percent. Presumably, it is also the worst crises that typically prompt official intervention. As neither the FPC study nor the BCBS gives the identity of the banks/countries registering the most severe losses, it is not possible for an outsider to discuss the specifics/relevance of the outliers in these studies. But, as argued in chapter 4, the relevance of the worst historical crises for a future (UK) banking crisis is a key question that needs to be answered in judging the optimal leverage ratio for (UK) banks. The FPC study does not provide the information necessary to evaluate the extreme observations.

Low versus Higher-Frequency Data

A related issue that speaks to the choice between central tendencies and extremes is the frequency of the data. The BCBS (2010d, 9) relies primarily on annual data. The study notes, however, that use of annual data may introduce a downward bias to the results and that an annual horizon may not be the relevant one for market participants' assessment of bank solvency. "There may be a downward bias in the figures by focusing on a calendar year since these capture negative net income 'spells' only within a year…we do not know with any certainty that market participants focus on solvency at a one-year horizon."

In its review of peak bank losses, the FPC uses semiannual data. That choice can make a difference. Consider, for example, the following data on net income for all US FDIC-insured banks over the stress period, third quarter 2008 to second quarter 2009: 2008Q3, plus $1.7 billion; 2008Q4, minus $32.1 billion; 2009Q1, plus $7.6 billion; and 2009Q2, minus $3.7 billion. The net income figure for the fourth quarter of 2008 was the first decline for this aggregate of US banks since 1990. At least in the first half of 2009, using the semiannual data yields a different peak loss picture than the quarterly data. I suspect that the substitution of annual for quarterly data makes a much bigger difference in biasing down the peak loss numbers.[21]

What one would have liked to see but neither the FPC or BCBS studies publishes is the maximum quarterly loss sustained by banks in the sample during the 2007–09 crisis. The BCBS study provides the full range of losses only for banks that had negative cumulative net income between the third

Figure 5.4   Net income for US and EU banks, 2006–13

billions of US dollars/euros

Source: Schildbach and Wenzel (2013). Reprinted with permission.

quarter of 2007 and the fourth quarter of 2009; for the entire sample it provides only mean peak losses. The range of losses for banks with a quarterly loss any time during that period is not provided. The FPC study provides the mean and the range of peak losses during the recent global crisis but only on a semiannual basis.

Figure 5.4 shows the behavior of net income for US and (large) EU banks over the 2006–13 period. For large EU banks, the drop in net income during the 2007–09 crisis is best characterized as a deep narrow *V* centered on the fourth quarter of 2008. If the data are smoothed, the extent of that decline will be underestimated. For US banks, there is also a *V* pattern, albeit one that is shallower and wider. EU banks—in contrast to US ones— show a double dip for net income as the EU debt crisis kicks into gear.

Tail-Risk Dependence

The FPC's treatment of bank losses reveals nothing about the coincidence of those losses across banks, which can make an important difference to an optimal capital assessment. If a large bank—even a G-SIB—is on the edge of failure in a sea of tranquility in which no other banks are in trouble, the problem is usually manageable (think of the failure of Barings in the United Kingdom in 1995). By way of contrast, if a group of large banks are at failure's door all at once, as in the 2007–09 crisis, systemic risk becomes much more acute. Each troubled bank will find it harder to get liquidity from other banks, the simultaneous fire sale of assets will reverberate negatively on each bank's balance sheet, and the resources (financial and human) of the official crisis managers will be stretched thin.[22]

This coincidence issue is so much at the heart of systemic risk that some researchers have actually defined systemic risk in terms of it. Acharya et al. (2010) argue that what counts for a bank's contribution to systemic risk is its propensity to fail at the same time that the banking system as a whole is failing. They also argue that this contribution can be measured by looking at the bank's equity return during the worst 5 percent of days for the market during the year. They show that such tail dependence plus a measure of simple leverage do a much better job of explaining capital shortfalls in stress tests than do measures of bank risk that do not account for the coincidence of losses.

Using a contingent claims model on a group of 29 G-SIBs, Haldane (2012) generates estimates of default probabilities under alternative assumptions about the independence of defaults among the G-SIBs. When there are no G-SIB capital surcharges and the defaults are independent, expected losses for the system are about $200 billion a year. To reduce those expected losses to $5 billion, a G-SIB surcharge of over 7 percent would be needed. When these defaults are perfectly correlated across the 29 banks (closer to the real-world situation in a crisis), the expected loss for the system rises to $750 billion, and it takes a 15 percent G-SIB surcharge to reduce the expected loss to $5 billion.

In the October 2008 issue of its *Financial Stability Review*, the Bank of England (2008b, 26) shows that in both the United Kingdom and internationally, the comovement between banks' equity returns was unusually high in late 2008, contributing to a high level of systemic risk:

> A key feature of the market pressures at this stage (late October 2008) is that they were operating at a system-wide level. Heightened macroeconomic uncertainties were a common shock affecting the asset values of all institutions, as reflected in the high correlation between banks' equity returns in the United Kingdom and internationally.... This valuation uncertainty generated a system-wide rise in counterparty risk, which was amplified by the institutional features which took place during the summer and early autumn (of 2008). One consequence of this network contagion was a breakdown in interbank funding markets.

The FPC's analysis does not seem to take tail risk dependence into account.

Market Pressures to Maintain Capital Ratios above the Regulatory Minimum

The FPC pays scant attention to the question of why large banks typically maintain actual capital ratios (for both risk-based measures and leverage) well in excess of minimum requirements. The answer provided by Hanson,

Kashyap, and Stein (2011) is that markets—concerned about losses during previous crises—force them to do so. The authors argue that the relevant way to frame the issue is in terms of how much capital banks need to maintain to absorb the losses suffered during the worst recent crisis and still meet the market-imposed minimum. The FPC calculations consider only the losses, not the market-imposed minimum. This distinction can make a large difference to the optimal capital estimates (as shown in chapter 4).

The July 2015 *Financial Stability Review* (Bank of England 2015a) reported that major UK banks were maintaining a common equity tier 1 ratio of just over 11 percent, even though the regulatory minimum was only 7 percent.[23] Similarly, according to the 2015 CCAR, large US banks (G-SIBs plus non-G-SIBs) were maintaining a tier 1 leverage ratio of nearly 9 percent in the third quarter of 2014, even though the regulatory minimum was only 4 percent.[24] Likewise, in stress tests the stressed capital hurdle is always set well above zero (in the 2016 CCAR test, the stressed hurdle rates in the severely adverse scenario were set at 4.5 percent for common equity tier 1 and 4 percent for the tier 1 leverage ratio). In short, ignoring the buffers above the minimum regulatory requirement that banks need to maintain to meet market pressures yields an unrealistically low estimate of the optimal capital ratio.

Lending Growth and the Optimal Capital Ratio

In putting banks' losses during past severe crises into perspective, the FPC does not address the question of how much capital the banking system needs after a crisis to maintain enough lending to the real economy to contribute to a satisfactory rate of economic growth. This question is at the heart of the macroprudential approach to bank supervision. It should also be of keen interest to the UK authorities. Indeed, in 2012 the Bank of England launched the "funding for lending" scheme with the explicit purpose of reinvigorating bank lending to the UK economy. The BCBS (2010d, 5) study explicitly warns that the amount of capital banks need to survive losses is not the same as the amount needed to avoid a credit crunch: "Most of the analysis focuses on losses incurred by banks and does not reflect how much additional capital would be needed to maintain a reasonable level of lending during the crisis to help avert adverse 'credit crunch' effects."

I have many misgivings about the BCBS estimates of mean losses of banks as a good indicator of the acute distress faced by large banks during the 2007–09 crisis. Nevertheless, when the BCBS does offer an estimate of the risk-weighted capital ratio needed to maintain a reasonable level of lending to the real economy, the range suggested (7 to 12 percent of risk-weighted assets) is considerably higher than its estimate of mean losses (5 percent of risk-weighted assets).

It is hard for me to see how the capital needed to meet market pressures and the capital needed to sustain healthy lending to the real economy can be accommodated with a minimum leverage ratio of 3 to 5 percent—even without bringing in the other factors (considered earlier in this chapter) favorable to a higher minimum leverage ratio.

Threshold Analysis of Optimal Capital Ratios

The FPC supplements its analysis of bank losses during the global crisis with a threshold analysis of capital ratios. Such analysis seeks to determine the capital ratio just before the crisis (end-2006) that best discriminated between stressed/failed banks and nonstressed/surviving banks during the 2007–09 crisis.

The FPC seems to have relied mainly on two studies, BCBS (2010d) and Aikman et al. (2014). These results are of interest because they seemingly sidestep the thorny issue of what is the most appropriate measure of bank losses to derive optimal capital ratios in favor of a more direct search procedure for the optimal capital ratio.

The first notable result of the threshold analysis was referred to earlier in the analysis of risk-based capital versus leverage ratios. The BCBS (2010d, 17) found that "there is little evidence that risk-based capital ratios were consistently higher for the group of nonstressed banks before the crisis." In contrast, each of four measures of leverage turned out to be higher in nonstressed banks than in stressed ones, and in six of the test runs this difference was statistically significant. In Aikman et al. (2014), the Basel I risk-based ratio is just slightly higher for surviving banks than for the failed ones, but this measure of capital turns out to be a much inferior leading indicator of bank survival/failure than a simple leverage ratio.

The second main result of the threshold analysis is that both studies find that the critical threshold for the leverage ratio lies in the 3 to 5 percent range.[25] Aikman et al. (2014) also compute the critical threshold for the Basel I risk-based capital ratio, which they estimate at 8.7 percent.

In interpreting these capital threshold results, one needs to consider two issues: (1) how the massive government intervention during the crisis affects the identification of the thresholds and (2) what the loss function is that evaluates "hits" versus "false alarms." True, banks that were intervened during the crisis are included in the "stressed" banks category. But this definition does not capture the full effects of the crisis interventions.

The problem is a familiar one in empirical work. If the "treatment" (in this case government crisis intervention) affects not only the treatment group but also the control group, the total impact of the treatment will not be revealed simply by looking at the difference in outcomes between the treatment and control groups. One also has to take into account the (unobserved) effect of the treatment on the control group.[26]

To illustrate this point, assume that in the threshold exercise a good bank capital signal (a "hit") occurs either when a bank with a relatively low capital ratio fails/is intervened or when a bank with a relatively high capital ratio survives/is not intervened. A bad bank capital signal (a "miss") occurs either when a bank with a relatively low capital ratio survives/is not intervened or a bank with a relatively high capital ratio fails/is intervened.

Now consider two examples of how the treatment in the 2007–09 crisis could affect the control group of banks. Example number one is a large Midwestern bank (Bank A) that made large loans before the crisis to General Motors and Chrysler as well as to autoworkers and to workers in auto parts suppliers for their home mortgages. If the US crisis management package had not included emergency loans to General Motors and Chrysler, those firms might well have had to declare bankruptcy, and Bank A, if it had relatively low capital, could well have failed or had to be intervened. But the threshold analysis will (incorrectly) record Bank A as a miss, because it survived even in the face of low capital. The treatment indirectly affected firms in the control group of banks even though those banks themselves were not intervened.

Now consider an international bank (Bank B) with strong counterparty links to RBS, Lloyds Bank, and Citigroup. If those three megabanks were not rescued via government intervention, Bank B (if it had relatively low capital) might well have failed or required intervention. But the threshold analysis will (incorrectly) record Bank B as a miss, because it survived even in the face of low capital. In this example the treatment also spilled over into the control group. In both examples failure to adjust for the effects of the treatment on the control group will lead to an underestimate of the optimal capital threshold.

Next consider the specification of the loss function used to evaluate the optimal capital threshold. Aikman et al. (2014) and BCBS (2010d) use a loss function that weights hits and false alarms equally. They thus select a threshold that would get at least half of the predictions right for both failed and surviving banks. The BCBS authors acknowledge that this is an arbitrary standard and not a particularly stringent one.

The cost-benefit approach, reviewed in chapter 4, looks at the same issue but can produce dramatically different results, because it does not assume that the (positive) benefits of higher capital (in terms of lower probability and cost of crises) are just offset by the (adverse) effects of higher capital on cost of financing. Instead, it values each separately for different capital levels. The FPC adopts the finding of Aikman et al. (2014) that the optimal level for the tier 1 risk-based capital ratio is about 8.5 percent. Using a cost-benefit approach that values more highly the benefits of a higher capital ratio than the costs, another BCBS study (2010c) finds the optimal risk-based ratio to be around 14 percent. The BIS (2015b) quantitative impact study of the total loss-absorbing capacity (TLAC) initiative finds that even under the most conservative assumption, the 18 percent minimum risk-based TLAC requirement cum the minimum 6.75 percent leverage ratio generates an estimated net benefit of 15 to 20 basis points of annual GDP.

In short, I do not regard the critical leverage ratios coming out of the threshold analysis as persuasive that a 3 to 5 percent minimum leverage ratio, inclusive of G-SIB surcharges, is adequate.

The Countercyclical Capital Buffer

The FPC notes that it is comfortable with a 3 percent minimum leverage ratio in large part because it has the authority to activate the 2.5 percent countercyclical capital buffer (CCL) to counter the systemic risk associated with credit booms. Using the 35 percent proportionality factor, this CCL surcharge adds 0.9 percent to the 3.0 percent minimum leverage ratio. The key question is: Will it work and can they pull the trigger during the boom?

On the first question, the conditions necessary for the countercyclical capital buffer to be effective do not seem to be satisfied, according to Cecchetti (2014), who looks at the 2009–13 experience for the advanced economies as a group. In particular, lending spreads do not seem to be very sensitive to higher capital requirements; as long as banks are reasonably well capitalized, loan volumes do not seem sensitive to changes in capital ratios; and during a credit boom, banks are likely to be profitable enough to raise equity easily and cheaply. More broadly, Cecchetti and Schoenholtz (2014) point out that information and recognition lags, response and decision lags, and transmission lags all work against the countercyclical capital buffer working as well as advertised.

On this score, the FPC might respond that the Bank of England has conducted a series of empirical studies for UK banks that suggest that the confidential and highly individualized changes in (Pillar 2) capital requirements enacted over the 1990–2011 period did have sizable (temporary) effects on bank lending (see Bridges et al. 2014 for a summary of those studies). But as the authors of those studies concede, the lending effects they identified may not translate to a publicly announced, banking system–wide increase in capital requirements, especially for large banks.[27]

In addition, there appear to be sizable "leakage" effects of such capital increases, particularly from the branches of foreign banks operating in the United Kingdom.[28] Former Bank of England Governor Mervyn King (2013, 4) has been clear about how he sees the link between bank capital and bank lending: "Those who argue that requiring higher levels of bank capital will necessarily restrict bank lending are wrong. The reverse is true. It is insufficient capital that restricts lending.... Capital supports lending and provides resilience." Bank of England Deputy Governor Andrew Bailey (2014, 7–8) offered the following assessment:

> there remains a perception in some quarters that higher capital requirements are bad for lending and thus for a sustained recovery.... Looking at the broader picture, the post-crisis adjustment of the capital adequacy standard is a welcome and necessary correction of the excessively lax underwriting and pricing of risk which caused the build-up of fragility in the banking system and led to the crisis. I do not, however, accept the view that raising capital standards damages lending. There are few, if any, banks that have been weakened as a result of raising capital.

If the countercyclical capital buffer does not deliver what it promises (in terms of curbing bank lending), the reaction could make it a "one and done" policy.[29]

One cannot have it both ways. If it is the lack of a bank lending response to increased capital requirements that in large part keeps down the "cost" of bank capital reform, the absence of that link dooms the efficacy of a countercyclical capital buffer. This does not mean that regulators and central bankers are helpless against credit booms. It just means that they have to use policy instruments other than time-varying capital requirements to address that problem. Loan-to-value limits on lenders and loan-to-income limits on borrowers in housing markets are examples of instruments that offer higher prospects for success. In addition, the People's Bank of China has shown how a string of old-fashioned increases in reserve requirements can counter bank lending surges.

On the time consistency side, the problem with the countercyclical capital buffer is that (temporary) capital increases are likely to be unpopular. As Cecchetti and Schoenholtz (2014) point out, unlike increases in interest rates, which offer immediate candy to the broad constituency of savers, higher countercyclical capital requirements are a harder sell because the benefits to society are tougher to see and take longer to show up.[30]

Given these doubts about the efficacy and time consistency of the countercyclical capital buffer, I would argue that the minimum leverage ratio in the United Kingdom is lower de facto than it is de jure.[31] The Federal Reserve also has the authority to activate a countercyclical capital buffer for its larger banks (Tarullo 2014c), but it does not (rightly) count it as part of the G-SIB leverage surcharge. Likewise, when the TLAC initiative set a final leverage ratio target for G-SIBs of 6.75 percent, it did not agree that 4.25 percent should be kept in place and that the remaining 2.50 percent would be added as needed in the form of a countercyclical capital buffer.

Without the countercyclical capital buffer, the minimum leverage ratio for the four most systemic UK banks would be just 4 percent (inclusive of the supplementary buffer) and the G-SIB leverage surcharge for those banks would be under 1 percent.[32] These levels are simply too low to offer adequate loss absorbency, provide enough lending to support the macroeconomy, and motivate G-SIBs to reduce the size of their systemic footprint over time. If all one needed to worry about for G-SIBs during the global crisis was a mean net income loss (relative to total exposure) of 2 percent or so, why was there such a massive and unprecedented government intervention to save those banks and why were the declines in market capitalization and in price-to-book ratios for those banks so deep?[33] If a 4 to 6 percent minimum leverage ratio for G-SIBs provides plenty of loss absorbency to meet the challenges of the future, why does even the (flawed) TLAC initiative ask for minimum TLAC that (if fully triggered) would amount to roughly 9 to 10 percent of total exposure?

Kindred Spirits on the Optimal Capital Ratio for UK Banks

I am not the only one who thinks that the Bank of England's current take on the appropriate minimum capital ratios for its largest banks (inclusive of systemic risk surcharges) is too lax. In a set of recent papers, Dowd (2016a, 2016c, and 2016d) argues that the comforting verdict from the Bank of England's 2014 and 2015 stress tests on its seven major banks rests on a weak foundation—and that with more reasonable hurdle rates, the results could easily be overturned. Examining the 2015 stress test results (Bank of England 2015b), Dowd (2016d) focuses on the (stressed) leverage ratio results. Using a 3 percent hurdle rate for the Basel III leverage ratio, the Bank of England found that all seven banks passed the test, with an average leverage ratio of 3.5 percent. But the best performer (Nationwide) had a surplus of only 110 basis points; four banks (Barclays, HSBC, Lloyds, and Santander) had surpluses of less than 100 basis points; and the remaining two (Standard Chartered and RBS) had no surplus at all (falling exactly on the 3 percent minimum).

Dowd (2016d) then asks what the results would be if the numerator of the Basel III leverage ratio, tier 1 capital, were replaced with common equity tier 1 capital, a superior measure of loss absorbency, but still sticking with a 3 percent hurdle rate. In this scenario, one bank fails, four have wafer-thin surpluses, and only two have surpluses that are more than insignificantly over the stressed minimum.

Dowd (2016d) then calculates what the results would be if one used a hurdle rate of 6 percent for the leverage ratio with common equity tier 1 capital in the numerator. He notes that from 2018 on, the federally insured subsidiaries of the eight US G-SIBs would have to meet a minimum Basel III leverage ratio of 6 percent.[34] For the 6 percent common equity tier 1 leverage ratio, all of the seven major UK banks would fail the test, with an average deficit of 300 basis points. In his longer and more comprehensive review of the UK stress tests, Dowd (2016c) cites use of extremely low pass standards and inadequate (capital ratio) metrics as one of the tests' key flaws.

In a separate study, Dowd (2016b) looks at all available measures of leverage (in terms of both book value and market value) for the major UK banks and how these ratios have changed since 2007. He concludes that "there has been only a modest increase in banks' capital standards since 2007 and UK bank leverage ratios are still very low. These leverage ratios indicate that UK banks are highly exposed to a renewed financial crisis" (1).

In a trio of recent papers (Vickers 2016a, 2016b, 2016c), John Vickers, the former chair of the United Kingdom's Independent Commission on Banking (ICB), has questioned the Bank of England's stance on systemic capital buffers, as well as its conclusion on broader optimal equity capital requirements. The UK framework for bank-capital regulation includes two kinds of systemic capital buffer (surcharges), one that covers G-SIBs and one that applies to ring-fenced banks that are domestically systemically important.[35] Whichever is the higher of the two applies.

Vickers (2016b) notes that the ICB thought that the Basel III minimum capital requirements were too low and therefore recommended in 2011 that the retail operations of major UK banks have a domestic systemic equity buffer of 3 percent of risk-weighted assets. About six banks—representing the bulk of British retail banking—would have qualified for this 300-basis-point capital surcharge; a few others would have faced smaller surcharges. In contrast, under the current proposal, no British bank would be required to maintain a 3 percent buffer, and the surcharge proposal for such retail (ring-fenced) banks would add just 0.5 percent of risk-weighted assets to equity capital in the system. Vickers argues that none of the reasons the Bank of England advances for this lower surcharge is persuasive, that its contention that its surcharge proposal is actually tougher than the ICB's recommendation on an apples-to-apples basis is faulty (the reverse is true), and that the relevant banks could easily achieve this higher systemic risk buffer by 2019.[36]

Vickers (2016c, 12) underlines a fundamental difference between the ICB and the Bank of England on optimal bank capital:

> Beyond this point-by-point comparison is a fundamental policy difference. The ICB considered global capital standards for equity capital to be too weak by some margin, and recommended that the UK should go well beyond them in respect of all major ring-fenced banks. Governor Carney, by contrast, is satisfied that post-crisis banking reform is substantially complete, and is proposing a systemic risk buffer for ring-fenced banks that would add relatively little equity capital to the UK system net of international requirements, and would be weaker than global requirements for major UK banking groups.

Vickers (2016c) is also critical of a recent staff study by Brooke et al. (2015) that concludes that the optimal equity requirement for British banks is 10 to 14 percent of risk-weighted assets.[37] He believes this study merits scrutiny, because it appears to be the foundation for the Bank's policy position. Among the reasons he offers for finding the study's results "very questionable" are the following: (1) The study does not recognize that equity capital is a more certain and straightforward loss absorber in a crisis than gone-concern loss absorbency; (2) the study pays too little attention to the important findings of a recent BIS study (Gambacorta and Shin 2016) that finds that better-capitalized banks lend more than weakly capitalized ones and that keeping back more of their profits for retained earnings would appreciably reduce banks' cost of equity funding; (3) the study's results focus on the costs and benefits of higher capital for normal risk conditions, when the benefits of higher capital are greatest under conditions of elevated risk;[38] and (4) the study assumes agile and clairvoyant use of the countercyclical capital buffer, which is improbable and cannot be relied upon.

Vickers' (2016c, 19) conclusion is that "equity capital of UK banking is fundamental to the country's financial stability. Equity capital has been far too thin and remains too low."

Admati (2016b) finds the analysis by Brooke et al. (2015) "fundamentally flawed." She observes that they confine the benefits of higher capital to crisis prevention and ignore other benefits, including the reduced externalities linked to intense asset sales in distress. She also takes the authors to task for presuming (falsely) that all bank lending is valuable and ignoring the fact that low capital can lead to too much risky lending, with adverse implications for bank solvency.

On the cost side of the ledger, Admati notes that Brooke et al. fail to make the critical distinction between private and social costs of higher bank capital. She argues that they provide no coherent framework for how any social costs would come about. Like Vickers (2016c), she is also critical of Brooke et al. for overestimating the benefits and underestimating the difficulties of allowing banks to go into resolution relative to the alternative of higher equity requirements.

To sum up, for all the reasons outlined above and for an economy in which resident bank assets are more than five times domestic GDP, the Bank of England's soft-touch view of optimal bank capital and of optimal systemic capital buffers just does not add up.[39]

The Federal Reserve's "Estimated Impact" Approach

The Rationale

In July 2015 the Federal Reserve published a report (Board of Governors 2015a) that explains how the risk-based capital surcharge for US G-SIBs is calibrated. The Fed calls this framework the "estimated impact" approach. It is very different from the Bank of England's symmetry and proportionality approach.

Taking its cue from the Dodd-Frank Act, the Fed study argues that one appealing definition of eliminating too big to fail is that the expected systemic loss from the failure of a G-SIB is no greater than the expected systemic loss from the failure of a large non-G-SIB. The expected systemic loss can in turn be represented as the product of its two components: the probability of default and the systemic loss given default (LGD). The goal of the G-SIB surcharge is to make the expected system loss from failure of a G-SIB equal to the expected systemic loss from the failure of a non-SIB. As by definition the systemic LGD is higher for a G-SIB than for a non-G-SIB, the only way to make the expected losses equal is to reduce the probability of default for the G-SIB enough so that it exactly offsets its higher LGD. If, for example, the failure of a G-SIB would produce twice the systemic loss of the failure of a non-G-SIB, then the probability of default for the G-SIB needs to be half as large as for a non-G-SIB. The role of the G-SIB capital surcharge is to generate that decline in the default probability for G-SIBs. The higher the score for a G-SIB's systemic LGD (relative to the reference non-SIB), the higher the surcharge needs to be.

Making the Estimated Impact Approach Operational

Three measures are needed to operationalize this calibration: a reference non-G-SIB, a way to create LGD scores for both G-SIBs and non-G-SIBs, and a function that relates a bank's capital ratio to its probability of default. In choosing a reference non-G-SIB, the Federal Reserve employs four options: a bank holding company with $50 billion in assets, a bank holding company with $250 billion in assets, the US non-G-SIB with the highest LGD score, and a hypothetical bank holding company at the cutoff line between G-SIBs and non-G-SIBs.

To create LGD scores, the Fed relies on the BCBS framework for scoring G-SIBs' systemic impact—the 12 financial indicators related to size, interconnectedness, complexity, cross-jurisdictional activity, and substitutability. In one set of LGD calculations, they use the standard 12 indicators shown in table 5.3. In another they replace the substitutability category with a measure of the firm's reliance on short-term wholesale financing.

To relate the probability of default to the risk-based capital ratio, the Fed first looks at the probability distribution of returns on risk-weighted assets for the 50 largest bank holding companies over the 1987–2014 period, with particular attention to the link between the size and probability of negative returns. It then makes a set of assumptions to relate capital levels to this probability distribution of returns. In the end the Fed is able to show that the formula for the G-SIB surcharge depends on only two factors: (1) the ratio of LGD of non-G-SIBs to G-SIBs and (2) the slope of the function that relates negative returns on risk-weighted assets to probabilities of those returns occurring. Interestingly enough, under the maintained assumptions, the G-SIB surcharge is invariant to both the level of the capital ratio at which banks fail and to the capital level (ratio) that the G-SIB surcharge is applied on top of.

With these inputs, the Fed then calculates a range of G-SIB surcharges for each of the eight G-SIBs. It calculates a range because the estimated surcharge for a given G-SIB varies with the choice of the reference non-G-SIB and the LGD scoring method (with or without wholesale financing as an indicator).[40] With these estimated G-SIB surcharges in hand, the Fed can (arguably) assign the eight G-SIBs to the right surcharge buckets shown in table 5.2

Criticism of the Methodology

I am supportive of almost any effort to increase the minimum loss absorbency of the largest banks. In addition, the concept of trying to make the expected systemic loss for a G-SIB equal to that of non-G-SIBs is attractive. Still, I am doubtful of some of the arguments and methodologies the Fed has used, as well as the conclusion that the top (risk-based) surcharge needs to be only 450 basis points.

Many of the criticisms I directed at the FPC's leverage ratio study (Bank of England 2014b) earlier in this chapter also apply to the Fed's G-SIB calibration study. Rather than repeat myself, I therefore concentrate on four particular shortcomings of the Fed study, only the first of which also applied to the FPC leverage ratio study: (1) the relevance of the historical data as a guide to future optimal capital requirements, (2) the use of the return on risk-weighted assets as the preferred measure of risk, (3) the choices made about non-G-SIB reference groups, and (4) the treatment of the probability of default.

Pitfalls of Relying Too Heavily on Historical Data

Here is what the Fed (Board of Governors 2015b, 7–8) has to say about the relevance of the historical data for drawing inferences about future optimal capital ratios:

> Data from the past three decades may be an imperfect predictor of future trends, as there are factors that suggest that default probabilities in the future may be either lower or higher than would be predicted on the basis of the historical data.

> On the one hand, these data do not reflect many of the regulatory reforms implemented in the wake of the 2007–08 financial crisis that are likely to reduce the probability of very large losses and therefore the probability of default associated with a given capital level. For example, Basel 2.5 and Basel III capital reforms are intended to increase the risk sensitivity of the risk weightings used to measure risk-weighted assets, which suggests that the risk of losses associated with each dollar of risk-weighted assets under Basel III will be lower than the historical pre–Basel III trend. Similarly, post-crisis liquidity initiatives (the liquidity coverage ratio and the net stable funding ratio) should reduce the default probabilities of large banking firms and the risk of fire sales. Together, these reforms may lessen a G-SIB's probability of default and potentially imply a lower G-SIB surcharge.

> On the other hand, however, extraordinary government interventions during the time period of the dataset (particularly in response to the 2007–08 financial crisis) undoubtedly prevented or reduced the large losses that many of the largest bank holding companies would otherwise have suffered. Because one core purpose of post-crisis reform is to avoid the need for such extraordinary interventions in the future, the G-SIB surcharge should be calibrated using the severe losses that would have materialized in the absence of such interventions; because the interventions in fact occurred, using historical RORWA (return on risk-weighted assets) may lead us to underestimate the future trend. Although the extent of the over- and under-estimations cannot be rigorously quantified, a reasonable assumption is that they roughly cancel each other out.

I am not buying it. As explained in chapter 4, if we used peak credit write-downs over the 2008–10 period (7.6 percent of total assets) as a proxy for the shocks facing US banks during the worst banking crisis since the Great Depression and if we wanted large banks, after absorbing a loss of this size, to meet a tangible leverage ratio (at the bottom of the financial cycle) of, say, approximately 6 percent, they would need a leverage ratio (at the top of the financial cycle) of about 14 percent.

This calculation does not take account of the extraordinary government intervention during that crisis, absent which credit losses could well have been 50 or even 100 percent larger, pushing the optimal leverage ratio to roughly 20 percent. One can, of course, estimate much lower optimal leverage ratios from the 2007–09 crisis experience by measuring the shock in terms of net income over several quarters or a year, because as one moves away from the nadir of the crisis, positive revenue offsets the negative influence of credit write-downs on net income. But this latter procedure presupposes that banks are stabilized enough to have the time to earn those revenues. During the nadir of the crisis, the largest and most important US financial institutions were stabilized by the very same extraordinary interventions that the Fed study now says it wishes to rule out in the future. Hence the relevant stand-alone measure of losses is the optimal leverage ratio based on the credit write-downs, not smoothed net income.

The Fed G-SIB study seems to argue that the United States could withstand another severe crisis without the extraordinary interventions employed last time and without a capital ratio (leverage ratio) anywhere near 20 percent because of postcrisis reforms to the sensitivity of risk weights and the addition of two new liquidity standards. Such a notion is surely a stretch—and a mighty big one at that.

Most of the reform on risk weights in the postcrisis period has sought to undo the damage caused by the rush to create more risk sensitivity in Basel II, especially via the internal ratings approach, an approach that Federal Reserve Governor Tarullo (2014c) has publicly branded as unhelpful and overdue for elimination (see chapter 3). Yes, the fundamental review of the trading book has now been completed and has resulted in a much needed increase in risk weights, but this increase is small potatoes relative to the huge undercapitalization outlined above (see BCBS 2015b).[41] As I argue in chapters 3 and 7, there are potentially much larger gains from eliminating the risk-based capital ratios as a Pillar 1 measure, but the official community has so far not been prepared to go there. The Basel III liquidity requirements (the liquidity coverage ratio and the net stable funding ratio) represent a step forward and will help discourage bank funding runs—but these liquidity reforms would be climbing uphill if during a severe crisis the largest banks were still regarded as severely undercapitalized or borderline insolvent.

The Fed study does not take account of the setbacks to the crisis management inventory that have taken place in the wake of the crisis (see Geithner 2016).[42] Important among them are the restrictions the US Congress has placed on the Fed's emergency lending authority. Emergency loans must now be part of programs with "broad-based eligibility" and approved by the secretary of the Treasury, leaders of Congress must be briefed promptly, and procedures must be in place to preclude lending to an insolvent institution (see Geithner 2016 and Cline and Gagnon 2013). Reflecting on these congressional restraints as well as Congressional antipathy toward quantitative easing, Posen (2016, 1) concludes that "financial stability has not yet been adequately addressed and even presents more risk now than before the crisis due to congressional distrust of the Fed." The FDIC's guarantee authority for bank debt is now also subject to prior congressional approval (Baily and Klein 2014).[43] To date the experiment with "living wills" has to be regarded as a disappointment, with little evidence that such plans are credible.[44]

On monetary policy, Summers argues that the fragile nature of the recovery will limit the speed with which the Fed can raise interest rates, which in turn limits its scope to lower interest rates, if needed, to combat the next recession or financial crisis.[45] On fiscal policy, Blanchard, Mauro, and Acalin (2015, 1) note that "the global economic and financial crisis that started in 2008 led to the most pronounced and pervasive increase in public debt ratios since World War II." In the United States, the ratio of net general government debt to GDP rose from 45 percent in 2006 to 80 percent at end-2015 (IMF 2015b). The comparable figures for G-20 advanced economies, taken as a group, are similar.

On top of this, the US Congress remains deeply divided—and sometimes paralyzed—on the relative merits of tax increases/decreases versus expenditure cuts/increases. The implication is that the room for massive fiscal support in the next severe crisis is apt to be narrower than it was in 2007–09. The less help that is available from other crisis management tools, the higher the premium on having banks reach and maintain a comfortable capital cushion.[46]

I am not the only one who is skeptical that the postcrisis improvement in the safety of large banks is as big as some officials—drawing mainly on the increase in risk-based capital ratios—claim. The market apparently also had its doubts. Sarin and Summers (2016a, 2016b) look at a group of market measures of the riskiness of banks. Five are volatility measures: historical volatility, future volatility as implied by option prices, put option data, beta (from the capital asset pricing model), and the systemic risk measure pioneered by Acharya et al. (2010). Three more are expected return measures: credit default swap spreads, preferred stock yields, and earnings-price ratios. Sarin and Summers compare the precrisis period (2002–07) with the postcrisis period (2010–15 and 2015) for three groups of banks: the 6 largest US G-SIBs, the next 50 largest US banks, and a group of large (non-Chinese) international banks. "To our surprise," they conclude, "we find that financial market information provides little support for the view that major financial institutions are significantly safer than they were before the crisis and some support for the notion that risks have actually increased" (2016a, 1).

Sarin and Summers (2016a) highlight that there has been a major decline in the market value of common equity to assets on both a risk-adjusted and risk-unadjusted basis and that this decline makes banks more vulnerable than would be indicated by book values of capital.[47] They put forward three explanations for the increase in vulnerability: Markets underestimated risk precrisis and have adjusted their views since then, regulatory capital measures are flawed and may have become more flawed over time, and banks are suffering from a decline in their franchise value. They argue that the third explanation—declining franchise value—is the most persuasive. They hint that it may have some link to regulation but do not investigate it. They also go to pains to underline that their findings do not make a case against the regulatory approaches pursued during and after the crisis.[48]

Although it did not come up in their paper, I suppose the Fed might argue that it could still salvage its position by the positive discipline effect that the TLAC initiative would have on reducing risk taking by large banks (BIS 2015b). The argument is that if large banks truly believe they will not be bailed out in a severe crisis, they will reduce their risk taking enough to appreciably lower the probability of a crisis, reducing it enough to make do with only a relatively small addition to current capital levels—that is, a minimum leverage ratio of 6.75 percent and an all-in (once the bail-in bonds are triggered) leverage-like ratio equivalent of, say, 10 percent. But as argued earlier in this chapter, TLAC capital is not big enough or assured enough and the bail-in bonds instrument is not battle-tested enough (in a systemic crisis) to convince banks (or anybody else) that it will end too big to fail.

The last two Great White Hopes for market discipline fared badly in the Great Recession. One was the alleged canary-in-the-coal-mine, disciplining role of subordinated debt. This discipline effect required that subdebtholders not be bailed out in a crisis. As Elliott, Salloy, and Santos (2012, 27) explain, this is not what happened in 2007–09:

The theory was that subordinated debtholders could be hit with losses without doing harm to constituencies that were of concern to regulators, such as depositors, senior bondholders, etc. In practice, very few regulators felt that they could allow such losses in the widespread and severe financial crisis experienced in 2008–09. The signaling and legal effects concerning the health of the troubled bank, and the potential to trigger a drying up of funding for other banks that might become troubled, were viewed as too severe to be worth the benefits of having subordinated debt holders shoulder some losses.

The other disciplining device was the prompt corrective action (PCA) guidelines present in US banking legislation since the Federal Deposit Insurance Corporation Improvement Act of 1991. The PCA guidelines were put into effect to discourage regulatory forbearance after the US savings and loan crisis. The idea was to simulate, via various capital level triggers, the discipline that the market would impose on an errant bank if there were no deposit insurance. A key part of the PCA guidelines was a closure rule that would resolve the bank at least cost to the taxpayer once its capital ratio declined to 2 percent.

In reviewing the operation of PCA in small and medium-size banks, Garcia (2010, 1) concludes that it failed: "Failed institutions avoided PCA restraints by artificially maintaining their well-capitalized status, sometimes with supervisor assistance, almost until they failed." I presume that at the worst point in the crisis, the arc of severely troubled institutions became so wide as to make the "systemic exception" to the PCA guidelines more the rule than the exception.

I think one could perhaps reap much of this discipline effect if US regulatory authorities implemented a plan to raise minimum tangible leverage ratios in US G-SIBs to, say, 14 to 18 percent, as outlined in chapter 7. Such a large increase in bank equity would be big enough and immune enough to public bailout to make plausible a stand-alone policy for large banks (as long as these banks could also count on emergency liquidity support from the central bank when needed). But such a large increase in capital requirements runs counter to the Fed's assumption that the next huge crisis could be weathered without recourse to a large increase in capital requirements.

So, no, I do not believe the Fed line that these under- and overestimations "roughly cancel each other out"—and neither should the reader.[49] What we have here is a problem of potentially misleading advertising. US G-SIBs could likely survive a severe crisis like that of 2007–09 with capital ratios not much above where they are now if US authorities and their foreign counterparts were again willing and able to do all the extraordinary crisis interventions they did last time. Alternatively, they could survive a crisis absent all those interventions if US and foreign leaders were prepared to implement a large increase in minimum leverage ratios for US G-SIBs (much beyond what is already included in TLAC). But to say that these G-SIBs could survive without either the extraordinary interventions of 2007–09 or a large increase in capital requirements is—in my opinion—trying to pull a fast one.

Return on Risk-Weighted Assets as a Measure of Risk

The Fed study argues that return on risk-weighted assets is a better measure of risk than return on total assets, because the risk weightings have been calibrated to ensure that two portfolios with the same risk-weighted assets contain roughly the same amount of risk. But this contention flies in the face of the evidence summarized in chapter 3. Numerous studies find that large banks produce very different levels of risk-weighted assets for the identical portfolio. The evidence also points to manipulation of risk weights being most severe at the largest banks. Moreover, the Fed is able to obtain a long time series on risk-weighted asset only by assuming that a dollar of risk-weighted asset measures essentially the same thing over the entire 1987–2014 period, something that is unlikely to be the case, because Basel I did not permit large banks to use their own internal models to calculate risk weights and studies suggest that risk-weight manipulation was greatest when the internal ratings approach was in its heyday. All of this means that risk-weighted assets are likely to be measured badly, both across banks in the study and over time.

These factors raise the risk that noise in the denominator of risk-weighted assets could suppress the signal in the numerator. One can, of course, argue that whatever the warts on the risk-weighted asset metrics, they will be much less troublesome than those on total assets. But then one has to explain why the leverage ratios using total assets have predicted large bank failures (both in the United States and globally) better than capital measures using risk-weighted assets in the denominator. Here the Fed should have followed the Bank of England and replaced risk-weighted assets by total assets in the denominator.

Sensitivity of the Capital Surcharge to the Choice of Non-G-SIB Reference Groups

The Fed uses four different reference groups of non-G-SIBs to estimate the expected loss for a non-G-SIB; only one of these reference groups is a "small" bank holding company (i.e., one with $50 billion or less in total assets). The Fed defends the other three reference groups by showing that their estimated LGD scores, while larger than the score for the $50 billion bank holding company, are still pretty far from the LGD scores for the eight G-SIBs.

I see three problems with the "large" reference bank holding companies. The first is that the most recent empirical evidence shows that the too big to fail subsidy cuts in at an asset size smaller than that for the larger non-G-SIB reference bank holding companies.

Cetina and Loudis (2015) look at the relationship between banks' observed (five-year) credit default swap spreads and various measures of systemic importance for an international sample of 71 banks. They find a significant negative relationship between the spreads and the measures of systemic importance, with banks perceived as too big to fail having spreads 44 to 80 points lower than other banks. Market participants appear to pay more attention to asset size than to more complex measures, such as G-SIB designation, in assessing too big to fail, and asset size acts as a threshold effect on the too big to fail subsidy, with the best-fitting models indicating asset size thresholds of $50 billion to $150 billion.

These findings raise a red flag for the Fed's G-SIB surcharge calculation: It is not sufficient to show that the expected loss from the failure of a G-SIB is equal to that of a reference non-G-SIB bank holding company if the latter carries nontrivial systemic risk. Afonso, Santos, and Traina (2014) provide empirical evidence that banks that benefit from too big to fail protection make poorer credit decisions (i.e., have higher loan impairment rates) than banks that are not too big to fail. In concert with Cetina and Loudis's (2015) finding that the too big to fail threshold cuts in at $50 billion to $100 billion in assets, this finding implies that banks that size could generate a nontrivial expected loss, even though their LGD is not that big, because their probability of default is higher than for banks without too big to fail protection. In operational terms, the implication seems clear: The Fed should choose reference bank holding companies for the surcharge calibration that have less than $50 billion of assets. Doing so would rule out all the bank holding companies that participate in the CCAR exercise. Since the size of the estimated G-SIB surcharge is lower, ceteris paribus the smaller the non-G-SIB bank holding company. Cetina and Loudis' findings also suggest that the appropriate G-SIB surcharge range is larger than the range estimated by the Fed for the $50 billion reference bank holding company. This would put the G-SIB surcharge ranges way above the ones actually chosen by the Federal Reserve (see discussion below).

A second potential problem is that the methodology used to create the LGD scores does not cover all drivers of systemic risk. Contagion can operate through large and abrupt changes in expectations as well as via traditional network effects, as shown in chapter 3. Two potential triggers for such a shift in expectations can be a perceived change in the regulatory rules of the game and a failure at a bank that uncovers a wider vulnerability than had previously been appreciated. The larger and more visible the bank is at ground zero, the more likely its experience is regarded as paradigm shifting.

A good case in point is the September 2008 failure of Washington Mutual, the largest US savings and loan bank at the time. Although it had roughly $300 billion in total assets—within shouting distance of the $250 billion reference bank holding company—it probably would not have been classified as a G-SIB because it had few G-SIB characteristics other than size. It was basically a large bank with a high exposure to the subprime mortgage market. It failed when the subprime market collapsed.

The FDIC decided to let Washington Mutual fail (and then be acquired by JPMorgan Chase), using its traditional least cost resolution. In addition to docking the shareholders and the subdebtholders, it applied a significant haircut to senior unsecured bondholders.[50] Given Washington Mutual's size, the market apparently viewed this haircutting of senior bondholders as precedent setting and as changing the rules of the game for bank debt going forward.

Washington Mutual's failure took place at the depth of the 2007–09 crisis. Contagion from the Washington Mutual precedent soon significantly reduced the market price of the senior debt of Wachovia and, soon after, that of Citigroup (Geithner 2014). As the contagion spread, the US Treasury and Federal Reserve put pressure on the FDIC to activate its systemic exception to least cost resolution and to issue a blanket FDIC guarantee on all new unsecured bank debt.

Washington Mutual turned out to carry systemic risk, even if it was not the kind of risk covered by the standard G-SIB classification methodology. Although the counterfactual is hardly straightforward, one might speculate that if a $40 billion bank holding company had haircut its senior bondholders as part of its resolution, it might well have flown beneath the radar, without triggering a wide-ranging run from senior bank debt. The operational implication is that it is better to choose a relatively small bank holding company as the reference bank holding company.

Yet a third reason for not choosing a reference bank holding company that is relatively close in size and systemic importance to a G-SIB is to avoid a methodological pitfall. The Fed study implicitly assumes that systemic LGD in the reference non-G-SIB is independent of that in the G-SIB. But consider a large non-G-SIB that is close to the G-SIB dividing line. Its size and activities are likely to be influenced by the size of the G-SIB capital surcharge as well as by the other more stringent regulatory requirements placed on G-SIBs. Indeed, one of the purposes of the G-SIB surcharge is to get the largest banks to reduce their systemic footprint. This creates the same methodological problem discussed earlier in this chapter—namely, that treatment affects not only the treatment group (in this case G-SIBs) but also the control group (non-G-SIBs). The rub is that the effect may be hard to estimate.[51]

When three of the four non-G-SIB reference groups are considerably larger than the $50 billion Dodd-Frank guideline, more systemic risk is introduced into the reference groups than is either necessary or desirable. I am pressing the reference group issue, because in the Fed's estimated impact methodology, the choice of a reference group has an enormous impact on the calculated surcharge. Consider the estimated surcharges for the largest G-SIB, JPMorgan Chase. When using a bank holding company with $50 billion in assets as the reference non-G-SIB under Method 1 (the standard G-SIB scoring index), JPMorgan Chase's surcharge range was 960 to 1,240 basis points. In contrast, it was 250 to 320 basis points when the reference group was the hypothetical bank holding company on the dividing line between G-SIBs and non-G-SIBs. For the US G-SIB with the lowest systemic score, State Street Bank, under the $50 billion reference bank holding company and Method 1, its surcharge range is 740 to 960 basis points versus 20 to 30 basis points under the dividing-line bank holding company. What's more, when calculating G-SIB surcharges under four reference group options, only one of which uses a small bank holding company, there is a natural tendency to think of the "average" calculated surcharge as a reasonable central estimate. Had the Fed stuck with the Dodd-Frank $50 billion reference non-G-SIB, the calibrated G-SIB surcharges would be in the 740 to 1,270 range, not the 100 to 450 surcharge schedule finally selected.

Treatment of Default Risk

The Fed study allows LGD to differ from one bank to the next, but my reading of their model is that bank-by-bank characteristics (outside of those already captured in its LGD) are not allowed to influence the probability of default. Consider three characteristics: dependence on wholesale financing, complexity, and too big to fail status. In one of the methods the Fed uses to calculate a bank's LGD (Method 2), a bank with high dependence on short-term wholesale financing gets (all else equal) a higher LGD than one with a lower dependence. But higher dependence on short-term wholesale financing does not apparently increase that bank's relative probability of default—despite the message from the 2007–09 crisis that banks with high dependence on wholesale financing showed themselves to be (all else equal) more vulnerable than those with a more secure retail deposit base. Indeed, it seems to me that the wholesale financing characteristic fits more comfortably in the probability of default matrix than in the LGD one.

Next consider complexity. A G-SIB that is large and very complex is not only likely to be difficult to resolve (increasing its LGD), it also is likely to be difficult to manage well, increasing its probability of default.

Finally, recall the link between too big to fail status and credit risk highlighted in Afonso, Santos, and Traina (2014) and BIS (2015b). If the largest G-SIBs have official support credit ratings higher than those of smaller bank holding companies, then the same channel that produced roughly 70 percent of the expected benefits from the TLAC proposal (see BIS 2015b) implies that these banks should have a higher probability of default than smaller G-SIBs or non-G-SIBs.

If some bank characteristics affect both the LGD and the probability of default (in the same direction), it will not be legitimate to derive the needed decline in the probability of default for a G-SIB just from the ratios of LGDs (for the G-SIB and the non-G-SIB) and the slope of the default function. G-SIBs would then have two undesirable features relative to non-G-SIBs: a higher LGD and a higher probability of default. Both would have to be taken into account in solving for the appropriate G-SIB surcharge. The implication is that the G-SIB surcharges would be larger than when one assumes that the G-SIBs and non-G-SIBs differ only because of their LGDs.

A further strong hint that the Fed's estimated impact approach is underestimating the appropriate G-SIB surcharge comes from a study by Laeven, Ratnovski, and Tong (2014). They examine the relationship between bank size and systemic risk using an international sample of 1,250 banks from 52 countries. They concentrate on systemic risk during the July 2007–December 2008 period, using as their measure of systemic risk Acharya et al.'s (2010) SRISK (a bank's contribution to the deterioration of the capitalization of the financial system as a whole during a crisis). They find that large banks contribute more to systemic risk when they have less capital and fewer deposits and engage more in market-based activities, as indicated by the share of noninterest income in total income or the share of loans in assets. They estimate how much additional capital would be necessary to equalize the systemic risk associated with banks of different sizes. Their estimates suggest that a bank with $1 trillion in total assets would need an additional 10 percentage points in risk-weighted capital (or roughly an additional 6 percentage points in the leverage ratio if using the ratio of risk-weighted assets to total assets for US banks) to generate the same amount of systemic risk as a bank with $100 billion in assets.[52] The difference between a $2 trillion bank and a $50 billion one would be much larger.

Summing Up on Estimated Impact Approach

The arguments and evidence presented in this chapter indicate that the Fed's current G-SIB risk-based surcharge range (100 to 450 basis points) is too low and too flat. Since the estimated impact methodology for calculating the G-SIB surcharge is independent of the base level of the capital ratio,[53] these findings would apply with even greater force to the current G-SIB surcharge on the Basel III leverage ratio, where G-SIBs face a minimum leverage ratio of 5 to 6 percent (under the enhanced supplementary leverage ratio) versus a minimum for other large banks of 3 percent, and a minimum tier 1 leverage ratio of 4 percent for all US banks (regardless of size). The current spread of 200 to 300 basis points between the minimum leverage ratio for the largest, most systemically important bank (JPMorgan Chase) and a bank with assets of less than $50 billion is way too low.

Conclusions

The gap between current capital ratios and ratios that would be desirable from a social point of view looks particularly large for leverage ratios. The current Basel III minimum leverage ratio is only 3 percent, and the Financial Stability Board's TLAC proposal for G-SIBs, even if it were fully implemented in 2022, calls for a final minimum leverage-like ratio of just 6.75 percent.

Likewise, in view of the evidence put forward in this chapter, the US G-SIB surcharge for the Basel III leverage ratio of only 2 to 3 percent (encased in the enhanced supplementary leverage ratio)—bringing the minimum to 5 to 6 percent—looks inadequate. Equally telling, US regulatory and supervisory officials have applied essentially the same capital hurdle rate to all bank holding companies participating in the CCAR stress tests, without regard to the large variations in their systemic importance.[54] Using the same hurdle rate seems inconsistent with the "differentiated" approach taken with other supervisory tools.

The bottom line is straightforward: Stress tests should introduce higher and more differentiated capital hurdle rates, in order to ease the way toward a more socially optimal bank funding structure. The proposal I introduce in chapter 7 calls for minimum leverage ratios for banks in the United States of 10 percent for small banks, 11 to 13 percent for large banks, and 14 to 18 percent for G-SIBs.

Endnotes

1. After laying out the additional requirements applicable to banking firms with at least $250 billion in assets or $10 billion in on-balance-sheet foreign assets, Tarullo (2014c, 2) lists the special requirements that apply to the eight US firms designated as G-SIBs: "risk-based capital surcharges, the enhanced Basel III supplementary leverage ratio, tighter single counterparty credit limits, and a long-term debt requirement designed to support the effectiveness of orderly resolution processes. In addition, the supervision of these firms is overseen by the Large Institution Supervision Coordinating Committee (LISCC), an interdisciplinary group created by the Federal Reserve Board in 2010."

2. Of the world's 75 largest banks, approximately 45 are not classified as G-SIBs.

3. In GAAP terms, G-SIB leverage ratio differences with non-G-SIB and with smaller banks are less marked than for IFRS comparisons, but nevertheless are still evident.

4. As a cautionary note, these size comparisons for tier 1 risk-based capital ratios need to be supplemented with comparisons using other (better) measures of risk-based capital (like CET1 ratios) before a more definitive conclusion can be reached.

5. The label "symmetry and proportionality" is mine, not the FPC's.

6. The Bank of England calls these surcharges "buffers," in line with the language of Basel III.

7. The 35 percent proportionality factor is 3.0 percent divided by 8.5 percent.

8. Goodhart's law states that any statistical relationship will break down once it is used for policy purposes. In the case of leverage ratios, the argument is that since all bank assets will then have the same risk weight, banks will game the system by loading up on high-risk assets—with adverse consequences for both the diagnostic performance of leverage ratios and financial stability.

9. In the Bank of England (2014b) model, the critical risk weight is the ratio of the minimum leverage ratio to the minimum risk-weighted measure. Hence the 35 percent magic constant indicates that the 3 percent leverage ratio would bind on UK banks with an average risk weight of 35 percent or less, versus an average observed risk weight for major UK banks of roughly 40 percent. According to the Bank of England, "a 3 percent minimum requirement is consistent with the FPC's leverage ratio framework playing a complementary role alongside the risk-weighted framework."

10. The three components of the 5 percent minimum leverage ratio are the 3 percent minimum leverage ratio, the 1.05 percent G-SIB surcharge, and the 0.9 percent countercyclical capital buffer.

11. A 2008 Federal Reserve study by Bassett and King (2008) on the condition of US banks in 2007 notes that "the share of assets at well-capitalized banks remained above 99 percent in 2007."

12. The Liikanen Report (2012, 22) highlights the cross-country effects of bailouts of banks: "Had the US allowed AIG to fail, it is not clear how any of the banks exposed to AIG counterparty risk would have fared faced with additional losses (EU banks included), the drain on their capital, and the indirect effects of the turmoil that would have followed in markets to which they were exposed."

13. Cohen et al. (2014) find that earnings management at US banks was positively related to CEO pay for performance sensitivity and negatively to board independence.

14. How the fair value of an asset is determined depends on the quality of the market in which it is traded. Level 1 assets are traded in a broad, deep, liquid secondary market. Level 2 assets are assets that do not have a liquid secondary market of their own but for which close substitutes are traded in a liquid market. Level 3 assets are assets in which the market for close substitutes is also illiquid. An asset may be shifted from one level to another if secondary markets change.

15. Most financial institutions use mixed attribute accounting, which combines features of fair value accounting and historical cost accounting. Herring (2013) points out that classifying assets by intended holding period provides protection against the volatility of fair value accounting. If assets are classified as trading assets, the change in their fair value has to be included in the income statement. In contrast, if classified as held to maturity, changes in their fair value need to be included in reported earnings only if the asset is judged to be impaired or if it is sold at a value other than at amortized cost. If the asset is classified as available for sale, it is excluded from earnings but is reported in a special account (called "other comprehensive income").

16. "Backfilling" refers to the practice of substituting a new fund manager's (usually favorable) historical returns for the (usually less favorable) returns of the departing fund manager.

17. See also my summary in chapter 9 of the new report on ending too big to fail by the Federal Reserve Bank of Minneapolis (2016). By paying particular attention to the large losses suffered during the Japanese banking crisis of 1997–2001 and the Icelandic banking crisis of 2008, the Minneapolis Fed concludes that the optimal leverage ratio for US banks is roughly 15 percent—versus estimates of 4 to 6 percent when only mean peak losses from a sample of banking crises in advanced economies is employed.

18. For a broader discussion of efforts by regulators to identify where the risk was hiding in the run-up to the 2007–09 global crisis, see Knight (2007).

19. These figures refer to all losses, not just peak losses.

20. Looking at the negative tail of the loss distribution for six countries over a longer period, the BCBS (2010d) finds that the mean of the maximum loss was 10 percent but that the largest of the maximum losses was more than 41 percent.

21. Of course, when one goes from peak losses to cumulative losses, a longer time horizon can contribute to a higher estimate of bank losses.

22. Bernanke (2015, 399) emphasizes the importance of fire sale of assets for contagion: "Perhaps the most dangerous channel of contagion...is a fire sale of assets.... If many institutions are trying to unload difficult-to-sell assets at the same time, then the market price of those assets will plunge. As asset values fall, institutions' financial conditions deteriorate further, increasing their creditors' fears and possibly leading to even more widespread runs."

23. For expositional purposes, I omit here the issues connected with the identification of the bottom of the financial cycle (see chapter 4).

24. The FPC does allude to the need for adequate capital buffers in its discussion of the 8.5 percent minimum for tier 1 risk-weighted capital. But if one took actual tier 1 holdings plus bank losses during the 2007–09 crisis, there is no way to get anywhere close to an 8.5 percent minimum risk-based capital metric.

25. The highest leverage ratio in the sample used by Aikman et al. (2014) is about 9 percent; it is not possible to arrive at a critical threshold higher than that. In contrast, in studying

US banking crises all the way back to the 1860s, Barth and Miller (2017) have observations on bank leverage ratios that extend up to 40 percent or so—and they find optimal leverage ratios for US banks that hover around 20 percent. One of their findings bears repeating:

> One implication of our findings is that it may be important to include periods when capital was higher when measuring the association between changes in capital and changes in the probability of a banking crisis. (Barth and Miller 2017, 24)

26. The classic example of treatment effect is the impact of unionization on wages. Comparing the wages of workers in unionized (treatment group) and nonunionized (control group) firms would not necessarily reveal the impact of unionization on wages, because employers in nonunion firms may set wages for their workers with the aim of deterring unionization; the treatment (unionization) affects the control group as well as the treatment group (see Ashenfelter, Johnson, and Pencavel 1972).

27. For example, Noss and Toffano (2014) note that when capital ratios are relatively low, increased systemwide capital requirements could improve confidence and reduce banks' cost of funding enough to allow them to increase capital levels without reducing their lending.

28. Aiyar, Calomiris, and Wieladek (2012) find that unregulated banks (resident foreign branches) increase lending enough in response to higher capital requirements on regulated banks to offset roughly a third of the initial impulse.

29. Even if the countercyclical capital buffer does not restrict bank lending, the increase in capital would still be of benefit (in loss absorbency terms) once the boom ends and the losses from it erode capital. If, however, the buffer offers only a loss absorbency side benefit, there is no point in having it rather than permanent and unconditional increases in bank capital requirements.

30. Hartmann (2015) offers an additional caution about the downside of the countercyclical capital buffer. The Bank of England's intention is to reduce capital requirements once the credit cycle turns down. But if the initial level of the capital requirement is not high, then although the initial effect of the capital decrease is stimulatory, the medium-term effect could be contractionary if the lower capital level is not sufficient to absorb the higher level of losses in the downturn.

31. One could, of course, regard the countercyclical capital buffer as solely increasing loss absorbency, not as having any countercyclical effect (leaving that to other macroprudential instruments). But then it would seem preferable to just have the full leverage amount available all the time, without the uncertainty attached to whether the Bank of England would actually activate the countercyclical capital buffer.

32. According to a UK Treasury (2015) report on the leverage ratio, the total leverage requirement (exclusive of the countercyclical capital buffer) for HSBC, Barclays, RBS, and Standard Chartered would be 3.875 percent, 3.70 percent, 3.525 percent, and 3.35 percent, respectively. For ring-fenced banks and large building societies, the total leverage requirement (exclusive of the countercyclical capital buffer) would be 3.35 to 4.05 percent.

33. According to the Bank of England (2008b), the market capitalization of major UK banks fell from over $700 billion in July 2007 to about $350 billion in October 2008. The de-

cline for US commercial banks was similar, from $650 billion to roughly $375 billion. Price-to-book ratios at UK banks fell from 2 in 2007 to less than 1 in October 2008.

34. The 6 percent minimum for the insured depositories of the eight US G-SIBs will have tier 1 capital, not common equity tier 1, in the numerator. In addition, the hurdle rates in the US stress tests do not yet include any G-SIB capital surcharges; all banks participating in the test face essentially the same hurdle rate. In the 2016 CCAR test, the average stressed tier 1 leverage ratio for the 33 banks was 5.9 percent versus a hurdle rate of 4.0 percent. The tier 1 leverage ratio used in the US tests has total assets, not total leverage exposure, in the denominator. Total leverage exposure is considerably larger than total assets for US G-SIBs taken as a group. Although on an apples-to-apples basis US G-SIBs appear to have higher Basel III leverage ratios than major UK banks, I suspect that most US G-SIBs would also fail a test with a stressed 6 percent common equity tier 1 Basel III–type leverage ratio.

35. Vickers (2016b, 2) defines ring-fenced banks as "independently capitalized entities (which may be part of wider banking groups) that carry out core retail banking activities and are prohibited from engagement in investment banking activities."

36. Vickers (2016b, 3) writes "Thus the Bank of England's policy (on domestic systemic risk buffers) is significantly softer."

37. I did not review Brooke et al. (2015) earlier in this chapter because my criticisms of it overlap to a substantial degree with my criticism of Bank of England (2014a).

38. Vickers (2016a) emphasizes that estimated crisis probability would be six times higher if conditioned on peak risk conditions rather than normal ones. Brazier's (2015) rationale for the Bank of England's relatively low minimum leverage requirements suffers from the same misunderstanding.

39. The corresponding figure for the United States—even including Fannie Mae and Freddie Mac—is 145 percent (see Pagano et al. 2014).

40. Because the LGD is lower for a small reference non-G-SIB (e.g., $50 billion in assets) than for a larger non-G-SIB (e.g., the largest non-G-SIB that is not a G-SIB), the estimated capital surcharges will be smaller when the former is used as the reference bank than when the latter is used. Similarly, because of the way the Fed weights wholesale financing in computing its LGD scores, G-SIBs that have relatively high dependence on such financing will generate relatively high LGD scores and as such will (all else equal) be subject to a higher estimated surcharge.

41. The increase in risk weights is expected to be less than 5 percent of the overall Basel III minimum capital requirement. It will take effect January 1, 2019.

42. Geithner (2016, 19) evaluates postcrisis limitations on the financial crisis toolkit in three areas: lending programs, guarantee programs, and capital programs. For each of 21 financial crisis tools, he asks: Could we do it today? His answer is "no" for 4 of 9 lending programs, 4 of 5 guarantee programs, and 4 of 4 capital programs. He draws the following implication (p. 20): "Together, these characteristics of the post-crisis emergency regime create a heightened vulnerability to a future systemic financial crisis. The combination of a more limited lender of last resort, no standing guarantee or broader capital authority, and a resolution regime designed to prevent the use of public resources and impose losses on current creditors is a dangerous combination. And when considered in the context of a much more constrained power of the monetary and fiscal policy tools, this mix of constraints threatens to leave us even less well prepared to deal with future crises than we were in 2007." Geithner (2016) is less optimistic than I am about the abil-

ity of much higher capital ratios to resolve this problem. He points to the coexistence in the United States of high capital ratios and a host of costly banking crises in the five decades before the Great Depression. Barth and Miller (2017), however, present new empirical evidence that, after holding other factors constant, higher capital ratios reduced significantly the probability of banking crises in that era. Scott (2016) argues that the US Congress has dramatically weakened the power of the government to respond to contagion in financial markets, including limitations on the Fed's LOLR actions.

43. Because of the size of the potential government liability attached to FDIC guarantees on bank debt, I am in favor of subjecting this FDIC authority to congressional approval. However, as Baily and Klein (2014) argue, such conditionality could result in costly delays to government action in a severe crisis.

44. Kashkari's (2016, 3) assessment of living wills is to the point: "Of the eight largest US banks, both the FDIC and the Federal Reserve recently deemed the living wills of five of them 'not credible.' Two of the eight banks were deemed 'not credible' by either the FDIC or the Federal Reserve, but not both. The living will of the one final bank, the best of the group, wasn't actually rated 'credible.' It was just not 'not credible.' This does not inspire a lot of confidence."

45. Summers argues as follows: "Historical experience suggests that when recession comes it is necessary to cut interest rates by more than 300 basis points. I agree with the market that the Fed likely will not be able to raise interest rates by 100 basis points a year without threatening to undermine the recovery. But even if this were possible, the chances are very high that recession will come before there is room to cut interest rates enough to offset it" ("Preparing for the Next Recession," *Washington Post*, December 6, 2015).

46. After reviewing postcrisis reforms to reduce the probability and cost of banking crises, Eichengreen (2015, 56) concludes: "The one thing we know for sure is that bank failures will happen. Whether their systemic consequences will now be less as a result of postcrisis reforms remains to be seen. There are reasons for doubt."

47. Sarin and Summers (2016a, 31) note: "Even though banks…are much less levered than previously, the declines in market valuation of banks have been so large that *measured on a market basis they have less equity relative to assets than they did previously*" (emphasis in original).

48. I am less surprised by the findings of Sarin and Summers than the authors seem to be, for at least four reasons. First, market indicators vastly underestimated the risk at large banks right before the crisis (see Greenspan 2010); the average credit default swap spread for the six largest US banks in early 2007 stood at 17 basis points. Second, low leverage ratios at large banks sent the right signal of high vulnerability just before the crisis (Hoenig 2013). Third, the change in average tangible leverage ratios for large international banks between, say, 2006 and 2015 is considerably smaller than the change in risk-weighted capital ratios that the authors and most officials highlight. Fourth, there have been some setbacks to the crisis management architecture and to the potential ammunition for fiscal and monetary policy that make the "net" positive effect of postcrisis reforms smaller than officials imply. I think one can get a better assessment of bank risk by using an eclectic indicator system than by relying on market measures of risk alone or book values of capital alone, as I suggest in chapter 7. The relationship between franchise value and bank risk taking needs more investigation. Martynova, Ratnovski, and Vlahu (2014) find, in contrast to Sarin and Summers' conjecture, that higher franchise value can increase risk taking, because it makes it easier for banks to borrow more.

49. In Fed folklore is a piece of advice attributed to former Governor Henry Wallich. The preferred answer to an impossible question, such as how many cats and dogs there are on the moon, is "an equal number." Perhaps the authors of the Fed estimated impact approach were appealing to the Wallich rule when gauging the net impact of past and future government intervention on the optimal capital ratio.

50. Bovenzi (2015) reports that holders of Washington Mutual's subdebt and senior debt suffered losses of about $11 billion in the global financial crisis.

51. If the presence of a sizable G-SIB surcharge induces the reference bank holding company to shrink in size or systemic importance, the Fed's formula will overstate what the appropriate G-SIB surcharge should be.

52. I am indebted to Lev Ratnovski of the IMF for producing this estimate from the regression estimates in Laeven, Ratnovski, and Tong (2014).

53. As a robustness check, it would need to be determined by how much the slope of the relationship between the probability and the size of net income losses changes when one redefines the return on assets to have total assets in the denominator instead of risk-weighted assets.

54. As summarized in chapter 9, in 2016 the Fed (see Tarullo 2016) proposed to include the risk-based surcharge for G-SIBs in its CCAR stress tests, beginning no earlier than 2018.

6

Lessons from the US and EU-Wide Stress Tests

This book reviews the experience of US and EU-wide supervisors with bank stress tests since 2009, with an eye toward identifying lessons and policy recommendations for supervisors in the United States, Europe, and other countries that may be considering whether and how to alter their own stress test exercises. This chapter lays out seven key lessons gleaned from that experience.

First, bank stress tests are likely to become the central pillar of banking supervision, because they respond to a demand that other parts of the supervisory toolkit cannot easily accommodate and because they offer more flexibility to meet country-specific needs than the Basel international regulatory regime. As such, there is a strong case for having supervisors around the globe upgrade their stress testing systems to increase their credibility.[1]

The global economic and financial crisis of 2007–09 demonstrated in spades just how costly systemic banking crises can be. In such crises the opacity of bank financial statements, combined with elevated uncertainty about macroeconomic and market risks, make it extremely difficult for market participants and the public alike to get an accurate picture of the solvency of the banking system as a whole as well as that of individual banks. Bank-capital ratios are static and backward looking and do not address tail risk within a forward-looking set of severe but still plausible scenarios. With stress tests, supervisors can consider risk configurations that are relevant but do not exist in the historical record. Analysis of one bank at a time—be it from on-site or off-site inspection—does not offer the horizontal comparison of banks that is available in a stress test, making the former less useful than the latter for sorting weak banks from stronger ones. Statements by senior bank managers about the health of their banks are likely to be regarded by the public as less objective than those of supervisors charged with protecting the public interest. Stress tests also provide a simple and understandable metric with which to evaluate the capital adequacy of banks—namely, a comparison of what the capital ratio would be under extremely adverse conditions with the capital hurdle rate. Pairing stress tests with remedial actions to eliminate undercapitalization provides an integrated solution to banking problems at hand.

Second, stress tests have the potential to contribute to financial stability, but their effectiveness in practice depends on the institutional framework and design. Just conducting a set of stress tests does not necessarily make the results credible. Stress test managers should therefore evaluate their stress test designs and frameworks against best practice.

Participating banks should account for a substantial part of the banking system's assets. If the country has a financial system that is not bank dominated, a way needs to be found to assess how fragilities in the nonbank sector and in systemically important nonbanks could affect the banking system. This guideline is particularly relevant for the United States, where the nonbank sector is dominant and played an important role in the 2007–09 crisis.

The supervisor coordinating the tests should have not only the resources and authority to obtain the necessary private data inputs from the banks but also the capacity to evaluate independently the quality of those inputs, as well as the impact of the shocks assumed in the scenarios on bank capital. Over time supervisors should seek to develop their own suite of models, both to guard against model risk from a particular model or two and to validate the reasonableness of models used by the banks in any bank-run tests.

Test coordinators must also have the political independence to be able to report the results of the tests as they see them. If markets perceive that the tests are rigged to produce an overly optimistic and politically convenient pattern of outcomes for bank failures and the aggregate capital shortfall, publication of results is likely to do little to bolster confidence. This caveat applies with particular force to the EU-wide stress tests, where far too much national discretion in the definition of bank capital has weakened their quality, and outmoded provisioning and credit write-down practices (in some EU economies) have allowed a large stock of nonperforming loans to languish on banks' books.[2]

The scenarios should address the major risks currently and prospectively facing the economy and the banking system. Since such scenarios are meant to be "what if" exercises, it is not helpful to rule out certain scenarios just because they run counter to current policy objectives. Likewise, it detracts from their credibility if the scenarios cover only a minor part of the relevant risk exposures or the "look-back" periods used to estimate the impact of the shocks are not long enough to encompass some of the most severe banking crises in the country's history. The 2009 Supervisory Capital Assessment Program (SCAP) scenarios took as a benchmark for some loan losses the historical loss rate during the Great Depression, which occurred more than 80 years earlier. In short, stress tests are not likely to be reassuring if they do not contain much stress.

Finding a way to link the results of the stress test with remedial actions to correct undercapitalization is crucial. The innovation of the US Comprehensive Capital Analysis and Review (CCAR) exercises—to embed the stress tests in the capital planning process of banks—is a good one that merits consideration in other jurisdictions. Bank supervisors need to have not only a mandate to suspend temporarily dividend payments and to share buybacks, and parts of executive compensation when capita hurdle rates in stress tests are not achieved, but also the will to enforce that mandate.

Third, bank stress tests do not operate in a vacuum. Even when the design of the stress test itself is sound, it will be difficult in a severe crisis to sell a finding that the "banks are safe" if other crisis management policies are so weak that the distribution for bank prospects contains a fat catastrophic tail. One reason the market accepted the 2009 SCAP results as credible is that they were embedded in an aggressive, governmentwide crisis management initiative that included, among other interventions, the Economic Stimulus Act of 2008, the Troubled Asset Relief Program (TARP), the Term Asset-Backed Securities Loan Facility (TALF), the Commercial Paper Funding Facility, the federal purchase of government-sponsored enterprises' debt and of mortgage banking securities, term auction credit, the Federal Reserve's supplementary financing account, guarantees of bank debt by the Federal Deposit Insurance Corporation (FDIC), the American Recovery and Reinvestment Act of 2009, and the passage of additional emergency unemployment benefits—all carried out against a backdrop of very easy monetary policy.

In contrast, the early EU-wide stress tests had a hard time gaining credibility, in part because the crisis management effort was less forceful and effective. European Central Bank (ECB) monetary policy was not consistently accommodative enough, and the introduction of quantitative easing was late in coming, as detailed in chapter 1.[3] The burden of balance of payments adjustment fell too heavily on debtor countries in the euro area periphery and not heavily enough on surplus countries; fiscal policy adjustment in the periphery was too rapid for such weak economies; too much of support programs in the periphery went to pay off bank creditors relative to the amounts allocated to funding the fiscal deficit; the right kind of bank recapitalization was too small and the long-standing policy of "no exit" for the weakest banks contributed to low profitability; and reform of the European Union's crisis management architecture took too long.

A **fourth** lesson concerns the use of bank stress tests in crisis prevention. Important parts of the 2009–16 stress test experience in the United States and European Union have been for crisis management. It is in that context that stress tests have been judged (with both positive and negative verdicts).

But as emphasized in chapter 3, it is troubling that stress tests performed so poorly in the run-up to the worst economic and financial crisis since the Great Depression, failing to provide early warning of the banking system's vulnerability not just in the United States but in almost all the economies that subsequently underwent systemic banking crises in 2007–09. Two corrective measures are called for.

The first is to draw more heavily on the empirical literature on early warning models of banking crises and to integrate that analysis better into the stress testing exercise. Top-down, dual-threshold models find that banking system vulnerability is greatest when there is both an abnormally rapid rate of growth in credit to the nonfinancial private sector and an abnormally rapid rise in real property prices. These models should be an integral part of the toolkit, because they performed well in forecasting most of the major systemic banking crises of the past several decades, including the 2007–09 episodes. Fortunately, these models are parsimonious and can be estimated and evaluated in any economy with time series data on credit aggregates and property prices.

The second fix is tougher. It involves getting enough feedback, contagion, and amplification effects into the modeling of the financial sector during a crisis that a seemingly moderate shock to the banking system can produce the kind of real economy and bank-capital effects observed in an actual severe crisis. The "stresses" and changes in the behavior of market participants that are incorporated in today's bank stress tests are still removed from those that occur in a real banking/financial crisis. The former do not incorporate enough elements of the leverage cycle, enough shifts in expectations, enough funding problems, enough fire sales of assets, enough nonlinearities and fat tails, enough interaction between the bank and nonbank financial sectors, and enough adaptation by agents. In addition, there are some tentative signs that the outcomes of the past few CCAR tests are becoming too predictable for comfort.

(a) Note that when former Federal Reserve Chairman Ben Bernanke testified to Congress in 2007 about the subprime crisis, he estimated that it would generate total losses in the neighborhood of $50 billion to $100 billion (Wessel 2009, 93).[4] (b) But as noted earlier, when Bernanke gave testimony in an AIG court case (Da Costa 2014), he explained that, by September and October of 2008, 12 of 13 of the most important financial institutions in the United States were at risk of failure within a period of a week or two. The question for stress test architects and modelmakers is, How do you make your models generate a transition from (a) to (b) in the course of, say, a year or two? This is not a technical sideshow. In stress modeling, it is the main event.

Even the most advanced stress testing programs acknowledge that they are in the earlier stages of dealing with this tough analytical issue. But they also argue that they are making progress. Accelerating that progress will probably mean that the scenarios in future stress tests—and the models that underpin them—will be more complex and varied than today's versions. In the face of added complexity, it will also be challenging to keep readable and understandable the annual reports summarizing the methodology and the results of the stress tests.

In the end, stress test managers have little choice. If they want the results of the tests to be credible, they will have to look for their keys where they lost them, not under the lamp post.

The **fifth** lesson comes from the macroprudential approach to bank supervision. When banking supervisors make the determination that the banking system is undercapitalized and banks need to reach a higher capital ratio, it is important for economic growth that they translate that higher capital target into an absolute amount of capital that should be raised. The target must be expressed in terms of the numerator of the capital ratio. If instead supervisors allow banks to choose how they will achieve the higher capital ratio, there is a good chance that the banks will opt to make much of the adjustment by cutting back on loans, engaging in fire sales of assets, and derisking (that is, rearranging their portfolio or redoing their internal risk-weight models, all with the aim of lowering their risk-weighted assets). These methods of lowering the denominator of the capital ratio—even if they seem to be the lowest-cost option to banks themselves—will not be the lowest-cost option for the macroeconomy. They will be contractionary.

As highlighted in chapter 1, the contrast between these two approaches to dealing with a capital shortfall was clearly illustrated by the 2009 post-SCAP recapitalization in the United States and the 2011 EU-wide capital exercise. In the United States, the 10 banks with capital shortfalls were required to raise absolute dollar amounts of new capital. In contrast, EU banks that fell below the 9 percent capital hurdle rate were left to choose how they would achieve the higher ratio. The April 2014 IMF *Global Financial Stability Report* (IMF 2014a) reported the results of that European Banking Authority decision. Between the third quarter of 2011 and the third quarter of 2013, EU banks raised their core tier 1 capital ratios by 2.4 percentage points, but over 60 percent of that increase (1.5 percentage points) was accounted for by deleveraging and derisking; less than 40 percent (0.9 percentage points) came from raising new capital.[5] Given the priority rightly placed on achieving a satisfactory rate of global growth, it is important that future efforts to raise bank capital ratios follow a recapitalization strategy that is growth friendly.

The **sixth** lesson is about the bank-capital metric that would convey the most useful diagnostic information in stress tests. Basel III rightfully put a lot of focus on the numerator in bank-capital ratios and helped move the system in the direction of higher-quality capital. Unfortunately, it did not do enough for the denominator. Although it introduced a leverage ratio for the first time in global bank regulation, this unweighted measure of bank assets was seen as a backup to the more traditional risk-weighted measures. In addition, the measure of capital that it settled on for the numerator of the leverage ratio (tier 1 capital) represented a backward step from the message it was sending elsewhere that the emphasis should be on the highest-quality capital (common equity tier 1).

The empirical evidence is now very strong that for large global banks, leverage ratios do a much better job than risk-weighted measures of differentiating the sick from the healthy. With hindsight it should have been obvious fairly early on in the global crisis that measures of bank capital based on risk-weighted assets just didn't smell right. Almost all the largest US financial institutions that ran into trouble during the crisis had risk-weighted capital measures that allowed them to be classified as "well capitalized" on their last reports, whereas low leverage ratios were simultaneously pointing to very thin capital cushions (Hoenig 2012).

In Europe the story was similar. The bank with the highest core tier 1 capital ratio (over 20 percent) in the 2011 EU-wide stress test (Irish Life and Permanent) had to be placed in a government restructuring plan in 2012. Dexia passed the 2011 test with flying colors, only to fail several months later.

Vestergaard and Retana (2013) show that the early warning properties of core tier 1 capital in identifying subsequent bank failures (after the 2011 EU-wide stress test) were much inferior to a leverage ratio.[6] Econometric analysis on a wider sample of large international banks reaches the same qualitative conclusion (Blundell-Wignall and Rochet 2012). Moreover, the risk-based measures of bank capital create an uneven playing field internationally as well as domestically (between large and small banks), and they correlate less well than leverage ratios with market-based measures of bank health, as argued in chapter 3. And none of this even takes into account the huge cost differential associated with producing internal bank estimates of these risk weights.

All of this suggests that if one were designing Basel III from scratch, it would make much more sense to build minimum bank-capital standards around a leverage ratio. Doing so would bypass (for regulatory purposes) the difficult task of trying to gauge the correct risk weights; eliminate incentives that work against revitalizing loan growth in recoveries because of their relatively high risk weights; and, most important, put an end to manipulation of risk weights for the purpose of artificially boosting a bank's regulatory capital ratio.

Unfortunately, we are not starting with a blank slate. Basel III has been agreed to, it is being implemented mostly ahead of schedule, and regulatory officials on the Basel Committee on Banking Supervision as well as officials in the United States and the European Union show little inclination to abandon risk-weighted capital measures. Two alternative strategies could therefore be adopted: a minimalist approach and a more ambitious one.

The minimalist approach could adopt the proposal offered by Fed Governor Daniel Tarullo (2014c) to jettison the internal ratings–based approach to calculating risk weights in favor of the (revised) standardized approach.[7] Under the (revised) standardized approach, banks would not be able to use their internal models to engineer reductions in risk-weighted assets (because those risk weights would be beyond the control of the bank).

A second-best proposal, which the Basel Committee on Banking Supervision is discussing, would be to get international agreement on a "floor" in calculating risk-weighted assets. This proposal is reportedly being supported by US bank supervisors but opposed by EU and Japanese bank supervisors. If, one way or another, "manipulation" of risk weights by banks can be curtailed, the diagnostic performance of risk-based capital measures should improve.

Another essential element of a minimalist approach would be to obtain agreement that all future bank stress tests contain a leverage ratio test, along with the existing risk-based tests (i.e., at least one of the capital hurdle rates in these tests would be a leverage ratio). The US CCAR tests have done so since 2012.

The downside of the minimalist approach to risk-weight reform was raised in chapter 5, in the discussion of the Bank of England's symmetry and proportionality approach. The coexistence of two Pillar 1 capital measures and the desire to have them both be binding simultaneously would likely result in a leverage ratio that is far too low from a loss absorbency point of view. Moreover, the official regulatory community would likely continue to be misled by a high headline minimum for risk-weighted capital measures, much as it has with the total loss-absorbing capacity (TLAC) initiative.

The more ambitious alternative, laid out more fully in chapter 7, seeks to enshrine the leverage ratio as the sole Pillar 1 capital measure in bank stress tests, as well as in US national banking legislation. In this plan risk weights derived from the standardized approach would still play some role, albeit as a Pillar 2 rather than Pillar 1 measure. These risk weights would serve as one among a set of indicators used to derive a risk surcharge. That surcharge would sit on top of the minimum leverage ratio and hence would not compete with it. The bank-capital regime would thus retain some risk sensitivity, albeit in a more eclectic and limited way.

A good deal of persuasion will be needed to get the official sector to buy into the more ambitious approach to risk-weight reform. I believe the prospective benefits are well worth that effort. I am not persuaded by the argument that the costs of transitioning from risk-based to leverage ratios as the primary bank capital metric would be costly. In response to the poor performance and conflict of interest problems of credit rating agencies in the run-up to the 2007–09 global economic and financial crisis, the Dodd-Frank Act barred the use of credit ratings for regulatory purposes. Although there was much foreboding at the time, including by the credit rating agencies, that the reform would spell disaster for the operation of financial markets, US markets seem to have adjusted to this change without missing a beat. If leverage ratios were to supplant risk-based capital measures as (the) Pillar 1 standard, banks could continue to use the latter for their internal risk management, but they would have no regulatory role beyond their use as an indicator for the risk surcharge.

Seventh and finally, when designing bank stress tests, more thought needs to be given to not just how to define the capital ratio but also how high to set the capital hurdle rate and how to relate the hurdle to longer-term plans to set appropriate capital standards. The results of a stress test are not informative for financial stability if meeting the capital hurdle rate under severely adverse scenarios still means that in a real crisis the largest banks will not be able to survive and generate healthy loan growth without exceptional government assistance and intervention.

In chapter 4 I reviewed three approaches to how high to set minimum regulatory requirements for bank capital: an approach that looks at bank losses during the global economic and financial crisis, a macroprudential approach that focuses on the propensity of unguaranteed wholesale creditors to run at a higher capital ratio than retail depositors, and a cost-benefit approach that weighs the funding cost disadvantage of heightened capital requirements against the benefits in terms of reduced crisis vulnerability. In chapter 5, I reviewed three approaches to setting appropriate capital surcharges for global systemically important banks (G-SIBs): an approach that compares systemic risk indicators to existing leverage ratios, a symmetry and proportionality approach that sets leverage ratio surcharges for G-SIBs as a proportion of the risk-based surcharges on those firms, and an estimated impact approach that derives G-SIB risk-based surcharges by trying to equate expected losses for G-SIBs and non-G-SIBs.

The strong conclusion that emerges is that the socially optimal level of the capital ratio is likely to be far above both the minimum ratios set out under Basel III and the actual capital ratios prevailing around the world. Thus when regulators seek to bolster confidence by saying that their banks are displaying capital ratios that are "close to that of their global peers," what this really means is that their banks are just as undercapitalized as the banks of partner countries. My review of the evidence suggests that bank regulators and supervisors ought to be pursuing a goal of increasing the minimum leverage ratio for G-SIBs to roughly 15 percent—about five times higher than the Basel III standard and about three times as high as the minimum for G-SIBs currently prevailing in the United States.

Since there is such a significant difference between the socially optimal funding mix for banks and the bank-capital hurdle rates used in today's stress tests, the message for stress test architects is clear: Over time they need to raise those hurdle rates.

In addition, the "differentiated" approach to banking supervision needs to extend to bank stress tests. It makes no sense for the most systemic G-SIBs to face the same capital hurdle rate in stress tests as large banks with much more modest systemic footprints. If the most systemically important banks require a capital surcharge to bring their expected systemic loss in line with those of smaller, less systemic banks, they also require a higher capital hurdle rate in supervisor-led stress tests.

Endnotes

1. Fischer (2014a, 4) argues that bank stress tests are likely to add significantly to the quality and effectiveness of financial sector supervision and are an innovation that should "spread internationally as best practice."

2. In a front-page article in early October 2016, the *Financial Times* reported that a special concession boosted Deutsche Bank's result in the July 2016 EU-wide test. Deutsche Bank reportedly included $4 billion in proceeds from selling its stake in Chinese lender Hua Xia, even though the deal was not finalized by the end of February 2015, the official cutoff point for such transactions to be completed ("Deutsche Bank Received Special Treatment in EU Stress Test via ECB Concession," *Financial Times*, October 11, 2016).

3. Posen (2016) interprets the difference between US and ECB monetary policy during the last crisis as follows: "One need look no further than the divergence between the Federal Reserve in 2008 and 2009 facing the overt crisis and the European Central Bank's conscious and deliberate inaction in the period of 2010 to 2012 in the face of mounting threats to Southern Europe.... monetary inaction led to far higher unemployment, far greater drops in output, far faster declines in prices, and far more human suffering in the euro area than when monetary action was taken in the United States. This is not just a comparison across countries that can be blamed on this strangeness of continental labor market institutions or European fragmentation...once the [ECB] did commit to monetary expansion, the policy was effective."

4. By April 2009 the IMF was estimating that total credit losses in the 2007–09 crisis would total about $2.7 trillion (Wessel 2009).

5. By now it is acknowledged even within the EU official sector that the way bank recapitalization was done after the 2011 EBA capital exercise was procyclical (see Mésonnier and Monks 2015).

6. Pagano et al. (2014) show that (non-risk-based) book and regulatory (risk-based) measures of bank capital were highly correlated for large EU banks in the late 1990s but that this correlation broke down in the early 2000s. By 2012 the correlation between the two capital ratios had turned negative, with the coefficient statistically significant at the 1 percent level.

7. The current standardized approach uses external credit ratings to generate risk weights. However, the BCBS (2014b) is in the process of revising the standardized approach to credit risk, operational risk, and market risk; it has already published proposals for revising credit risk. Under the proposed approach, a number of simple "drivers" would substitute for the role of external credit ratings. For bank exposures, for example, the drivers of risk weights would be the capital adequacy ratio and the asset quality ratio; for corporate exposures, the drivers would be revenue and leverage.

7

A Plan for Bank-Capital Reform

Basel III and the Dodd-Frank Act of 2010 in the United States have moved the ball forward on designing and implementing tougher bank capital standards. They have not gone nearly far enough, however, particularly in three areas:

- upgrading the leverage ratio from a supplementary backup to the dominant measure of regulatory capital,

- setting the minimum leverage ratio high enough so that large banks could cope with losses in a crisis as severe as the 2007–09 one on their own, without extraordinary government intervention, and

- setting the capital surcharge for global systemically important banks (G-SIBs) high enough that their expected systemic losses are no higher than those for a nonsystemic bank holding company, and so that G-SIBs have a strong incentive to shrink their systemic footprint.

The $64,000 question is, How do we get from here to there?

This chapter describes the outlines of a plan for getting to much higher minimum leverage ratios and to a steeper leverage-based G-SIB surcharge schedule. The plan is not yet detailed enough to form the basis for legislation or comprehensive enough to answer all the relevant operational questions that would arise in making such a de facto—if not de jure—regime shift. Many of the elements in the plan come from earlier proposals made by others, although I would like to think I have provided some value added. If I thought an idea or proposal helped build a better mousetrap, I used it (with proper attribution).

To give some specificity, I assume that the plans would be implemented (first) in the United States and I draw on some data for US banks to approximate the relevant magnitudes.

Outline of the Plan

The Federal Reserve would announce that consistent with its mandate for stress testing and for establishing more stringent standards for bank holding companies with more than $50 billion in total consolidated assets under the Dodd-Frank Act, it would be making some important changes to its bank-capital regime. These changes would occur in five areas:

- A single standard—the tangible leverage ratio—would replace four existing bank-capital standards (the common equity tier 1 ratio, the tier 1 risk-based capital ratio, the total risk-based capital ratio, and the tier 1 leverage ratio).

- Long-term minimums for the tangible leverage ratio would be established for three classes of US banks: G-SIBs, other large bank holding companies participating in the Comprehensive Capital Analysis and Review (CCAR) stress tests, and other (smaller) banks. For G-SIBs the long-term target would be 14 to 18 percent (depending on the bank's systemic importance). For other "large" banks, the long-term target would be 11 to 13 percent (depending on their size and systemic importance). For smaller banks, the long-term target would be 10 percent. These new minimum leverage ratios would be phased in over a 10-year period, beginning in 2017; they would replace the existing minimum leverage ratios established under the supplementary leverage ratio and the enhanced supplementary leverage ratio.[1] The Federal Reserve would also have the authority to lower minimum leverage ratios when, based on its assessment of the leverage/economic/financial cycle, it judged that economic conditions warranted such a reduction.[2]

- Although risk-based capital standards would no longer serve as Pillar 1 minimum capital requirements, some risk sensitivity in the capital regime would be retained by a new (Pillar 2) risk surcharge. This surcharge would sit "on top" of the basic minimum leverage ratio, and it would apply (in a given year) only to G-SIBs and other large banks whose assets (and/or off-balance-sheet commitments) were judged to be unusually risky relative to those of their peers. A set of indicators would be used to evaluate the riskiness of each bank participating in the stress test. The ratio of risk-weighted assets to total assets—obtained from a revised standardized approach to risk weighting—would be but one of those indicators. The purpose of the risk surcharge would be twofold: to compensate for some of the weaknesses of existing stress tests (e.g., no test for tail risk dependence, no test for rapid credit expansion paired with overvalued property prices, too little attention to market prices vis-à-vis book values, etc.) and to discourage larger banks from responding to the new leverage ratio standard by shifting unduly into risky assets.

- The new leverage ratio minimums for G-SIBs and other large bank holding companies would be translated into the baseline (unstressed) capital hurdle rates in the annual CCAR stress tests. The stressed hurdle rates in the adverse and severely adverse scenarios would be set below the baseline hurdle rate, depending on the severity of the scenarios and the model parameters that link the shocks to bank capital. The increases in the baseline hurdle rate would take place in roughly 10 equal annual installments, so that by the end of the 10-year phase-in period (2027) the baseline hurdle rates would be at their long-term target levels. During the first half of the phase-in period, almost all the increase in capital ratios would need to come from the numerator of the capital ratio; during the second five-year period, this requirement could be relaxed somewhat to provide more room for the very largest banks to reduce the size of their systemic footprint.[3]

- Just before the middle of the phase-in period (2022), the Federal Reserve would conduct a study assessing the effects of these higher bank-capital standards on the banking and financial system and on the broader US economy. If that assessment were positive, the second five-year period of hurdle rate increases would commence as planned. If the assessment were negative, the Fed would have the authority to recommend either a slower rate of increase in hurdle rates or the suspension of those increases.

Features of the Plan

Which Leverage Ratio?

The benefits of replacing risk-based capital standards with a leverage ratio are straightforward. The leverage ratio is much better (for large banks) at distinguishing sick banks from healthy ones, it is easier to understand and less costly to compute and maintain, and it is less susceptible to manipulation by banks seeking to inflate the capital ratio artificially for regulatory purposes.

There are three candidates for the official leverage ratio: the tangible leverage ratio, the Basel III leverage ratio, and the tier 1 leverage ratio currently used in US stress tests. The Basel III leverage ratio is not bad in a backup role for the risk-based standards and carries the advantages of both familiarity and international comparability (because of its compromise solution to the different treatment of derivatives netting under US Generally Accepted Accounting Principles [GAAP] versus International Financial Reporting Standards [IFRS]). It would not be the best choice as the sole Pillar 1 capital standard, however, because its numerator (tier 1 capital) does not possess the desired degree of loss absorbency. After all the effort in Basel III to improve such loss absorbency and to move away from tier 1 capital in favor of common equity tier 1, going back to tier 1 as the sole capital standard would be a nontrivial and unnecessary setback.[4]

A second candidate would be the tier 1 leverage ratio, currently the choice in US stress tests and a regulatory requirement for all US banks. It has the same weakness as the Basel III ratio, using (less loss-absorbent) tier 1 capital in the numerator. It also has a narrower denominator (total assets) than the Basel III leverage ratio, thereby providing less coverage of potential risks, particularly for the largest banks. Yet an additional disadvantage is that the leverage surcharges for larger US banks as implemented in the supplementary and enhanced supplementary leverage ratios are defined using total leverage exposure in the denominator (as with the Basel III leverage ratio), not total assets. Hence if and when these leverage surcharges are reflected in the hurdle rates in US stress tests, the tier 1 leverage ratio will not be able to accommodate that needed upgrade. For all of these reasons, I believe the tier 1 leverage ratio is dominated by the Basel III leverage ratio, at least for larger banks.

The third candidate is the tangible leverage ratio. Its primary selling point is that it has the highest degree of loss absorbency. Although it has not been employed for regulatory purposes, financial professionals have long used it to analyze bank solvency. Its denominator is much narrower than total leverage exposure, but leverage exposure could and should still be retained to measure systemic importance and to compute the appropriate G-SIB surcharge for the very largest banks. Because of the different treatment of the netting of derivatives in GAAP and IFRS accounting standards, one has to use a conversion factor to compare tangible leverage ratios in US and foreign G-SIBs. But this conversion factor is known and is regularly published by the Federal Deposit Insurance Corporation (FDIC) in its Global Capital Index (see, for example, Hoenig 2016b). Moreover, in only five of the eight US G-SIBs does the GAAP/IFRS difference have any significant effect on reported leverage ratios; the issue is not important for the other 25 banks participating in the CCAR stress tests or for smaller banks.

If a tangible leverage ratio replaced the Basel III measure, it would not be the first time that US supervisors introduced a higher-quality measure of capital outside the Basel framework. When US authorities were designing the first US stress test (the Supervisory Capital Assessment Program [SCAP]), they introduced tier 1 common capital to bolster the credibility of the stress test results. That unilateral decision proved to be successful and helped pave the way for the introduction in Basel III of common equity tier 1 as the preferred measure of high-quality capital in that regime. Why, then, should a similar-quality upgrade be regarded as unwarranted for the leverage ratio?

In the end, because of its superior loss absorbency, the tangible leverage ratio would be the best choice for the sole Pillar 1 capital standard, even if it does break more china than the other candidates. The Basel III leverage ratio would be my second choice.

Size of the Capital Adjustment

Table 7.1 shows the cumulative and average annual adjustments in capital ratios that global systemically important banks (G-SIBs), large non-G-SIBs, and smaller banks need to make to reach the final leverage ratio targets (16, 12, and 10 percent, respectively) for two alternative definitions of the leverage ratio.[5,6] The main takeaway is that the size of the bank-capital adjustment would be much larger for G-SIBs than for large non-G-SIBs or smaller banks. This higher adjustment burden for G-SIBs reflects both a somewhat lower starting leverage ratio and a considerably higher final target. Table 7.1 also reveals that the size of the adjustment path is somewhat larger for the tangible leverage ratio than for the tier 1 leverage ratio, because the starting position of the latter is higher.

In table 7.2 I take a more disaggregated look at the adjustment path for bank capital, treating each of the eight US G-SIBs individually. I examine those paths under two definitions of the leverage ratio. This time, instead of using the average final target ratio for the group, I give them individual targets, maintaining the same ordinal ranking used in the 2015 risk-based G-SIB surcharge schedule:[7]

- JPMorgan Chase: 18 percent,
- Citigroup: 17 percent,
- Bank of America, Goldman Sachs, Morgan Stanley: 16 percent,
- Wells Fargo: 15 percent, and
- Bank of New York Mellon (BNYM) and State Street: 14 percent.

The message coming out of table 7.2 is that JPMorgan Chase faces the largest capital adjustment, followed by BNYM. The two G-SIBs facing the lowest adjustment burdens are Wells Fargo and Goldman Sachs. As with the group averages, adjustment is somewhat lower for the tier 1 leverage ratio than for the tangible leverage ratio, owing to the higher starting position for the former.

Having different minimum leverage ratios for different sizes and systemic classes of banks allows one to put the largest increases where they will do the most good. In my view that means requiring the highest level and largest increases in minimum leverage ratios for G-SIBs.

Table 7.1 Leverage ratio targets and implied adjustments for G-SIBs, non-G-SIBs, and small banks

A. Tangible leverage ratio (adjusted tangible equity/adjusted tangible assets)

	(1) Actual end-2015 (percent)	(2) Cumulative adjustment to target (percent)	(3) Annual adjustment over 10 years (basis points)
G-SIBs (8)		to 16 percent	
GAAP (weighted average)	8.1	7.9	79
Large non-G-SIBs		to 12 percent	
10 largest non-G-SIBs	8.8	3.2	32
GAAP (weighted average)			
Smaller banks		to 10 percent	
10 largest ≤ $50 billion in assets	8.3	1.7	17
GAAP (weighted average)			
10 largest ≤ $1 billion in assets	9.8	0.2	2
GAAP (weighted average)			

B. Tier 1 leverage ratio (tier 1 capital/total assets)

	(1) Actual 2015Q4 (percent)	(2) Cumulative adjustment to target (percent)	(3) Annual adjustment over 10 years (basis points)
G-SIBs (8)		to 16 percent	
Unweighted average	8.4	7.6	76
Weighted average	8.9	7.1	71
Large non-G-SIBs (25) (CCAR participants with ≥ $50 billion in assets)		to 12 percent	
Unweighted average	10.3	1.7	17
Weighted average	10.1	1.9	19

GAAP = Generally Accepted Accounting Principles; CCAR = Comprehensive Capital Analysis and Review

Note: Cumulative adjustment to target is the difference between the actual leverage ratio in column 1 and the target leverage ratio in column 2. Annual adjustment over ten years is the cumulative adjustment shown in column 2 divided by 10 and expressed in basis points.

Sources: Tangible leverage ratios: FDIC Global Capital Index, December 2015, www.fdic.gov/about/learn/board/hoenig/capitalizationratios4q15.pdf. Tier 1 leverage ratios: Board of Governors (2016a).

Table 7.2 Leverage ratios for US G-SIBs: Starting position and implied adjustments for 10-year phase-in

Bank	Actual 2015 (GAAP)	Target in 2027 (percent)	Adjustment	
			Cumulative (basis points)	Annual (basis points)
Tangible leverage ratio				
JPMorgan Chase	8.3	18.0	970	97
Bank of America	7.6	16.0	840	84
Citigroup	8.8	17.0	820	82
Wells Fargo	8.5	15.0	650	65
Goldman Sachs	9.2	16.0	680	68
Morgan Stanley	7.7	16.0	830	83
Bank of New York Mellon	4.4	14.0	960	96
State Street	5.6	14.0	840	84
Tier 1 leverage ratio				
JPMorgan Chase	8.5	18.0	950	95
Bank of America	8.6	16.0	740	74
Citigroup	10.2	17.0	680	68
Wells Fargo	9.4	15.0	560	56
Goldman Sachs	9.3	16.0	670	67
Morgan Stanley	8.3	16.0	770	77
Bank of New York Mellon	6.0	14.0	800	80
State Street	6.9	14.0	710	71

Sources: See tables 5.4 and 7.1. Cumulative and annual adjustment as defined in table 7.1.

Opponents of higher capital requirements are fond of noting that 85 percent of the insured US banks that failed over the 2008–11 period had assets of less than $1 billion each. This statistic is thoroughly misleading. Only about 3 percent of small US banks failed (ICBA 2013). The failure-cum-rescue rate for very large US and global banks during the crisis was much higher. Twelve of the 13 largest US financial institutions were within two weeks of failure in the fall of 2008, according to former Federal Reserve Chair Ben Bernanke (Da Costa 2014). Aikman et al. (2014) analyze almost all global banks that had more than $100 billion in assets at end-2006. Using the definition of bank failure/rescue of Laeven and Valencia (2013), they find that 36 percent of these banks failed between 2007 and the end of 2009—a failure rate roughly 10 times as high as for small US banks. Haldane (2010) finds that banks with assets of more than $100 billion each accounted for 90 percent of the bailout costs for financial institutions during the crisis. Make no mistake: In the 2007–09 global crisis, very large banks (and large nonbanks), not small banks, were the key actors.

Another attribute of having both different minimum leverage ratios for the three banking groups and a wider range of minimums within the G-SIB group itself is that the G-SIB surcharge schedule is much steeper than under current US or international regulatory regimes. In the United States, the top minimum leverage ratio for G-SIBs under the enhanced supplementary leverage ratio is 5 to 6 percent. It is 3 percent for large (advanced-approach) non-G-SIBs under the supplementary leverage ratio and 4 percent for the narrower tier 1 leverage ratio at all other banks. The maximum difference in the minimum leverage ratio is thus just 3 percent. For risk-based capital standards, the current US G-SIB surcharge schedule provides a maximum surcharge of 4.5 percent for the largest G-SIB (JPMorgan Chase) relative to non-G-SIBs. In the international regime, the (November 2015) G-SIB surcharge schedule envisions a maximum difference of 3.5 percent, although no G-SIB is currently subject to a surcharge of more than 2.5 percent. Contrast these differences with the minimum leverage ratio differences in the plan outlined above: an 8 percent difference in minimum leverage ratios between the most systemic G-SIB and smaller banks and a 7 percent difference between the most systemic G-SIB and the least systemic non-G-SIB bank holding company (with $50 billion or more in total consolidated assets).

Operational Issues

Having a three-level system of minimum leverage ratios is not all milk and honey; it raises some thorny operational issues. Two of them are the boundary problem between and within different sizes and systemic classes of banks and the challenges of keeping the CCAR stress test framework relatively simple and understandable.

Boundary Problems

Any time one bank is subject to different regulatory treatment from another, there is apt to be controversy. The Dodd-Frank Act calls for banks with total assets greater than $50 billion to be subject to stricter standards. As such, the CCAR stress tests and the accompanying regulation already incorporate differential treatment of banks depending on their perceived/estimated systemic risk. For example, in the 2015 CCAR, six of the eight G-SIBs were subject to a global market shock scenario and a counterparty default scenario, respectively, that do not apply to other CCAR participants. In the qualitative section of the CCAR, the Federal Reserve holds bank holding companies that are part of the Large Institution Supervision Coordinating Committee (LISCC) to higher standards for risk management and capital planning practices than other bank holding companies (Board of Governors 2015a). Differential minimum leverage ratio requirements and risk-based surcharges already apply to different sizes and systemic risk classes of US banks.

Still, the plan's three-level minimum leverage ratio schedule raises a few questions that do not exist under the current differential approach. Some non-G-SIB bank holding companies—which face an 11 to 13 percent minimum leverage ratio under the plan versus 10 percent for smaller banks—may complain that they are subject to unfair treatment.

Going beyond the answer that Dodd-Frank has size criteria one has to live with, one response—which has other attractive properties—is to couple the 10 percent minimum ratio for small banks with side conditions that the larger bank holding companies are unlikely to be able or want to meet.

FDIC Vice Chair Thomas Hoenig (2015) has advanced just such a proposal. He suggests that because the 6,400 non-G-SIB banks in the United States have had much lower failure rates than the largest banks and because these smaller banks have higher (tangible) leverage ratios than the G-SIBs, they have a good case for some regulatory relief. His eligibility criteria for that relief are the following:

- banks that hold effectively zero trading assets or liabilities,
- banks that hold no derivative positions other than interest rate or foreign exchange derivatives,
- banks whose total notional value of derivatives is less than $3 billion, and
- banks that maintain a leverage ratio (defined as the ratio of equity to assets in GAAP terms) of at least 10 percent.

None of the banks with more than $100 billion in assets would meet these criteria, but the vast majority of banks smaller than that, including community banks, would. As to the form of regulatory relief, it would include, among other elements, exemption from Basel capital standards and risk-weight calculations, exemption from stress test exercises, less frequent examinations, and laxer reporting requirements. Hoenig points out that a 10 percent minimum leverage ratio would not be a burden for smaller banks, because the vast majority of them already have leverage ratios very close to or at that level (see table 7.1).

If the 10 percent minimum leverage ratio for smaller banks comes with Hoenig's side conditions, there is no discontinuity between the two smaller size groups in the plan. For a bank holding company that has a profitable derivatives business, meeting those side conditions to qualify for the lower 10 percent rate could be costly. If it is, there is no arbitrage opportunity.[8] The "effective" minimum leverage rate with side conditions is higher than 10 percent; there is thus no incentive for the bank holding company in the middle bank group (labeled "large non-G-SIBs" in table 7.1) to want to migrate to the small bank group. At the end of 2015, 17 of the 25 bank holding companies in the non-G-SIB group had more than $100 billion of total assets; only 4 had total assets of $50 billion to $75 billion.

The other boundary issue is how to set the minimum leverage ratios within the top two bank groups (the 8 G-SIBs and 25 non-G-SIB bank holding companies). The Federal Reserve uses its estimated impact approach to calibrate the G-SIB risk-based surcharges, as noted in chapter 5. That methodology could be easily applied to estimate where each G-SIB should fit on the 14 to 18 percent G-SIB leverage ratio schedule. Under the estimated impact approach, the Fed already estimates the expected systemic loss for non-G-SIBs as a reference group. It would therefore be straightforward to estimate where the 25 non-G-SIB bank holding companies should lie on the proposed 11 to 13 percent minimum leverage ratio schedule. Under the current regime, the Fed assigns stricter standards to the six (larger) non-G-SIBs that are classified as "advanced approach" bank holding companies. If one did not want to rely exclusively on the estimated impact approach to estimate appropriate minimum leverage ratios within the non-G-SIB group, the bank holding companies with "advanced-approach" designation could be assigned the (top) 13 percent minimum.

Number of Capital Hurdle Rates

The second thorny operational issue is how many capital hurdle rates to have in the CCAR stress test for the 33 participating banks. Under the current regime, all 33 participating banks face the same unstressed and stressed hurdle rate for each of the four capital ratio metrics (the tier 1 leverage ratio and three risk-based capital measures), whether the bank is JPMorgan Chase (with $2.3 trillion in total consolidated assets at end-2015) or Zions Bancorporation (with $60 billion in total consolidated assets). Having a single hurdle rate simplifies the reporting of stress test results, but it pays little attention to the very large differences in expected systemic losses across a varied group of 33 large bank holding companies.

In contrast, the plan laid out here would have at least eight different hurdle rates for the tangible leverage ratio (three minimum leverage ratios within the non-G-SIB group and five within the G-SIB group). I do not see this increased degree of differentiation as a negative;[9] it is the price of properly internalizing externalities and the mechanism for inducing too big to fail banks to reduce their systemic footprint. Still, if a compromise were needed for operational feasibility, a workable model might be to assign to each bank within a group the midpoint of the minimum leverage ratio for that group. Doing so would mean that for the purpose of specifying the baseline hurdle rates, G-SIBs would face a 16 percent final minimum leverage ratio target, and non-G-SIBs would face a 12 percent ratio. This compromise loses the surcharge sensitivity within groups but retains it across the two groups of CCAR participants—not optimal, but still much better than a uniform hurdle rate for all institutions.

Replacement of Existing Risk-Based Capital Measures with a Unitary Risk Surcharge

I move next to the issue of how to replace the (three) Pillar 1 risk-based capital metrics with a unitary risk surcharge, modeled on the systemic risk-scoring approach used by the FSB, the BCBS, and others to calculate G-SIB surcharges. By "replacing" the risk-based Pillar 1 measures, I mean that these capital metrics would no longer have any official role as minimum capital requirements. Banks could, of course, keep constructing and maintaining risk based capital ratios for their own internal risk management purposes, but doing so would be strictly voluntary.

Recall from chapter 5 (table 5.3) that the systemic importance indicator for G-SIBs is based on five sets of indicators (representing size, interconnectedness, substitutability, complexity, and cross-jurisdictional activity), each with a 20 percent weight. The risk score could also be based on a set of indicators. To put a little flesh on the bones, one might think of six types of risk indicators:

- a measure of tail risk dependence, perhaps along the lines of the "systemic expected shortfall" in Acharya et al. (2010),
- the rate of loan growth cum a measure of the overvaluation of property prices,
- market-based measures of bank health (e.g., contingent claim analysis of distance to default, leverage ratios that depend on market capitalization rather than book values),
- risk derived from "reverse scenarios," in which one solves for the shocks that will produce a given decline in the capital ratio,
- areas of risk where the supervisors have special concerns (e.g., leveraged loans, commercial real estate, etc.), and
- the ratio of risk-weighted assets to total assets, where risk-weighted assets come from a revised "standardized" approach to risk weighting.

Part of the trick is to choose indicators that deal with sources of risk that are not already being addressed, either in the scenarios of the stress test themselves or through other supervisory tools, such as the Basel III liquidity ratios (the liquidity coverage ratio and the net stable funding ratio). The idea of having a set of indicators is that each of them has strengths and weaknesses and that when used in combination (rather than as competing standards) they should do better at identifying dangerous levels of asset risk than a single indicator.[10]

Each of these indicators has been shown to be useful in a given context. Tail dependence indicators pick up the crucial difference between a solitary bank failure and simultaneous bank failures. The rate of loan growth has been shown to be a useful early warning indicator of deteriorating credit quality and, when paired with a measure of the overvaluation of property prices, of subsequent banking crises (Borio and Drehmann 2009).[11] Market-based indicators of bank health often perform better in diagnosing bank vulnerability than slower-moving accounting (book value) measures (Haldane and Madouros 2012, Aikman et al. 2014). Reverse scenarios are useful because they are portfolio specific in a way that traditional stress test scenarios are not. Allowing supervisors to assign a relatively high risk weight to asset concentrations that are of particular current concern guards against the risk that the nature of risk changes over time.[12] Finally, the ratio of risk-weighted assets to total assets—if obtained from a revised "standardized" approach to risk weights—combines credit, market, and operational risk, without the noise created by manipulation from bank internal models.

Once these indicators have been calculated and weighted to form a risk score, it should be possible to group the 33 banks into, say, four groups: low, normal, elevated, and highly elevated risk. Banks in the normal risk group would be subject to a zero risk surcharge, banks with low risk to negative surcharges, and banks with elevated or highly elevated scores to positive surcharges. The aim would be to get the ordinals right rather than to aim for one decimal point precision. Because the risk surcharge would sit on top of the basic minimum leverage ratio, just like the G-SIB surcharge does, it should be binding, but without constraining the height of the basic leverage ratio itself.

Some critics may claim that by classifying bank portfolios into broad risk categories instead of employing a continuous time series on risk-weighted assets the plan is throwing out valuable information. But if that information is so valuable, why did supervisors relying on it in the run-up to the 2007–09 crisis make so many errors, and why have leverage ratios (employing no risk weighting at all) consistently outperformed risk-weighted capital measures in identifying failures at large banks?

In this connection, Bailey (2014, 5) offers a revealing glimpse into the failure of Royal Bank of Scotland (RBS):

> The acquisition of ABN AMRO meant that RBS's trading book assets almost doubled between end-2006 and end-2007. The low risk weights assigned to trading assets suggested that only £2.3 billion of core tier 1 capital was held to cover potential trading losses which might result from assets carried at around £470 billion on the firm's balance sheet. In fact, in 2008, losses of £12.2 billion arose in the credit trading area alone.... A regime which inadequately evaluated trading book risk was, therefore, fundamental to RBS's failure.

Other skeptics might argue along similar lines that any risk assessment that did not involve a hard-number measure of risk would be too fuzzy to be of much use in a stress test context. But the qualitative part of the CCAR uses no such hard number and yet manages to make judgments about individual banks' risk management and capital planning—and to back up those judgments with pass/fail verdicts on banks' original capital plans. In fact, over the past two years, more banks failed the qualitative part of the CCAR than the quantitative part. Surely the risk assessment process outlined in the plan would not be fuzzier than the existing qualitative part of the CCAR.[13]

How Large Would the Risk Surcharge Need to Be?

How high the surcharge should be is a tough question to answer before one has information on the distribution of the risk scores. Nevertheless, my suspicion is that it would not have to be large to be effective. The surcharge would be applied at the margin, and banks would be in a challenging environment to meet the secular annual increases in the hurdle rate as they made their way toward the final minimum leverage targets. Banks that do not meet the capital hurdle rate in the CCAR need to submit revised capital plans, affecting their dividend payouts, share buybacks, and, potentially, executive compensation.

Some information from the 2015 CCAR is instructive. Of the 14 advanced approach bank holding companies (including the 8 G-SIBs), 6 had a tier 1 leverage ratio in the severely adverse scenario that was within 1 percent of the stressed hurdle rate, and 1 (JPMorgan Chase) fell below the hurdle rate in its original capital plan and had to submit a revised one (which passed by only 0.2 percent). The average margin above the tier 1 stressed hurdle rate for these 14 bank holding companies was 1.6 percent. For the remaining non-advanced-approach bank holding companies in the 2015 CCAR, the margin over the stressed (leverage) hurdle rate was considerably larger (3.5 percent), with only three banks within 1.5 percent. Given the need to meet more ambitious minimum leverage requirements under the plan and given the likelihood that the Federal Reserve will (eventually) incorporate G-SIB surcharges into the CCAR stress tests, I would expect the buffers over the minimum requirement to shrink some.[14] If, therefore, the risk surcharge for the banks falling in the "elevated" and "highly elevated" categories were set at, say, 0.75 and 1.5 percent, respectively, I would expect those surcharges to have an impact in discouraging a loading-up of risky assets.[15]

Would the Risk Surcharge Be Less Vulnerable to "Gaming"?

Although only time will tell, I expect the risk indicator system outlined above to be less vulnerable than the current system to gaming by banks. Risk-weighted assets would be based on a standardized approach to risk weighting in which the weights are not derived from banks' own internal models. As the risk score depends on a set of indicators with different properties, this makes gaming more difficult than when only one indicator is involved. The total asset/exposure denominator of the leverage ratio would preclude efforts to ramp up risk by engaging in trades with low margins but in very large volumes ("going big"). The new Basel III liquidity coverage ratio puts some constraints on asset shifting, because a certain quantity of liquid assets has to be maintained to meet the guidelines. The "worrisome" assets that would be selected by the stress test architects for a higher risk rating would be expected to change from year to year. And to the extent that the construction of the new risk surcharge indicator made the CCAR stress tests less predictable, it would be responsive to critics who have charged that the current stress testing regime has become too repetitive and routine.

Length of the Phase-in Period

My defense of the 10-year phase-in is a Goldilocks one: not too short and not too long. The main argument for allowing a 10-year transition is that the proposed increase in capital requirements is considerably larger than previous increases and that the 2010–13 experience with the implementation of Basel III is consistent with the view that a gradual phase-in produces few disruptive macroeconomic effects. As highlighted in chapter 4, between end-2009 and end-2013, a large sample of global banks raised their risk-based (common equity tier 1/risk-weighted assets) capital ratios by about 4.5 percentage points, with roughly two-thirds of the increase coming from retained earnings and with barely a ripple on net interest margins or on operating costs (Cecchetti 2014). Moreover, the increases in capital ratios were paired with the introduction of two new quantitative liquidity standards that, according to Elliott, Salloy, and Santos (2012), should have been expected to increase lending spreads by more than the increase in capital requirements. Banks participating in the 2014 CCAR increased their tier 1 common capital ratios by more than 500 basis points over the 2009–14 period. The plan proposes a weighted increase (across the three size groups of US banks shown in table 7.1) in tangible leverage ratios of 600 basis points to be implemented over a period twice as long.

With reasonable assumptions about bank profitability, asset growth, and capital distributions, a ballpark estimate—gleaned from a simple simulation model—is that the group of eight US G-SIBs could increase their weighted average tangible leverage ratios from 8 to 16 percent over a 10-year period, with virtually all of the increase coming from retained earnings.[16]

The contribution that dividend suspensions can make to building capital is often underappreciated. Greenlaw et al. (2012) indicate that about $80 billion of bank capital (roughly half the public capital injection into SCAP banks) could have been retained in the 19 banks participating in the 2009 SCAP had dividend payments been suspended at the beginning of the financial crisis in the summer of 2007.[17] The Independent Community Bankers of America (2013) had this to say about the effect of dividend payments on bank capital at the largest US banks:

> Over the past five years (2007–12), during the worst financial crisis since the Great Depression, the five largest banks have paid out $233 billion in dividends. If 60 percent of those dividends had been retained, these banks would have attained a leverage equity ratio of 10 percent. This does not even take into account the additional amount that was paid out of earnings in stock and cash bonuses.

Total dividends paid out by euro area banks since 2007 amount to about half of their aggregate end-2013 retained earnings, the core of banks' book equity (Gambacorta and Shin 2016). What should prevail is the wider public interest of maintaining financial stability, not the narrower one of keeping bank shareholders happy. Stein (2016) notes that only 20 percent of US firms now pay dividends and that many successful firms (e.g., Google) seem to do fine without them. He also reminds us that a dividend cut does not send a negative signal to markets if it is mandatory (in which case it carries no information content).

On the other side of the coin, some analysts may regard a 10-year transition as excessively long and/or hard to sustain over a period that might well encompass sharp political shifts, among other developments. This claim is hardly self-evident. Basel III allowed for a nine-year phase-in period, but almost all large banks had completed the transition to the stricter capital and liquidity standards by 2015, four years ahead of schedule. Although banks often claim that maintaining a higher capital ratio than their peers would put them at a competitive disadvantage, the response to Basel III suggests otherwise, as more weakly capitalized banks were the ones that eventually came under market pressure to close the gap with their better-capitalized rivals.

Successful public policy programs that are implemented over long periods are not unknown. My favorite example is the corporate average fuel economy standard (CAFE) in the United States, enacted in 1975 in the wake of the Arab oil embargo and still going strong. Although there is some debate on the role played by the standards versus gasoline prices, and some critics assail the effects on highway safety, there seems to be a consensus that CAFE had a significant effect on increasing fuel efficiency for passenger cars and light trucks (the 2015 Volkswagen scandal notwith-standing). The fuel efficiency standard for passenger cars in 1978 was 18 miles per gallon; the target for 2016 is 37.8. If such a long-term effort to achieve energy fuel independence can be sustained in the United States, in the face of strong initial opposition from the industry, why could it not be sustained in pursuit of financial stability?

Some critics, perhaps from the banking industry, will argue that banks will simply not be able to raise the amounts of capital proposed under the plan over 10 years. Admati and Hellwig (2013a, 12) reject this claim: "Solvent banks can always raise equity by selling additional shares to existing shareholders through rights offerings or to new shareholders in the market. If a bank cannot raise equity at any price, the bank may well be insolvent." One should also remember that the largest banks, which are being asked to raise the most capital, represent some of most storied banking franchises in the world. To claim that such banks cannot over a decade raise enough capital to bring their leverage ratios to a level less than half that of major global nonfinancial corporations seems farfetched.

Consistency with US International Obligations

Some observers may worry that a decision by the United States to (unilat-erally) drop the use of risk-based capital measures as Pillar 1 minimum requirements would be inconsistent with the US agreement to implement Basel III and could even, in a worst-case scenario, result in US withdrawal from the BCBS.

I think not.

Given the important role of US financial intermediaries in the global financial system and the key role played by the United States, along with the United Kingdom, in pressing for the first broad-based international agreement on capital adequacy requirements (Basel I), it is hard to conceive of a well-functioning international body on banking supervision that did not include the United States.[18] Symmetrically, in a world of cross-border banking with large potential spillovers, and with the risk of national banking regulation being made less effective by international arbitrage, the United States has a strong self-interest in remaining an active member of the BCBS.

All of this suggests that there would be a mutual interest in a compromise solution. In the run-up to the 2007–09 crisis, the United States chose not to implement Basel II at its smaller banks, but that disagreement did not produce a split.[19] The Dodd-Frank Act restricts the use of external credit ratings for regulatory purposes—credit ratings that, under Basel II and III, were a key driver of risk weights under the standardized approach to risk weighting. No split took place.[20]

Basel I, II, and III have always been minimum standards; the understanding has always been that countries could go beyond these minimums in their national banking regulation. It would be hard to argue that a US minimum leverage schedule of 10 to 18 percent, coupled with the use of various risk-based indicators as part of a Pillar 2 risk surcharge, represents a retreat from international minimum standards. Such measures are considered so controversial precisely because they represent such a substantial upgrading of existing standards.

What might a compromise between the BCBS and the United States look like? Instead of offering countries just one choice of minimum risk-based capital and leverage ratio requirements, a menu could be provided. For countries wedded to risk-based capital requirements as Pillar 1 measures, the system would stay the same. For the United States (and any other countries that wanted to join it), there would be a second choice with a much higher minimum leverage requirement, coupled with use of risk-based indicators as a Pillar 2 risk surcharge measure. Such a menu approach could be agreed to as a transition regime, until the market and the BCBS membership decided which option they preferred. Such an approach has already been employed for calculating risk-weighted assets (i.e., the internal ratings approach versus the standardized approach). I do not see it as beyond the pale that a similar approach might be applied in a broader context.

Advantages of the Plan

I see five important advantages to moving from the status quo to a three-tier minimum leverage ratio, with a top tier of 14 to 18 percent for G-SIBs.

Quantum Jump in Loss Absorbency

The plan would deliver a quantum jump to the amount of loss-absorbing, high-quality capital in our largest banks. With a much larger capital cushion, these banks would be able to withstand not only the scale of losses suffered during the crisis of 2007–09 but also even larger (hypothetical) losses under a no-more-too-big-to-fail scenario. Under that scenario, the government's crisis interventions (aside from expansionary monetary and fiscal policies) would be limited to lender of last resort liquidity injections by the central bank. The much higher capital cushion would also diminish the prospect of large-scale runs on banks by wholesale creditors, because they could be more confident that their bank counterparties were solvent. The taxpayer would not be on the hook. What's more, large banks would have enough capital left in a severe crisis to provide sufficient loan growth to support a recovery. This is what should be meant by appropriate self-insurance for banks.

Consider the group of eight G-SIBs. According to the plan, after the 10-year phase-in period was completed, they would probably be maintaining leverage ratios of 16 to 20 percent (the 14 to 18 percent minimum plus a buffer of, say, 200 basis points). Even if they faced an extraordinary loss equal to, say, 10 percent of their assets, they would still have ample capital left to support lending to the real economy. This is simply not true for existing regulations or proposals that call for a 3 to 6 percent minimum leverage ratio. They are a Maginot Line. The plan is not.

Perfectly Consistent with Maintaining Satisfactory Macroeconomic Performance

The plan's proposed range and pace of capital increases are perfectly consistent with maintaining satisfactory macroeconomic performance.

Let's face it. The chief obstacle to moving ahead with plans that would put bank-capital ratios where they need to be at the largest banks has been the fear that such increases would so adversely affect the availability of bank lending and the cost of bank funding that the economy's performance would suffer unduly. That fear is unwarranted.

As shown in chapter 4, despite repeated and continued claims to the contrary by the banking industry, the strongest and most recent evidence does not indicate that well-capitalized banks lend less than poorly capitalized ones. Indeed, the evidence goes almost entirely the other way (see, for example, Bailey 2014, Cecchetti 2014, Gambacorta and Shin 2016, and Enria 2014b). Only in cases where capital raising plans allow banks to meet the higher capital ratio via deleveraging or risk-weight shenanigans or where banks initially have such low capital as to be in a debt overhang situation is the result different—and both exceptions are avoidable with sensible policy.

This leaves the impact on the cost of bank funding and on bank lending rates. My best estimate of the effect of a 1 percentage point increase in the (actual) leverage ratio on the cost of bank funding is about 3 basis points (see chapter 4). Moreover, recent evidence from the 2009–13 period strongly suggests that large banks will absorb some of these higher costs without passing them on fully to bank customers. In fact, none of the increase in bank funding costs that standard models suggest should have been linked to bank capital increases was visible in the behavior of interest margins or operating costs over this period (Cecchetti 2014). The weighted-average (tangible) leverage ratio (in GAAP terms) for US banks at end-2015 was just about 8½ percent (see table 7.1);[21] the weighted-average final-target leverage ratio under the proposed plan is roughly 14½ percent. The plan thus envisages an increase in the weighted-average leverage ratio of 600 basis points, to take place over a 10-year transition period. The cost of bank funding would increase by approximately 18 basis points. If one assumes further that 80 percent of this increase in funding costs would be passed on to bank customers, overall bank lending rates would go up by roughly 14 basis points over a 10-year period.[22]

It is useful to put such an increase in lending spreads into perspective. The empirical evidence, reviewed in chapter 4 (see table 4.2), suggests that for large (systemically important) US banks, the unwarranted too big to fail subsidy during normal (noncrisis) periods is at least 15 basis points. During crisis periods, that subsidy rises to approximately 75 basis points. These too big to fail subsidies are much larger for EU banks.[23]

A second point of reference is the rule of thumb that says a 100-basis-point increase in the US federal funds rate (which boosts the entire term structure of interest rates) reduces the level of real GDP by about 100 basis points over eight quarters. A similar-size increase in overall bank lending rates should produce just a fraction of that effect given its narrower impact. On the basis of this rule of thumb, a 14-basis-point increase in overall bank lending rates spread over a 10-year period is likely to be so small as to be barely detectable in the macro data. Moreover, any macro effect could be easily offset by the Fed lowering the path for the funds rate infinitesimally.

So the key question is, Do we, as a society, want to give up the substantial financial stability benefits linked to a quantum jump in minimum leverage ratios for a 14-basis-point cumulative increase in overall bank lending rates spread out over 10 years? Is such an increase the Armageddon that the banking industry has frequently told us lies just around the corner if we implement bold reform of the bank-capital regime? The net benefits of a large increase in bank-capital requirements are decidedly large and positive in virtually all the objective studies of that thought experiment. To be consistently put off from taking action because of the banks' repeated doomsday claims would be—in the terms of Akerlof and Shiller (2015)—allowing ourselves to be "phished for phools."[24]

The plan goes the extra mile to ensure that the macroeconomic effects of much heightened capital requirements are benign. As the first five-year period during the transition is drawing to a close, the Federal Reserve would report the results of its study of the macroeconomic effects of the move to higher minimum leverage ratios. If the effects were satisfactory, the annual increases would continue; if they were not, either the pace of increase could be slowed or the process could be suspended entirely.[25] What could be fairer and more prudent than that?

Putting the Largest Increase in Capital Ratios Where It Is Most Needed

The plan's three-level structure puts the largest required increase in bank capital where it is needed most: at the nation's largest and most systemically important banks. These banks were the recipients of the lion's share of official assistance during the Great Recession and currently have lower leverage ratios than smaller banks with less systemic importance. By mandating lower minimum leverage ratios for non-G-SIBs and smaller banks (including more than 6,000 community banks), the plan is able to offer 14 to 18 percent minimum leverage ratios for G-SIBs while maintaining an overall weighted-average minimum leverage ratio target of just under 14.5 percent. As one does not know whether and by how much the next crisis will resemble the last one, the plan also specifies prudent minimum leverage ratios for large non-G-SIBs (11 to 13 percent) and for smaller banks (10 percent). Because non-G-SIBs have higher starting leverage ratios than G-SIBs and lower final targets, the capital adjustments for these groups are lower than they are for G-SIBs. Indeed, for small banks, although the minimum leverage ratio is considerably above the current level (4 percent), their current leverage ratios are high enough that the new minimum will require only a small increase in capital—and in exchange, these smaller banks would obtain some regulatory relief.

Using the Leverage Ratio and Risk Sensitivity in Tandem

The plan offers a new answer to the important question of how an unweighted leverage ratio and risk-weighted assets can best be used in tandem. The conventional answer is that both kinds of capital ratios should be regarded as Pillar 1 minimum requirements, with the risk-based ratio(s) regarded as the primary constraint and the leverage ratio serving as a backup. If both requirements are to be binding—so says the current consensus—the minimum leverage ratio should not be set much higher than the current 3 to 6 percent range, unless the risk-based ratios are raised simultaneously by enough to establish the original level of proportionality between the two.

I reject this answer. Raising the minimum risk-based capital ratio to, say, 29 percent (to pair up with a 14.5 percent weighted minimum leverage ratio) would be an exercise in implementing "if it's not working, do more of it." The conventional dual standard (both Pillar 1) bank-capital model has been a failure, as I show in chapters 3 and 4. If a single standard is to be the alternative, that standard should have three properties:

- It should provide superior loss absorbency.
- It should be easy to understand and measure but tough to manipulate.
- It should perform better than the alternatives in distinguishing sick (large) banks from healthy ones.

By no stretch of the imagination do the existing risk-based capital ratios fit this job description. After nearly 30 years of slogging on with a dual standard and the wrong capital ratio as the "front stop," it is high time to acknowledge that "Basel, we have a problem" and to look for a workable repair. The plan provides such a repair.

The leverage ratio is much closer to what one should want from a single Pillar 1 minimum capital requirement. The plan shows how the leverage ratio can be supplemented with a Pillar 2 risk surcharge framework. The proposed framework would compensate for some omissions and weaknesses in the existing supervisor-led stress test exercises, it would address the leverage ratio's lack of risk sensitivity, and it would provide some deterrence against the possibility of banks loading up on risky assets. Just as important, because the risk surcharge would sit on top of the basic leverage ratio, rather than competing with it as a separate Pillar 1 minimum requirement, it would be binding without constraining the height of the minimum basic leverage ratio itself. As Federal Reserve Vice Chair Stanley Fischer (2015a) remarked, "Regulation is a cat-and-mouse game." If so, I submit that this is a smarter cat.

Steepening the G-SIB Surcharge Schedule

The plan would steepen the (leverage) surcharge schedule for G-SIBs, by increasing the minimum leverage ratios the most at the very top end and increasing them less (relative to actual leverage ratios) at the lower end. Small US banks currently face a 4 percent minimum (tier 1) leverage ratio while the very largest banks face a 5 to 6 percent (Basel III) one. Under the plan, the minimum leverage ratios for US G-SIBs would rise to 14 to 18 percent and that for small banks would go up to 10 percent. The difference in the minimum leverage ratio between the largest, most systemically important bank and a small bank would thus be 800 basis points, not the 200- to 300-basis-point differential currently prevailing. The differential between G-SIBs and large non-G-SIBs would also increase.

Incentives matter. If real progress is to be made on ending too big to fail and direct restrictions on bank size are not the route the Executive and the Congress want to take to get there, another way has to be found to motivate the largest banks to decrease their systemic footprint over time.[26] It is hard to see that happening without much higher minimum capital requirements.

The proposed plan provides such an incentive. Speaking at an investor day in February 2015, JPMorgan CEO Jamie Dimon defended his bank's scale, commenting that "We still want that preeminent position, and we're not giving that up for anyone."[27] Maybe. But under the plan, JPMorgan Chase would have to pay for it with a much higher self-insurance premium.

Stress Tests Can Help

The plan gives an important role to stress tests as a framework for implementing the plan. Stress tests have advantages over other supervisory tools in the flexibility of their design, the forward-looking way they assess risks, the way they collect and use horizontal information across banks, the space they leave for supervisory judgments, and the immediate consequences that they impose for inadequate capital. All of these features will be helpful in facilitating and motivating a transition to much higher capital ratios.

But so, too, in the opposite direction. In chapter 3, I argue that if stress tests are to become more credible, greater attention will have to be paid to contagion and amplification mechanisms, because even moderate shocks can generate crises. If starting capital ratios were considerably higher via bank-capital reform, stressed capital ratios could fall by much more without causing so much concern. I fear that it is only with this increased range of motion that stress test architects will feel comfortable doing the experimentation with their models and scenarios that, over time, would make the crisis simulations resemble a real crisis.

Stress test architects are now struggling to maintain and validate the huge number of models (reportedly running into the thousands at the European Central Bank and Single Supervisory Mechanism) necessary to evaluate banks' risk models and produce their own estimates of the effects of the adverse scenarios. A simplified risk-weighting system would make that task easier and free resources up for other stress test challenges. By putting more emphasis on the easily computed leverage ratio, the proposed plan would lighten their load.

Endnotes

1. Note that while the phase-in period for Basel III and for the new risk-based G-SIB surcharge schedule does not end until 2019, almost all large banks already meet the final Basel III capital and liquidity requirements and all US G-SIBs—with the exception of JPMorgan Chase—already have risk-based capital ratios that meet or exceed the new surcharge levels.

2. The ability to lower minimum capital ratios in a downturn is essential if bank-capital cushions are to be used when needed and not just for show. The point is illustrated by the story of the traveler who arrives at a train station late at night only to find that he cannot hire the sole taxi remaining because of a local regulation that requires that there must always be at least one taxi at the stand. (The example comes from D. H. Robertson's 1922 book *Money*, published by Cambridge University Press. I am indebted to Charles Goodhart for the reference and for keeping the story alive.)

3. The extent to which required increases in capital ratios for G-SIBs could come from decreases in the denominator of the capital ratio should depend, inter alia, on macroeconomic conditions and the ability of non-G-SIBs, smaller banks, and shadow banks to absorb (at non-fire-sale prices) activities that are being downsized by the G-SIBs.

4. See Goldstein (2016) on why the quality of capital becomes especially important in a crisis.

5. I did not include the Basel III leverage ratio in table 7.1 because it has not been published for the 33 banks participating in the 2016 CCAR.

6. For the G-SIB calculations in table 7.1, I used the middle of the 14 to 18 percent final target range and the GAAP definition of the tangible leverage ratio. For the IFRS definition, the starting point would be an average of 6 percent (not 8.1 percent). The adjustment to the final target would thus be about 21 basis points higher per year.

7. The 2016 US risk-based G-SIB surcharge schedule was not available at the time of writing.

8. I am reminded of one of my favorite arbitrage stories. A man goes to the butcher to buy lamb chops. He asks how much they cost. The butcher tells him they are $9 a pound. The man says, "That price is outrageous! The butcher down the street charges only $7 a pound." The butcher then asks, "So why don't you go buy the chops from him?" The man answers, "Because he doesn't have any." The butcher answers, "When I don't have any, I'll sell them to you for $5 a pound."

9. The Federal Reserve apparently now agrees with me; see Tarullo (2016) and the discussion in the postscript (chapter 9) of the proposed new stress capital buffer (SCB); under the SCB, a BHC's stressed hurdle rate would depend, in part, on the size of its capital decline in the severely adverse scenario. Since these capital declines are bank specific, introduction of the SCB implies a much larger number of stressed hurdle rates in the CCAR than presently exist.

10. Aikman et al. (2014) report that using a set of bank vulnerability indicators increased the percentage of correct calls in distinguishing failing from safe banks from just over 50 percent to just over 80 percent.

11. The countercyclical capital buffer in Basel III addresses excessive credit growth—but only at an aggregate level (not bank by bank) and not in combination with a measure of property price overvaluation. The adverse and severely adverse scenarios in CCAR stress tests

typically include property prices—but usually not in combination with credit developments, as noted in chapter 2.

12. US bank supervisors already issue such official "guidance" via warning letters to banks. They did so in 2013 and 2014 for leveraged loans (i.e., loans made by banks to companies that were already highly indebted) and in December 2015 for commercial real estate loans. An advantage of including this indicator as a component of the risk surcharge is that it provides a direct incentive (beyond moral suasion) for the banks to comply—namely, that failure to reduce the targeted exposures increases the risk surcharge and, in turn, the capital hurdle rate, exposing the bank to a higher probability of having the Federal Reserve reject its capital plan. If there was a concern that banks could be blind-sided by changing official views of what is and is not a worrisome credit development, the Fed could indicate—when it sends out information on the scenarios for the next CCAR exercise—what types of loans would fall into the worrisome category.

13. In a recent report, the US Government Accountability Office (GAO 2016) criticized the Federal Reserve's stress test program for (among other things) not providing enough information for banks to fully understand its qualitative assessment approach or the reasons for the Fed's decision to object to a bank's capital plan.

14. Because the existing G-SIB surcharge for leverage ratios in the United States is defined in terms of the Basel III leverage ratio, not the tier 1 leverage ratio, and the average Basel III leverage ratio for US G-SIBs is lower than that for the tier 1 leverage ratio, switching to a Basel III leverage test in the CCAR would probably shrink the existing cushion over minimum leverage ratio requirements for G-SIBs.

15. Admati and Hellwig (2013b, 16) are also doubtful of the banking industry's claims that making the leverage ratio the sole Pillar 1 capital requirement would induce large changes in banks' asset portfolios: "These may be empty threats but if they are not, the claim raises serious concerns about governance.... If risks are worth taking on behalf of banks' investors, why aren't the banks already taking them? If the risks are not worth taking, why would the banks take them when they are funded with more equity?"

16. In this model, retained earnings are defined as net income less dividend payments and net stock purchases. Suppose we assume that return on assets (ROA) is fixed at 90 basis points, that annual asset growth is zero percent, and that capital distribution—the sum of dividend payments and net (purchases minus sales) stock purchases—is 10 percent of net income. Then one can move from an 8 percent leverage ratio to a 16 percent target in roughly 10 years (with retained earnings accounting for 90 percent of net income). We could still get there in 10 years if annual asset growth were minus 1 percent but the capital distribution was raised to 20 percent. Similarly, by assuming minus 2 percent annual asset growth but a capital distribution of 30 percent, one again reaches the target in 10 years. If return on assets were 80 basis points (instead of 90), annual asset growth minus 2 percent, and capital distribution 25 percent, one could again reach the leverage ratio target in 10 years. Finally, combining minus 2 percent annual asset growth with a return on assets of 100 basis points would allow a 45 percent capital distribution and still would be consistent with a 10-year phase-in period. For simulation purposes, I think it is reasonable to assume some shrinkage in the size of G-SIBs if their minimum leverage ratio were increased over 10 years to 16 percent. I am most grateful to Chuck Morris and Kristen Regehr for their help in building this model and applying it to data on US G-SIBs.

17. Jeremy Stein (2016), who served as an advisor to the US Treasury secretary in 2009, notes that one outrageous feature of the $125 billion US government capital injection to nine large banks in October 2008 was that the TARP 9 were on track to pay $25 billion of this $125 billion out as dividends in the next year alone; $250 million of that would go to officers and directors of those firms. See Goldstein (2012b) for a criticism of dividend payouts at large EU banks.

18. In the definitive history of the early years (1974–97) of the Basel Committee on Banking Supervision (BCBS), Goodhart (2011) recounts how the 1982 emerging-market debt crisis not only revealed the inadequacy of capital in the US money center banks but also highlighted the potential competitive disadvantage of trying to raise capital adequacy requirements (CAR) unilaterally. With the US Congress concerned about the latter effect, Federal Reserve Chair Paul Volcker was dispatched to go to the G-10 governors to seek an internationally equivalent capital adequacy regime. The BCBS had been working on this issue for some time; a roadblock was that attitudes and practices toward CAR were initially sufficiently different across major countries to make a consensus unreachable. The United States and the United Kingdom reached agreement on the separate adoption of a common accord on CAR in the autumn of 1986. According to Goodhart, this agreement had the intended effect of putting extra pressure on the BCBS to reach a compromise solution. The Basel I agreement was adopted in 1988.

19. See Herring (2007) on why the United States chose to have a bifurcated implementation of Basel II.

20. Goodhart (2011, 5–6) notes: "The BCBS always emphasized it had no formal role whatsoever and also that it could apply no sanctions to any country failing to implement its proposals."

21. This calculation assumes (total consolidated asset) weights of 62, 24, and 14 percent respectively for US G-SIBs, large non-G-SIBs that participated in the 2016 CCAR tests, and smaller banks (with less than $50 billion in assets); it also assumes the weighted-average tangible leverage ratio for smaller banks was approximately 9.5 percent at end-2015.

22. As discussed in chapter 4, this calculation employs what I have called a "loans-plus" approach to the link between increased financing costs and increases in loan rates.

23. Cetina and Loudis (2015) find that, all else equal, banks perceived as too big to fail had credit default swap spreads 44 to 80 basis points lower than other banks.

24. Akerlof and Shiller (2015, xi) define phishing as "getting people to do things that are in the interest of the phisherman, but not in the interest of the target." Their definition of a "phool" is "someone who, for whatever reason, is successfully phished."

25. Cecchetti and Schoenholtz (2014, 4) suggest a similar strategy: "Being pragmatists, we think regulators should continue to ratchet up bank-capital requirements until the trade-off between banking efficiency and financial safety shifts appreciably in favor of the latter. Importantly, as capital levels rise, we will be able to measure the costs, in terms of increased lending spreads, reduced loan volumes, and shifts in activity to less-regulated intermediaries. Over time, these responses will give us the information we need to determine the desirable level of capital requirements. And during the transition, the safety of the financial system will be on the rise."

26. The Dodd-Frank Act specifies that any insured depository or systemically important nonbank could be prohibited from merging or acquiring substantially all the assets or control of another company if the combined total consolidated liabilities would exceed 10 percent of the aggregate consolidated liabilities of all financial companies. This liabil-

ity size cap, however, would not require any existing US financial institution to shrink. In May 2010 US Senators Sherrod Brown (D-Ohio) and Ted Kaufman (D-Delaware) went farther, proposing an amendment to the Dodd-Frank Act. Their bill would have capped deposits and other liabilities and restricted bank assets to 10 percent of GDP. Three large US G-SIBs (JPMorgan Chase, Wells Fargo, and Bank of America) would have had to shrink to meet that requirement. The bill was defeated by a 61–33 vote.

27. "Fed Lifts Capital Requirements for Banks," *Wall Street Journal*, July 20, 2015.

8

Potential Objections to the Plan for Bank-Capital Reform and Closing Remarks

Despite having considerable curb appeal (at least for me), I anticipate that a plan to increase minimum leverage ratios to 10 percent for smaller banks, 11 to 13 percent for large non–global systemically important banks, and 14 to 18 percent for global systemically important banks (G-SIBs) will encounter some stiff opposition. The main criticisms (beyond those discussed thus far) are likely to be the following:

- The proposed minimum leverage ratio schedule is out of the mainstream and therefore unlikely to be implemented.

- If implemented, the plan would shrink the size of the largest banks, the banking system, and the financial system as a whole, with adverse consequences for economic growth.

- The plan would encourage and accelerate the growth of the shadow banking system, with adverse consequences for financial stability.

- The plan is no longer needed, because G-20 leaders have endorsed the Financial Stability Board's total loss-absorbing capacity (TLAC) proposal to require G-SIBs to hold 18 percent of their risk-weighted assets (exclusive of surcharges) in the form of equity plus long-term debt.

10/11–13/14–18 Percent Minimum Leverage Ratios: A Step Too Far?

Earlier Proposals for Much Higher Capital Requirements

I am not of course the first economist to recommend much higher minimum leverage ratios for banks. Among those who have made earlier calls for the same remedy and have taken a stab at putting a number or range on what the minimum should be, I draw the reader's attention to the following (in descending order of the proposed minimum requirement).

In their book *The Bankers' New Clothes*, Admati and Hellwig (2013a, 179) call for a minimum leverage ratio for banks of 20 to 30 percent:

> Requiring that banks' equity be at least on the order of 20–30 percent of their total assets would make the financial system substantially safer and healthier. At such levels of equity, most banks would usually be able to cope on their own and require no more than occasional liquidity support.

In a May 2014 interview, Nobel Laureate Eugene Fama called for a 20 to 25 percent minimum equity share for the largest banks:

> One way to take [too big to fail] off the table is to increase equity requirements. Not like they have been talking about them though. They have to go up to maybe 20, 25 percent equity finance for these too-big-to-fail banks (cited in Pethokoukis 2014).

In a November 2010 letter to the *Financial Times*, 20 distinguished professors of finance (including two Nobel Laureates) reached the following conclusion: "Basel III is far from sufficient to protect the system from recurring crises. If a much larger fraction, at least 15 percent, of banks' total non-risk-weighted assets were funded by equity, the social benefits would be substantial. And the social cost would be minimal, if any."[1]

In 2013 US Senators Sherrod Brown (D-Ohio) and David Vitter (R-Louisiana) unveiled a bill (the Terminating Bailouts for Taxpayer Fairness Act, or Too Big to Fail Act) that would increase minimum leverage requirements for large US banks. Under their plan six US G-SIBs with total assets of more than $500 billion would be required to meet a 15 percent minimum leverage ratio, and midsized and regional banks would be subject to an 8 percent minimum leverage ratio. Community banks would be unaffected by the legislation. They would also receive some regulatory relief under this legislation. The bill did not receive enough support to become law.

In a 2010 paper on the 2007–10 financial crisis, former Federal Reserve Chair Alan Greenspan (2010, 224) analyzed what size public capital injection might have been necessary during the crisis to reduce credit default spreads for the six largest US banks to levels seen just before the crisis (in 2007). Adding that figure to the book leverage ratio for US banks in 2010, he concluded that the minimum leverage ratio should be 13 to 14 percent.

In his new book on the financial crisis, *The End of Alchemy*, Lord Mervyn King (2016, 280), the former governor of the Bank of England, endorses a 10 percent minimum leverage ratio for banks: "A minimum ratio of equity to total assets of 10 percent would be a good start."

Thomas Hoenig (2013), the vice chair of the Federal Deposit Insurance Corporation (FDIC), also recommends a minimum 10 percent leverage ratio for all US banks. Charles Calomiris (2013) parts company with other economists who claim that much heightened capital requirements would come with practically no social costs but nevertheless believes that the benefits of higher capital requirements would be large enough to justify a 10 percent minimum leverage ratio.

What Is Feasible?

The feasibility of agreeing on and implementing much higher capital ratios is in the eye of the beholder.[2] At least in its public stance, the banking industry continues to strongly oppose making the leverage ratio the primary or sole capital standard,[3] dropping the use of internal models in the calculation of risk-weighted assets (IIF 2015), and requiring any increases in minimum capital beyond what was agreed to under Basel III or US banking legislation.[4]

But the strategy of stonewalling against much higher capital requirements is not necessarily a winning one for the largest banks over the medium to long run. These banks have seen their reputations badly tarnished not only by the massive credit losses suffered during the 2007–09 global economic and financial crisis but also by a series of scandals (LIBOR, foreign exchange, etc.) that have led (as of end-2016) to more than $300 billion in fines, with no assurance that their legal liabilities are yet fully behind them.[5]

The official sector response has been a more intrusive effort to limit excessive risk taking, via the Volcker Rule, higher G-SIB capital surcharges, and recent (September 2016) proposals by the Federal Reserve to prohibit banks from buying and selling commodities and engaging in merchant banking activity.[6] Speaking on July 20, 2015, after the decision to raise the risk-based surcharge on G-SIBs, Fed Chair Janet Yellen painted the options facing the largest banks in stark terms: "In practice, this final rule confronts these financial institutions with a choice: They must either hold substantially more capital, reducing the likelihood that they will fail, or else they must shrink their systemic footprint, reducing the harm that their failure would do to the financial system."[7]

What Chair Yellen did not say—but is nevertheless implied by the official actions of the past few years—is that the largest banks face another related choice. If those banks refuse to reduce their systemic footprint (loss given default) and increases in capital requirements are not large enough to reduce the probability of default enough to bring their expected loss down to a tolerable level, the official sector could consider imposing structural activity measures that also reduce the probability of default. The Volcker Rule, for example, has generated significant changes in the organization and business models of some large banks.[8]

Some Democratic politicians think change has not gone far enough. Presidential candidate Hillary Clinton proposed the following:

> We need to further rein in major financial institutions. My plan proposes legislation that would impose a new risk fee on dozens of the biggest banks—those with more than $50 billion in assets—and other systemically important financial institutions to discourage the kind of hazardous behavior that could induce another crisis. I would also ensure that the federal government has—and is prepared to use—the authority and tools necessary to reorganize, downsize, and ultimately break up any financial institution that is too large and risky to be managed effectively. No bank or financial firms should be too big to manage.[9]

Senator Elizabeth Warren (D-Massachusetts) argued that "If big banks want to engage in high-risk trading, they can go for it but then they don't get access to insured deposits and put the taxpayer on the hook for some of that risk."[10]

Vermont senator and former presidential candidate Bernie Sanders favored breaking up too big to fail institutions. "If a bank is too big to fail, it is too big to exist.... These institutions have acquired too much economic and political power, endangering our economy and our political process."[11]

On the Republican side of the aisle, as a candidate, Donald Trump promised to scale back government regulation (including presumably the Dodd-Frank Act) but did not release a detailed financial sector plan. Congressman Jeb Hensarling (R-Texas), the chair of the House Financial Services Committee, released a plan called the Financial Choice Act.[12] Under this plan, US banks with a CAMELS rating of 1 or 2 would have the option of maintaining a simple leverage ratio of 10 percent (as measured by the US supplementary leverage ratio) in exchange for being granted wide-ranging regulatory relief.[13] Banks choosing this option would be functionally exempt from the post-Dodd-Frank regulatory regime, the Basel III capital and liquidity standards, and a number of other regulatory features that predate Dodd-Frank. The bill would also create a new subchapter of the bankruptcy code to address the failure of a large, complex, financial institution, replacing the orderly liquidation authority of Dodd-Frank.

I do not regard a minimum 10 percent leverage ratio as adequate protection against a wholesale dismantling of the Dodd-Frank and Basel III regulatory reforms.[14] Far from it, especially since as of the end of 2015, the eight US G-SIBs maintained a Basel III leverage ratio of about 6.5

percent (see Hoenig 2016a).[15] That said, I take the broader point that if banks were much better capitalized, they would be on stronger ground in arguing that some existing structural reforms are not needed.[16] At some point, one would think that one or more CEOs of G-SIBs would come to the conclusion that higher capital ratios are the neatest, least intrusive, and least costly mechanism for satisfying regulators and the general public that their institutions are safe enough.[17]

It is well, too, to keep in mind that the largest banks are not the only ones in Washington with political clout. Almost every small town in America has a community bank, and the group that represents them (the Independent Community Bankers of America [ICBA]) has influence. In a 2013 report, ICBA expressed its strong desire to end too big to fail. It supported the Brown-Vitter proposal of a 15 percent minimum leverage ratio for the nation's six largest banks.

US regulators and supervisors have been moving in the right direction on minimum capital ratios and raising capital hurdle rates in the CCAR stress tests. But they have not moved far enough. Maybe they reason that taking many small bites out of the apple generates less opposition than supporting a major bank-capital reform. But standing pat or close to it after Dodd-Frank and Basel III invites its own risks.

One risk is that standing pat offers opportunities for forces opposed to banking reform to chip away at earlier reforms, through, for example, hidden language in legislative deals to, say, keep the government open or increase the debt ceiling.[18] Such a tactic is facilitated by the fact that many aspects of financial reform are arcane and matter more to the industry than to the average voter. So far concessions have been outside the bank-capital area, such as in swaps carveouts. But maybe next time the industry will press for rollbacks in the de facto quality of bank capital. All of this leads some reformers (including me) to argue that the best defense against an erosion of existing banking reforms is a good offense: a major new initiative that lays out a schedule and timetable for new higher minimum capital standards.

As emphasized in chapter 5, despite the overall advances made in Dodd-Frank, the crisis management ship of state has taken a few torpedoes below the waterline. In particular, the Federal Reserve is now more constrained than before Dodd-Frank in how it can apply its lender of last resort emergency lending instrument, and fiscal policy is more constrained than before because of the much higher public debt ratio and the continued/increased politicization of the tax/spending debate. In view of these challenges, US officials might well conclude that the premium on having well-capitalized banks that can meet shocks largely on their own has increased.

For all of the above reasons, I do not see the plan for much heightened capital requirements as pie in the sky. The timing is admittedly uncertain and more persuasion (hence this book) is needed. But reform can happen.

Large Banks, Large Banking Systems, and Too Little/Too Much Finance

A second potential criticism of the plan is that were it implemented and were the largest banks, the banking system, and the financial sector as a whole to shrink, the results would hurt the macroeconomy, slowing economic growth.

Bank Size

Defenders of the present size of America's largest banks argue that reducing their size would give up significant economies of scale and scope. The Liikanen Report (2012) and studies by the chair of the Financial Stability Oversight Council (FSOC 2011), Haldane (2012), and Pagano et al. (2014) provide empirical evidence on economies of scale and scope. There is considerable consensus in these four reports (summarized below), and I support their findings.

Economies of scale mean that unit costs decline as the level of output (or size, measured by total assets) increases. Up until about 2010, the consensus was that economies of scale in banking were exhausted well before banks reached the size cutoff for participating in the Comprehensive Capital Analysis and Review (CCAR) stress tests ($50 billion in total consolidated assets). More recent empirical studies for US banks (Hughes and Mester 2011, Wheelock and Wilson 2012) overturned that earlier conclusion, with economies of scale evident in bank sizes running up even to $1 trillion to $2 trillion in total assets. These economies of scale stem largely from payments and clearing systems and information technology.

The rub, however, is that these efficiency benefits at the largest banks come about in large part because of the lower funding costs linked to their perceived too big to fail status. Once that advantage is eliminated, economies of scale disappear beyond $100 billion in assets. Points above the dotted line in figure 8.1 denote economies of scale; points below it denote diseconomies. In panel (a) of figure 8.1 no account is taken of the implicit too big to fail funding subsidy. Economies of scale are therefore visible all the way up to the size of the very largest banks ($2 trillion or more in total assets). Panel (b) accounts for the too big to fail funding subsidy. It shows no economies of scale beyond $100 billion in bank assets. The conclusion of the Liikanen Report (2012, 41) on economies of scale in banking is representative: "Although there is no agreement on the maximum efficient scale

Figure 8.1 Estimated scale economies

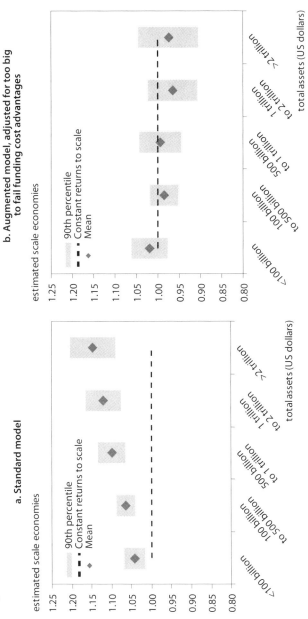

a. Standard model

b. Augmented model, adjusted for too big to fail funding cost advantages

Notes: The results are for estimated scale economies over the period 2001 to 2010. A value equal to one, less than one, or greater than one implies constant returns to scale, scale diseconomies, and scale economies, respectively. Presented results are estimated at the mean and standard error of the estimated scale economies for each bank in each time period. Total assets have been adjusted to constant year-2010 prices using country level inflation rate data.

Source: Davies and Tracey (2014). Reprinted with permission.

of banking, the available estimates tend to suggest levels that are relatively low compared to the current size of the largest EU banks."[19]

Economies of scope stem from the benefits of diversification and vertical integration, including cross selling and one-stop shopping. The earlier empirical literature held out hope that the more diversified product and funding mix of large universal banks would generate substantial cost savings and resilience. The diversification benefits linked to the removal of interstate banking regulations in the United States held out the promise that large banks with subsidiaries and branches around the world would be in a favored position.

Although synergies exist between traditional lending and deposit taking and some geographic diversification remains valuable, the promised benefits did not materialize. According to the Liikanen Report (2012, 46), "Economies of scope, including operating cost and revenue synergies as well as risk diversification benefits, are appealing in theory, but the empirical evidence on their existence is weak."

In explaining why economies of scale and scope have delivered a less favorable benefit-cost result than expected, the literature emphasizes the following points.[20]

1. The near doubling of the size of the EU banking system relative to GDP since 1966 is due entirely to the growth of the largest 20 banks.[21] The same trend is also evident in the United States, but the growth of large banks has been about twice as rapid in the European Union as in the United States. After 2000 large EU banks moved more aggressively into lines of business other than deposit taking and credit origination, especially securities trading and issuance activity (Pagano et al. 2014).

2. The median leverage ratio for the 20 largest banks in the European Union in 2006 was about half its level in the late 1990s, so rapid expansion was paired with a declining capital cushion (Pagano et al. 2014). An expectation by too big to fail banks that their gains would be privatized while their losses would be socialized increased their incentives to both take on excessive risks and hold lower levels of self-insurance.

3. Using five different measures of bank risk on a sample of 195 EU banks over the 1994–2012 period, Pagano et al. (2014) find that, all else equal, bank risk is higher the larger the bank.[22] They report the same finding when the estimation is redone on a panel of 1,179 global banks over the same period.

4. The universal banking model (in which traditional lending is paired with other activities, such as securities business, derivatives trading, and lending to governments) seems to have imposed higher social costs than more specialized intermediaries. Much of this is due to the former's greater exposure to securities markets and hence the stronger link between asset price shocks on the one hand and the supply of

credit and real economic activity on the other (Pagano et al. 2014). The aggregate balance sheet of monetary-financial institutions in the euro area shows that in 2013 only 31 percent of their assets represented credit to households and firms (Pagano et al. 2014).[23]

5. At least in the European Union, bank size seems to be negatively related to a bank's loan to total assets ratio. Large banks with low lending ratios also seem to generate higher capital shortfalls at the same time as the market is suffering a shortfall (Pagano et al. 2014). Large universal banks thus have higher tail risk dependence and hence generate higher systemic risk. Pagano et al. also report that any cost efficiency shown by large European universal banks stems entirely from public subsidies. All of this leads Pagano et al. to the following conclusion: "On balance, therefore, the preponderance of universal banking in Europe appears to be socially harmful, in the sense that its social costs far outweigh any private benefits" (p. 34).

6. Diversification for a single bank does not translate into diversification for the banking system as a whole. Goodhart and Wagner (2012, 1) offer the following assessment: "Financial institutions—in particular the very large ones—have become very similar to each other. The biggest institutions are now operating in the same global markets, undertaking similar activities, and are exposed to the same funding risks.... This lack of diversity is very costly to society. Similar institutions are likely to encounter problems at the same time."

7. Diversification at large banks tends to increase their complexity, which makes them harder to manage, reduces their transparency, and complicates resolution (Liikanen Report 2012). Herring and Carmassi (2010) use the number of majority-owned subsidiaries as a rough proxy for the complexity of large and complex financial institutions (LCFIs). By this measure, 16 LCFIs have 2.5 times as many majority-owned subsidiaries as the 16 largest multinational manufacturing firms. Eight of the 16 LCFIs in the sample had more than 1,000 subsidiaries each, and one (Citigroup) had nearly 2,500, half of which were chartered abroad. Diversified banks trade at a discount to a portfolio of comparable stand-alone firms (Laeven and Levine 2005).

8. Other things equal, large banks are more likely to be intervened and supported by public funds than small banks (see Altunbas, Manganelli, and Marques-Ibanez 2011 for US and EU banks and Rose and Wieladek 2012 for UK banks). Large sovereign bailouts of large banks in turn generate a higher risk of sovereign default. Using 2011 data, the Liikanen Report (2012) finds that eight large EU banks had assets equal to 100 percent or more of national GDP and that the largest EU bank had assets equal to 17 percent of EU GDP. The experiences of Iceland in 2008–09 and Ireland in 2010 serve as dramatic reminders of that sovereign risk.

Given this body of evidence on the costs and benefits of having very large banks, reducing the size of the largest banks in the United States and the European Union would be a blessing, not a curse.

Banking System Size

The plan proposes increased minimum leverage ratios not just for G-SIBs but also for other banks. Critics would likely charge that it would lead to a smaller US banking system as a whole and that such shrinkage would be bad for macroeconomic performance and economic growth.

Here, too, recent empirical evidence has led to a change in views. In the earlier empirical literature on the relationship between financial development and economic growth (summarized in Levine 1997), what mattered (after controlling for other determinants of economic growth) was the total amount of finance—that is, financial depth, often defined as the sum of bank credit to the private sector, stock market capitalization, and public and private bond market capitalization (all expressed as a ratio to GDP) (see, for example, Khan and Senhadji 2000). The greater the financial depth, the higher the economic growth. The composition, or "structure," of that finance between bank and market finance was not found to be important for economic growth (Levine 2002).

More recent research suggests that bank-dominated financial systems are less friendly to higher economic growth than market-based ones. Pagano et al. (2014) review these studies and provide some new evidence of their own. They redo Levine's (2002) study, substituting annual observations for the 1989–2011 period for the original 1980–95 observations. The financial structure variable compares (in log ratio form) domestic equities traded on domestic exchanges (relative to GDP) to deposit money bank credits to the private sector (also relative to GDP). The authors find the estimated coefficient on the structure variable to be positive and significant at the 5 percent level and report that this result holds up to various robustness checks. Their results imply that if Germany's financial structure had followed that of the United States over the past 20 years, its level of GDP would have been roughly 2 percent higher than it was in 2014.

Using data for 71 economic downturns in 24 countries over the 1960–2013 period, Gambacorta, Yang, and Tsatsaronis (2014) find that although bank-based and market-based financial systems perform about the same during normal downturns, bank-based systems perform approximately three times worse when downturns are accompanied by a financial crisis. Bank-based systems are also associated with weaker recoveries from financial crises.

Using data on a sample of 195 EU banks and the same five measures of bank risk discussed earlier, Pagano et al. (2014) find that, all else equal, bank risk is higher the larger the size of the banking system. They attribute these results to three features of bank-based financial systems:

- The volatility of bank credit growth is much higher than that for the growth in net debt securities issuance.
- Bank-denominated systems are better able to deter entry to competing suppliers of credit.
- The bilateral monopoly relationship that develops between bank lenders and their borrowers contributes to excessive loan forbearance.

This message about the perils of overdependence on bank financing in Europe seems to be getting through. In his maiden policy speech as president-elect of the European Commission in July 2014, Jean-Claude Juncker argued that the European Union should move toward creating a capital markets union to go along with its banking union.[24] In September 2015 European Commissioner for Financial Markets Jonathan Hill offered an action plan for moving toward such a union.[25]

In the United States, where the financial system is much more market based than in Europe, there is no public policy initiative to reduce the size of the banking system for economic growth objectives.[26] But there is nothing in the empirical evidence reviewed above to indicate that doing so would slow economic growth.

Size of the Financial Sector: Too Little or Too Much Finance

The third member of this unholy trinity argues that in order to prevent higher minimum capital ratios in the banking sector from leading via regulatory arbitrage to a larger nonbank sector, regulations would have to be stiffened for nonbanks, with the outcome that the whole financial sector would be become smaller, which would slow economic growth. Like its two big-is-beautiful siblings, this assertion also runs counter to the latest evidence.

In the 1990s empirical tests on the relationship between financial development and economic growth showed a significant, positive relationship based on both aggregate cross-country data (King and Levine 1993, Levine 1997) and pooled industry and country samples (Rajan and Zingales 1998). New empirical research has qualified the earlier conclusion in an important way (see Arcand, Berkes, and Panizza 2012; Cecchetti and Kharroubi 2012; and Sahay, Cihak, and N'Diaye 2015, among others).[27] It turns out that when a quadratic term for financial development is added to the growth equation (alongside the level of financial development and a set of control variables), the estimated coefficient has a negative sign and is consistently statistically significant, indicating that at some point, the influence of financial development on growth turns negative. Here is what the authors have to say about their results:

> We use different empirical results to show that there can indeed be "too much finance." In particular, our results suggest that finance starts having a negative effect on output growth when credit to the private sector reaches 100 percent of GDP. (Arcand, Berkes, and Panizza 2012, 1)

> As is the case with many things in life, with finance you can have too much of a good thing. That is, at low levels, a larger financial system goes hand in hand with higher productivity growth. But there comes a point—one that many advanced economies passed long ago—where more banking and more credit are associated with lower growth.[28] (Cecchetti and Kharroubi 2012, 1)

> Our analysis uncovers evidence of "too much finance" in the sense that beyond a certain level of financial development, the positive effect on economic growth begins to decline, while costs in terms of economic and financial volatility begin to rise.... High financial development does not impede capital accumulation. However, it leads to a loss of efficiency in investment. (Sahay, Cihak, and N'Diaye 2015, 1)

Two of the results of the recent too much finance literature are of special interest. The first is that on the eve of the 2007–09 crisis, the United States, along with Iceland, Ireland, the United Kingdom, Spain, and Portugal, were well beyond the negative threshold (see Arcand, Berkes, and Panizza 2012 and Cecchetti and Kharroubi 2012). The second is that the United States still has greater financial depth than optimal from an economic growth standpoint (Sahay, Cihak, and N'Diaye 2015).

The most popular explanation for this negative threshold effect of financial development on growth is twofold (Pagano et al. 2014): Too much finance leads to a misallocation of financial and human capital (in part by attracting, via excessively high wages, human resources from more productive sectors elsewhere in the economy), and larger financial systems, especially larger banking systems, are more prone to financial crises, which reduce growth.[29]

An important question is how robust the findings of the too much finance empirical studies are. Cline (2017) argues that the negative growth impacts should be taken with a large grain of salt, because they could reflect spurious attribution of causality and because the estimated growth effects from reducing the size of the financial sector appear too large to be credible.

Arcand, Berkes, and Panizza (2015) provide what seems to me to be a persuasive rejoinder to Cline's (2017) criticisms. I also find it reassuring that the findings of Cecchetti and Kharroubi (2012); Arcand, Berkes, and Panizza (2013); and Sahay, Cihak, and N'Diaye (2015) appear to hold up under many different formulations, including different country samples and time periods, different definitions of the financial development variable, the use of aggregate and firm-level data, the inclusion or exclusion of financial crisis periods, and many other iterations. Although more empirical research will shed light on the relationship between the size of the financial sector and economic growth, I see the burden of proof as now falling on the traditional more-finance-improves-growth advocates to show that the "too much finance" conclusions are faulty.

The bottom line is that a reduction in the size of the US financial sector as a whole would more likely be growth enhancing than growth reducing.

Shadow Banking and the Migration Problem

The third potential criticism of the plan is that heightened capital requirements for banks would cause financial activity to migrate to nonbank financial institutions, where regulation is less strict, with unhappy consequences for financial stability. This issue is sometimes known as the migration problem. Among all the potential objections to the plan, I consider this to be the weightiest one.

Excellent work on shadow banking has been done over the past few years (Group of Thirty 2009, Gorton and Metrick 2010a, FSB 2013, Adrian 2014, IMF 2014a, Pozsar 2014, Fischer 2015a, Ricks 2016, Volcker Alliance 2016). These studies provide a good summary of the nature of the problem and a menu of policy prescriptions.

What Is Shadow Banking?

There is more than one definition of shadow banking. Probably the most popular one comes from the Financial Stability Board (FSB 2011), which defines it as credit intermediation outside the conventional banking system. By that definition, roughly a quarter of total financial intermediation worldwide resides in the shadow banking system, with the largest shadow banking systems (as a share of GDP or total banking assets) in the United States, the United Kingdom, and the euro area (IMF 2014a).[30]

Adrian (2014, 1) prefers a definition that emphasizes the difference in regulation cum government backstops between traditional and shadow banking: "maturity transformation, liquidity transformation, and credit risk transfer outside of institutions with direct access to government backstops, such as depository institutions, i.e., traditional commercial banks." He notes that whereas most shadow banking is regulated to some extent, unlike the traditional banking system it is usually not subject to prudential regulation.

Figure 8.2 (taken from Adrian 2014), shows that the no-government-backstop definition of shadow banking encompasses much of the financial system. While commercial banking liabilities as a share of US GDP were roughly constant (at 70 percent) for the past 50 years, shadow credit intermediation expanded from less than 1 percent in 1960 to about 80 percent in 2007–08 at the time of the global financial crisis. Liabilities of the parent in bank holding companies and liabilities of broker-dealer subsidiaries are treated separately in figure 8.2 because unlike commercial bank subsidiaries (of BHCs), such parents and broker-dealers do not have access to either the discount window or deposit insurance.[31]

The IMF (2014a) observes that instead of defining shadow banking by the nature of the entity that carries it out, some analysts prefer definitions focused on instruments or markets. It recently introduced yet another definition based on the type of funding linked to a financial activity (IMF 2014b). It classifies an activity as shadow banking if it funds itself with nontraditional (noncore) funding. Thus, for example, securitization would be called shadow banking, regardless of whether it is carried out on the balance sheet of a bank or via a special purpose vehicle. IMF (2014a) shows that the different measures of shadow banking share a similar growth trend until 2007 but not after that. The FSB (2011) measure indicates that, after a mild drop in 2008, shadow banking activity recovered in the United States, the United Kingdom, and the euro area, whereas the narrower definitions suggest stagnation.

Why Is Shadow Banking of Concern?

Federal Reserve Vice Chair Stanley Fischer (2015a, 2) offers seven complementary explanations for why regulators in the United States should and do care about the shadow banking system:

1. The nonbank financial sector has produced material benefits, including more diversity in funding sources and greater market liquidity.

2. The sector is much larger and plays a more important role in the US economy than in most other countries, with about two-thirds of nonfinancial credit market debt held by nonbanks.

3. The 2007–09 financial crisis manifested itself first in the nonbank sector, beginning with nonbank mortgage companies, spreading to asset-backed commercial paper vehicles, moving on to nonbank finance companies dealing with auto and credit card loans and then to investment banks (including Bear Stearns, Lehman Brothers, Merrill Lynch, and others), and it was worse for nonbanks than for banks.

Figure 8.2   Shadow banking and traditional banking in the United States, 1960–2014

total liabilities as percent of nominal GDP

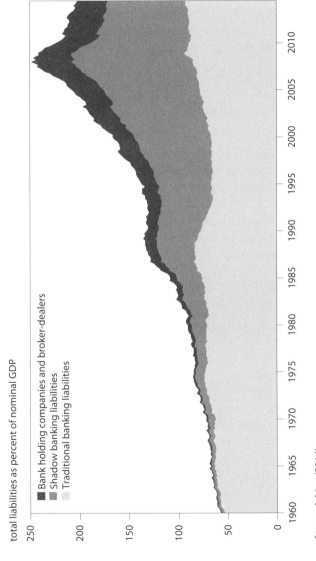

■ Bank holding companies and broker-dealers
▨ Shadow banking liabilities
░ Traditional banking liabilities

Source: Adrian (2014).

4. Nonbank distress has shown that it can inflict real harm on the real economy.

5. Many of the problems encountered by nonbanks in the crisis were similar to those that plagued banks, including insolvency, illiquidity, and a general loss of confidence.

6. The crisis management tools available during the crisis for nonbanks were much more limited than those for banks (resolution and lender of last resort lending by the central bank).

7. Nonbank distress can be transmitted to the banking sector via a variety of channels, including counterparty relationships, disruptions in funding markets, and the knock-on effects of asset fire sales.

In analyzing what has driven the strong growth of the shadow banking system more generally, analysts point to a variety of incentives and motivations. The IMF (2014a) highlights three factors:

- search-for-yield (low government bond yields generate a search for higher returns and the shadow banking system supplies those assets)

- regulatory arbitrage (financial institutions use nonbank intermediation to circumvent tighter bank regulation, including higher capital requirements), and

- complementarities with the rest of the financial system (growth of insurance and pension funds and the demands of institutional cash pools for alternatives to insured deposits and safe assets).[32]

Drawing on the literature, Adrian (2014) identifies six economic mechanisms that motivate shadow banking activities:[33]

1. Specialization (vertical disintegration). The shadow banking system transforms risky long-term loans into seemingly credit-free, money-like instruments, using a chain of wholesale-funded, securitization-based lending.

2. Mispriced government backups. Some shadow-banking liabilities are able to benefit from indirect access to government backstops (e.g., access to credit lines from commercial banks, credit guarantees written by insurance companies that benefit from high credit ratings because of state insurance funds, implicit guarantees under the umbrella of bank holding companies, etc.).

3. Regulatory arbitrage. The restructuring of financial activity to avoid taxes, disclosure, and/or capital requirements (e.g., asset-based commercial paper consolidated onto bank balance sheets that did not need to be included in the measurement of risk-based capital).

4. Neglected risk. Shadow banks are able to take advantage of risk myopia in the market by accumulating assets that are particularly sensitive to tail risk.

5. A host of agency problems. These problems allow shadow banks to take advantage in the securitization process of various forms of asymmetric information (between issuers and investors, lenders and loan originators, lenders and investors, beneficiaries of invested funds and credit rating agencies, etc.).

6. Private money creation. Shadow banking liabilities can serve as substitutes for high-power money and thus expand in line with increasing money demand (shadow banking money creation takes place mainly in the commercial paper market and the repo market).

Focusing on the rapid growth of shadow banking in the United States, Gorton and Metrick (2010b) emphasize the role of regulatory arbitrage. They note that money market mutual funds in the United States were a response to interest ceilings on demand deposits (Regulation Q) and that whereas banks pay for deposit insurance, the promise to pay $1 per share cost the money market mutual funds nothing. Assets of US money market mutual funds grew from roughly $4 billion in the late 1970s to a peak of $3.8 trillion in 2008.

In addition to the rapid growth of money under management by institutional investors, pension funds, mutual funds, states and municipalities, and nonfinancial firms, Gorton and Metrick (2010a) argue that the explicit exclusion of repo agreements from Chapter 11 (and its automatic stay provisions) helped fuel the US repo market's growth, to perhaps $10 trillion (in gross amounts) at end-2007. Among other factors, they cite the lower regulatory capital requirements of off-balance-sheet securitizations as aiding its rapid growth from 2000 to 2006.

What Can Be Done to Address the Risks Associated with Shadow Banking?

Despite the vulnerability and externalities raised by the rise of shadow banking, there is actually a rather large set of potential policy actions that regulators can take to limit the buildup of risk in that sector and its transmission to the banking sector and the real economy. Drawing on research by the Group of Thirty (2009); Gorton and Metrick (2010a); Hanson, Kashyap, and Stein (2011); Adrian (2014); Pozsar (2014); Fischer (2015a); King (2016); and Ricks (2016), let me mention both some of the measures already taken and others that could be activated.

As a result of the Dodd-Frank Act, the Federal Stability Oversight Council (FSOC) has the authority to designate a nonbank as systemically important and to subject it to prudential regulation by the Federal Reserve. Four nonbanks (AIG, Prudential Financial, General Electric Capital Corp., and MetLife) have been so designated, and more nonbanks could be added to the list.[34] Systemically important nonbanks could also be included in the annual (supervisor-led) Dodd-Frank Act stress test exercise, although including them might entail the design of special adverse scenarios for them.

As a complement to regulation by type or systemic importance, regulation could also be established by type of product, in a way that affects all investors in that product. Hanson, Kashyap, and Stein (2011) have proposed that regulatory minimum haircut requirements be established on asset-backed securities, so that no investor who takes a position in credit assets can avoid constraints on short-term leverage.

Pozsar (2014) suggests that the Federal Reserve use its reverse repurchase facility to set minimum haircuts on safe assets such as treasuries. He argues that minimum haircut requirements could become the equivalents of minimum capital requirements for backing of shadow money claims, giving the Fed macroprudential control over market-based credit cycles—control it lacked before the crisis, when competition drove haircuts to excessively low levels. The Fed might also be able to expand the scope of Regulation T (on margin requirements for securities purchases), to underpin a more activist and more product-based response to leverage cycles.

The creation of an orderly resolution authority in Title II of the Dodd-Frank Act and the Single Point of Entry (SPOE) provision in the proposed G-20 TLAC initiative should make the resolution of a systemically important shadow bank (somewhat) less of a potential nightmare than it was precrisis (see the discussion of the G-20 and FSB TLAC initiative later in this chapter).

To reduce information asymmetries and externalities in the securitization process, US regulatory authorities have put in place a measure that requires securitizers to have more skin in the game by retaining some of the risk of the securities they create. Securitizers must retain no less than 5 percent of the credit risk of any asset sold through the issuance of any asset-backed security, they cannot hedge or transfer the retained credit risk, and they must disclose the amount and form of the retention to investors (Adrian 2014). To deal with the conflicts of interest at credit rating agencies—the results of which were so damaging during the run-up to the 2007–09 crisis—these agencies are now prohibited from structuring the same product they rate, analysts cannot receive gifts exceeding $25 from the companies they rate, agencies are required to publish statistics about the performance of their ratings, and sales and analysis within crediting rating agencies have been separated (Adrian 2014). Adrian proposes that credit rating agencies also be required to hold a slice of any securities they rate before they can disclose ratings on that security to investors.

Since 2016 the Securities and Exchange Commission (SEC) has required prime institutional money funds in the United States to publish a floating net asset value rather than a stable value of $1 per unit. Funds will also be able to impose limitations on withdrawals of liabilities and can also impose liability redemption fees. Both of these measures were approved in the wake of the 2007–09 crisis to discourage runs (Fischer 2014b). Minimum capital requirements for money market funds were apparently considered and (unfortunately in my view) rejected, but this proposal could be reconsidered.

To address fragilities in the triparty repo market, triparty repo clearing banks are reportedly in the process of making technological changes that will reduce the excessive reliance on intraday credit extension, and the supervision of the largest dealers in this market has been heightened (Adrian 2014).

Several reforms have been implemented to deal with vulnerabilities in the derivatives markets. Standardized derivatives have moved to central counterparties, and initial and variation margins have been put in place for noncleared derivatives (Fischer 2014b). In November 2014 the International Swaps and Derivatives Association (ISDA) issued a protocol that ended the automatic termination of covered derivative contracts when there is a bankruptcy or public resolution of a systemic financial institution; 18 of the largest global financial institutions, representing a majority of the swaps market, agreed voluntarily to adhere to it.[35] A large-scale monitoring and data collection effort (the latter coordinated by the new Office of Financial Research at the US Treasury) has also been mounted, to improve tracking and understanding of risks in the nonbank sector.

Run-Proofing and King's Pawnbroker for All Seasons

But what if much higher capital requirements for banks speed further migration to shadow banks? And what if, despite the initiatives outlined above, there remains a serious risk of another systemic run on shadow banks because of the maturity/liquidity mismatch between their liabilities and their assets? What more could be done to "run-proof" the system?

Several bold initiatives would put the regulation and supervision of shadow banks that issue short-term, redeemable-at-par liabilities on a more equal footing with that of banks. These initiatives (Group of Thirty

2009, Gorton and Metrick 2010a, Gorton 2012, King 2016, Ricks 2016) share a number of elements.

First, they view runs or panics by short-term debtholders as particularly damaging to the real economy, because they generate a cascade of fire sales of bank and shadow bank assets; because they leave little time for officials and market participants to engineer a workout; and because the "moneyness" or near moneyness (cash equivalence) of such short-term debt implies larger effects on real expenditure when these money markets are disrupted.

Second, they typically do not see higher capital ratios alone as being able to preempt such runs. Instead, they rely on funding maturity restrictions, combined with some mix of government insurance, access to the lender of last resort, and collateral/portfolio restraints to preempt runs. The collateral/portfolio restraints are meant to limit the moral hazard linked to granting shadow banks the same insurance/lender of last resort protection accorded to banks. By limiting entry into certain activities to firms with approved funding structures and portfolio requirements, some of these proposals also aim to create franchise value for "licensed" banks, thereby reducing their incentives to take on excessive risk.

Third, financial institutions that are not willing to sign on to the maturity funding restrictions, the portfolio restrictions, and (in some proposals) risk-based insurance premiums would not be permitted (i.e., granted an official "license") to offer certain financial products or to engage in certain financial activities, nor would they be eligible for government insurance or lender of last resort assistance in a crisis. Put in other words, they would be restricted to funding themselves with longer-term (usually defined as one-year or longer) liabilities and allowed to fail if they got in trouble.

Fourth, these initiatives take a decidedly "functional" approach to regulation. They argue that short-term claims (on banks or shadow banks) that serve largely the same function and create similar risks should be subject to equivalent (if not identical) regulation (see Crawford 2016).

There are also some notable differences in the various proposals. Some (King 2016, Ricks 2016) would impose the same regulatory treatment on all shadow banks that wish to use short-term debt. Others (Gorton and Metrick 2010a) would offer customized regulatory packages for different shadow banking entities/activities (money market mutual funds, securitization, repo markets).

Some proposals (Ricks 2016) maintain that the only regulatory tool that can be relied on to preempt a true panic by short-term debtholders is credible government insurance. Others (King 2016) are more confident that certain fundamentals-based tools—specifically, a new form of liquidity buffer—could also do the job, with fewer adverse side effects.

Among the "run-proofing" schemes currently on offer, I favor the "pawnbroker for all seasons" (PFAS) initiative put forward by former Bank of England Governor Mervyn King (2016).[36] He argues that the traditional Bagehot (1873) lender of last resort guideline for central banks—to lend freely against collateral at a penalty rate—is no longer up to the task in a world in which there is radical uncertainty and banks and shadow banks do not have enough high-quality liquid assets to cover their runnable short-term liabilities. When a systemic crisis like the 2007–09 one comes along, central banks will find themselves lending against bad collateral, at inadequate haircuts, and at low or zero penalty rates, because the alternatives to not doing so would be worse for the macroeconomy.

King proposes that the Bagehot rule be replaced by having the central bank act as a pawnbroker for all seasons. The basic idea is to ensure that banks (and shadow banks) always have sufficient cash to meet the demands of depositors and holders of their short-term unsecured debt. King (2016, 271–72) describes the basic building blocks of the PFAS as follows:

> Each bank would decide how much of its assets it would position in advance at the central bank—that is, how much of the relevant assets the central bank would be allowed to examine and which would then be available for use as collateral.
>
> For each type of asset, the central bank would calculate the haircut it would apply when deciding how much cash it would lend against that asset. Adding up all the assets that had been positioned, it would then be clear how much central bank money the bank would be entitled to borrow at any instant. Because these arrangements would have been put in place well ahead of any crisis, there would be no difficulty in the central bank agreeing to lend at a moment's notice.... The amount which a bank was entitled to borrow against prepositioned collateral, added to its existing central bank reserves, is a measure of the 'effective liquid assets' of a bank.
>
> The second step is to look at the liabilities side of a bank's balance sheet—its total demand deposits and short-term unsecured debt (up to, say, one year)—which could run at short notice. That total is a measure of the bank's 'effective liquid liabilities.' The regulatory requirement on banks and other financial intermediaries would be that their effective liquid assets should exceed their effective liquid liabilities.

Cecchetti and Schoenholtz (2016) and Wolf (2016) have reviewed King's PFAS proposal. I summarize the potential benefits of this scheme drawing on their analysis and reactions of my own:

1. Since the PFAS applies to all financial intermediaries offering fixed-value liabilities with a maturity of less than one year, it should deter

(and maybe even stop) runs on shadow banks. It should also deter runs from uninsured depositors and short-term debtholders in traditional banks.

2. The PFAS offers a middle ground between the status quo and 100 percent reserve banking, allowing banks to retain much of their role as traditional lenders.

3. The PFAS would be compatible with a higher minimum leverage ratio for banks while still streamlining existing financial regulation. King favors a minimum leverage ratio of 10 percent as a good starting point and has indicated his support for higher minimum leverage ratios over time. He envisages his PFAS being implemented gradually over 10 to 20 years (in the same ballpark as the plan outlined in this book). The haircuts on collateral posted with the central bank could also be thought of as a substitute for existing regulatory risk weights; requiring effective liquid liabilities to be smaller than effective liquid assets could eventually replace both the existing liquidity coverage ratio and the net stable funding ratio, which apply only to traditional banks. The PFAS liquidity requirements would apply to both traditional and shadow banks.

4. Unlike some other run-proofing schemes, King's proposal provides run-proofing without requiring the permanent extension of insurance to a wide swath of shadow banks or the negotiation of detailed portfolio and collateral requirements for each kind of shadow bank.

5. The scheme recognizes that only the central bank can create liquidity in a crisis, and it takes advantage of the reserves created by quantitative easing and the infrastructure created by central banks to evaluate and manage collateral.

6. The small number of moving parts in the scheme makes it less US-centric and suggests that it would travel well to other economies. Indeed, as Cecchetti and Schoenholtz (2016) remark, the PFAS would probably be easier to implement in economies with more centralized regulatory and supervisory structures (like the United Kingdom) and smaller shadow banking systems. If the PFAS helped motivate a consolidation of the US financial regulatory structure, that would be no bad thing either (see Volcker Alliance 2015).

7. The political economy of the PFAS might be useful in spurring shadow banking reform. Traditional banks are apt to see the PFAS as leveling the playing field with their shadow banking competitors and helping them regain some of the market share lost over the past several decades to their less heavily regulated rivals.

No plan for regulatory reform comes without a host of conceptual and operational questions; King's PFAS is no exception.[37] But none of the challenges raised by commentators strikes me as insurmountable.

To sum up, yes, one does have to worry about the effects of higher bank capital requirements on migration of risk to the nonbank sector and about the risk of runs on the short-term liabilities of shadow banks. But there is no shortage of policy instruments available to the US authorities to deal with sources of systemic risk in the shadow banking sector. Some important reforms have already been put in place. Other, more ambitious ones, like the PFAS, could be implemented if the existing menu proved inadequate.

I favor a pragmatic approach. In outlining the plan for higher bank capital requirements, I suggest that midway through the 10-year implementation period, the Federal Reserve undertake a study to assess how these bank capital requirements were affecting the US macroeconomy. As part of that study, the Fed should evaluate the impact of those capital requirements on the shadow banking system. In addition, the study should assess whether other (noncapital) elements of the Dodd-Frank reform package that deal with the shadow banking system seem to be operating in a direction that would significantly reduce the risk of runs on short-term liabilities of shadow banks. If that assessment were positive, policymakers could stick with the existing set of reforms.[38] If the verdict were negative, one could propose implementing some version of the PFAS initiative as a complement to higher capital requirements.

True, sometimes necessary reforms to shadow banks are delayed, perhaps because of strong lobbying by the industry and political impasses in Congress. To borrow a phrase from former Fed Chair Ben Bernanke's memoir about the crisis (Bernanke 2015), there can be a shortfall in the "courage to act." But that shortage hardly seems like a good excuse to amplify systemic risk in the US economy by failing to implement appropriate minimum capital requirements for US banks.

Are Higher Equity Minimum Capital Requirements Still Needed After TLAC?

Yet a fourth potential objection to the plan is that one of its key provisions (much higher minimum capital requirements for G-SIBs) is no longer necessary, because, at the behest of the G-20 leaders, the FSB, the BIS, and the Basel Committee on Banking Supervision (BCBS) have agreed on a new minimum capital standard for such institutions (TLAC).

The main features of the TLAC proposal are spelled out in a 2015 report by the Financial Stability Board (FSB 2015). The primary objective of the proposal is to see to it that a failing G-SIB can be resolved without either drawing on taxpayer support or generating such disruption in financial markets that the real economy is severely damaged. Toward that end, as of January 1, 2019, G-SIBs will be required to hold TLAC-eligible instruments equal to 16 percent of their risk-weighted assets and 6 percent of the resolution entity's total leverage exposure (recall that total leverage exposure is the denominator of the Basel III leverage ratio). By January 1, 2022, G-SIBs will have to reach the TLAC final targets of 18 percent of risk-weighted assets and 6.75 percent of total leverage exposure.

Both the risk-weighted and leverage ratio TLAC requirements are exclusive of prevailing regulatory capital buffers, that is, exclusive of the capital conservation buffer, the countercyclical buffer, and any BCBS G-SIB surcharges. If one assumes that the countercyclical buffer is inactive, then for US G-SIBs, the all-in final (2022) TLAC minimum requirements could go as high as (the greater of) 23.5 percent of G-SIB risk-weighted assets and 8.75 percent of G-SIB total leverage exposure.[39] TLAC-eligible instruments will consist of tier 1 regulatory capital plus eligible long-term debt of the BHC. Cline's (2017) summary description of TLAC-eligible instruments is common equity, subordinated debt, and contingent convertible debt (CoCos). Long-term debt is expected to make up at least one-third of the TLAC requirement.[40]

The structure of G-SIBs would be altered if necessary to ensure that "losses" in bank subsidiaries performing critical economic functions could be passed upward to the bank holding company, thereby allowing these crucial subsidiaries to remain solvent and keep operating. Goodhart (2014) and Tucker (2014) summarize how the TLAC proposal would operate.

> It (TLAC) aims to do this primarily by dividing G-SIBs into a holding company (hold-co) and an operating subsidiary (or subsidiaries) (op-co). The hold-co is then required to have a sufficiency of loss-absorbing capital (LAC), so that in the event of a major loss anywhere within the group, the external LAC of the hold-co can be written down and the hold-co liquidated (if necessary), with the capital thus released/transferred, e.g., to the main operating subsidiary (via internal LAC), so as to recapitalize the op-co. The idea is that the op-co can soldier on after recapitalization without taxpayer support, providing necessary banking functions. Instead, the recapitalization is to be obtained by bailing-in the equity holders and bail-inable creditors providing eligible external TLAC in the hold-co. (Goodhart 2014, 1)[41]

> Groups must have simpler legal, financial, and organizational structures that positively enable orderly resolution. This is *the* big structural reform. Regulators and resolution authorities must deliver it…. Firms must be structured so that, either for the worldwide group as a whole or for well-defined subgroups, losses are transmitted upwards to a group or intermediate holding company. And if the holding company is broken as a result, it is resolved by converting into equity as much as necessary of externally

issued bonds, whose holders become the new owners. A plan for the group to be resolved as whole is known as single-point-of-entry (SPOE) resolution. When a group would be split up, it is multiple point of entry.... The FDIC's plans for resolving US SIFIs (systemically important-financial-institutions) under its new Dodd-Frank powers fall firmly within this global model.... A necessary condition for it to work is that financial groups maintain a critical mass of bonds which can be "bailed-in" to cover losses and recapitalize firms to the required equity level. (Tucker 2014, 7)

What's not to like about this proposal? After all, relative to the status quo, the total loss-absorbing capacity of G-SIBs is increased; the extra capital needed to keep crucial subsidiaries solvent and open after a big loss is created automatically and just in time via the conversion feature of the bail-in bonds; bail-in bonds will be cheaper for banks than pure equity; the cooperation between home and host-country bank supervisors needed to prevent local ring-fencing of assets during a crisis will be hard-wired into the SPOE structural reform;[42] and creditor runs can be discouraged if the bail-in bonds are limited to unsecured longer-term instruments and if they are made clearly subordinate to short-term bonds.[43]

I think there are some good things in the TLAC proposal (particularly the SPOE structural measure), but there are also troubling aspects and many unanswered questions. Persaud (2014), Goodhart (2014), Goodhart and Avgouleas (2015), Hoenig (2016a), and Kashkari (2016) identify a number of key pitfalls.

Much Lower Loss Absorbency than Under the Proposed Plan

At first glance, the all-in 23.5 percent (of risk-weighted assests) TLAC requirement looks quite large. Loss absorption is, however, much smaller upon closer examination. The final all-in (inclusive of buffers) minimum leverage ratio requirement in the TLAC proposal is just 8.75 percent—a level that I show in chapters 4 and 5 (and in the earlier part of this chapter) to be too low given both counterfactual bank losses during the 2007–09 crisis and the huge negative externalities that (multiple) failure of such G-SIBs would produce. The 8.75 percent final leverage ratio target in TLAC also includes in the numerator long-term debt that is not currently included in tier 1 capital—so it is weaker than and not directly comparable to the Basel III leverage ratio.[44] No wonder then that the largest US banks are not in screaming revolt over TLAC.[45] By way of comparison, recall that the plan's minimum tangible leverage ratio for US G-SIBs is 14 to 18 percent—with a weighted average of just over 16 percent.[46] Recall too that the plan's minimum leverage ratio for G-SIBs is defined in terms of tangible equity—the highest quality of equity—and that there is no lower-quality nonequity filler included. Comparing the TLAC proposal to the plan outlined in chapter 7 is thus comparing apples to oranges in a key loss-absorbing dimension. My plan does not count long-term debt as loss absorbing: The TLAC plan does.

Bail-In Bonds Are Not Like Pure Equity

Equity already in place is not the same as a bond that converts to equity contingent on a set of prespecified criteria, for several reasons. First, there is a question of where to set the trigger for conversion of bail-in bonds. Too high a trigger can give the false impression that the bank is about to topple over; too low a trigger in effect converts the instrument directly into a loss, as Persaud (2014) argues. Pure equity has no trigger issue: It is already equity.

Second, in a severe crisis involving the simultaneous survival of many systemically important financial institutions, crisis managers may be reluctant to allow the triggers to be pulled on several large institutions at once no matter what the contract for those bonds says.[47] Such crises are the time when new precedents get set, rules get broken, and systemic exemptions get called.

In the 2007–09 crisis and the 2010–12 euro area debt crisis, despite the urgent need for more bank capital, there were very few haircuts on bonds. As Blanchard (2015a) explains, there was a reluctance to give senior bondholders of French and German banks a haircut on their sovereign debt exposure to Greece and Ireland because the euro area banking system was seen as still in fragile recovery mode. Precrisis arguments for a minimum capital requirement expressed in terms of subordinated debt emphasized that since subdebtholders would almost never be bailed out, they would be ideal monitors of banking health. Yet in the 2007–09 crisis, subdebtholders were bailed out. As debt accounts for the lion's share of bank financing, crisis managers view anything that roils the debt markets in a severe crisis as extremely threatening. Ask yourself: Which is going to produce the better crisis dynamics—trying to bail in bondholders at the very time in a severe crisis when banks are trying to keep their funding sources from drying up, or having a comfortable equity cushion in place and allowing that equity capital to be drawn down to reflect mounting credit losses?

Pulling the trigger on a CoCo the first time a major bank is in trouble is not the real test. The real test comes from allowing the trigger to be pulled in the second case if the first case was followed by a run of bank creditors. When the haircut imposed on senior bank creditors of Washington Mutual in 2008 was followed by a run on bank bonds, it was not long before US crisis managers reversed course and issued a guarantee on all new bank debt, as noted in chapter 4. Goodhart and Avgouleas (2015) point out that if a bail-in is triggered before a fiscal backstop is secured for other parts of the financial system, a creditor flight from banks will be certain. They cite former US Treasury Secretary Timothy Geithner's (2014, 306) appraisal of the time-consistency problem associated with haircuts on bondholders: "The overwhelming temptation [in a crisis] is to let the most egregious firms fail, to put them through a bankruptcy process like the FDIC had for community banks and then haircut the bondholders. But unless you have the ability to backstop every other systemic financial institution that's in a similar situation, you'll just intensify failures and haircuts."

Haldane (2012, 5) also emphasizes the time-consistency dilemma associated with bail-ins, be they rule based or discretionary: "Whether a rule is followed in practice depends on the balance of costs and benefits at the time the crisis strikes, not at the time the rule is written.... The history of big bank failure is a history of the state blinking before private creditors."

Minneapolis Fed President Neel Kashkari (2016, 4) offers a similar assessment: "Do we really believe that in the middle of economic distress when the public is looking for safety that the government will start imposing losses on debt holders, potentially increasing fear and panic among investors? Policymakers didn't do that in 2008. There is no evidence that their response in a future crisis will be different."

Although the new EU resolution regime requires a haircut on bank creditors as a prior action to the unlocking of public funds, Hellwig (2014b) remains skeptical that it will be implemented as written. The objections of the Italian government to a bail-in of bondholders amid strong market pressure on Italian banks in the summer of 2016 is consistent with Hellwig's skepticism.

The contrast between bail-in bonds and pure equity is instructive. Episodes of bailing out equity holders in a severe crisis are few and far between.[48] As equity is already equity, there is no time-consistency issue or need to get approval from a resolution board. And because equity constitutes a much smaller share of bank funding than debt, the effects of a temporary disruption of that market in a crisis are easier to withstand than one in which debt financing dries up.

Potential Amplification Mechanism during Crises with Multiple Bank Failures

Bail-in bonds may work tolerably well when one large bank fails, according to Persaud (2014), Goodhart (2014), and Goodhart and Avgouleas (2015), but they become a crisis amplification mechanism when many banks get into trouble at roughly the same time. Persaud's (2014, 5) evaluation is telling:

A simple test of whether a new policy instrument will help deal with a liquidity crisis is whether it will moderate the collective enthusiasm to buy assets during a boom or the crowd mania to sell them during a crisis. The dynamics of financial markets suggest that bail-in securities will fail this test.... Short-term investors...who buy these instruments do so today and will do so in the future because they see no near-term risk of a bail-in.... The more these yields fall, the more the banks will be encouraged to issue more of these securities, enabling them to lend more.... It is therefore unlikely that these instruments would temper bank lending prior to a crash.... When an event changes perception of risk, short-term investors in these securities will trample over each other to reach the exit before bail-in.... Funds that trade in liquid debt securities cannot easily become owners of illiquid bank equity. As they form a disorderly queue at the exit, the price of these securities will collapse, triggering a series of contagious mechanisms.... Faced with collapsing prices and declining confidence, the rating agencies will downgrade bail-in securities. More stoic holders...who had resisted the urge to sell in the first wave will now be forced to sell as a result of investment mandates limiting the holding of low-rated instruments.... Bail-in securities will bring forward and spread a crisis, not snuff it out.

Goodhart (2014, 3) is also skeptical:

Once a failing bank has been put into resolution, a forensic auditor will no doubt be sent in to estimate the necessary size of creditor haircuts required to recapitalize the op-co sufficiently. There can hardly be two bites at this, if only because transactions in such assets will begin once the initial write-downs have been established.... My own expectation is that the forensic auditor will aim to err on the side of austere caution in such valuations...the haircuts will be larger than previously expected on the basis of the last preresolution accounts. The market will be shocked. The bail-inable debt will, almost by definition, have previously been bought by optimists (and the ill-informed) and their optimism will suddenly appear misguided. There must be a good chance that, after the first newsworthy resolution, the market for such bail-inable debt will completely dry up for some period of time before re-opening at a much higher (and to bank CEOs unattractive) yield. What then happens as bail-inable debt rolls over?....Is this not another example where the T-LAC approach would reinforce the cycle and make the financial sector even more prone to systemic crisis?

As Cline (2017) notes, the experience with CoCos in March 2016, when there were fears that Deutsche Bank might miss a coupon payment, provides a hint of this instrument's potential market panic dynamics: A leading index of CoCo bonds fell from a 2015 high of 104.6 to 88.8 cents on the euro in March 2016.

True, equity markets have also shown a tendency to collapse in a crisis. But the burden of proof is on the new policy instrument to show that it can deliver improved crisis resiliency relative to a bank funding structure that, say, has the same total amount of (nominal) loss absorption but more of that absorption in the form of pure equity. I see no compelling argument why bail-in bonds should do so.

Different but not Necessarily Better Burden Sharing in a Crisis

Even if bail-in bonds do not diminish liquidity risk in a crisis, wouldn't they still be a big improvement over the status quo by eliminating taxpayer liability for systemic bank resolution? I would argue that the right answer is maybe but probably not. If bail-in bonds were activated during a systemic crisis, taxpayers would initially pay less than they would have in the absence of such bonds. But bail-in bonds would not necessarily reduce the burden individuals and families face during and after a crisis, because their pension and insurance benefits would be reduced if those institutions wound up being the main holders of bail-in bonds (unless the government bailed out pension and insurance companies for these losses, which takes us right back to the taxpayer bailout case).

The TLAC plan devotes too little attention to who would be the holders of TLAC bonds and what the consequences would be for different ownership patterns. The FSB and the BCBS have made it clear that they do not want banks to be holding one another's TLAC bonds for fear of creating a new contagion mechanism. Similarly, money market funds are unlikely to be the preferred holders, because even with the reforms recently agreed to improve their resilience, TLAC bonds would be beyond their risk tolerance.

The architects of the TLAC plan have also stipulated that the TLAC bonds must have a minimum maturity of at least a year, because holders of shorter-term instruments could evade the bail-in by refusing to roll over their investments. This feature presumably leaves pension funds, insurance companies, sovereign wealth funds, hedge funds, and other nonbanks as the target holders of these bonds.[49] Persaud (2014) and Goodhart and Avgouleas (2015) shed light on some of the key pitfalls.

> The right economic and investment strategy for an investor is to hold those risks for which they have a natural ability to hedge and to rid themselves of risk they cannot hedge. That strategy will lead pension funds and life insurance companies away from bail-in securities.... To hedge liquidity

risk, one must have time to wait—perhaps through long-term funding or the long-term liabilities that pension and life insurance companies have. But having time does not help to hedge credit risks. The longer the credit risk is held, the more time there is for it to blow up.... Credit risk is best hedged by diversifying across a wide range of credit risks and actively managing the spread of risk—in the way that a bank or credit hedge can do far more easily than a traditional pension fund. The right instruments for institutions with long-term liabilities are instruments offering a higher return because they are illiquid...these instruments include infrastructure bonds..., asset-backed securities, and real estate development—the exact type of assets they have traditionally purchased. (Persaud 2014, 4)

If pension funds suffered losses on CoCos, taxpayers would very likely be pressured into bailing them out. Given the greater fragmentation of the savings markets such a bailout will probably be even more complicated, messy, and politically sensitive than bailing-out a handful of banking institutions. (Persaud 2014, 3)

The effect of shifting bail-out to bail-in will, therefore, primarily transfer the burden of loss from one set of domestic payers, the taxpayers, to another, the pensioners and savers. It is far from clear whether, and why, the latter have broader backs and are better placed to absorb bank rescue losses than the former. One argument, however, is that savers and/or their financial agents have made an ex ante choice to purchase the claim on the bank, whereas the taxpayer had no such option, and that having done so, they could/should have played a monitoring role. While this is a valid point, the counter argument is that charities, small or medium-sized pension funds, or individual savers, e.g., via pension funds, do not really have the expertise to act as effective bank monitors. Thus, forcing them to pay the penalty of bank failure would hardly improve bank governance. On the contrary, it would only give rise to claims that they were "tricked" into buying bail-in-able debt. (Goodhart and Avgouleas 2015, 26–27)[50,51]

No Suspension of Debt Interest Payments Allowed

Hoenig (2016a, 2) notes that debt interest payments on CoCos cannot be suspended and that the history of trust-preferred securities offers a valuable cautionary tale:

To appreciate the potential effects that TLAC might have, it is useful to look at the history of trust-preferred securities (TRuPS) at banks before the last crisis.... [R]egulators permitted firms to issue these instruments at the holding company and to include them as part of capital. Although TRuPS are essentially long-term debt instruments, it was argued that they would be available to help absorb losses in a crisis, relieving these firms from having to hold equity. As the crisis unfolded, the weaknesses of

TRuPS revealed themselves as firms often had to remove resources from the operating banks in an effort to move cash to the holding company and avoid default. TRuPS placed significant pressures on insured banks to continue making large debt-servicing payments which most certainly exacerbated losses to the banking system.... Congress wisely eliminated the use of these instruments as part of industry capital when it passed Dodd-Frank.

Unanswered Questions about Liquidity for the Surviving Crucial Subsidiaries

In addition to the operational problems outlined above, Goodhart (2014, 2) argues that there remain important questions in a number of G-20 jurisdictions about the ability of the surviving subsidiary (op-co) to obtain the liquidity it will need and to compete with G-SIBs that have not had to go through resolution:[52]

> Sufficiency of liquidity is by no means assured. The resolution process is bound to be noteworthy. The overall strength of the banking group will have become undoubtedly impaired when the hold-co is liquidated or drastically written down.

> The name and reputation of the bank will have been brought into question. The likelihood is that the initial reaction of both the informed and uninformed investors (as with Northern Rock) will be to flee.... Without protection from that eventuality in the guise of an associated commitment by the relevant Central Bank to provide sufficient lender of last resort (LOLR) support, the whole exercise stands at risk of failing disastrously at the first hurdle.

> ...[W]ith the hold-co liquidated or sharply written down, the overall valuation of and strength of the banking group will have been much impaired. The op-co will have sufficient capital of its own, but will no longer have the hold-co as buffer above it. Thus, the op-co will be significantly weaker than all the competitive banks around it. The op-co by itself will no longer have the T-LAC support deemed necessary for everyone else. What happens then? Presumably, the op-co cannot then pay-out dividends or do buy-backs until it can fully reconstitute a hold-co that meets standard requirements. Is this the intention?

Tiny Cost Saving Relative to Real Equity

To sum up, if the only choice available were to stay with the status quo or to vote for the TLAC initiative, I would probably hold my nose and opt for TLAC, because of the increase in loss absorbency and the benefits of a SPOE structural reform for resolution. But this in no way suggests that TLAC reduces the attractiveness of the plan put forward in this book for a much heightened minimum leverage requirement for G-SIBs. Compared with the TLAC proposal, the plan offers a significantly higher level of G-SIB loss absorption, greater certainty that this higher level of loss absorbency would actually be there when it is most needed; less operational complexity; and a broader, more diverse investor base to hold the loss absorbing capital. SPOE resolution can also be implemented more easily under the proposed plan than under TLAC, because the bank holding company would be more highly capitalized, losses in crucial subsidiaries could still be passed up the chain to the bank holding company, and those subsidiaries could remain in operation to fulfill functions deemed important for the economy. Moreover, the higher starting level of loss absorbency in the plan would leave the holding company itself better capitalized after internal bail-in than under TLAC.

But the real kicker is this: For all the additional risks that the TLAC initiative brings with it for the economy relative to the plan, it is not much cheaper in terms of bank funding costs and bank lending rates than the proposed plan.[53] My best estimate of the cumulative increase in overall bank lending rates associated with increasing the weighted-average tangible leverage ratio for US banks by 600 basis points (from roughly 8½ to 14½ percent) over a 10-year period is a little less than 15 basis points. The macroeconomic effects of such a lending rate increase would be barely detectable in terms of US economic growth and could easily be offset with a tiny reduction in the fed funds rate.

The BIS (2015b) published the results of its quantitative impact study of TLAC implementation. The bottom line is that the cost saving I estimate from implementing the (wannabe-equity) TLAC initiative instead of the (real equity) plan outlined in this chapter is about 7 to 12 basis points in overall bank lending rates.[54] I repeat: 7 to 12 basis points in overall bank lending rates, spread over a 10-year period. If the macroeconomic effects of a 14-basis-point increase in overall bank lending rates spread over a decade is barely detectable, the macroeconomic effects of anything smaller than that is virtually invisible, akin to a rounding error.[55]

Overall Assessment: Penny Wise and Pound Foolish

Now think about the difference in expected benefits from TLAC versus the proposed plan. The main positive output effects from TLAC are alleged (in BIS 2015b) to derive from the better credit decisions that G-SIBs will make once they know that they will no longer be bailed out in a crisis. But these improved "discipline" effects are completely contingent on TLAC bondholders not being bailed out in a severe crisis. Surely, the probability of such a bailout of TLAC bondholders is higher than the probability of a bailout for holders of equity. Moreover, the increase in bank capital proposed under the plan is much larger than that under the TLAC initiative. Hence anyway you cut it, the expected benefits from the plan have to be larger than under TLAC.

If the difference in expected benefits under the plan are significantly higher than under TLAC and the cost difference between the two initiatives is trivial, the proposed plan offers a much better benefit-cost tally than TLAC. As the BIS (2015b) estimates net benefits under TLAC to be highly positive, net benefit for the plan must also be positive and larger.[56] In view of all this, there is only one way to characterize the TLAC initiative relative to the plan: penny wise and pound foolish.

Closing Remarks

Like the convicted murderer who upon ascending the steps to the gallows was heard to remark "this will certainly be a good lesson for me," the 2007–09 global economic and financial crisis taught us all a good lesson about the social costs of severely undercapitalized large banks. Bank stress tests are a potentially valuable supervisory tool for guarding against the danger that such a misreading of banks' capital adequacy happens again. The rub here is the qualifier: potential. Stress tests are not going to be able to reach their potential until the modeling of contagion, feedback, fire sales, and funding runs better resembles what happens in a real crisis; bank capital is measured properly; the capital hurdle rates set in those tests get much closer to socially optimal capital ratios; and a revised G-SIB surcharge schedule gives the largest banks more incentive to become smaller and less complex. Some progress has been made on all four of these fronts over the past half-dozen years. But taken as a group, these initiatives are just too timid for the challenge at hand.

This book lays out the outlines of a more ambitious agenda that covers not only the design of the stress tests but also reform of the US bank-capital regime under which US stress tests operate. I think the main obstacle to getting to a safer financial system is fear that a quantum jump in minimum equity requirements and a reorientation of the Basel capital regime away from risk-based capital metrics and toward a (sole) Pillar 1 leverage requirement (with a risk surcharge backup) would be too costly and too disruptive.

Drawing on empirical evidence and recent experience, I have tried to demonstrate that such a fear is unwarranted. Highly capitalized banks lend more, not less. The increase in bank funding costs linked to reaching almost a 15 percent weighted-average leverage ratio for America's banks is too modest to hurt the US macroeconomy. Smaller banks, a smaller banking system, and a smaller financial system are more likely to increase US economic growth, not decrease it. The United States has enough tools to control systemic risk in the shadow banking system as long as it has the courage to use them.

Seemingly cheaper methods of providing adequate loss absorption for the world's G-SIBs (like bail-in bonds) are unlikely to deliver the same benefits as real equity, and the cost savings from buying the costume jewelry version rather than the real thing are tiny. Transferring the burden of resolution of G-SIBs in a severe crisis from taxpayers to pensioners does not make the too big to fail problem go away.

Finally, it is possible to reap the simplicity, lower cost, and superior diagnostic benefits of a leverage ratio while still discouraging banks from loading up on high-risk assets. It just requires slipping off the straitjacket of the Basel dual Pillar 1 capital regime. That regime is supposed to serve us, not the other way around. We have changed that regime before. We can change it again.

All plans are imperfect, but I have been encouraged by the sage advice of two luminaries. One is the great Hall of Fame catcher Yogi Berra, who counseled "if you don't know where you are going, you may never get there." The other is the principal architect of the US stress testing program, former US Treasury Secretary Tim Geithner (2014), who reminds us that "a plan beats no plan."

This book puts forward a plan for reforming the US (and eventually international) bank-capital regime. It consists of three elements: equity and plenty of it, a better thermometer (a leverage ratio) for measuring bank capital, and bigger incentives for the most systemically important banks to shrink their systemic footprint. If you know of a better plan, show it to me.

Endnotes

1. "Healthy Banking System Is the Goal, Not Profitable Banks," *Financial Times*, November 9, 2010.

2. In the postscript (chapter 9), I discuss how the election of Donald Trump as president of the United States might change the outlook for bank-capital reform.

3. The chief executive of Standard Chartered, Peter Sands, for example, writes: "I guarantee that a required framework that has the leverage ratio as the primary measure will make banks and the banking system more prone to crises" (Peter Sands, "In Banking, Too Much Simplicity Can be Costly," *Financial Times*, August 26, 2013, www.ft.com/content/15ba8044-f46a-11e2-a62e-00144feabdc0).

4. According to James Gorman, CEO of Morgan Stanley, "We are not capital short.... if anything, we're capital heavy." Tim Pawlenty, president of the Financial Services Roundtable argues that "regulators should reasonably address risk, but this rule—the proposed increased G-SIB surcharge in July 2015—will keep billions of dollars out of the economy" ("Fed Lifts Capital Requirements for Banks," *Wall Street Journal*, July 20, 2015).

5. Gavin Finch, "World's Biggest Banks Fined $321 Billion Since Financial Crisis," Bloomberg, March 2, 2017.

6. See "Regulators Seek Tighter Curbs on Investments by Big Banks," *New York Times*, September 8, 2016. It describes "merchant banking" as banks owning large, private equity-like stakes in private companies.

7. Board of Governors of the Federal Reserve System, press release, July 20, 2015.

8. The Volcker Rule restricts US commercial banks from engaging in proprietary trading or investing in or sponsoring private equity or hedge funds. There have been parallel structural reforms in Europe (see the Vickers Report 2011 and the Liikanen Report 2012).

9. Clinton proposed requiring firms that are too large and too risky to reorganize, downsize, or break apart (www.hillaryclinton.com/briefing/factsheets/2015/10/08/wall-street-work-for-main-street).

10. See Holly LaFon, "Elizabeth Warren Calls for Breaking Up the Big Banks," *US News & World Report*, April 15, 2015.

11. See Reforming Wall Street, https://berniesanders.com /issues/reforming-wall-street.

12. Remarks to the Economic Club of New York, June 7, 2016.

13. CAMELS stands for capital adequacy, assets, management capability, earnings, liquidity, and sensitivity to market risk. It is a ratings system for banks used by US bank supervisors.

14. Senator Warren has criticized the Hensarling proposal, suggesting that it be called the Wet Kiss for Wall Street Act (Jesse Westbrook, "Super Capitalized Banks Free from Rules in Republican's Plan," Bloomberg, June 6, 2016).

15. These figures on Basel III leverage ratios for US G-SIBs come from the banks' annual reports. Hoenig (2016a) cautions that they have not been screened by the FDIC and do not specify whether the figures are transitional or fully loaded Basel III leverage ratios.

16. As long as the largest banks have leverage ratios well below the minimum set out in the proposed plan, I am in favor of structural reforms that would reduce their probability of default. If they achieve those much higher capital ratios, it could be a different story.

17. There are some tentative signs in at least a few EU G-SIBs of a change in view about the sustainability of a low capital strategy. In 2015 John Cryan, the new CEO of Deutsche Bank, announced a new capital raising strategy, including a two-year suspension of dividend payments ("Investors Question Whether Cut Can Turn Tide for Deutsche Bank," *Financial Times*, October 29, 2015). Tidjane Thiam, the new Credit Suisse CEO, has also embarked on a capital strengthening program, noting that the low capital strategy had not worked and that it was thus time to try a high capital one (Patrick Jenkins, "Tidjane Thiam: Credit Suisse Boss Introduces a Quiet Revolution," *Financial Times*, October 26, 2015).

18. Trade policy reformers often invoke the "bicycle theory" (you fall over if you are not moving forward) to explain why major new trade initiatives are needed. It may apply even better to financial reform.

19. The conclusion of the report of the chair of the Financial Stability Oversight Council (FSOC 2011, 10) is similar: "There is no clear evidence that the scale economies continue increasing as financial institutions approach a very large size."

20. Two additional arguments for maintaining the current size of the largest US and EU banks are also dubious. One is that JPMorgan Chase's takeover of Bear Stearns and Washington Mutual as well as Bank of America's takeover of Merrill Lynch during the 2007–09 crisis show that large banks are needed to resolve weak financial institutions when the government chooses not to do so. The relevant counterfactual is that if those weak institutions had had adequate capital ratios and a good resolution regime had been in place, no one would have needed to take over those institutions. The second weak argument for very large banks is that they are needed to meet the sophisticated financial service requirement of very large multinational corporations. But there is no reason why a group of somewhat smaller banks cannot meet these needs. The Liikanen Report (2012) observes that most multinational corporations already have relationships with more than one bank and the sharing of business among a larger group of banks reduces the risk that the largest banks with the most market power could abuse that power to set socially suboptimal prices.

21. The growth of bank assets in the European Union over the 1996–2013 period was also rapid relative to household wealth (Pagano et al. 2014).

22. The five measures of bank risk are the following: a market-based estimate of the amount of equity capital that a bank would need to raise in the event of systemwide stress; the bank-level probability of default from the National University of Singapore's Credit Research Initiative; the bank-level probability of default calculated by Moody's KMV (derived from an extension of the Black-Scholes-Merton model of option pricing); the credit default swap spread; and Altman's (1968) *Z*-score, a standard measure of bank risk using balance sheet information.

23. The remaining shares of euro area monetary-financial institution assets are distributed as follows: claims on other financial institutions (30 percent), claims on governments (9 percent), claims on non–euro area residents (13 percent), and remaining assets, which are mostly derivatives (13 percent). The weighted distribution of loan to total assets ratios for EU banks has an inverted *U*-shape, with most assets held by universal banks with intermediate ratios. In contrast, for US banks this distribution is more uniform, with investment banks having very low ratios and retail banks having very high ones. All of these figures come from Pagano et al. (2014).

24. Jean-Claude Juncker, A New Start for Europe: My Agenda for Jobs, Growth, Fairness and Democratic Change, address to the European Parliament, Strasbourg, July 15, 2014.

25. Jonathan Hill, "Capital Markets Union: An Action Plan to Boost Business Funding and Investment Financing," European Commission, Brussels, September 30, 2015.

26. Pagano et al. (2014) gauge the structure of the financial system by looking at the ratio of stock market capitalization to bank credit to the private sector. That ratio for the United States is roughly 2. It is well below 1 for the five largest EU economies (France, Germany, Italy, Spain, and the United Kingdom).

27. Pagano et al. (2014) provide a review of this "too much finance" empirical literature.

28. Cecchetti and Kharroubi (2012) also find that rapid growth in finance—measured as growth in employment or value added—is bad for aggregate real growth. They interpret this second major finding as suggesting that financial booms are inherently bad for trend growth. Sahay, Cihak, and N'Diaye (2015) similarly find that there is a clear positive relationship between the speed with which financial institutions grow and financial instability.

29. See Philippon and Reshef (2012) for evidence on the relative and excess wages in finance and Pagano et al. (2014) for a fuller discussion of how too much finance reduces the marginal product of capital.

30. As a percent of GDP, the United Kingdom has the largest shadow banking system; as a share of banking assets, the United States is the leader (IMF 2014a). The Financial Stability Board definition of shadow banking includes non-money-market funds; some other definitions do not.

31. If one adds in the liabilities of both parents of BHCs and broker-dealers to the liabilities of shadow banks as shown in figure 8.2, then the all-in liabilities of shadow banks hits a peak of about 120 percent of US GDP in 2008. If I interpret correctly the data underlying figure 8.2, the all-in liabilities of shadow banks in 2014 declined to roughly 80 percent of GDP in 2014.

32. See Pozsar (2014). The IMF (2014a) provides some econometric evidence to buttress its story.

33. Adrian (2014) adds susceptibility to short-term funding and runs as a seventh factor but does not explain why it would motivate the growth of shadow banking. For this reason I did not include it.

34. In March 2016 MetLife won a decision in US federal court challenging its designation as a systematically important financial institution. It is not known whether the US government will appeal this decision. In June 2016 the FSOC decided that GE Capital had shrunk its assets enough that its "systemically important" designation could be dropped.

35. Martin Gruenberg, A Progress Report on the Resolution of Systemically Important Financial Institutions, talk given at the Peterson Institute for International Economics, Washington, May 12, 2015.

36. King (2016, 8) titled his book *The End of Alchemy*. By alchemy, he means "the belief that all paper money can be turned into an intrinsically valuable commodity, such as gold, on demand and that money kept in banks can be taken out whenever depositors ask for it." The main policy initiative in the book—turning the central bank into a "pawnbroker for all seasons"—is meant to end alchemy.

37. Cecchetti and Schoenholtz (2016) raise a set of operational complexities about King's PFAS scheme, including how often collateral would need to be evaluated by the central bank, how new financial instruments would be handled, and whether political pressure in a crisis would push the central bank to set haircuts too low. Another issue is the penalties for a financial institution found to be in violation of the PFAS rule.

38. Hanson (2016), writing in late 2016, argues that US shadow banking is at its nadir—with the share of shadow banking claims as a share of private money-like claims at a lower level than before the start of the 2007–09 financial crisis.

39. For US G-SIBs, one can think of the risk-based 23.5 percent TLAC requirement as consisting of an 18 percent base, plus the 2.5 percent capital conservation buffer, plus a 3.0 percent G-SIB surcharge. Similarly, the 8.75 percent leverage ratio–based TLAC requirement can be seen as the sum of a 6.75 percent base plus a 2.0 percent G-SIB surcharge under the enhanced supplementary leverage ratio.

40. The Federal Reserve Bank of Minneapolis (2016, p. 17) has suggested that a 23.5 percent risk-based TLAC requirement would, in the case of US G-SIBs, be made up roughly of 10.5 percent of eligible long-term debt and 13 percent of common equity.

41. By "internal" TLAC, Goodhart (2014) means bonds or equity issued by the op-co and held by the hold-co, so that the loss in the op-co can be transferred to the hold-co. By external TLAC, he means bail-in bonds issued by the hold-co and held by external investors.

42. Huertas (2013) contrasts the unified, top-down approach to resolution under SPOE with a fragmented "territorial" approach. Using the example of a bank with a foreign branch, he explains that under the territorial approach, the host country will have the right "to ring fence the assets and liabilities of the branch in the host country, liquidate the assets of the branch, and use the proceeds to meet the liabilities of the branch to host-country creditors" (p. 15). The host country may have the right to initiate resolution. The territorial approach creates a bias toward liquidation, with a greater loss of value to creditors and greater possibility of disruption to the economy as a whole.

43. See Huertas (2013) Tucker (2014), and Gruenberg (2015) on the advantages of the TLAC-SPOE initiative. Guynn (2015) argues that although US G-SIBs had substantial potential TLAC (roughly 17 percent of risk-weighted assets) in the run-up to the 2007–09 crisis, available TLAC was much lower (roughly 5 percent), because there was then no way to bail in longer-term unsecured bonds without also bailing in short-term bonds and doing the latter would have generated widespread turbulence in financial markets. He claims that US G-SIBs have now restructured their liabilities to give short-term debt instruments priority over longer-term ones.

44. According to the BCBS (2016), the end-2015 weighted-average Basel III fully loaded leverage ratio of 30 G-SIBs was 5.2 percent. No separate official figure for US G-SIBs has been published, but data collected from bank annual reports and published in the end-2015 FDIC Global Capital Index suggest that the comparable US figure is about 6.5 percent.

45. I say only half tongue in cheek that whenever the largest global banks are not in full combat mode over a financial reform proposal, it is almost always a sign that the proposal is unlikely to deliver substantial reform.

46. Even if one converted the 23.5 percent risk-based TLAC requirement into a total asset (leverage ratio) requirement using a 63 percent risk-weight density for US G-SIBs and made the additional (erroneous) assumption that TLAC-eligible instruments were just

as good in loss absorbency as tangible equity, the resulting 14.8 percent leverage-ratio facsimile would still be short of the 16.2 percent weighted tangible leverage ratio for G-SIBs under the plan.

47. If the triggers on the bail-in bonds are not pulled, then the argument for the automaticity of timely recapitalization—touted by Calomiris and Herring (2013) for CoCos—collapses as well.

48. There are sometimes temporary bans on short selling of equities in a severe crisis; large-scale government assistance to ailing banks also benefits equity holders of those banks, albeit not as much as bondholders. Still, there seems to be widespread understanding on the part of the public that losses as well as gains on equities need to remain private, not socialized.

49. Pension fund assets in advanced economies total nearly $22 trillion; the cumulative assets of sovereign wealth funds (roughly $6 trillion) are considerably smaller (Persaud 2014).

50. In 2014 the United Kingdom's new Financial Conduct Authority suspended the sale of CoCos to retail investors on the argument that they were highly complex and inappropriate for mass retail markets. In the summer of 2016, the Italian government made clear its opposition to bailing in retail holders of Italian bank bonds (Persaud 2014).

51. In 2015 the Italian government opted to bail in junior, or subordinated, bondholders at four small regional banks that had run into difficulties. The move caused a political uproar, because retail investors had been one of the main buyers of such bonds. One pensioner later committed suicide. This controversy prompted the government to promise a hardship "compensation" fund ("Bondholders Cry Foul over Bank Bail-Ins," *Financial Times*, January 8, 2015). Imagine a similar saga writ large during the simultaneous failure of a group of G-SIBs or systemically important financial institutions.

52. Goodhart and Avgouleas (2015) argue that differences in the resolution of systemically important financial institutions in the United States (solely a closed-bank, bail-in process) and the European Union (either open-bank or closed-bank bail-in) will likely lead to problems down the road.

53. Kashkari (2016, 5) has expressed doubts about the cost savings available from TLAC bail-in bonds versus common equity: "This [TLAC] approach defies market logic.... On the one hand, regulators are saying believe us, contingent debt is as good as common equity in its power to absorb losses if a bank runs into trouble. We will really force bondholders to take losses. On the other hand, the same regulators are saying investors will price these securities closer to debt than equity. But if these securities truly do face equity-like downside risk (by the way, without the upside of equity), why would investors price them more like debt?"

54. The BIS (2015b) study concluded that the TLAC would wind up increasing lending rates for the median G-SIB by about 8 basis points. Once one converts this increase in G-SIB lending rates into an increase in overall lending rates using the US ratio of G-SIB assets to total bank holding company assets of 62 percent, this translates into an increase in overall lending spreads of about 5 basis points. In the plan outlined in chapter 7, the increase in overall lending rates for an 800-basis-point increase in the leverage ratio for G-SIBs is 12 basis points; hence, this bottom-line comparison leads to a difference of 7 basis points (12 minus 5). One can get a little closer to an apples-to-apples comparison by extending to the BIS estimate my loan-plus approach to estimating the link between increased funding costs and increases in loan rates. On this basis, a back-of-the-envelope

estimate is that this increases the difference between the two plans to roughly 12 basis points in overall lending rates (that is, 14 basis points minus 2 basis points). This is still far from a full apples-to-apples comparison, but it captures the basics behind my conclusion.

55. Sorry, but I cannot resist an analogy. Iris, the 77-year-old founder of an interior design firm, has just announced that she will retire at the end of the year. As a retirement present to herself, she decides to take an around-the-world trip. To the shock of her friends, she announces that her 79-year-old husband Saul (her partner for over 50 years) will not be accompanying her on the trip. Instead, she will be going with Nigel, a 78-year-old man she met at a bridge tournament the previous month. When asked why she decided to leave Saul for Nigel, Iris replies: "I guess I just wanted to know what it would be like to be with a younger man." Program guide: For today's performance, the role of Nigel will be played by TLAC.

56. The BIS (2015b, 1) estimates that TLAC will produce overall annual benefits of 45 to 60 basis points in terms of GDP versus costs of 2 to 5 basis points.

9

Postscript

Much happened between September 2016, when most of this volume was written, and mid-January 2017, when this postscript was completed. For bank-capital reform and stress testing, two recent developments merit particular attention.[1,2]

On November 8, 2016, Donald Trump was elected the next president of the United States. While the specifics of his administration's economic policies have yet to be announced, Trump reiterated his intention to make financial deregulation an important element of his plan to raise economic growth in the United States from its 2016 level of 1.6 percent to a target of 3 to 4 percent.

In a speech in late September 2016, Federal Reserve Governor Daniel Tarullo (2016) outlined the next steps in the evolution of the US stress testing program, including bringing risk-based capital surcharges for global systemically important banks (G-SIBs) into the tests' (baseline) capital hurdle rates.

In this postscript, I discuss the issues tied to these two developments and provide my preliminary reactions.

The Trump Administration and Financial Deregulation

Profiles of the Trump economic plan have emphasized large tax cuts, increased infrastructure spending, sweeping deregulation, and imposition of protectionist trade policies. On banking deregulation, the idea seems to be to "unleash the banks" in order to reduce regulatory compliance costs, increase risk taking, strengthen the role of market forces, and spur loan growth. As noted earlier, there has already been a sharp increase in bank equity prices since the election—presumably driven by the expectation that bank profitability will increase on the back of higher interest rates, an increased spread between long- and short-term interest rates, improved trading results linked to higher market volatility, and increased loan demand.

A Banking Industry Wish List

While it is still too early to know what specific proposals will be put forward by the new administration, there has been a lot of speculation on what the banking industry hopes to get in any broad deregulation program.[3] I have therefore put together a representative "wish list" for the industry. If nothing else, it should be informative about what kinds of issues are likely to be on the negotiating table with Democrats in Congress. My list includes the following:[4]

- Appoint individuals with a "light touch" regulatory philosophy to key regulatory positions, including the now vacant vice chair for supervision at the Federal Reserve. As the old saying goes, "People are Policy."
- Increase the threshold in the Dodd-Frank Act for enhanced supervision from $50 billion in total assets for bank holding companies (BHCs) to, say, $250 billion—or even to $500 billion.
- Rewrite Title II of the Dodd-Frank Act and replace the Orderly Liquidation Authority (OLA) with a new Chapter 14 special bankruptcy code (Scott and Taylor 2012). Resist efforts to have the banking industry fund (either ex ante or ex post) debtor-in-possession (DIP) financing.
- Repeal or weaken the Volcker Rule.
- Redesign the Financial Stability Oversight Council (FSOC) and remove its authority to designate large nonbanks as "systemically important."
- Replace the director of the Consumer Financial Protection Bureau (CFPB) with a board of commissioners appointed by the president. Also, narrow the CFPB's mandate and limit its funding.
- Restrict the mandate of the Office of Financial Research and perhaps seek to reduce its budget as well.
- Roll back the Durbin amendment (which limits the fees banks can charge on credit cards).
- Block any reform effort that proposes to increase minimum capital requirements for banks or to elevate the role of the leverage ratio in banking supervision. In this connection, attempt to delay or modify the proposed increases in capital requirements in the trading book;

repeal the Collins amendment and, working with European and Japanese bank supervisors, block the initiative in the Basel Committee on Banking Supervision to put a floor on risk-weighted assets (RWAs) (calculated from banks' internal models); and try to delay or derail the Federal Reserve's proposed incorporation of risk-based G-SIB capital surcharges into the Comprehensive Capital Analysis and Review (CCAR) stress tests.

- Seek to expand the definition of liquid assets in the liquidity coverage ratio, as well as the definition of instruments eligible for the Financial Stability Board's (FSB) total loss-absorbing capacity (TLAC) initiative.

- Reduce the severity in the CCAR stress tests by, among other things, reducing the stressed hurdle rates, reducing the assumed rise in the unemployment rate in the severely adverse scenario, and liberalizing further the treatment of capital distributions.

- Weaken the criteria for approval of living will submissions.

- Seek additional carveouts from regulations on the central clearing of derivatives.

- Seek to weaken mortgage underwriting standards.

- Seek additional regulatory relief for community and regional banks.

- Lower disclosure standards on compensation for senior management.

- Eliminate the Department of Labor's fiduciary duty standard for investment advice.

- Pay less attention to the standards promulgated by international regulatory agencies (e.g., Basel Committee on Banking Supervision, Financial Stability Board), so that priority can be given to US objectives.

A Different Perspective

Not everyone thinks that the Trump administration's policies on financial regulation will amount to an across-the-board rollback of the post-2008 regulatory architecture.[5] Here, it is pointed out that in the election campaign Trump called for breaking up big banks and restoring Glass-Steagall; that at least two of the (alleged) leading candidates for the Fed's vice chair for supervision have in the past proposed a minimum leverage ratio of at least 10 percent; that big banks have already met the final targets for capital and liquidity in Basel III; that drastic regulatory regime switching—only seven years after the Dodd-Frank Act and Basel III—is costly to banks themselves; and finally, that both banks and the Trump administration understand that overdoing it on financial liberalization and deregulation will heighten market anxiety and ultimately raise risk premiums.

In their view, deregulation will be more measured and selective and a matter of trading off deregulation in some areas for higher capital ratios. As noted earlier, House Financial Services Chair Jeb Hensarling's (R-Texas) "Financial Choice Act" would swap elimination of the Volcker Rule and curbing the CFPB's powers (among other deregulation initiatives) for a 10 percent minimum leverage ratio combined with a high (CAMELS) rating by bank supervisors. As explained in chapter 8, I do not see that trade as a good one for financial stability: Hensarling is offering too little in terms of higher capital ratios and asking for too much in deregulation—but others may have different assessments.

Reactions

Speculation—even informed—is not a good substitute for seeing the new administration's detailed financial deregulation proposals themselves. Still, let me offer three cautionary reactions to the initiatives being discussed.

First, the Dodd-Frank Act and other financial reforms that were put in place after the 2007–09 global financial crisis did not come out of thin air. They were enacted because during the run-up to and during that crisis itself, major abuses (e.g., predatory lending), large gaps in regulation (e.g., resolution regimes for systemically important financial institutions, including nonbanks), and significant regulatory deficiencies (capital standards that were way too low) were revealed.[6] It is folly to assume that many of the risks that had such a devastating impact on Main Street less than a decade ago could not reappear if the policies put in place to contain those risks were removed. Thus, while some moderate pruning here and there in light of experience may be justified, a wholesale dismantling of those reforms would be dangerous. It would show that we have learned next to nothing from the worst financial crisis since the Great Depression.

In this connection, it is wise to recall the debate in US policy circles that led up to the 2007–09 crisis. Here, Reinhart and Rogoff (2009, 214) document that many senior officials concluded that risks were extremely low because "this time was different." Defending that view, they offered the following argument: "The United States, with the world's most reliable system of regulation, the most innovative financial system, a strong political system, and the world's largest and most liquid capital markets, was special." We should therefore be wary of claims that new broad-brush deregulation will be "special" and free of the defects that led many earlier financial deregulation initiatives to end in tears (see Reinhart and Rogoff 2009 for the link between deregulation and banking crises in a large sample of earlier banking crises around the world).

Second, if a bank lending boom is the mechanism by which "unleashing the banks" is to lead to much higher US economic growth, one should again consider the risks involved. Chief among them is the risk that the lending boom turns out to be larger and last longer than originally anticipated, that no one in officialdom is prepared to take away the punch bowl in time, and that not enough high-quality bank capital is in place to absorb the large losses.

Parsons (2016) reports that US bank lending growth eventually reverts to the mean when the industry's loan balances grow more than twice as fast as GDP. He reports that over the 1984–2016 period, bank loan growth averaged about 1.7 times GNP growth. But during 2003–07, loan growth jumped to 3.4 times GNP growth. And when this loan growth reverted to the mean with a vengeance soon after that, the sharp deceleration in loan growth brought a major crisis with it. When bank loan growth accelerates into double digits and stays there for an extended period, credit quality deteriorates, usually with dire consequences.[7] As emphasized in chapter 3, the leading early warning model of banking crises is a dual threshold one that forecasts a banking crisis when the ratio of credit to the private sector and real property prices simultaneously reach certain thresholds relative to their trend lines (e.g., Borio and Drehmann 2009). According to recent BIS (2016a) figures (for the second quarter of 2016), US credit ratios and real property prices are not yet near the danger zone—but that would of course change if unleashing the banks led to a large and sustained credit boom.[8] Moreover, higher bank profitability would not necessarily be a guarantee against a capital shortage if deregulation also meant that banks were free to distribute most of their higher retained earnings in the form of higher dividend payments and increased share buybacks. In that case, the numerator of the capital ratio would likely be growing more slowly than the denominator and, sooner or later, the market would notice.

Third, let me reiterate a point made frequently in this volume: What happens in the banking sector reflects to a large degree what is happening elsewhere in the macroeconomy. Here, it is relevant to take note of another key element of the Trump economic program—namely, a large fiscal stimulus. Many would argue that the US economy is already close to full employment. While the sorry state of US infrastructure and very low long-term interest rates make it attractive to expand public investment in infrastructure, combining that with a large tax cut is likely to put increased pressure on the Federal Reserve to increase interest rates at a faster pace than they would otherwise. And that rise in interest rates will in turn almost surely result in a higher dollar, a larger trade deficit, and larger capital inflows.

If this increase in capital inflows to the US economy is large and persistent, it too could increase vulnerability to a banking crisis. Listen to what former Federal Reserve Chair Ben Bernanke (2010, 25) had to say about the relationship between capital inflows and crisis vulnerability in the run-up to the 2007–09 crisis:

> ...whatever complex story we wind up telling about this crisis, clearly part of it was the fact that a lot of capital flowed into the industrial countries. The United States, of course, had a current-account deficit of about 6 percent of GDP, corresponding to large capital inflows, which would not be a problem if we had invested and managed that money appropriately. But evidently we were not able to do that. Our financial regulatory system, financial private-sector, and risk management mechanisms were overwhelmed and did not do a good job. As a result, there is a close association, I think, between capital inflows and the financial regulatory system.... [T]here's a clear parallel to literally dozens of crises that we've seen previously. We were too smug. We saw this happening in emerging markets. We said it wouldn't happen in the United States, but a very similar pattern existed here as existed in other countries.

Bernanke's (2010) conclusion about the link between banking crises and large capital inflows is supported by Reinhart and Rogoff's (2009) examination of the association between the two in 66 country cases over the 1960–2007 period. In short, they find that the probability of a country experiencing a banking crisis is higher when it also experiences large capital inflows (what the authors call "capital flow bonanzas").

Summing up, within say the next three or four months, we will get a clearer picture of the scope and structure of the Trump administration's financial deregulation plan, as well as its ideas on minimum capital requirements for banks. And if the administration does decide to go ahead with sweeping deregulation and a freeze on further increases in bank-capital requirements, we will see four years or so later the results of that experiment. Based on the evidence presented in this book and on the cautionary notes raised in this chapter, I fear that the outcome will not be one that makes America great again.

Next Steps for the US Stress Tests

Proposed Changes

After the 2015 stress testing cycle, the Federal Reserve conducted a review of its stress-testing program, including input from bank officials, debt and equity-side market analysts, public interest groups, and academics. In his speech on September 26, Tarullo (2016) announced the broad outlines of how the CCAR stress testing exercise is likely to be altered. From the perspective of this volume, five such proposed changes are most relevant.

First, the existing schedule of G-SIB risk-based capital surcharges will be included in the CCAR's baseline capital hurdle rates. He did not say that existing G-SIB surcharges would also be included for the leverage ratio.

Second, the existing (2.5 percent of RWA) capital conservation buffer (CCB) will be replaced by a firm-specific stress capital buffer (SCB). The SCB will be set equal to the decline in the BHC's common equity tier 1 (CET1) ratio during the severely adverse scenario. If that decline exceeds 2.5 percent of RWA, the actual decline will be used; if the decline is less than 2.5 percent, the SCB will be 2.5 percent—in order to avoid a decline in the severity of the test. To illustrate how the baseline hurdle rate would change, Tarullo (2016) offers the following example. Suppose that the decline in a BHC's CET1 ratio under the severely adverse scenario is 5 percent,[9] and that it is subject to a risk-based G-SIB surcharge of 3 percent. Then its baseline CET1 capital hurdle under the new procedures would be 12.5 percent—the sum of a 4.5 percent basic CET1 minimum, a 5 percent SCB charge, and a 3 percent G-SIB surcharge.[10]

Third, the treatment of planned dividends and share repurchases will be changed. Under the existing CCAR, the maintained assumption is that the BHC would implement its planned dividends and share repurchases over the two-year planning horizon regardless of the amount of stress the bank is under. Since capital distributions drain capital, assuming instead that the BHC suspends capital distributions or reduces them from planned levels under stress will produce a higher poststress capital ratio, thereby decreasing the severity of the test. Under the new CCAR procedures, the Fed will assume that the BHC will maintain its dividends for one year while reducing its share repurchases. This new treatment of capital distributions will also replace the existing "soft limit" on dividend payouts under which the Fed has closely scrutinized planned dividend payout ratios of more than 30 percent.

Fourth, after considering suggestions for improving the treatment of contagion and amplification mechanisms and for improving interactions between the banking and shadow banking sectors, the Fed will intensify its research in this direction and work toward including funding shocks and fire-sale dynamics in some future scenarios. That said, the Fed also concludes (Tarullo 2016, 5) that "to this point, even the most conceptually promising of the ideas are a good ways from being realized in specific and well-supported elements of our economic models." Going farther, Tarullo (2016) explains that modeling the knock-on effects of first-round losses in the financial system depends on the vulnerabilities and responses of other (nonbank) major actors in the financial system—including many that the Fed does not regulate—and that information on the latter's behavior may not be observable either to those firms or to the Fed.

And fifth, the Fed is proposing that banks with less than $250 billion in total assets and without significant international or nonbank activity would no longer be included in the qualitative part of the CCAR tests. Instead, these BHCs' progress on risk management and capital planning would be evaluated through the normal supervisory process, supplemented with horizontal reviews of discrete aspects of capital planning. This proposal would be implemented in 2017; in contrast, the other proposals summarized above would not be implemented before 2018.

Reactions

My preliminary reactions to the Fed's revised stress testing program can be summarized as follows.[11]

Incorporation of the G-SIB risk-based surcharges into the CCAR tests is a welcome step forward, as it will increase the minimum risk-weighted CET1 ratio for G-SIBs. That said, I can give it only one thumb up because there is no indication in the Tarullo (2016) speech that the Fed is yet prepared to incorporate the leverage-based G-SIB surcharge into the CCAR, and because treatment of the minimum leverage ratio is more important than the minimums for the risk-based capital measures.

On replacement of the capital conservation buffer with the new stress capital buffer, I agree with the Fed that the previous coexistence of dividend restrictions in the CCB and in the CCAR was prone to inconsistency and that the establishment of the SCB removes it. In addition, because there is a floor of 2.5 percent of RWA in the SCB and because the likely average size of the SCB appears to be about 5 percent, the introduction of the SCB into the CCAR should raise the minimum baseline hurdle rate for CET1 capital. Since the decline in the CET1 ratio in the severely adverse scenario differs across BHCs, the SCB also introduces more risk differentiation (across banks) into the tests—generally a good thing. However, basing the SCB exclusively on the capital decline in the severely adverse scenario increases the risk that the test may miss other important risks. In a recent review of the Fed's stress tests, the Government Accountability Office (GAO 2016, iii) concluded that "while there are advantages to using one scenario—including simplicity and transparency—many different types of financial crises are possible, and the single selected scenario does not reflect a fuller range of possible outcomes."[12] It was partly because of this single-scenario risk that the plan outlined in chapter 7 includes a firm-specific risk surcharge based on a set of indicators. In other words, I think the SCB would work better if it were supplemented by other firm-specific risk factors not currently captured in the severely adverse scenario.

The proposed more lenient treatment of capital distributions in the CCAR is a retrograde step. As Tarullo (2016) acknowledges and as emphasized in chapters 4 and 7, large US banks—including those that received assistance under the Troubled Asset Relief Program (TARP)—made large dividend payments during the 2007–09 crisis, depleting capital that was sorely needed (see Stein 2016). There is no assurance that in a future severe crisis, those banks would not wish to do so again—or that the Federal Reserve will have the requisite determination to say no to those requests. As such, I see no point in allowing banks to get, by assumption in the CCAR tests, a treatment of dividends that does not accord with their (less than responsible) behavior in crises.

Moreover, switching to a more lenient treatment on capital distributions dilutes the increase in (risk-based) capital requirements derived from incorporation of G-SIB surcharges and from substitution of the SCB for the CCB. Indeed, Tarullo (2016, 7) explains that, for the eight US G-SIBs, the new assumptions on capital distributions (in concert with a slightly more lenient treatment of balance sheet assumptions) would forfeit less than half of the capital increases owing to the G-SIB surcharges and the SCB. In a context in which capital ratios held by G-SIBs—inclusive of the new CCAR proposals—would still be way below their optimal levels, making concessions on capital distribution assumptions is unwarranted.

On the integration of contagion and amplification effects into the modeling of crises, the Fed's conclusion that existing approaches are not yet ready for prime time (in the CCAR tests) is, at least to my taste, too pessimistic. To be sure, and as acknowledged in chapters 2 and 3, this is a formidable analytical challenge. Yes, incorporating stronger contagion and amplification effects before they are fully refined carries risk of model error. But *not* incorporating these effects—which were proven to be so potent during the 2007–09 global crisis—also carries risks of model error. In short, the risks of underdoing it may well be larger than doing it imperfectly.

Finally, eliminating the qualitative part of the CCAR tests for BHCs with less than $250 billion in total assets (and without significant international or nonbank activity) is ill advised. In explaining the rationale for this decision, Tarullo (2016, 3) observes that officials from these smaller CCAR participants complained that:

> CCAR qualitative assessment was unduly burdensome because it created pressure to develop complex processes, extensive documentation, and sophisticated stress test models that mirrored those in use at the largest, most complex firms, in order to avoid the possibility of a public objection to their capital plan.[13]

The question is: Can these concerns of the smaller BHCs be addressed without having them drop out of the qualitative part of the CCAR tests? I think they can. The Fed has on many occasions indicated that it sets lower risk-management standards for smaller, less complex BHCs than for the largest, most complex ones. Maybe the problem is one of communication. In this regard, the GAO (2016, i) concluded in its review of the qualitative part of the CCAR that "The Federal Reserve...has not disclosed information needed to fully understand its assessment approach or the reasons for decisions to object to a company's capital plan." If the (lower) standards expected of smaller CCAR participants were better explained, these firms would not feel that they had to mirror the costlier risk management practices of the larger test takers. I am afraid what will be lost by dropping the qualitative test for these smaller firms is the incentive for improvement provided by potential "public" objection to their capital plans in the CCAR; this public spotlight of the CCAR has no analogue in what Tarullo (2016, 6) calls "the normal supervisory process." Remember too that these "smaller" CCAR participants all have at least $50 billion in total assets, and that BHCs in the $50 billion to $250 billion asset class are hardly free of systemic risk.

To sum up, the Federal Reserve's new set of proposals for the CCAR stress tests represents at best a mixed bag. The de facto increase in risk-based capital requirements for G-SIBs—especially those with the largest G-SIB surcharges—is welcome. The switch to a more lenient treatment of capital distributions is not. The most disappointing aspect of the new approach to the CCAR is what is *not* being recommended. The Fed does not propose integrating the existing G-SIB surcharges for the leverage ratio into the CCAR, nor does it propose increasing the size of these surcharges. In fact, because there is no proposed SCB mechanism or surcharge integration for the leverage ratio and because of the proposed easing of the capital distribution assumption, the de facto hurdle rate for the leverage ratio in the CCAR will actually be *lower* than before. With an (estimated) gap of roughly 800 basis points between the actual leverage ratio for G-SIBs and the optimal ratio, such a setback is precisely the opposite of what is needed.

If the broad Trump financial deregulation initiative (discussed above) is actually implemented, there is also a risk that the administration would abandon or delay the Fed's plans to incorporate G-SIB surcharges into the test and to replace the CCB with the SCB but simultaneously go ahead with plans to ease the capital distribution assumptions and exempt smaller CCAR-participating BHCs from the qualitative part of the tests. In my view, this would amount to a serious setback to the US bank stress testing program.

Taking a broader and longer-term view post–2007–09 crisis, the Fed has been moving in the right direction on capital standards for the largest banks. But when it comes to minimum leverage ratios—the most important of the bank-capital metrics—it is making progress at a snail's pace. Pardon the urgency, but if US regulators and supervisors are going to get minimum leverage ratios within shouting distance of their socially optimal levels, I (at 72 years old) admit to having a preference for getting it done while I am still above ground.

Endnotes

1. It is also worth mentioning several market developments that took place during the last quarter of 2016. The Standard and Poor's 500 bank index for the United States gained 22 percent since Trump's election, while the Euro Stoxx banks index registered a 26 percent gain in the fourth quarter of 2016 and an even larger 40 percent gain from its low in the weeks after June's Brexit referendum in the United Kingdom (see Eric Platt, "Ascent of Trump Caps an Exceptionally Testing Year Marked by Wide Asset Price Fluctuations," *Financial Times*, December 31, 2016). Deutsche Bank's share price has climbed over 50 percent since September 2016. The latest (December 2016) EMED Consensus Survey forecasts US and euro area (real GDP) growth in 2017 at 2.2 and 1.5 percent, respectively, and 2017 consumer price inflation at 2.3 and 1.3 percent, respectively. Note that in 2016, euro area consumer price inflation was only 0.2 percent, so deflation risk there has fallen considerably. In Italy, the ECB recently informed Italian officials that the capital shortfall for Monte dei Paschi di Siena (MPS) had increased to 8.8 billion euros (up substantially from the estimate in the July 2016 EU-wide stress test). After attempts to fill the MPS shortfall with private funds failed, the Italian government pushed through legislation for a 20 billion euro bank recapitalization fund, of which about 6.5 billion euros are expected to be used for MPS. The size of haircuts for MPS debtholders—in line with the provisions of the EU Bank Recovery and Resolution Directive—is not yet final, but retail holders of junior bonds are expected to be compensated because of alleged mis-selling (see James Politi, "Rome Attacks ECB Over 'Rigid' Approach to Monte dei Paschi," *Financial Times*, December 30, 2016).

2. In November 2016 the Federal Reserve Bank of Minneapolis (2016) released the initial draft of its plan (the Minneapolis Plan) to end "too big to fail" at the largest US banks. In brief, the plan has four steps: (1) a minimum risk-weighted capital ratio of 23 percent of risk-weighted assets (that is, a minimum 15 percent leverage ratio) for all US bank holding companies (BHCs) with total assets of $250 billion or more; (2) an additional capital requirement equal to 5 percent of risk-weighted assets each year after the five-year transition to step 1 for those BHCs deemed "systemically significant" by the US Treasury secretary—until either they are no longer systemically important or their capital reaches a maximum of 38 percent of risk-weighted assets; (3) a financing-cost equalization tax equal to 120 basis points on shadow banks with more than $50 billion in assets (so as to prevent large-scale migration to the shadow banking system); and (4) a commitment to reform the supervisory regime for community banks to make it simpler and less burdensome.

   Although the Minneapolis Plan concludes that the optimal leverage ratio is 15 percent for banks with more than $250 billion in assets—close to the 16 percent optimal leverage ratio for G-SIBs proposed in chapter 7 of this volume—I have doubts about several of the study's findings and recommendations. Cline (2017) argues that the Minneapolis Plan significantly overestimates the optimal leverage ratio because it greatly underestimates the probability of banking crises at the lower end of the capital ratio spectrum. I am also skeptical of the implicit assumption that the Japanese banking crisis of the 1990s and the Korean banking crisis of 1997, both of which drive much of the results on optimal leverage ratios for systemically important banks (SIBs), are good reference points for expected losses in a future US banking crisis; instead, as explained in chapter 4, I find the US banking crisis of 2007–09 a much better comparator. Finally, I worry that the intended deleveraging induced by such large differences in proposed minimum leverage ratios across the three groups of banks (38 percent for SIBs, 15 percent for banks with more than $250 billion in assets, and 4 percent for all other banks)—will be a recipe for a huge fire sale of assets if implemented over a relatively short period. Such discontinuities in minimum leverage ratios across different groups of banks do not exist under my plan: Recall that they are 10 percent for smaller banks, 11 to 13 percent for non-G-SIB large banks, and 14 to 18 percent for G-SIBs. Also, the transition period under my plan is 10 years, not five. I am grateful to Bill Cline for helpful discussions on the pros and cons of the Minneapolis Plan.

In December 2016, the Board of Governors of the Federal Reserve System (2016c) issued its final rule on TLAC and eligible long-term debt for US G-SIBs. In brief, this final rule is likely to result in an all-in (inclusive of regulatory buffers) risk-based TLAC requirement of 21.5 to 23.0 percent of RWA for the eight US G-SIBs, with JPMorgan Chase and Citigroup at the high end of this range and State Street and Bank of New York Mellon at the low end; see Davis Polk and Wardwell (2017). The all-in TLAC leverage ratio requirement will be 9.5 percent of total leverage exposure. The risk-based requirement for external long-term debt will be 6 percent of RWA plus applicable regulatory surcharges (that is, about one-third the size of the external TLAC minimum); the leverage-based requirement for long-term debt will be 4.5 percent of total leverage exposure (that is, one-half the size of the TLAC leverage ratio requirement). The Fed estimated that implementation of the TLAC initiative would result in a rise in G-SIB lending rates of between 1 and 6 basis points—an increase it regards as too small to meaningfully affect the level of real US GDP. The Fed also decided on a more rapid phase-in of TLAC than outlined in the international (FSB) TLAC proposal. US G-SIBs have to comply with the US final TLAC rule by January 1, 2019. Since the final US TLAC rule is so similar to the international TLAC rule discussed in chapter 8, the comments I offered on the international version also apply to the US version.

3. See, for example, William Cohan, "Why Wall Street Is Suddenly in Love with Trump," *Politico*, November 14, 2016; Steven Solomon, "Conflicts Exist, but Financial Overhaul Proposals Have Merit," *New York Times*, November 23, 2016; "Small Banks Cheer Trump's Victory. So, After a Pause, Do Big Ones," *New York Times*, November 23, 2016; and Ben Mcannahan and Barney Jopson, "What Wall Street Wants," *Financial Times*, January 12, 2017.

4. I put aside here the question of whether Senate Republicans will have the votes necessary to repeal the Dodd-Frank Act.

5. See, for example, Adam Creighton and Ryan Tracy, "Donald Trump Might Be Bad News for Banks After All," *Wall Street Journal*, December 26, 2016.

6. Departing US Treasury Secretary Jacob Lew (2016) recently offered a comprehensive and spirited defense of the Wall Street reforms enacted over the past eight years.

7. Lee and Rose (2010) report that annual growth of US bank loans and leases was in double digits continuously throughout the 2004–07 period. In 2016, bank loans and leases grew by 6½ percent (Board of Governors of the Federal Reserve System, Assets and Liabilities of Commercial Banks in the United States). It is not clear in Parsons (2016) which series on US bank loan growth he is using for his analysis.

8. The Bank for International Settlements (BIS 2016a) credit-to-GDP gap figures define credit as total credit to the private, nonfinancial sector. This means that it includes both bank credit and credit from shadow banks.

9. In the 2016 CCAR, the average decline in the CET1 ratio under the severely adverse scenario was 5.1 percent (see Board of Governors 2016a).

10. This example also assumes that the countercyclical capital buffer (CCL) is not active during this period. If it were active, this could add as much as 2.5 percent to the baseline hurdle rate.

11. I say "preliminary" because not all the relevant details of the revised approach have been published.

12. Although the CCAR tests contain two stressed scenarios—adverse and severely adverse—the second is basically a more extreme version of the first. While the Federal Reserve was, on the whole, quite receptive to the recommendations of the Government Accountability Office (GAO 2016), it pushed back on the criticism of the single scenario, arguing that "promulgating and evaluating more scenarios would increase the burden on the banks participating in the exercise and the Federal Reserve" (GAO 2016, 110).

13. Tarullo (2016, 6) also notes that the smaller BHCs have already met supervisory expectations on their capital planning and risk management processes and could continue their progress through the normal supervisory process.

References

Acemoglu, Daron, Asuman Ozdaglar, and Alireza Tahbaz-Salehi. 2015. Systemic Risk and Stability in Financial Networks. *American Economic Review* (February).

Acharya, Viral, and Sascha Steffen. 2014a. *Benchmarking the European Central Bank's Asset Quality Review and Stress Test: A Tale of Two Leverage Ratios*. VoxEU, November 21.

Acharya, Viral, and Sascha Steffen. 2014b. *Falling Short of Expectations? Stress Testing the European Banking System*. CEPS Policy Brief 315. Brussels: Centre for European Policy Studies.

Acharya, Viral, and Sascha Steffen. 2014c. *Making Sense of the Comprehensive Assessment*. VoxEU, October 29.

Acharya, Viral, Dirk Schoenmaker, and Sascha Steffen. 2011. *How Much Capital Do European Banks Need? Some Estimates*. VoxEU, November 22.

Acharya, Viral, Deniz Anginer, and Joseph Warburton. 2013. *The End of Market Discipline? Investor Expectations and Implicit State Guarantees*. New York: Stern Business School, New York University.

Acharya, Viral, Dianne Pierret, and Sascha Steffen. 2016. Capital Shortfalls of European Banks since the Start of the Banking Union. New York: Stern School of Business, New York University.

Acharya, Viral, Lasse Pedersen, Thomas Philippon, and Matthew Richardson. 2010. Measuring Systemic Risk. New York: Stern School of Business, New York University. Available at http://pages.stern.nyu.edu/~sternfin/vacharya/public_html/MeasuringSystemicRisk_final.pdf.

Acharya, Viral, Tim Eisert, Christian Enfinger, and Christian Hersch. 2015. Whatever It Takes: The Real Effects of Unconventional Monetary Policy. Paper presented at the 16th Annual Jacques Polak Research Conference, Washington, November 5-6.

Admati, Anat. 2014. Testimony at Hearing on Examining the GAO Report on Expectations of Government Support for Bank Holding Companies. US Senate, Subcommittee on Financial Institutions and Consumer Protection, July 31. Washington: US Senate.

Admati, Anat. 2016a. How Effective Capital Regulation Can Help Reduce the Too-Big-to-Fail Problem. Paper presented at the conference on Ending Too Big to Fail, Federal Reserve Bank of Minneapolis, April 4.

Admati, Anat. 2016b. The Missed Opportunity and Challenge of Capital Regulation. *National Institute Economic Review* 235: R4–R14.

Admati, Anat, and Martin Hellwig. 2013a. *The Bankers' New Clothes: What's Wrong with Banking and What to Do about It.* Princeton, NJ: Princeton University Press.

Admati, Anat, and Martin Hellwig. 2013b. *The Parade of the Bankers' New Clothes Continues,* June 23. Palo Alto, CA: Stanford Graduate School of Business. (An updated version of this paper is available at http://bankersnewclothes.com/wp-content/uploads/2016/01/Parade-Continues-2015.pdf.)

Admati, Anat, Peter DeMarzo, Martin Hellwig, and Paul Pfleider. 2015. *The Leverage Ratio Effect.* Working Paper 3029. Palo Alto, CA: Stanford Graduate School of Business. (A later version is forthcoming in 2017 in the *Journal of Finance.*)

Adrian, Tobias. 2014. *Financial Stability Policies for Shadow Banking.* Staff Report 664 (February). New York: Federal Reserve Bank of New York.

Adrian, Tobias, Daniel Covitz, and Nellie Liang. 2014. *Financial Stability Monitoring.* Staff Report 601 (revised June). New York: Federal Reserve Bank of New York.

Afonso, Gara, A. C. Santos, and James Traina. 2014. Do Too-Big-to-Fail Banks Take on More Risk? *Economic Policy Review.* New York: Federal Reserve Bank of New York.

Ahmed, Enam, Andrea Appeddu, Melanie Bowler, Tomas Holinka, Juan Licari, Olga Loiseau-Aslanidi, and Zach Witton. 2011. Europe Misses Again on Bank Stress Test. *Regional Financial Review* (July). Moody's Analytics.

Ahluwalia, Pavan. 2000. *Discriminating Contagion: An Alternative Explanation for Contagious Currency Crises.* IMF Working Paper 00/14. Washington: International Monetary Fund.

Aikman, David, Mirta Galesic, Gerd Gigerenzer, Sujit Kapadia, Konstantinos Katsikopoulos, Amit Kothiyal, Emma Murphy, and Tobias Neumann. 2014. *Taking Uncertainty Seriously: Simplicity versus Complexity in Financial Regulation.* Financial Stability Paper 28. London: Bank of England.

Aiyar, Shekhar, Charles Calomiris, and Tomasz Wieladek. 2014. *Does Macro-Pru Leak? Evidence from a UK Policy Experiment.* NBER Working Paper 17822. Cambridge, MA: National Bureau of Economic Research.

Aiyar, Shekhar, Wolfgang Bergthaler, José Garrido, Anna Ilyina, Andreas Jobst, Kenneth Kang, Dmitriy Kovtun, Dermot Monaghan, and Marina Morett. 2015. *A Strategy for Resolving Europe's Problem Loans.* IMF Staff Discussion Note (September). Washington: International Monetary Fund.

Akerlof, George, and Robert Shiller. 2015. *Phishing for Phools: The Economics of Manipulation and Deception.* Princeton, NJ: Princeton University Press.

Alessandri, Piergiorgio, and Andrew Haldane. 2009. Banking on the State. Paper based on a presentation at the Federal Reserve Bank of Chicago twelfth annual International Banking Conference on "The International Financial Crisis: Have the Rules of Finance Changed?" Chicago, September 25. Available at www.bankofengland.co.uk/archive/Documents/historicpubs/speeches/2009/speech409.pdf.

Allahrakha, Maraj, Paul Glasserman, and H. Peyton Young. 2015. *Systemic Importance Indicators for 33 US Bank Holding Companies: An Overview of Recent Data*. Office of Financial Research Policy Brief 15-01. Washington: US Treasury.

Alessi, Lucia, and Carsten Detkin. 2009. *Real-Time Early Warning Indicators for Costly Asset Price Boom/Bust Cycles: A Role for Global Liquidity*. ECB Working Paper 1039. Frankfurt: European Central Bank.

Altman, Edward. 1968. Financial Ratios, Discriminant Analysis and the Prediction of Corporate Bankruptcy. *Journal of Finance* (September): 189–209.

Altunabas, Yenar, Simone Manganelli, and David Marques-Ibanez. 2011. *Bank Risk During the Financial Crisis: Do Business Models Matter?* ECB Working Paper 1394 (November). Frankfurt: European Central Bank.

Anand, Kartik, Guillaume Bédard-Pagé, and Virginie Traclet. 2014. Stress Testing the Canadian Banking System. *Financial Stability Review* (June). Ottawa: Bank of Canada.

Angeloni, Ignazio. 2014a. The SSM Sails Past the Starting Line: Seeking High-Quality Supervision and a Level Playing Field. Paper presented at the conference on the Start of the European Banking Union, London School of Economics, November 10.

Angeloni, Ignazio. 2014b. Stress-Testing Banks: Are Econometric Models Growing Young Again? Speech at the School of Management, Yale University, New Haven, CT, August.

Arcand, Jean-Louis, Enrico Berkes, and Ugo Panizza. 2012. *Too Much Finance?* IMF Working Paper 12/161. Washington: International Monetary Fund.

Arcand, Jean-Louis, Enrico Berkes, and Ugo Panizza. 2015. *Too Much Finance or Statistical Illusion: A Comment*. Working Paper 12-2015. Geneva: Graduate Institute of International and Development Studies.

Ashenfelter, Orley, George Johnson, and John Pencavel. 1972. Trade Unions and the Rate of Change of Money Wages in US Manufacturing Industries. *Review of Economic Studies* 39, no. 1: 27–54.

Atkinson, Tyler, David Luttrell, and Harvey Rosenblum. 2013. *How Bad Was It: The Costs and Consequences of the 2007-09 Financial Crisis*. Staff Papers no. 2 (July). Dallas: Federal Reserve Bank of Dallas.

Bailey, Andrew. 2014. The Capital Adequacy of Banks: Today's Issues and What We Have Learned from the Past. Speech at Bloomberg, London, July 10. Available at www.bankofengland.co.uk/publications/Documents/speeches/2014/speech745.pdf.

Baily, Martin, and Aaron Klein. 2014. The Impact of the Dodd-Frank Act on Financial Stability and Economic Growth. Paper presented at the University of Michigan Conference, Ann Arbor, MI, October 24.

Bair, Sheila. *Everything the IMF Wanted to Know about Financial Regulation and Wasn't Afraid to Ask*. VoxEU, June 9.

Baker, Malcolm, and Jeffrey Wurgler. 2015. Do Strict Capital Requirements Raise the Cost of Capital? Bank Regulation, Capital Structure, and the Low Risk Anomaly. *American Economic Review* (May).

Ball, Lawrence. 2014a. *The Great Recession's Long-Term Damage*. VoxEU, July 1.

Ball, Lawrence. 2014b. Long-Term Damage from the Great Recession in OECD Countries. *European Journal of Economics and Economic Policies* 11, no. 2: 149–60.

Bank of England. 2008a. *Financial Stability Review* (May). London.

Bank of England. 2008b. *Financial Stability Review* (October). London.

Bank of England. 2009. *Financial Stability Review* (June). London.

Bank of England. 2013a. *Financial Stability Review* (November). London.

Bank of England. 2013b. *A Framework for Stress Testing the UK Banking System: A Discussion Paper.* London.

Bank of England. 2014a. *The Financial Policy Committee's Review of the Leverage Ratio: A Consultative Paper* (October). London.

Bank of England. 2014b. *Stress Testing the UK Banking System: 2014 Results.* London.

Bank of England. 2015a. *Financial Stability Review* (July). London.

Bank of England. 2015b. *Stress Testing the UK Banking System: 2015 Results* (December). London.

Bank of England. 2016. *Financial Stability Review* (July). London.

Barth, James, and Stephen Miller. 2017 (forthcoming). *Benefits and Costs of a Higher Bank Leverage Ratio.* Fairfax, VA: Mercatus Center, George Mason University.

Bassett, William, and Thomas King. 2008. Profit and Balance Sheet Developments at US Commercial Banks 2007. *Federal Reserve Bulletin* 94. Washington: Board of Governors of the Federal Reserve System.

BCBS (Basel Committee on Banking Supervision). 2010a. *An Assessment of the Long-Term Economic Impact of Stronger Capital and Liquidity Requirements* (April). Basel.

BCBS (Basel Committee on Banking Supervision). 2010b. *Assessing the Macroeconomic Impact of the Transition to Stronger Capital and Liquidity Requirements.* Final Report with the Financial Stability Board (December). Basel: Bank for International Settlements.

BCBS (Basel Committee on Banking Supervision). 2010c. *Basel III: A Global Framework for More Resilient Banks and Banking Systems* (revised June). Basel.

BCBS (Basel Committee on Banking Supervision). 2010d. *Calibrating Regulatory Minimum Requirements and Capital Buffers: A Top-Down Approach.* Basel.

BCBS (Basel Committee on Banking Supervision). 2013. *Revised Basel III Leverage Ratio Framework and Disclosure Requirements* (September). Basel.

BCBS (Basel Committee on Banking Supervision). 2014a. *Consultative Document, Standards: Capital Floors: The Design of a Framework Based on Standardized Approaches* (December). Basel.

BCBS (Basel Committee on Banking Supervision). 2014b. *G-SIBs as of November 2014 Allocated to Buckets Corresponding to Required Levels of Additional Loss Absorbency* (November). Basel.

BCBS (Basel Committee on Banking Supervision). 2014c. *Reducing Excessive Variability in Banks' Regulatory Capital Ratios* (November). Basel.

BCBS (Basel Committee on Banking Supervision). 2014d. *Regulatory Consistency Assessment Program: Assessment of Basel III Regulations—European Union* (December). Basel.

BCBS (Basel Committee on Banking Supervision). 2014e. *Regulatory Consistency Assessment Program: Assessment of Basel III Regulations—United States of America* (December). Basel.

BCBS (Basel Committee on Banking Supervision). 2014f. *Review to the Standardized Approach to Credit Risk. Consultative Document* (August). Basel.

BCBS (Basel Committee on Banking Supervision). 2015a. *Basel III Monitoring Report* (March). Basel.

BCBS (Basel Committee on Banking Supervision). 2015b. *Fundamental Review of the Trading Book: Interim Impact Analysis* (November). Basel.

BCBS (Basel Committee on Banking Supervision). 2015c. *TLAC Quantitative Impact Study Report* (November 15). Basel.

BCBS (Basel Committee on Banking Supervision). 2016. *Basel III Monitoring Report* (March). Basel.

Beck, Thorsten. 2014. *After AQR and Stress Tests: Where Next for Banking in the Eurozone?* VoxEU, November 10.

Behn, Markus, Rainer Haselmann, and Vikrant Vig. 2016. *The Limits of Model-Based Regulation.* ECB Working Paper no. 1928 (July). Frankfurt: European Central Bank.

Berger, Allen, and Christa Bouwman. 2013. How Does Capital Affect Bank Performance During Financial Crises? *Journal of Financial Economics* 109: 146–76.

Bernanke, Ben. 2009. The Supervisory Capital Assessment Program. Speech given at Federal Reserve Bank of Atlanta 2009 Financial Markets Conference, Jekyll Island, Georgia, May 11.

Bernanke, Ben. 2010. General Discussion: Asia and the Global Financial Crisis. Asia Economic Policy Conference series, Federal Reserve Bank of San Francisco, October 19.

Bernanke, Ben. 2013. Stress Testing Banks: What Have We Learned? Paper presented at the Financial Markets Conference sponsored by the Federal Reserve Bank of Atlanta, April 8.

Bernanke, Ben. 2015. *The Courage to Act: A Memoir of a Crisis and Its Aftermath.* New York: W.W. Norton and Company.

Berger, Bennet, Pia Hüttl, and Silvia Merler. 2016. *Total Assets versus Risk Weighted Assets: Does It Matter for MREL?* Policy Contribution (August 9). Brussels: Bruegel.

Better Markets. 2015. *The Cost of the Crisis: $20 Trillion and Counting.* Washington.

BIS (Bank for International Settlements). 2014. *84th BIS Annual Report, 2013/2014* (June). Basel.

BIS (Bank for International Settlements). 2015a. *85th BIS Annual Report* (June). Basel.

BIS (Bank for International Settlements). 2015b. *Assessing the Economic Costs and Benefits of TLAC Implementation* (November). Basel.

BIS (Bank for International Settlements). 2016a. *Credit-to-GDP Gaps* (December). Basel. Available at www.bis.org/statistics/c_gaps.htm

BIS (Bank for International Settlements). 2016b. *86th BIS Annual Report.* Basel.

Bisias, Dimitrios, Mark Flood, Andrew Lo, and Stavros Valavanis. 2012. *A Survey of Systemic Risk Analytics.* Office of Financial Research Working Paper 0001. Washington: US Treasury.

Blanchard, Olivier. 2015a. *Greece: Past Critiques and the Path Forward.* iMFdirect, July 9. Washington: International Monetary Fund.

Blanchard, Olivier. 2015b. *Rethinking Macroeconomic Policy: Introduction.* VoxEU, April 20.

Blanchard, Olivier, and Daniel Leigh. 2013. *Growth Forecasts and Fiscal Multipliers.* IMF Working Paper 13/01. Washington: International Monetary Fund.

Blanchard, Olivier, Eugenio Cerutti, and Lawrence Summers. 2015. *Inflation and Activity: Two Explorations and their Monetary Policy Implications.* IMF Working Paper 15/230. Washington: International Monetary Fund. Available at www.imf.org/external/pubs/ft/wp/2015/wp15230.pdf.

Blanchard, Olivier, Paolo Mauro, and Julian Acalin. 2015. *The Case for Growth-Indexed Bonds in Advanced Economies Today*. PIIE Policy Brief 16-2. Washington: Peterson Institute for International Economics. Available at https://piie.com/publications/policy-briefs/case-growth-indexed-bonds-advanced-economies-today.

Blinder, Alan. 2013. *After the Music Stopped: The Financial Crisis, the Response, and the Work Ahead*. New York: Penguin Press.

Blinder, Alan, and Mark Zandi. 2010. *How the Great Recession Was Brought to an End* (July 27). Available at www.economy.com/mark-zandi/documents/End-of-Great-Recession.pdf.

Blinder, Alan, and Mark Zandi. 2015. *The Financial Crisis: Lessons for the Next One* (October 15). Washington: Center on Budget and Policy Priorities.

Blundell-Wignall, Adrian, and Caroline Roulet. 2012. Business Models of Banks, Leverage, and the Distance to Default. *Financial Market Trends*. Paris: Organization for Economic Cooperation and Development.

Blundell-Wignall, Adrian, and Patrick Slovik. 2010. *The EU Stress Test and Sovereign Debt Exposures*. Working Paper on Finance 4. Paris: Organization for Economic Cooperation and Development.

Board of Governors. 2009a. *The Supervisory Capital Assessment Program: Design and Implementation* (April). Washington: Federal Reserve.

Board of Governors. 2009b. *The Supervisory Capital Assessment Program: Overview of Results* (May). Washington: Federal Reserve.

Board of Governors. 2011. *Comprehensive Capital Analysis and Review: Objectives and Overview* (March). Washington: Federal Reserve.

Board of Governors. 2012. *Comprehensive Capital Analysis and Review 2012: Methodology and Results for Stress Scenario Projections* (March). Washington: Federal Reserve.

Board of Governors. 2013a. *Comprehensive Capital Analysis and Review: Assessment Framework and Results* (March). Washington: Federal Reserve.

Board of Governors. 2013b. *Dodd-Frank Act Stress Test 2013: Supervisory Stress Test Methodology and Results* (March). Washington: Federal Reserve.

Board of Governors. 2013c. *Supervisory Scenarios for Annual Stress Tests Required under the Dodd-Frank Act Stress Testing Rules and the Capital Plans Rule* (November). Washington: Federal Reserve.

Board of Governors. 2014a. *Comprehensive Capital Analysis and Review 2014: Assessment Framework and Results* (March). Washington: Federal Reserve.

Board of Governors. 2014b. *Dodd-Frank Stress Test 2014: Supervisory Stress Test Methodology and Results* (March). Washington: Federal Reserve.

Board of Governors. 2015a. *Calibrating the GSIB Surcharge* (July 20). Washington: Federal Reserve.

Board of Governors. 2015b. *Comprehensive Capital Analysis and Review 2015: Assessment Framework and Results* (March). Washington: Federal Reserve.

Board of Governors. 2015c. *Dodd-Frank Act Stress Test 2015: Supervisory Stress Test Methodology and Results* (March). Washington: Federal Reserve.

Board of Governors. 2016a. *Comprehensive Capital Analysis and Review 2016: Assessment Framework and Results* (June). Washington: Federal Reserve.

Board of Governors. 2016b. *Dodd-Frank Act Stress Test 2016: Supervisory Stress Test Methodology and Results* (June). Washington: Federal Reserve.

Board of Governors. 2016c. *Total Loss-Absorbing Capacity, Long-Term Debt, and Clean Holding Company Regulations for Systemically Important US Bank Holding Companies and Intermediate Holding Companies of Systemically-Important Foreign Banking Organizations* (December). Washington: Federal Reserve.

Bookstaber, Richard. 2012. *Using Agent-Based Models for Analyzing Threats to Financial Stability.* Office of Financial Research Working Paper no. 3 (December 21). Washington: US Treasury.

Bookstaber, Rick, R. Citina, J. Feldberg, G. M. Flood, and Paul Glasserman. 2013. *Stress Tests to Promote Financial Stability: Assessing Progress and Looking to the Future.* Office of Financial Research Working Paper 13-10. Washington: US Treasury.

Borio, Claudio. 2012. *The Financial Cycle and Macroeconomics: What Have We Learnt?* BIS Working Paper 395. Basel: Bank for International Settlements.

Borio, Claudio, and Mathias Drehmann. 2009. Assessing the Risk of Banking Crises Revisited. *BIS Quarterly Review* (March): 29–46.

Borio, Claudio, Mathias Drehmann, and Kostas Tsatsaronis. 2012. *Stress Testing Macro Stress Tests: Does It Live Up to Expectations?* BIS Working Paper 369. Basel: Bank for International Settlements.

Bovenzi, John. 2015. *Inside the FDIC: Thirty Years of Bank Failures, Bailouts, and Regulatory Battles.* New York: John Wiley and Sons.

Brazier, Alex. 2015. The Bank of England's Approach to Stress Testing the UK Banking System. Presentation at the LSE Systemic Risk Centre Conference on Stress Testing and Macro-prudential Regulation, London School of Economics, October 29–30.

Brei, Michael, and Leonardo Gambacorta. 2014. *The Leverage Ratio over the Cycle.* Working Paper 471. Basel: Bank for International Settlements.

Bridges, Jonathan, David Gregory, Mette Nielsen, Silvia Pezzini, Amar Radia, and Marco Spaltro. 2014. *The Impact of Capital Requirements on Bank Lending.* Working Paper 486. London: Bank of England.

Brooke, Martin, Oliver Bush, Robert Edwards, Jas Ellis, Bill Francis, Rashmi Harimohan, Katherine Neiss, and Caspar Siegert. 2015. Measuring the Macroeconomic Costs and Benefits of Higher UK Bank Capital Requirements. *Financial Stability Paper* 35. London: Bank of England.

Buch, C., and E. Prieto. 2014. Do Better Capitalized Banks Lend Less? Long-Run Panel Evidence from Germany. *International Finance* 17, no. 1: 1–24.

Bulow, J., J. Goldfield, and P. Klemperer. 2013. *Market-Based Capital Regulation.* VoxEU, August 29.

Calomiris, Charles. 2013. *Is a 25% Bank Equity Requirement Really a No-Brainer?* VoxEU, November 28.

Calomiris, Charles, and Gary Gorton. 1991. The Origins of Banking Panics: Models, Facts, and Bank Regulation. In *Financial Markets and Financial Crises*, ed. Glenn Hubbard. Chicago: University of Chicago Press.

Calomiris, Charles, and Richard Herring. 2013. How to Design a Contingent Convertible Debt Requirement that Helps to Solve Our Too-Big-to-Fail Problem. *Journal of Applied Corporate Finance* 25, no. 2: 39–62.

Candelon, Bertrand, and Amadou Sy. 2015. *How Do Markets React to Stress Tests?* IMF Working Paper 15/75. Washington: International Monetary Fund.

Carney, Mark. 2014. The Future of Financial Reform. 2014 Monetary Authority of Singapore Lecture, Bank of England, London, November 17.

CEBS (Committee of European Banking Supervisors). 2009. Press Release on the Results of the EU-Wide Stress Testing Exercise, October. Brussels.

CEBS (Committee of European Banking Supervisors). 2010. Aggregate Outcome of the 2010 EU-Wide Stress Test Exercise Coordinated by the CEBS in Cooperation with the ECB, July. Brussels.

Cecchetti, Stephen. 2014. The Jury Is In. *CEPR Policy Insight* 76. London: Centre for Economic Policy Research.

Cecchetti, Stephen, and Enisse Kharroubi. 2012. *Reassessing the Impact of Finance on Growth.* Working Paper 381. Basel: Bank for International Settlements. Available at www.bis.org/publ/work381.pdf.

Cecchetti, Stephen, and Kim Schoenholtz. 2014. *Making Finance Safe* (June 16). Available at www.moneyandbanking.com/commentary/2014/10/6/making-finance-safe.

Cecchetti, Stephen, and Kim Schoenholtz. 2016. *Making Banking Safe* (June 13). Available at www.moneyandbanking.com/commentary/2016/6/10/making-banking-safe.

Cetina, Jill, and Bert Loudis. 2015. *The Influence of Systemic Importance Indicators on Banks's Credit Default Swap Spreads.* Office of Financial Research Working Paper no. 15-09 (May 13). Washington: US Treasury.

Chari, Anusha, and Peter Henry. 2013. Two Tales of Adjustment: East Asian Lessons for European Growth. Paper presented at the Annual IMF Research Conference in Honor of Stanley Fischer, Washington, November 7.

Chopra, Ajai. 2014. Stimulating Demand to Foster Structural Reform in the Euro Area. In *Rebuilding Europe's Common Failure: Combining Growth and Reform in the Euro Area.* PIIE Briefing 14-5 (December). Washington: Peterson Institute for International Economics.

Chouinard, Eric, and Graydon Paulin. 2014. Making Banks Safer: Implementing Basel III. *Financial Stability Review* (June). Ottawa: Bank of Canada. Available at https://pdfs.semanticscholar.org/4ed7/e357cb90a6c7dfba458212ad2172f9a98e82.pdf.

Cline, William. 2015a. The Financial Sector and Growth in Emerging Asian Economies. In *From Stress to Growth: Strengthening Asia's Financial Systems in a Post-Crisis World,* ed. Marcus Noland and Donghyun Park. Washington: Asian Development Bank and Peterson Institute for International Economics.

Cline, William. 2015b. *Too Much Finance or Statistical Illusion.* PIIE Policy Brief 15-9. Washington: Peterson Institute for International Economics.

Cline, William. 2017 (forthcoming). *The Right Balance for Banks: Theory and Evidence on Optimal Capital Requirements.* Washington: Peterson Institute for International Economics.

Cline, William, and Joseph Gagnon. 2013. *Lehman Died, Bagehot Lives: Why Did the Fed and the Treasury Let a Major Wall Street Bank Fail?* PIIE Policy Brief 13-21. Washington: Peterson Institute for International Economics.

Cohen, Benjamin. 2013. How Have Banks Adjusted to Higher Capital Requirements? *BIS Quarterly Review* (September). Basel: Bank for International Settlements.

Cohen, Benjamin, and Michela Scatigna. 2014. *Banks and Capital Requirements: Channels of Adjustment*. BIS Working Paper 443. Basel: Bank for International Settlements.

Cohen, Lee, Marcia Cornett, Alan Marcus, and Hassan Tehranian. 2014. Bank Earnings Management and Tail Risk During the Financial Crisis. *Journal of Money, Credit, and Banking* 46, no. 1: 175–97.

Constâncio, Vítor. 2015. The Role of Stress Testing in Supervision and Macro-Prudential Policy. Speech at the LSE Systemic Risk Centre Conference on Stress Testing and Macroprudential Supervision, London School of Economics, October 29–30.

Covas, Francisco, Ben Rump, and Egon Zakrajsek. 2013. *Stress Testing U.S. Bank Holding Companies: A Dynamic Panel Quantile Regression Approach*. Finance and Economics Discussion Series 2013–55. Washington: Federal Reserve Board.

Crawford, John. 2016. Shining a Light on Shadow Money. *Vanderbilt Law Review* 69: 185–207. Available at www.vanderbiltlawreview.org/2016/04/shining-a-light-on-shadow-money/.

Da Costa, Pedro. 2014. Bernanke: 2008 Meltdown Was Worse Than the Great Depression. RealTime Economics blog, *Wall Street Journal*, August 26.

Dagher, Jihand, Giovanni Dell'Ariccia, Luc Laeven, Lev Ratnovski, and Hui Tong. 2016. *The Benefits and Costs of Bank Capital*. IMF Staff Discussion Note 16/04. Washington: International Monetary Fund. Available at https://www.imf.org/external/pubs/ft/sdn/2016/sdn1604.pdf.

Davies, Paul. 2014. ECB Should Stop Southern European Games with Bank Capital. *Wall Street Journal*, October 13.

Davies, Richard, and Belinda Tracey. 2014. Too Big to Be Efficient? The Impact of Implicit Subsidies on Estimates of Economies of Scale for Banks. *Journal of Money, Credit, and Banking* 46, no. 1: 219–53.

Davis Polk and Wardwell LLP. 2017. *Federal Reserve's Final Rule on Total Loss-Absorbing Capacity and Eligible Long-Term Debt* (January 11). New York.

De Grauwe, Paul. 2011. *The Management of a Fragile Eurozone*. Working Paper. Brussels: Centre for European Policy Studies.

De Grauwe, Paul. 2015. *Design Failures of the Euro-Zone*. VoxEU, September 7.

De Gunst, Eric. 2013. *Basel III and Banking Supervision: Taxes Are of Capital Importance* (April/May). Ernst and Young. Available at www.ey.com/Publication/vwLUAssets/Basel_III_and_banking_supervision_-_taxes_are_of_capital_importance/$FILE/Basel%20III%20and%20banking%20supervision%20taxes%20are%20of%20capital%20importance.pdf.

Demirgüç-Kunt, Asli, Enrica Detragiache, and Ouarda Merrouche. 2010. *Bank Capital: Lessons from the Financial Crisis*. IMF Working Paper 10/286. Washington: International Monetary Fund.

Dowd, Kevin. 2016a. *The Average Leverage Ratio across the UK Banking System: 2007 vs. Now* (June 3). London: Adam Smith Institute. Available at www.adamsmith.org/average-leverage-ratio.

Dowd, Kevin. 2016b. *The Bank of England Fails Its Stress Test, Again*. Cato at Liberty, January 15. Washington: Cato Institute.

Dowd, Kevin. 2016c. *Is Deutsche Bank Kaputt?* September 27. London: Cobden Centre. Available at www.cobdencentre.org/2016/09/is-deutsche-bank-kaputt.

Dowd, Kevin. 2016d. *No Stress: The Flaws in the BOE's Stress Testing Programme*, 2d. ed. London: Adam Smith Institute.

Drehmann, Mathias, Claudio Borio, and Kostas Tsatsaronis. 2012. *Characterizing the Financial Cycle: Don't Lose Sight of the Medium Term.* Working Paper no. 380 (May). Basel: Bank for International Settlements.

Dudley, William. 2012. US Experience with Bank Stress Tests. Paper presented at the G-30 Meeting, Bern, Switzerland, March 28.

Dudley, William. 2013. Ending Too Big to Fail. Remarks at the Global Economic Policy Forum, Federal Reserve Bank of New York, November 7.

EBA (European Banking Authority). 2010. *Aggregate Outcome of the 2010 EU-Wide Stress Test Exercise Coordinated by CEBS in Cooperation with the ECB* (July 23). London.

EBA (European Banking Authority). 2011. 2011 EU-Wide Stress Test: Aggregate Report (July 15). London.

EBA (European Banking Authority). 2012. *Results of the Basel III Monitoring Exercise, Based on Data as of 31 December 2011.* London.

EBA (European Banking Authority). 2013a. *EU-Wide Transparency Exercise 2013: Summary Report.* London.

EBA (European Banking Authority). 2013b. *Interim Results of the EBA Review of the Consistency of Risk-Weighted Assets: Top-Down Assessment of the Banking Book.* London.

EBA (European Banking Authority). 2014a. EBA Publishes Common Methodology and Scenario for 2014 EU-Banks Stress Test. Press release, April 29. London.

EBA (European Banking Authority). 2014b. EU-Wide Stress Test: Frequently Asked Questions, April 29. London.

EBA (European Banking Authority). 2014c. *Methodological Note: EU-Wide Stress Test 2014.* Version 2.0, April 29. London.

EBA (European Banking Authority). 2014d. *Report on Impact of Differences in Leverage Ratio Definitions* (March 4). London.

EBA (European Banking Authority). 2014e. *Results of the 2014 EU-Wide Stress Test. Aggregate Results.* London: European Banking Authority.

EBA (European Banking Authority). 2016a. EBA Publishes 2016 EU-Wide Stress Test Results (July 2). London.

EBA (European Banking Authority). 2016b. 2016 EU-Wide Stress Test: Frequently Asked Questions, July 2. London.

EBA (European Banking Authority). 2016c. *2016 EU-Wide Stress Test: Methodological Note* (February 24). London.

EBA (European Banking Authority). 2016d. *2016 EU-Wide Stress Test: Results* (July 29). London.

ECB (European Central Bank). 2013. *Financial Stability Review* (November). Frankfurt.

ECB (European Central Bank). 2014a. *Financial Stability Review* (May). Frankfurt.

ECB (European Central Bank). 2014b. *Financial Stability Review* (November). Frankfurt.

ECB (European Central Bank). 2014c. Opinion of the European Central Bank on Deferred Tax Assets. CON/2014/66, September 3. Frankfurt.

ECB (European Central Bank). 2015a. *Financial Stability Review* (May). Frankfurt.

ECB (European Central Bank). 2015b. *Financial Stability Review* (November). Frankfurt.

ECB (European Central Bank). 2016. *Financial Stability Review* (May). Frankfurt.

Eichengreen, Barry. 2015. The Next Financial Crisis. *Economia Politica*: 53–66.

Elliott, Douglas. 2010. *A Primer on Bank Capital*. Washington: Brookings Institution.

Elliott, Douglas, Suzanne Salloy, and André Santos. 2012. *Assessing the Cost of Financial Regulation*. IMF Working Paper 12/233. Washington: International Monetary Fund. Available at www.imf.org/extèrnal/pubs/ft/wp/2012/wp12233.pdf.

Engle, R. 2009. The Risk That Risk Will Change. *Journal of Investment Management* 7, no. 4: 24–28.

Enria, Andrea. 2013. Progress in Banking Sector and Institutional Repair in the European Union. Speech at the Institute of International Finance, Washington, April 2013.

Enria, Andrea. 2014a. Completing the Repair of the EU Banking Sector. Speech at the Oliver Wyman Institute Conference, London, October 1.

Enria, Andrea. 2014b. The Outlook for Europe Post Macro Stress Scenarios. Speech at the meeting of Roubini Global Economics and the European Banking Authority, London, May 21.

Enria, Andrea. 2015. Challenges for the Future of EU Banking. Speech at the Banking Forum of the IESE Business School, Madrid, January 14.

European Court of Auditors. 2014. European Banking Supervision Taking Shape, Say EU Auditors. Press release, July 2. Luxembourg.

ESRB (European Systemic Risk Board). 2014. *EBA/SSM Stress Test: The Macroeconomic Adverse Scenario*. April 17. Frankfurt.

ESRB (European Systemic Risk Board). 2016. Adverse Macro-Financial Scenario for the EBA 2016 EU-Wide Bank Stress Testing Exercise (January 29). Frankfurt.

Fama, Eugene, and Kenneth R. French. 2004. The Capital Asset Pricing Model: Theory and Evidence. *Journal of Economic Perspectives* 18, no. 3 (Summer): 25–46.

Farag, Marc, Damian Harland, and Dan Nixon. 2014. Bank Capital and Liquidity. *Bank of England Quarterly Review* 3Q: 201–15.

FDIC (Federal Deposit Insurance Corporation). 2010. *2010 Annual Report*. Washington.

Federal Reserve Bank of Minneapolis. 2016. *The Minneapolis Plan to End Too Big to Fail* (November). Minneapolis.

Federal Reserve Bank of St. Louis. 2016. *The Weighted Average Maturity for All Commercial and Industrial Loans, All Commercial Banks*. St. Louis.

Fender, Ingo, and Ulf Lewrick. 2015. *Calibrating the Leverage Ratio* (December). Basel: Bank for International Settlements.

Fernandez, Marcelo, Deniz Igan, and Marcelo Pinheiro. 2015. *March Madness in Wall Street: (What) Does the Market Learn from Stress Tests?* IMF Working Paper WP/15/271. Washington: International Monetary Fund. Available at www.imf.org/external/pubs/ft/wp/2015/wp15271.pdf.

Fisher, Peter. 2012. What Now? Speech at the Sixth Biennial Conference on Risk Management and Supervision, Financial Stability Institute, Basel, November 6.

Fischer, Stanley. 2014a. The Great Recession: Moving Ahead. Speech at a conference sponsored by the Swedish Ministry of Finance, Stockholm, August 11.

Fischer, Stanley. 2014b. *Financial Sector Reform: How Far Are We?* Martin Feldstein Lecture, National Bureau of Economic Research, Cambridge, MA, July 10.

Fischer, Stanley. 2015a. The Importance of the Non-Bank Financial Sector. Speech at the conference on Debt and Financial Stability, Bundesbank and German Ministry of Finance, Frankfurt, March 27.

Fischer, Stanley. 2015b. Non-Bank Financial Intermediation, Financial Stability, and the Road Ahead. Speech at the 20th Annual Financial Markets Conference, Federal Reserve Bank of Atlanta, Stone Mountain, GA, March 30.

Flannery, Mark, Beverly Hirtle, and Anna Kovner. 2015. *Evaluating the Information in the Federal Reserve Stress Tests.* Staff Report 744. New York: Federal Reserve Bank of New York.

Flannery, M. J., S. H. Kwan, and M. Nimalendran. 2010. *The 2007–09 Financial Crisis and Bank Opaqueness.* Working Paper. San Francisco: Federal Reserve Bank of San Francisco.

Freixas, Xavier, and Jean-Charles Rochet. 2008. *The Microeconomics of Banking,* 2d. ed. Cambridge, MA: MIT Press.

FSA (Financial Services Authority). 2009. *The Turner Report.* London.

FSB (Financial Stability Board). 2011. *Shadow Banking: Strengthening Oversight and Regulation.* Basel.

FSB (Financial Stability Board). 2013. *Strengthening Oversight and Regulation of Shadow Banking: An Overview of Recommendations* (August 29). Basel.

FSB (Financial Stability Board). 2014a. *Adequacy of Loss-Absorbing Capacity of Global Systemically Important Banks in Resolution* (November). Basel.

FSB (Financial Stability Board). 2014b. *Global Shadow Banking Monitoring Report 2014* (November). Basel.

FSB (Financial Stability Board). 2015. *Principles on Loss Absorption and Recapitalization Capacity of G-SIBs in Resolution: Total Loss-Absorption Capacity (TLAC) Term Sheet* (November). Basel.

FSB (Financial Stability Board), IMF (International Monetary Fund), and World Bank. 2011. *Financial Stability Issues in Emerging and Developing Economies.* Report to G-20 Finance Ministers and Central Bank Governors. Basel.

FSOC (Financial Stability Oversight Council.) 2011. *Study of the Effects of Size and Complexity of Financial Institutions on Capital Market Efficiency and Economic Growth.* Washington.

Gabrieli, Silvia, Dilyara Salakhova, and Guillaume Vuillemey. 2015. *Interconnectedness and Contagion Risk in the European Banking System.* Paris: Banque de France.

Gambacorta, Leonardo, and Hyun Shin. 2015. *On Book Equity: Why It Matters for Monetary Policy.* Basel: Bank for International Settlements.

Gambacorta, Leonardo, and Hyun Shin. 2016. *Why Bank Capital Matters for Monetary Policy.* Working Paper 558. Basel: Bank for International Settlements.

Gambacorta, Leonardo, Jing Yang, and Kostas Tsatsaronis. 2014. Financial Structure and Growth. *BIS Quarterly Review* (March). Basel: Bank for International Settlements.

GAO (Government Accountability Office). 2016. *Federal Reserve: Additional Actions Could Help Ensure the Achievement of Stress Test Goals.* Report to the Chairman, Committee on Financial Services, House of Representatives, November. Washington.

Garcia, Gillian. 2010. Failing Prompt Corrective Action. *Journal of Banking Regulation* 11: 171.

Geanakoplos, John. 2010. *Solving the Present Crisis and Managing the Leverage Cycle.* Cowles Foundation Paper 1305. New Haven, CT: Yale University.

Geanakoplos, John. 2014. *Leverage, Default, and Forgiveness: Lessons from the American and European Crises*. Cowles Foundation Paper 1419. New Haven, CT: Yale University.

Geithner, Timothy. 2014. *Stress Tests: Reflections on Financial Crises*. New York: Crown Publishers.

Geithner, Timothy. 2016. Are We Safer? The Case for Strengthening the Bagehot Arsenal. Per Jacobsson Lecture at the 2016 Annual Meetings of the International Monetary Fund and World Bank Group, Washington, October 8.

Glasserman, Paul, and Gowtham Tangirala. 2015. *Are the Federal Reserve's Stress Test Results Predictable?* Office of Financial Research Working Paper 15-02. Washington: US Treasury.

Goldman Sachs. 2013. *Measuring the TBTF Effect on Bond Prices*. New York: Goldman Sachs Markets Institute.

Goldstein, Itay, and Haresh Sapra. 2014. Should Banks' Stress Test Results Be Disclosed? An Analysis of Costs and Benefits. *Foundations and Trends in Finance* 8, no. 1: 1–54.

Goldstein, Morris. 1998. *The Asian Financial Crisis: Causes, Cures, and Systemic Implications*. Washington: Institute for International Economics.

Goldstein, Morris. 2012a. *The EU's Implementation of Basel III: A Deeply Flawed Compromise*. VoxEU, May 27.

Goldstein, Morris. 2012b. *Stop Coddling Europe's Banks*. VoxEU, January 11.

Goldstein, Morris. 2014. *The 2014 EU-Wide Bank Stress Test Lacks Credibility*. RealTime Economic Issues Watch blog, November 5. Washington: Peterson Institute for International Economics.

Goldstein, Morris. 2016. Stress Testing during Crises. Presentation at the Yale Financial Crisis Forum, New Haven, CT, July 26–28.

Goldstein, Morris, and John Hawkins. 1998. *The Origins of the Asian Financial Turmoil.* Reserve Bank of Australia Discussion Paper 980. Sydney: Reserve Bank of Australia.

Goldstein, Morris, and Nicolas Véron. 2011. *Too Big to Fail: The Transatlantic Debate*. PIIE Working Paper 11-2 (January). Washington: Peterson Institute for International Economics.

Goldstein, Morris, Graciela Kaminsky, and Carmen Reinhart. 2000. *Assessing Financial Vulnerability in Emerging Economies: An Early Warning System for Emerging Markets*. Washington: Institute for International Economics.

Goodhart, Charles. 2011. *The Basel Committee on Banking Supervision: A History of the Early Years 1974–97.* Cambridge: Cambridge University Press.

Goodhart, Charles. 2014. *Bank Resolution under T-LAC: The Aftermath*. VoxEU, December 24.

Goodhart, Charles, and Emilios Avgouleas. 2015. *Critical Reflections on Bank Bail-Ins* (January 12). London: London School of Economics.

Goodhart, Charles, and Wolf Wagner. 2012. *Regulators Should Encourage More Diversity in the Financial System*. VoxEU, April 12.

Gorton, Gary. 1988. Banking Panics and Business Cycles. *Oxford Economic Papers* 40: 751–81.

Gorton, Gary. 2012. *Misunderstanding Financial Crises: Why We Don't See Them Coming.* Oxford: Oxford University Press.

Gorton, Gary, and Andrew Metrick. 2010a. *Regulating the Shadow Banking System.* Brookings Papers on Economic Activity. Washington: Brookings Institution.

Gorton, Gary, and Andrew Metrick. 2010b. *Securitized Banking and the Run on Repo*. NBER Working Paper 15223. Cambridge, MA: National Bureau of Economic Research.

Greenlaw, David, Anil Kashyap, Kermit Schoenholtz, and Hyun Shin. 2012. *Stressed Out: Macro-Prudential Principles for Stress Testing*. Working Paper 12-08. Chicago: Booth School of Business, University of Chicago.

Greenspan, Alan. 2010. *The Crisis*. Brookings Papers on Economic Activity. Washington: Brookings Institution.

Grill, Michael, Jan Lang, and Jonathan Smith. 2015. The Leverage Ratio, Risk Taking, and Bank Stability. Paper presented at the Fourth European Banking Authority Policy Research Workshop, London, November 18–19.

Group of Thirty. 2009. *Financial Reform: A Framework for Financial Stability*. Washington.

Gruenberg, Martin. 2015. A Progress Report on the Resolution of Systemically Important Financial Institutions. Speech at the Peterson Institute for International Economics, Washington, May 12.

Guynn, Randall. 2015. The Role of Bankruptcy Reform in Addressing Too Big to Fail. Prepared statement submitted to the Senate Subcommittee on Financial Institutions and Consumer Protection, Washington, July 29.

Hagendorff, Jens, and Francesco Vallascas. 2013. *Bank Capital Requirements: Risk Weights You Cannot Trust and the Implications for Basel III*. VoxEU, December 16.

Haldane, Andrew. 2009. Rethinking the Financial Network. Speech at the Financial Student Association, Amsterdam, April 28.

Haldane, Andrew. 2010. The $100 Billion Question. Speech at the Institute of Regulation and Risk, Hong Kong, March 30.

Haldane, Andrew. 2011. Capital Discipline. Speech at the American Economic Association, Denver, January.

Haldane, Andrew. 2012. On Being the Right Size. Beesley Lecture, Institute of Directors, London, October 25.

Haldane, Andrew. 2013. Constraining Discretion in Bank Regulation. Paper presented at the Federal Reserve Bank of Atlanta Conference on Maintaining Financial Stability, Atlanta. April 9. Available at www.bankofengland.co.uk.

Haldane, Andrew. 2014a. The Age of Asset Management. Speech given at the London Business School, London, April 4.

Haldane, Andrew. 2014b. Ambidexterity. Presentation at the annual meeting of the American Economic Association, Philadelphia, January 3.

Haldane, Andrew, and Vasileios Madouros. 2012. The Dog and the Frisbee. Paper presented at the Federal Reserve Bank of Kansas City's 36th Economic Policy Symposium, Jackson Hole, Wyoming, August 31.

Hanson, Samuel. 2016. Banking Regulation: The Risk of Migration to Shadow Banking. Paper presented at the Fourth Symposium on Ending Too Big to Fail, Federal Reserve Bank of Minneapolis, September 26.

Hanson, Samuel, Anil Kashyap, and Jeremy Stein. 2011. A Macro-Prudential Approach to Financial Regulation. *Journal of Economic Perspectives* (Winter): 3–28.

Hartmann, Philipp. 2015. The Bank of England's Approach to Stress Testing the UK Banking System. Discussant comments at the LSE Systemic Risk Centre Conference on Stress Testing and Macro-prudential Supervision, London School of Economics, October 29–30.

Hellwig, Martin. 2014a. Systemic Risk and Macroprudential Policy. Paper prepared for the Nederlandsche Bank's High-Level Seminar on Making Macroprudential Policy Work in Practice, June 10. Published in *Making Macroprudential Policy Work*, ed. Aerdt Houben, Rob Nijskens, and Mark Teunissen. Occasional Studies 12, no. 7. Amsterdam: Nederlandsche Bank

Hellwig, Martin. 2014b. *Yes Virginia, There Is a European Banking Union! But It May Not Make Your Wishes Come True*. Reprints of the Max Planck Institute for Research on Collective Goods, Bonn 2014/12 (December). Available at www.coll.mpg.de/pdf_dat/2014_12online.pdf.

Henry, Jerome, and Christoffer Kok, eds. 2013. *A Macro Stress Testing Framework for Assessing Systemic Risks in the Banking System*. Occasional Paper 152. Frankfurt: European Central Bank.

Herring, Richard. 2007. *The Rocky Road to Implementation of Basel II in the United States*. Athens: Hellenic Bank Association.

Herring, Richard. 2013. Fair Value Accounting, Disclosure and Financial Stability: Does How We Keep Score Influence How the Game Is Played? In *Handbook of Key Global Financial Markets, Institutions, and Infrastructure*, ed. Gerard Caprio. Cambridge, MA: Academic Press.

Herring, Richard, and Jacopo Carmassi. 2010. The Corporate Structure of International Financial Conglomerates: Complexity and Its Implications for Safety and Soundness. In *Oxford Handbook of Banking*, eds. Allen Berger, Philip Molyneux, and John Wilson. Oxford: Oxford University Press.

Hirtle, Beverly, Anna Kovner, and Eric McKay. 2014. *Becoming More Alike? Comparing Bank and Federal Reserve Stress Test Results*. Liberty Street Economics, July 21. New York: Federal Reserve Bank of New York.

Hirtle, Beverly, and Andreas Lehnert. 2014. *Supervisory Stress Tests*. Staff Report 696. New York: Federal Reserve Bank of New York.

Hoenig, Thomas. 2012. Back to Basics: A Better Alternative to Basel Capital Rules. Paper presented at the American Banker Regulatory Symposium, Washington, September 14. Available at www.fdic.gov.

Hoenig, Thomas. 2013. Basel III Capital: A Well-Intended Illusion. Paper presented at the International Association of Deposit Insurers Research Conference, Basel, April 9. Available at www.fdic.gov.

Hoenig, Thomas. 2015. A Conversation about Regulatory Relief for the Community Bank. Speech at the 24th Annual Hyman Minsky Conference, National Press Club, Washington, April 15.

Hoenig, Thomas. 2016a. The Relative Role of Debt in Bank Resiliency and Resolvability. Speech at the Peterson Institute for International Economics, Washington, January 20. Available at https://piie.com/publications/papers/hoenig20160120.pdf.

Hoenig, Thomas. 2016b. Statement by FDIC Vice Chairman Hoenig on the Semi-Annual Update of the Global Capital Index (April 12). Washington: Federal Deposit Insurance Corporation. Available at www.fdic.gov/news/news/speeches/spapr1216.html.

Hogan, Thomas, Neil Meredeth, and Xuhao Pan. 2013. *Evaluating Risk-Based Capital Regulation*. Working Paper 13-12. Fairfax, VA: Mercatus Center, George Mason University.

Holmstrom, Bengt, and Jean Tirole. 1997. Financial Intermediation, Loanable Funds, and the Real Sector. *Quarterly Journal of Economics* 112, no. 3 (August): 663–91.

Huertas, Thomas. 2013. *Safe to Fail*. LSE Financial Markets Group Paper. London: London School of Economics.

Hughes, Joseph, and Loretta Mester. 2011. Who Said Large Banks Don't Experience Scale Economies: Evidence from a Risk-Return-Driven Cost Function. Working Paper no. 11-27 (July). Philadelphia: Federal Reserve Bank of Philadelphia.

ICBA (Independent Community Bankers of America). 2013. *End Too Big to Fail* (June 25). Washington.

IIF (Institute of International Finance). 2010. *Interim Report on the Cumulative Impact on the Global Economy of Proposed Changes in the Banking Regulatory Framework* (June). Washington.

IIF (Institute of International Finance). 2015. *Risk Sensitivity: The Important Role of Internal Models* (March). Washington.

IMF (International Monetary Fund). 2006a. *Belgium: Financial Sector Stability Assessment*. IMF Country Report 06/75 (February). Washington.

IMF (International Monetary Fund). 2006b. *Denmark: Financial System Stability Assessment*. IMF Country Report 06/343 (October). Washington.

IMF (International Monetary Fund). 2006c. *Greece: Financial System Stability Assessment*. IMF Country Report 06/6 (January). Washington.

IMF (International Monetary Fund). 2006d. Ireland: Financial System Stability Assessment Update. IMF Country Report 06/292 (August). Washington.

IMF (International Monetary Fund). 2006e. *Portugal: Financial Sector Assessment Program*. IMF Country Report 06/378 (October). Washington.

IMF (International Monetary Fund). 2006f. *Spain: Financial System Stability Assessment*. IMF Country Report 06/212 (June). Washington.

IMF (International Monetary Fund). 2007. *Global Financial Stability Report: Market Developments and Issues* (April). Washington.

IMF (International Monetary Fund). 2009. *Global Financial Stability Report: Responding to the Financial Crisis and Measuring Systemic Risk* (April). Washington.

IMF (International Monetary Fund). 2010a. *Global Financial Stability Report: Meeting New Challenges to Stability and Building a Safer System* (April). Washington.

IMF (International Monetary Fund). 2010b. *Global Financial Stability Report: Sovereign Funding and Systemic Liquidity.* (October). Washington.

IMF (International Monetary Fund). 2011a. *Global Financial Stability Report: Getting There from Here* (April). Washington.

IMF (International Monetary Fund). 2011b. *Global Financial Stability Report: Grappling with Crisis Legacies* (September). Washington.

IMF (International Monetary Fund). 2011c. *IMF Performance in the Run-up to the Financial and Economic Crisis: IMF Surveillance in 2004–07*. Washington: Independent Evaluation Office.

IMF (International Monetary Fund). 2011d. *People's Republic of China: Financial System Stability Assessment*. IMF Country Report 11/321 (November). Washington.

IMF (International Monetary Fund). 2012. *Regional Economic Outlook, Asia and Pacific* (April). Washington.

IMF (International Monetary Fund). 2013a. *People's Republic of China: 2013 Article IV Consultation*. IMF Country Report 13/211 (July). Washington.

IMF (International Monetary Fund). 2013b. *Singapore: Financial System Stability Assessment* (November). Washington.

IMF (International Monetary Fund). 2013c. *Technical Note on Stress Testing of Banks. Financial Sector Assessment Program: European Union* (March). Washington.

IMF (International Monetary Fund). 2014a. *Global Financial Stability Report: Moving from Liquidity to Growth-Driven Markets* (April). Washington.

IMF (International Monetary Fund). 2014b. *Global Financial Stability Report: Risk Taking, Liquidity, and Shadow Banking: Curbing Excess While Promoting Growth* (October). Washington.

IMF (International Monetary Fund). 2014c. *People's Republic of China, Hong Kong Special Administrative Region: Financial System Stability Assessment* (May). Washington.

IMF (International Monetary Fund). 2014d. *People's Republic of China, Hong Kong Special Administrative Region: Financial Sector Stability Assessment: Stress Testing the Banking System* (July). Washington.

IMF (International Monetary Fund). 2014e. *Regional Economic Outlook. Asia and Pacific: Sustaining the Momentum: Vigilance and Reforms* (April). Washington

IMF (International Monetary Fund). 2014f. *Republic of Korea: Financial System Stability Assessment*. IMF Country Report 14/126 (May). Washington.

IMF (International Monetary Fund). 2014g. Back to Work: How Fiscal Policy Can Help. *IMF Fiscal Monitor* (October). Washington.

IMF (International Monetary Fund). 2015a. *Greece: An Update of the IMF Staff's Preliminary Public Debt Sustainability Analysis*. IMF Country Report 15/186 (July 14). Washington.

IMF (International Monetary Fund). 2015b. *IMF Fiscal Monitor: The Commodities Roller Coaster* (October). Washington.

IMF (International Monetary Fund). 2015c. *World Economic Outlook: Adjusting to Lower Commodity Prices* (October). Washington

IMF (International Monetary Fund). 2015d. *Global Financial Stability Report: Navigating Monetary Policy Challenges and Managing Risks* (April). Washington.

IMF (International Monetary Fund). 2016a. *Global Financial Stability Report: Fostering Stability in a Low-Growth, Low-Rate Era* (October). Washington.

IMF (International Monetary Fund). 2016b. *World Economic Outlook. Subdued Demand: Symptoms and Remedies* (October). Washington.

Ingves, Stefan. 2014. Banking on Leverage. Paper presented at the 10th Asia-Pacific High Level Meeting on Banking Supervision, Auckland, New Zealand, February 25–27. Available at www.riksbank.se/en.

Jobst, Andreas, and Dale Gray. 2013. *Systemic Contingent Claims Analysis: Estimating Market-Implied Systemic Risk*. IMF Working Paper no. 13/54 (February). Washington: International Monetary Fund.

Johnson, Simon, and James Kwak. 2009. *13 Bankers*. New York: Crown.

Junge, G., and P. Kugler. 2013. Quantifying the Impact of Higher Capital Requirements on the Swiss Economy. *Swiss Journal of Economics and Statistics* 149, no. 3: 313–56.

Kashkari, Neel. 2016. An Update on Ending Too Big to Fail. Speech at Third Symposium on Ending Too Big to Fail, Peterson Institute for International Economics, Washington, DC, June 20.

Kashyap, Anil, Jeremy Stein, and Samuel Hanson. 2010. *An Analysis of the Impact of "Substantially Heightened" Capital Requirements on Large Financial Institutions*. Working Paper (May). Cambridge, MA: Harvard Business School.

Khan, Mohsin, and Abdelhak Senhadji. 2000. *Financial Development and Economic Growth: An Overview*. IMF Working Paper 00/209. Washington: International Monetary Fund.

King, Mervyn. 2013. A Governor Looks Back—and Forward. Mansion House Speech, London, June 9.

King, Mervyn. 2016. *The End of Alchemy: Money, Banking, and the Future of the Global Economy*. New York: W.W. Norton and Company.

King, Robert, and Ross Levine. 1993. Finance and Growth: Schumpeter Might Be Right. *Quarterly Journal of Economics* 108, no. 3: 717–37. Available at http://qje.oxfordjournals.org/content/108/3/717.abstract.

Kirkegaard, Jacob. 2014. *Whither Europe's Banks after the Stress Test?* RealTime Economic Issues Watch blog, October 29. Washington: Peterson Institute for International Economics.

Knight, Malcolm. 2007. Now You See It, Now You Don't: Risk in the Small and in the Large. Speech at the Eighth Annual Risk Management Meeting of the Global Association of Risk Professionals, February 27–28.

Koenker, Roger, and Kevin Hallock. 2011. *Quantile Regression: An Introduction*. University of Illinois, Urbana-Champaign. Available at www.econ.uiuc.edu/~roger/research/intro/rq3.pdf.

Kohn, Donald. 2008. Financial Regulation in a System Context: A Comment. *Brookings Papers on Economic Activity* 2008: 262–66. Washington: Brookings Institution.

Kuritzkes, Andrew, and Til Schuermann. 2007. *What We Know, Don't Know, and Can't Know About Bank Risk: A View from the Trenches*. Wharton Financial Institutions Center Working Paper 06-05 (September). New York: Wharton Financial Institutions Center.

Laeven, Luc, and Ross Levine. 2005. *Is There a Diversification Discount in Financial Conglomerates?* Washington: World Bank.

Laeven, Luc, and Fabian Valencia. 2010. *The Resolution of Banking Crises: The Good, the Bad and the Ugly*. IMF Working Paper 10/146 (June). Washington: International Monetary Fund.

Laeven, Luc, and Fabio Valencia. 2013. Systemic Crises Data Base. *IMF Economic Review* 61: 225–70. Washington: International Monetary Fund. Available at http://link.springer.com/article/10.1057%2Fimfer.2013.12.

Laeven, Luc, Lev Ratnovski, and Hui Tong. 2014. *Bank Size and Systemic Risk*. IMF Staff Discussion Note 14/04. Washington: International Monetary Fund.

Lardy, Nicholas. 2014. *Financial Instability in China*? Paper presented at the Global Economic Prospects Meeting, Peterson Institute for International Economics, Washington, April 9.

Larosière, Jacques de. 2009. *The High Level Group on Financial Supervision in the EU* (February 25). Brussels: European Systemic Risk Board.

Lautenschläger, Sabine. 2013. The Leverage Ratio: A Simple and Comparable Measure? Paper presented at the Deutsche Bundesbank/SAFE Conference on Supervising Banks in Complex Financial Systems, Frankfurt, October 22. Available at www.bis.org/review. Give specific URL.

Lautenschläger, Sabine. 2014. Start of the Single Supervisory Mechanism: From the Comprehensive Assessment to Day-to-Day Supervision. Speech at Euro Finance Week, Frankfurt, November 18.

Lee, Seung Jung, and Jonathan Rose. 2010. Profit and Balance-Sheet Developments at US Commercial Banks in 2009. *Federal Reserve Bulletin* (May).

Lehnert, Andreas. 2015. Overview of Independent Supervisory Stress Testing in the United States. Presentation at the LSE Systemic Risk Centre Conference on Stress Testing and Macro-prudential Regulation, London School of Economics, October 29–30.

Le Leslé, Vanessa, and Sofiya Avramova. 2012. *Revisiting Risk-Weighted Assets: Why Do RWAs Differ Across Countries and What Can Be Done about It?* IMF Working Paper 12/90. Washington: International Monetary Fund.

Levine, Ross. 1997. Financial Development and Economic Growth: Views and Agenda. *Journal of Economic Literature* 35 (June): 688–726. Available at http://pascal.iseg.utl.pt/~aafonso/eif/pdf/Levine.pdf.

Levine, Ross. 2002. Bank-Based or Market-Based Financial Systems: Which Is Better? *Journal of Financial Intermediation* 11, no. 4: 398–428.

Lew, Jacob. 2016. Eight Years After the Financial Crisis: How Wall Street Reform Strengthened Our Financial System and Laid the Foundation for Long-Run Growth. *NYU Journal of Legislation and Public Policy* 19, no. 61: 611–29.

Liikanen Report. 2012. *High Level Expert Group: Reforming the Structure of the EU Banking Sector* (October 2). Brussels: European Commission.

MacKinlay, A. Craig. 1997. Event Studies in Economics and Finance. *Journal of Economic Perspectives* (March): 13–39.

Mariathasan, Mike, and Ouarda Merrouche. 2013a. *Capital Adequacy and Hidden Risk*. VoxEU, June 29.

Mariathasan, Mike, and Ouarda Merrouche. 2013b. *The Manipulation of Basel Risk Weights*. CEPR Discussion Paper 9494. London: Centre for Economic Policy Research.

Martynova, Natalya, Lev Ratnovski, and Razuan Vlahu. 2014. *Franchise Value and Risk Taking in Modern Banks*. Working Paper 430. Amsterdam: De Nederlandsche Bank.

McCauley, Robert. 2014. *Is Basel III Enough for Macro-prudential Policy in Asia and the Pacific?* Pacific Trade and Development Working Paper 36-02. Canberra: Australian National University.

McKinsey and Company. 2014. *The Road Back: McKinsey Global Banking Annual Review 2014* (December). Available at www.mckinsey.com.

Mésonnier, Jean-Stéphane, and Allen Monks. 2015. *Heightened Capital Requirements and Bank Credit in the Crisis: The Case of the 2011 EBA Capital Exercise in the Euro Area*. Paris: Banque de France.

Miles, David. 2011. *What Is the Optimal Leverage for a Bank?* VoxEU, April 27.

Miles, D., J. Yang, and G. Marcheggiano. 2012. Optimal Bank Capital. *Economic Journal* 123, no. 567: 1–37.

Milgram, S. 1967. The Small-World Problem. *Psychology Today* 1, no. 1: 61–67.

Modigliani, Franco, and Merton Miller. 1958. The Cost of Capital, Corporation Finance, and the Theory of Investment. *American Economic Review* 48, no. 3: 261–97. Available at https://assets.aeaweb.org/assets/production/journals/aer/top20/48.3.261-297.pdf.

Montesi, Giuseppe, and Giovanni Papiro. 2015. Bank Stress Testing: A Stochastic Simulation Framework to Assess Banks' Financial Fragility. Paper presented at the LSE Systemic Risk Centre Conference on Stress Testing and Macro-Prudential Regulation, London School of Economics, October 29–30.

Moody's Investors Service. 2014. *Basel III Implementation in Full Swing: Global Overview and Credit Implications.* Special Comment (August 4). Available at www.btinvest.com.sg/system/assets/27262/Basel%20III%20Implementation%20in%20Full%20Swing%20-%20Global%20Overview%20and%20Credit%20Implications%204Aug14.pdf.

Moretti, Marina, Stephanie Stolz, and Mark Swinburne. 2008. *Stress Testing at the IMF.* IMF Working Paper 08/206 (September). Washington: International Monetary Fund.

Morris, Stephen, and Hyun Song Shin. 2008. Financial Regulation in a Systemic Context. *Brookings Papers on Economic Activity.* Washington: Brookings Institution.

Morris, Stephen, and Hyun Song Shin. 2009. *Identifying the Illiquidity Component of Credit Risk.* Working Paper, Princeton University, Princeton, NJ. Available at www.princeton.edu/~hsshin/www/IlliquidityComponent.pdf.

Myers, S. C., and N. S. Majluf. 1984. Corporate Financing and Investment Decisions When Firms Have Information that Investors Do Not. *Journal of Financial Economics* 13, no. 2: 187–221.

Noss, Joseph, and Patricia Toffano. 2014. *Estimating the Impact of Changes in Bank Capital Requirements during the Upswing.* Working Paper 494. London: Bank of England. Available at www.bankofengland.co.uk/research/Pages/workingpapers/2014/wp494.aspx.

Nouy, Daniéle. 2014a. *Marking the Inauguration of the ECB's New Supervisory Responsibilities* (November 20). Frankfurt: European Central Bank.

Nouy, Daniéle. 2014b. Regular Hearing of the Chair of the ECB's Supervisory Board at the European Parliament's Economic and Monetary Affairs Committee, European Parliament, Brussels, November 3.

Nouy, Daniéle. 2015. European Banking Supervision: Leveling the Playing Field. Speech at Corporate Program Roundtable, Council on Foreign Relations, New York, September 11.

Nouy, Daniéle. 2016. Risks and Resilience: The European Banking Sector in 2016. Speech at the Deutsche Bank Capital Forum, London, February 23.

OECD (Organization for Economic Cooperation and Development). 2013. *Economic Outlook: Focus: Strengthening Euro-Area Banks.* Paris.

Ong, Li Lian, ed. 2014. *A Guide to IMF Stress Testing: Methods and Models.* Washington: International Monetary Fund.

Ong, Li Lian, and Ceyle Pazarbasioglu. 2013. *Credibility and Crisis Stress Testing.* IMF Working Paper 13/178. Washington: International Monetary Fund. Available at www.imf.org/external/pubs/ft/wp/2013/wp13178.pdf.

Orphanides, Athanasios. 2014. *Stress Tests as a Policy Tool: The European Experience during the Crisis.* Sloan Working Paper 5122-14. Cambridge, MA: MIT.

Pagano, Mark, Sam Langfield, Viral Acharya, Amoud Boot, Markus Brunnermeir, Claudia Buch, Martin Hellwig, André Sapir, and Ieke van den Burg. 2014. *Is Europe Overbanked?* Report of the Advisory Scientific Committee of the European Systemic Risk Board.

Parsons, Richard. 2016. Don't Be Fooled by Overly Rosy Loan Growth. *American Banker* (March).

Paulson, Henry. 2010. *On the Brink: Inside the Race to Stop the Collapse of the Global Financial System*. New York: Business Plus.

Persaud, Avinash. 2014. *Why Bail-In Securities Are Fools' Gold*. PIIE Policy Brief 14-23 (November). Washington: Peterson Institute for International Economics.

Pethokoukis, James. 2014. Nobel Prize winning economist Eugene Fama: Crank up bank capital levels to 25%. AEI Ideas blog, May. Washington: American Enterprise Institute.

Philippon, Thomas, and Arielle Reshef. 2012. Wages and Human Capital in the US Finance Industry, 1909-2006. *Quarterly Journal of Economics* 127, no. 4 (November):1551–609.

Pierret, Diane. 2015. Systemic Risk and the Solvency-Liquidity Nexus of Banks. *International Journal of Central Banking* (June): 193–227. Available at www.ijcb.org/journal/ijcb15q3a5.pdf.

Posen, Adam. 2016. Bernanke, the Fed, and the Real Lessons of the Crisis: Review of Ben Bernanke's *The Courage to Act. Foreign Affairs* (January/February).

Posen, Adam, and Nicolas Véron. 2014. Europe's Half a Banking Union. *Europe's World* (June 15).

Pozsar, Zoltan. 2014. *Shadow Banking: The Money View*. Office of Financial Research Working Paper 14-04. Washington: US Treasury.

Rajan, Raghuram, and Luigi Zingales. 1998. Financial Dependence and Growth. *American Economic Review* 88, no. 3: 559–58.

Reinhart, Carmen, and Kenneth Rogoff. 2009. *This Time Is Different: Eight Centuries of Financial Folly*. Princeton, NJ: Princeton University Press.

Reynolds, Craig. 1987. Flocks, Herds, and Schools: A Distributed Behavioral Model. *Computer Graphics* 21, no. 4: 25–34.

Ricks, Morgan. 2016. *The Money Problem: Rethinking Financial Regulation*. Chicago: University of Chicago Press.

Rose, Andrew K., and Tomasz Wieladek. 2012. *Too Big to Fail: Some Empirical Evidence on the Causes and Consequences of Public Banking Interventions in the United Kingdom*. Working Paper 460. London: Bank of England. Available at www.bankofengland.co.uk/research/Pages/workingpapers/2012/wp460.aspx.

Rosengren, Eric. 2014. Broker-Dealer Finance and Financial Stability. Paper presented at the conference on the Risks of Wholesale Funding, Federal Reserve Banks of Boston and New York, August 13.

Sachs, Lee, and Matthew Kabaker. 2016. Targeted Capital Injections and Guarantees. Slide presentation at the Yale Financial Crisis Forum, New Haven, CT, July 26–28.

Sahay, Ratna, Martin Čihák, and Papa N'Diaye. 2015. *How Much Finance Is Too Much? Stability, Growth and Emerging Markets*. iMFdirect, May 4. Washington: International Monetary Fund.

Sarin, Natasha, and Lawrence Summers. 2016a. *Have Big Banks Gotten Safer?* Brookings Papers on Economic Activity. Washington: Brookings Institution.

Sarin, Natasha, and Lawrence Summers. 2016b. Have Big Banks Gotten Safer? Slide presentation at the Brookings Panel on Economic Activity, Brookings Institution, Washington.

Schoenmaker, Dirk, and Nicolas Véron. 2016. European Banking Supervision: Compelling Start, Lingering Challenges. Blog, June 8. Brussels: Bruegel. Available at http://bruegel.org/2016/06/european-banking-supervision-compelling-start-lingering-challenges/.

Schroth, Enrique, Gustavo Suarez, and Lucian Taylor. 2014. Dynamic Debt Runs and Financial Fragility: Evidence from the 2007 ABCP Crisis. *Journal of Financial Economics* 112, no. 2: 164–89.

Schuermann, Til. 2012. Stress Testing Banks. Speech at the Global Association of Risk Professionals New York Chapter Meeting, April 18. Available at www.garp.org/.

Schuermann, Til. 2013. The Fed's Stress Tests Risk to the Financial System. *Wall Street Journal,* March 19.

Schuermann, Til. 2015. Presentation on Stress Testing and Systemic Stability at the LSE Systemic Risk Centre Conference on Stress Testing and Macro-prudential Regulation, London School of Economics, October 29–30.

Schildbach, Jan, and Claudius Wenzel. 2013. *Bank Performance in the US and Europe: An Ocean Apart.* Current Issues, Global Financial Markets (September 26). Frankfurt: Deutsche Bank.

Schoenmaker, Dirk, and Nicolas Véron. 2016. Introduction and Executive Summary. In *European Banking Supervision: The First Eighteen Months*, ed. Dirk Schoenmaker and Nicolas Véron. Brussels: Bruegel.

Scott, Hal. 2016. Connectedness and Contagion: Protecting the Financial System from Panics. Cambridge, MA: MIT Press.

Scott, Kenneth, and John Taylor, eds. 2012. *Bankruptcy Not Bailout: A Special Chapter 14.* Palo Alto: Hoover Institution Press.

Sheng, Andrew. 2013. *Basel III and Asia.* Finance Working Paper. Hong Kong: Fung Global Institute.

Shin, Hyun Song, and Philip Turner. 2015. What Does the New Face of International Financial Intermediation Mean for Emerging Market Economies? *Financial Stability Review* (April). Paris: Banque de France.

Shleifer, Andrei, and Robert Vishny. 2011. Fire Sales in Finance and Macroeconomics. *Journal of Economic Perspectives* 25, no. 1: 29–48. Available at http://scholar.harvard.edu/files/shleifer/files/fire_sales_jep_final.pdf.

Shulock, Michael. 2014. *Another Unbelievable Stress-Free Test: Whitewash Myth and Deferred Tax Assets.* Mish's Global Economic Trend Analysis, October 26.

Sorkin, Andrew. 2009. *Too Big to Fail.* New York: Viking.

Squam Lake Working Group on Financial Regulation. 2009. *Reforming Capital Requirements for Financial Institutions* (April). New York: Council on Foreign Relations.

Steil, Ben, and Dinah Walker. 2014a. Europe's Dodgy Bank Stress Tests. *Wall Street Journal*, December 8.

Steil, Ben, and Dinah Walker. 2014b. *The ECB Fails to Stress Banks over the One Critical Variable It Controls: Inflation. Geo-Graphics* (November 3). New York: Council on Foreign Relations.

Stein, Jeremy. 2013. Overheating in Credit Markets: Origins, Measurement, and Policy Responses. Speech at research symposium, Federal Reserve Bank of St. Louis, St Louis. February 7.

Stein, Jeremy. 2014. Incorporating Financial Stability Considerations into a Monetary Policy Framework. Speech at the International Research Forum on Monetary Policy, Washington, March 21. Available at www.federalreserve.gov/newsevents/speech/stein20140321a.htm.

Stein, Jeremy. 2016. Targeted Capital Injections and Guarantees. Slide presentation at the Yale Financial Crisis Forum, Yale University, New Haven, CT, July 26–28.

Stein, Jeremy, Robin Greenwood, and Samuel Hanson. 2016. Central Bank Balance Sheets and Financial Stability. Paper presented at the Jackson Hole Economic Policy Symposium, Federal Reserve Bank of Kansas City, August 25–27.

Summers, Lawrence. 2000. International Financial Crises: Causes, Prevention, and Cures. Richard T. Ely Lecture. *American Economic Review* 90, no. 2: 1–16. Available at w.sfu.ca/~kkasa/summers_AER00.pdf.

Swensen, David. 2011. Guest Lecture at Professor Robert Shiller's Course on Financial Markets, Yale University, New Haven, CT.

Tarullo, Daniel. 2008. *Banking on Basel: The Future of International Financial Regulation*. Washington: Peterson Institute for International Economics.

Tarullo, Daniel. 2011. The Evolution of Capital Regulation. Speech at the Clearing House Business Meeting and Conference, New York, November 9.

Tarullo, Daniel. 2014a. Dodd-Frank Implementation. Testimony before the Committee on Banking, Housing, and Urban Affairs. US Senate. September 9. Available at www.bis.org.

Tarullo, Daniel. 2014b. Rethinking the Aims of Prudential Regulation. Speech at the Federal Reserve Bank of Chicago Bank Structure Conference, Chicago, May 8.

Tarullo, Daniel. 2014c. Stress Testing after Five Years. Speech at the Federal Reserve Third Annual Stress Test Modeling Symposium, Boston, June 25. Available at www.federalreserve.gov.

Tarullo, Daniel. 2016. New Steps in the Evolution of Stress Testing. Speech at the Yale University School of Management Leaders Forum, New Haven, CT, September 26.

Truman, Edwin. 2016. *The IMF and the Euro-Area Crises: Review of a Report from the Independent Evaluation Office*. PIIE Policy Brief 16-13. Washington: Peterson Institute for International Economics.

Tucker, Paul. 2014. *Regulatory Reform, Stability, and Central Banking*. Hutchins Center on Fiscal and Monetary Policy. Washington: Brookings Institution.

Turner, Philip. 2012. *Macro-Prudential Policies in Emerging Market Economies: Theory and Practice*. BIS Paper 62. Basel: Bank for International Settlements.

Turner, Philip. 2014. *The Global Long-Term Interest Rate, Financial Risks, and Policy Choices in Emerging Market Economies*. BIS Working Paper 441. Basel: Bank for International Settlements.

UK Treasury. 2015. FPC Leverage Ratio Consultation (February 2). London.

Véron, Nicolas. 2014. *The European Union Lags on Basel III Banking Reforms*. RealTime Economic Issues Watch blog, December 10. Washington: Peterson Institute for International Economics.

Vestergaard, Jakob. 2014. *European Banking Misery: Pretending Rather Than Mending Does No Favors to Lending* (November 4). GEG Watch: Trends in Global Economic Governance.

Vestergaard, Jakob, and Maria Retana. 2013. *Behind Smoke and Mirrors: On the Alleged Capitalisation of Europe's Banks*. Copenhagen: Danish Institute of International Affairs.

Vickers Report. 2011. *Independent Commission on Banking: Final Report* (December 30). London.

Vickers, John. 2012. Some Economics of Banking Reform. *Rivista di Politica Economica* (October/December). Available at www.rivistapoliticaeconomica.it/pdf/XIII-COSTA-LECTURE-VICKERS.pdf.

Vickers, John. 2016a. The Bank of England Must Think Again on Systemic Risk. *Financial Times*, February 14. Available at www.ft.com/content/674b16b8-d184-11e5-831d-09f7778e7377.

Vickers, John. 2016b. *How Much Equity Should UK Banks Have?* VoxEU, February 15.

Vickers, John. 2016c. *The Systemic Risk Buffer for UK Banks: A Response to the Bank of England's Consultation Paper.* Special Paper 244, LSE Financial Markets Group Series. London: London School of Economics.

Wall, Larry. 2013. *Measuring Capital Adequacy Supervisory Stress Tests in a Basel World.* Working Paper 2013-15. Atlanta: Federal Reserve Bank of Atlanta.

Wessel, David. 2009. *In Fed We Trust.* New York: Crown Business.

Wheelock, David, and Paul Wilson. 2015. *Evolution of Scale Economies in US Banking.* Working Paper no. 2015-21. St. Louis: Federal Reserve Bank of St. Louis.

Volcker Alliance. 2015. *Reshaping the Financial Regulatory System: Long Awaited, Now Crucial* (April). New York.

Volcker Alliance. 2016. *Unfinished Business: Banking in the Shadows* (December). New York.

Wolf, Martin. 2014a. Europe's Banks Are Too Feeble to Spur Growth. *Financial Times*, October 28.

Wolf, Martin. 2014b. *The Shifts and the Shocks: What We've Learned—and Have Still to Learn—from the Financial Crisis.* New York: Penguin Press.

Wolf, Martin. 2015. A Deal to Bring Modernity to Greece. *Financial Times*, February 3.

Wolf, Martin. 2016. Central Banks as Pawnbrokers of Last Resort. *Financial Times*, March 31. Available at www.ft.com/content/e4931794-2696-11e6-8b18-91555f2f4fde.

Index

leverage ratio vs. risk-based capital measures, 209

position on systemic capital buffers, 226

RAMSI model, 132n

requirements to strengthen bank capital, 97

stress testing regime, 89

on surcharges, 241n

symmetry and proportionality approach, 205–28

    dual vs. single bank capital regimes, 208–10

    Financial Policy Committee (FPC), 205–08

    problems with critical risk weight, 210–12

Bank of Ireland, 46

Bank of New York Mellon

    capital ratio target, 261

    global capital index, 2015, 194–95t

    leverage ratios, 263t

    risk-based capital surcharge, 190t

    systemic importance indicators reported by, 191–92t

Bank Recovery and Resolution Directive (BRRD), 62

bank regulations, primary capital standard for, 25

bank stock returns, downside risk of, 61

bank stress tests

    basics, 1–4

    existing weaknesses, 9

    and lending rates, 317

    other influences, 17

    study outline, 9–14

    transparency of, 3

bank supervision, macroprudential approach to, 152–55, 251

bank vulnerability indicators, 280n

The Bankers' New Clothes (Admati and Hellwig), 286

banking crises

    annual probability of, 183n

    definition, 170

    early warning models, 250

    early warning models of, 17

    effects of systemic, on actual vs. potential output, 171

    historical database on probability, 21–22

    indicators in US, 129n

    Minneapolis Federal Reserve study of, 184n

    occurrence, 172f

    output losses, 21

    prevention guideline, 22

    reduced probability of, 170–71

    waves of, 172

banks

    "advanced-approach," 6

    asset portfolios, leverage ratio and, 281n

    and credit for private US nonfinancial sector, 25

    decline in market value of common equity to assets, 233

    deregulation, Trump and, 325–30

    differential treatment, 264

    dividends, 271

    efforts to limit risk taking, 287–88

    funding costs

        effect on GDP, 168–69

        and lending rates, 275

    lending rates, 37n

    liquidity position, 3

    liquidity requirements, 177n

    losses, and optimal capital ratios, 212–19

        earnings management, 213

        lower vs. higher-frequency data, 217–18

        means/medians vs. extremes, 215, 217

        no counterfactual, 212

        survivorship bias, 214

        tail-risk dependence, 218–19

    losses during 2007-09 crisis, 137–52

        balance sheet vs. income statement approaches, 137–40

        calculations of optimal capital, 140–44

        credit losses during financial cycle upswing, 140

    market-based indicators of health, 268

    market measures of riskiness, 232–33

    minimalist approach to standards, 253

    minimum leverage ratio for smaller, 265

    peer group analysis of, 99

    profitability of major, 165t

    reform plan, and bank size, 290–94

    risk, 292

Other Publications from the
PETERSON INSTITUTE FOR INTERNATIONAL ECONOMICS

WORKING PAPERS

POLICY ANALYSES IN INTERNATIONAL ECONOMICS SERIES

* = out of print

Japan in the World Economy*   Bela Balassa and Marcus Noland
1988   ISBN 0-88132-041-2

America in the World Economy: A Strategy for the 1990s*   C. Fred Bergsten
1988   ISBN 0-88132-089-7

Managing the Dollar: From the Plaza to the Louvre*   Yoichi Funabashi
1988, 2d ed. 1989   ISBN 0-88132-097-8

United States External Adjustment and the World Economy   William R. Cline
May 1989   ISBN 0-88132-048-X

Free Trade Areas and U.S. Trade Policy*
Jeffrey J. Schott, ed.
May 1989   ISBN 0-88132-094-3

Dollar Politics: Exchange Rate Policymaking in the United States*   I. M. Destler and C. Randall Henning
September 1989   ISBN 0-88132-079-X

Latin American Adjustment: How Much Has Happened?*   John Williamson, ed.
April 1990   ISBN 0-88132-125-7

The Future of World Trade in Textiles and Apparel*   William R. Cline
1987, 2d ed. June 1999   ISBN 0-88132-110-9

Completing the Uruguay Round: A Results-Oriented Approach to the GATT Trade Negotiations*   Jeffrey J. Schott, ed.
September 1990   ISBN 0-88132-130-3

Economic Sanctions Reconsidered (2 volumes)
Economic Sanctions Reconsidered: Supplemental Case Histories*   Gary Clyde Hufbauer, Jeffrey J. Schott, and Kimberly Ann Elliott
1985, 2d ed. Dec. 1990   ISBN cloth 0-88132-115-X/
                            paper 0-88132-105-2

Economic Sanctions Reconsidered: History and Current Policy*   Gary Clyde Hufbauer, Jeffrey J. Schott, and Kimberly Ann Elliott
December 1990   ISBN cloth 0-88132-140-0
                           ISBN paper 0-88132-136-2

Pacific Basin Developing Countries: Prospects for the Future*   Marcus Noland
January 1991   ISBN cloth 0-88132-141-9
                           ISBN paper 0-88132-081-1

Currency Convertibility in Eastern Europe
John Williamson, ed.
October 1991   ISBN 0-88132-128-1

International Adjustment and Financing: The Lessons of 1985–1991*   C. Fred Bergsten, ed.
January 1992   ISBN 0-88132-112-5

North American Free Trade: Issues and Recommendations*   Gary Clyde Hufbauer and Jeffrey J. Schott
April 1992   ISBN 0-88132-120-6

Narrowing the U.S. Current Account Deficit*
Alan J. Lenz
June 1992   ISBN 0-88132-103-6

The Economics of Global Warming
William R. Cline
June 1992   ISBN 0-88132-132-X

US Taxation of International Income: Blueprint for Reform*   Gary Clyde Hufbauer, assisted by Joanna M. van Rooij
October 1992   ISBN 0-88132-134-6

Who's Bashing Whom? Trade Conflict in High-Technology Industries   Laura D'Andrea Tyson
November 1992 ISBN 0-88132-106-0

Korea in the World Economy*   Il SaKong
January 1993   ISBN 0-88132-183-4

Pacific Dynamism and the International Economic System*   C. Fred Bergsten and Marcus Noland, eds.
May 1993   ISBN 0-88132-196-6

Economic Consequences of Soviet Disintegration*   John Williamson, ed.
May 1993   ISBN 0-88132-190-7

Reconcilable Differences? United States-Japan Economic Conflict*   C. Fred Bergsten and Marcus Noland
June 1993   ISBN 0-88132-129-X

Does Foreign Exchange Intervention Work?
Kathryn M. Dominguez and Jeffrey A. Frankel
September 1993   ISBN 0-88132-104-4

Sizing Up U.S. Export Disincentives*
J. David Richardson
September 1993   ISBN 0-88132-107-9

NAFTA: An Assessment*   Gary Clyde Hufbauer and Jeffrey J. Schott, *rev. ed.*
October 1993   ISBN 0-88132-199-0

Adjusting to Volatile Energy Prices
Philip K. Verleger, Jr.
November 1993   ISBN 0-88132-069-2

The Political Economy of Policy Reform
John Williamson, ed.
January 1994   ISBN 0-88132-195-8

Measuring the Costs of Protection in the United States   Gary Clyde Hufbauer and Kimberly Ann Elliott
January 1994   ISBN 0-88132-108-7

The Dynamics of Korean Economic Development*   Cho Soon
March 1994   ISBN 0-88132-162-1

Reviving the European Union*
C. Randall Henning, Eduard Hochreiter, and Gary Clyde Hufbauer, eds.
April 1994   ISBN 0-88132-208-3

China in the World Economy   Nicholas R. Lardy
April 1994   ISBN 0-88132-200-8

Greening the GATT: Trade, Environment, and the Future   Daniel C. Esty
July 1994   ISBN 0-88132-205-9

Western Hemisphere Economic Integration*
Gary Clyde Hufbauer and Jeffrey J. Schott
July 1994   ISBN 0-88132-159-1

Currencies and Politics in the United States, Germany, and Japan   C. Randall Henning
September 1994   ISBN 0-88132-127-3

Estimating Equilibrium Exchange Rates
John Williamson, ed.
September 1994   ISBN 0-88132-076-5

Managing the World Economy: Fifty Years after Bretton Woods   Peter B. Kenen, ed.
September 1994   ISBN 0-88132-212-1

Trade Liberalization and International Institutions*   Jeffrey J. Schott
September 1994   ISBN 978-0-88132-3

Reciprocity and Retaliation in U.S. Trade Policy*
Thomas O. Bayard and Kimberly Ann Elliott
September 1994   ISBN 0-88132-084-6

SPECIAL REPORTS

Sales Representatives

In Asia, North America, and South America
Perseus Distribution
210 American Drive
Jackson, TN 38301
orderentry@perseusbooks.com

Tel. (800) 343-4499
Fax (800) 351-5073
Email: cup_book@columbia.edu

Secure online ordering is available on the CUP website at: www.cup.columbia.edu

In Africa, Europe, the Middle East, South Africa, South Asias, and the United States
Columbia University Press
c/o Wiley European Distribution Centre
New Era Estate
Oldlands Way, Bognor Regis
West Sussex PO22 9NQ

Tel. (1243) 843-291
Fax (1243) 843-296
Email: customer@wiley.com

(Delivery via Wiley Distribution Services Ltd., or you may collect your order by prior arrangement)

United States and Canada Sales and Publicity Representatives
Brad Hebel, Director of Sales and Marketing
61 West 62nd Street
New York, NY 10023

Tel. (212) 459-0600, ext. 7130
Fax (212) 459-3678
Email: bh2106@columbia.edu

Columbia University Sales Consortium Manager and Souther US
Catherine Hobbs

Tel. (804) 690-8529
Fax (434) 589-3411
Email: catherinehobbs@earthlink.net

Northeast US and Eastern Canada
Conor Broughan

Tel. (917) 826-7676
Email: cb2476@columbia.edu

Midwest US and Central Canada
Kevin Kurtz

Tel. (773) 316-1116
Fax (773) 489-2941
Email: kkurtz5@earthlink.net

Western US and Western Canada
William Gawronski

Tel. (310) 488-9059
Fax (310) 832-4717
Email: wgawronski@earthlink.net

United Kingdom and Europe
The University Press Group Ltd.
Lois Edwards
LEC 1, New Era Estate
Oldlands Way, Bognor Regis
PO22 9NQ England

Tel. 44 (1243) 842-165
Fax 44 (1243) 842-167
Email: lois@upguk.com

Ben Mitchell
U.K. Sales Manager
62 Fairford House
Kennington Lane
London SE11 4HR England

Tel. (44) 776-691-3593
Email: ben.mitchell.upg@gmail.com

Andrew Brewer
Managing Director
57 Cobnar Road
Sheffield S8 8QA England

Tel. (44) 114-274-0129
Mobile (44) 796-703-1856
Email: andrew.brewer@virgin.net

Middle East and Africa
Andrew Brewer
Managing Director
57 Cobnar Road
Sheffield S8 8QA England

Tel. (44) 114-274-0129
Mobile (44) 796-703-1856
Email: andrew.brewer@virgin.net

Asia
Brad Hebel
61 West 62nd Street
New York, NY 10023

Tel. (212) 459-0600, ext. 7130
Fax (212) 459-3678
Email: bh2106@columbia.edu